NonProliferation Treaty

NonProliferation Treaty

Hearings
before the
Committee On Foreign Relations
United States Senate

Ninetieth Congress
Second Session
on
Executive H, 90th Congress,
Second Session
Treaty on the NonProliferation of Nuclear Weapons

July 10, 11, 12, and 17, 1968

Protected under the Berne Convention. Published 2001

Printed in The United States of America
Ross & Perry, Inc. Publishers
717 Second St., N.E., Suite 200
Washington, D.C. 20002
Telephone (202) 675-8300
Facsimile (202) 675-8400
info@RossPerry.com

SAN 253-8555

Government Reprints Press Edition 2001

Government Reprints Press is an Imprint of Ross & Perry, Inc.

Library of Congress Control Number: 2001094513
http://www.GPOreprints.com

ISBN 1-931641-94-3

⊚ The paper used in this publication meets the requirements for permanence established by
the American National Standard for Information Sciences "Permanence of Paper for Printed
Library Materials" (ANSI Z39.48-1984).

CONTENTS

NONPROLIFERATION TREATY

WEDNESDAY, JULY 10, 1968

United States Senate,
Committee on Foreign Relations,
Washington, D.C.

The committee met, pursuant to notice, at 10 a.m., in room 318, Old Senate Office Building, Senator John Sparkman presiding.

Present: Senators Sparkman, Gore, Lausche, Symington, Pell, Hickenlooper, Aiken, Carlson, Williams of Delaware, and Case.

Also present: Senators Pastore, Anderson, and Bennett, members of the Joint Committee on Atomic Energy.

Senator SPARKMAN. Let the committee come to order, please.

The Committee on Foreign Relations begins its hearings this morning on the Nonproliferation Treaty. We are pleased to have the Secretary of State, the Honorable Dean Rusk, and the Director of the U.S. Arms Control and Disarmament Agency, the Honorable William C. Foster, with us this morning.

We are joined in these hearings this morning by Senate colleagues on the Joint Committee on Atomic Energy who have accepted the Foreign Relations Committee's invitation to sit with us during the hearings.

It is a particular pleasure for me to welcome Senator Pastore, Chairman of the Joint Committee on Atomic Energy. As my colleagues know, Senator Pastore introduced in 1966 a Senate resolution reflecting the feeling of the Senate that the President should be commended for his urgent efforts to negotiate an international agreement limiting the spread of nuclear weapons. There is no doubt that this resolution—Senate Resolution 179—which found the unanimous support of the Senate, played a major role in achieving the nonproliferation agreement now before us.

It is certainly not my intention this morning to comment at length on the Nonproliferation Treaty. Yet I find it appropriate at this time to commend the President and his Secretary of State for this significant achievement, the final realization of four and a half years of steady effort by the U.S. Government. I would also like to express my personal appreciation, which I am sure is shared by my colleagues, to the distinguished Director of the Arms Control and Disarmament Agency, Mr. Foster. Mr. Foster has been a veritable "Job" through these long and tortuous negotiations—his patience and forbearance has been outstanding.

CAREFUL SENATE CONSIDERATION URGED

As for the treaty itself, I believe that if the overwhelming majority of nations of the world embrace and fulfill both its principles and spirit, the Nonproliferation Treaty will rank as the most important international agreement brought before the U.S. Senate since the North Atlantic Pact. In my judgment, the responsibilities assumed by the signatories are so grave that the treaty itself must be subjected to the most careful and thoughtful consideration by the Senate.

This treaty is not merely a simple exchange of pledges not to give or receive nuclear weapons or skills but involves far-reaching national security considerations for the United States and a challenge to our ability and willingness to become a worldwide supplier of peaceful nuclear services and materials.

Experience has taught the Senate to proceed cautiously and vigilantly in our consideration of new national commitments. The Senate is now asked to give its advice and consent to the ratification of an immensely important step in the direction of an interdependent world. We can do nothing less here than to give this treaty the full and thorough consideration it deserves.

Mr. Secretary, I am sure you will understand that your appearance this morning may have to be considered in the nature of a preliminary hearing. The message of the President transmitting the Nonproliferation Treaty to the Senate, the accompanying report of the Secretary of State on the treaty, the treaty itself, and related documents arrived only late yesterday. I would like these documents inserted in the record.

(The documents referred to appear in the appendix.)

The Foreign Relations Committee is taking unprecedented action in considering this treaty less than 24 hours after the President submitted it to the Senate. Thus, we simply have not had the time to study the documents accompanying the treaty, and, therefore, must ask you to be prepared to return, although I hope that will not be necessary.

HEARING PROCEDURE

Finally, I would like, at this time, to indicate the general procedures I intend to follow during these hearings, assuming it is acceptable to the committee. Most of this week will be devoted by the committee to hearing witnesses appearing for the administration in support of the treaty. Deputy Secretary of Defense Paul H. Nitze and Chairman of the Joint Chiefs of Staff, Gen. Earle G. Wheeler will appear before the committee tomorrow morning. On Friday, we will hear from Dr. Glenn T. Seaborg, Chairman of the Atomic Energy Commission.

Next week we hope to hear public witnesses. The public witness list will be closed as of Tuesday of next week, July 16. Those citizens desiring to be heard should address their request to the clerk of the Committee on Foreign Relations.

I would like to suggest to the committee, since we have both Secretary Rusk and Director Foster testifying this morning, that we hear their statements, which I understand are rather brief, in tandem, and then direct our questions to the two of them afterward.

Mr. Secretary, we shall be very happy to have you proceed in your own way.

STATEMENT OF HON. DEAN RUSK, SECRETARY OF STATE

Secretary Rusk. Thank you very much, Mr. Chairman; Chairman Pastore, and distinguished Senators.

First, let me say, Mr. Chairman, that I am, of course, at the disposal of the Senate and these two distinguished committees in connection with this treaty. I owe that not only to you as Senators but also to the importance of the treaty itself, so that I am entirely available to return again if, in your judgment, you wish me to do so.

Today I am very glad to have this opportunity to discuss with you the recently signed Treaty on the Nonproliferation of Nuclear Weapons. I appreciate especially the promptness with which you are giving it your attention.

I understand that you have had this treaty in your hands only since yesterday. Actually, the international schedule made it difficult to bring the treaty before you sooner because it was considered by a special session of the General Assembly of the United Nations, and the signing took place in three capitals on July 1st, but we do believe that this is a subject with which Members of the Senate have been generally familiar and a number of you have been in close consultation about it, and it is directly related to the important resolution which you mentioned of 1966.

REFLECTION OF LONGSTANDING POLICY

This treaty, we believe, reflects a longstanding policy of both the legislative and the executive branches of the U.S. Government.

The Baruch plan in 1946 proposed an international authority to own or control all "dangerous" atomic materials from the mining process to the manufacturing of finished products. This plan would have removed nuclear energy entirely from the military field, but it was not accepted.

In that same year, the Congress prohibited, through the McMahon Act, the proliferation of nuclear weapons to any other country. The succeeding legislation—the Atomic Energy Act of 1954, as amended—likewise prohibits the transfer of our nuclear weapons to others. The basic undertaking of the nuclear-weapon parties to the Nonproliferation Treaty was deliberately patterned after that legislation.

In making the first U.S. test ban proposal, President Eisenhower noted that his purpose was to curtail the uncontrolled spread of nuclear weapons. And the International Atomic Energy Agency which resulted from his atoms for peace plan has, as one of its basic purposes, the prevention of proliferation.

When President Kennedy announced the successful negotiation of the nuclear Test Ban Treaty in 1963, he expressed the hope that it would be the opening wedge in a campaign to prevent the spread of nuclear weapons. He pointed out that a number of other nations could soon have the capacity to produce such weapons, and urged that we use whatever time remained to persuade such countries not to follow that course. If we should fail to do so, he said:

There would be no rest for anyone then, no stability, no real security, and no chance of effective disarmament. There would only be the increased chance of accidental war and an increased necessity for the great powers to involve themselves in what otherwise would be local conflicts.

In 1964, President Johnson, in his first message to the Geneva Disarmament Conference, proposed an agreement that nuclear weapons not be transferred to nonnuclear countries, and that all transfers of nuclear materials for peaceful purposes take place under international safeguards.

In 1966, the Senate unanimously adopted Senate Resolution 179. This resolution to which you, Senator Pastore, gave strong leadership, commended the efforts of the President to negotiate international agreements limiting the spread of nuclear weapons, and supported the principle of additional efforts by the President which were appropriate and necessary for the solution of nuclear proliferation problems. This expression of the sentiment of the U.S. Senate was extremely useful in the conduct of our negotiations.

OUTLINE OF TREATY

The treaty that resulted is now before you. In broadest outline, the treaty is designed to—

Commit the nations of the world which do not now have nuclear weapons, not to produce or receive them in the future;

Assure equally that such nations have the full peaceful benefits of the atom;

Provide assurance, through international safeguards, that the peaceful nuclear activities of states which have not already developed nuclear weapons will not be diverted to making such weapons; and

Give recognition to the determination of the parties that the treaty should lead to further progress toward arms control and disarmament.

Later this morning, William C. Foster, the principal negotiator of the treaty, will go over the specific provisions of the treaty with you briefly, and describe the negotiations that led up to it. It might be of use to the committee if I spelled out some of the reasons why nonproliferation is a major objective of our foreign policy—reasons that lead me to urge your advice and consent to the ratification of this treaty.

NONPROLIFERATION AS A FOREIGN POLICY OBJECTIVE

Secretary of State Herter indicated that general motivation behind our nonproliferation policy in 1960 when he said:

The more nations that have the power to trigger off a nuclear war, the greater the chance that some nation might use this power in haste or blind folly.

This general motivation lends itself to more specific analysis.

Nuclear weapons in the hands of more countries could have consequences for world security which no one can foresee. Every additional country having nuclear weapons, no matter how responsibly governed, is an additional center of independent decisionmaking on the use of nuclear weapons. International relations are thereby made more complex and more dangerous, and the risk that one of such centers could fall into irresponsible hands is increased.

Efforts of the present nuclear powers to negotiate mutually advantageous nuclear arms control agreements would be more complex and hence more difficult as the number of such powers increased, and, of course, the overall chance of accident or unauthorized use would increase as more nations acquired nuclear weapons.

Nuclear proliferation could add a new and dangerous dimension to historic ethnic and territorial disputes between nations. A decision by one party to acquire nuclear weapons could generate pressures on others to "go nuclear"—or to destroy the nuclear facilities of the acquiring state before the program reaches completion. In short, nuclear weapons proliferation could stimulate a preventive war.

Our efforts to maintain friendly relations with as many countries as possible would become more difficult by virtue of nuclear weapons spread. This is because we are seriously and solemnly committed to nonproliferation.

The spread of national nuclear capabilities would interfere with vitally needed economic growth in the less developed countries. Some potential nth countries are attempting to achieve their economic development with the support of the United States. The cost of developing nuclear weapons and delivery systems could force curtailment of economic development and tend to cancel out benefits of economic assistance provided by the United States and others.

INTERESTS OF NATO ALLIANCE

Another matter about which Senators have expressed an interest is the consistency between U.S. nonproliferation policy, as reflected in the treaty, and the interests of the NATO alliance. The United States has worked closely with its allies in the formulation of this treaty. Of concern to some of our NATO allies was the construction of articles I and II, containing the basic undertakings not to proliferate and not to acquire nuclear weapons. These articles were the first substantive articles to be included in their present form in the treaty text. Before any other substantive articles had been added, the United States allayed some of the concerns of our NATO allies about the treaty by giving them the following answers to questions they had posed:

The treaty deals only with what is prohibited, not with what is permitted. It prohibits transfer to any recipient whatsoever of nuclear weapons or control over them, meaning bombs and warheads. It also prohibits the transfer of other nuclear explosive devices, because a nuclear explosive device intended for peaceful purposes can be used as a weapon or can be easily adapted for such use. It does not deal with, and therefore does not prohibit, transfer of nuclear delivery vehicles or delivery systems, or control over them to any recipient, so long as such transfer does not involve bombs or warheads. It does not deal with allied consultations and planning on nuclear defense so long as no transfer of nuclear weapons or control over them results. It does not deal with arrangements for deployment of nuclear weapons within allied territory as these do not involve any transfer of nuclear weapons or control over them unless and until a decision were made to go to war, at which time the treaty would no longer be controlling. And, it does not deal with the problem of European unity, and would not bar succession by a new federated European state to the nuclear status of one of its former components. A new federated European state would have to control all of its external security functions, including defense and all foreign policy matters relating to external security, but would not have to be so centralized as to assume all governmental functions. While not dealing with succession by such a federated state, the treaty would bar transfer of nuclear weapons (including ownership) or control over them to any recipient, including a multilateral entity.

SAFEGUARDS

The other primary concern of our NATO allies was article III on safeguards. The United States effort involved working out a resolution of this problem satisfactory to us and to our NATO allies, and at the same time acceptable to the Soviet Union.

The safeguards problem arose out of the existence of two international safeguards systems: one, the International Atomic Energy Agency (IAEA), with headquarters at Vienna, and the other a system set up earlier by the European Atomic Energy Community (Euratom) of the six Common Market countries.

It had always been United States policy to work toward a single, worldwide system of safeguards. However, the Common Market countries were reluctant to allow the IAEA safeguards system to operate in their countries for fear that it would result in abandonment of the Euratom system, with unfavorable effects on progress toward European unity. As a result, the United States has been clear in its negotiations with the Soviets that both systems should be permitted to continue.

The Soviet Union was agreeable to mandatory safeguards from the nonnuclear signatories of the treaty but believes those safeguards should be administered by the IAEA. From the outset the Soviets opposed the idea of accepting Euratom safeguards as a complete substitute for IAEA safeguards under the treaty, on the ground that Euratom safeguards amounted to self-inspection of Euratom members.

There was an impasse in the negotiations over safeguards until the early fall of 1967. Then, after discussions in capitals of alliance members, in the North Atlantic Council and in Euratom, the United States, on November 2, submitted a revised compromise draft, which was given a "green light" by the North Atlantic Council as a basis for further negotiations. Throughout November and December we urged Soviet acceptance of the November 2 draft as the road to agreement.

When the 18-nation Disarmament Committee reconvened in Geneva on January 18, 1968, after a month's recess, the Soviet Union agreed to this draft. A complete draft treaty, including this article III on safeguards, was submitted to the Disarmament Committee. This article is the one in the treaty presently before you. In presenting it, the U.S. representative in Geneva set forth the three guiding principles enumerated in my letter to the President recommending ratification of the treaty, a letter which is in your hands.

In sum, the treaty that was negotiated took the concerns of our NATO allies into account and, I believe, went as far as we could to satisfy those concerns.

PROMPT ACTION URGED

We have asked for prompt action on the treaty because many countries, particularly our allies, are waiting to see what we do before starting their own parliamentary consideration of the treaty. We recognize that the effectiveness of the treaty will depend in large measure upon the adherences of other countries. But we have been among the leaders in securing agreement on this treaty, and other countries are looking to us now. If we want the treaty to receive widespread adherence in time to have reasonable prospects for dealing with the perils of proliferation, we should, if possible, proceed promptly with our own constitutional procedures.

Mr. Chairman, in addressing the United Nations General Assembly on the day it endorsed the Nonproliferation Treaty, President Johnson said:

"I believe that this treaty can lead to further measures that will inhibit the senseless continuation of the arms race. I believe that it can give the world time—very precious time—to protect itself against Armageddon. And if my faith is well founded, as I believe that it is," he said, "then this treaty will truly deserve to be recorded as the most important step toward peace since the founding of the United States."

I wholeheartedly concur in the President's statement. And one of the further arms control measures this treaty can help to promote is the limitation of strategic offensive and defensive nuclear weapons delivery systems.

MUTUALITY OF INTERESTS WITH THE SOVIET UNION

The United States has been seeking negotiations on a measure of this kind since early 1964. Recently our hopes for serious discussions were stimulated by Soviet Foreign Minister Gromyko's statement before the Supreme Soviet that the Soviet Union is now ready to talk. Subsequently, on July 1, the day the Nonproliferation Treaty was signed, Premier Kosygin referred to a Soviet memorandum to other governments which stated:

The Soviet Government declares its readiness to conduct an exchange of opinions with interested states on mutual limitations and subsequent reduction of strategic means of delivery of nuclear weapons.

On the same day, President Johnson announced that "agreement has been reached between the Governments of the Union of Soviet Socialist Republics and the United States to enter in the nearest future into discussions" on this subject.

This augurs well for meaningful further steps in the field of arms control. Despite our differences, the United States and the Soviet Union have a mutuality of interest in common with all humanity.

That interest, Mr. Chairman, simply is survival.

Thank you, Mr. Chairman.

Before Mr. Foster explains the meaning of the various articles of the treaty, permit me to associate myself with you, sir, in expression of my very great esteem for the dedication and the persistence and the negotiating skill which Mr. Foster has brought to his important task. You may now wish to hear from Mr. Foster.

Senator SPARKMAN. Very glad to hear from you, Mr. Foster.

STATEMENT OF HON. WILLIAM C. FOSTER, DIRECTOR, U.S. ARMS CONTROL AND DISARMAMENT AGENCY

Mr. Foster. Thank you, Mr. Chairman. Chairman Sparkman and Chairman Pastore, and gentlemen, having appeared before both the Foreign Relations Committee and the Joint Committee on Atomic Energy many times during the course of negotiations on this treaty— times when the prospects for agreement were less than encouraging— I am particularly pleased to be here with you today.

Before I get into the provisions of the treaty and some of the issues involved in the negotiations, I want to tell you that I am deeply appreciative of the suggestions and encouragement you gentlemen have given to me. I firmly believe that the agreement we have now concluded commends itself to ratification.

The treaty consists of a preamble and 11 articles.

PREAMBLE

Paragraphs 1 through 3 of the preamble reflect the importance and urgency of preventing nuclear weapons proliferation.

Paragraphs 4 and 5 express support for international safeguards on peaceful nuclear activities, and for continuing improvements in safeguards techniques.

The importance of such safeguards has increased with the vast expansion of the nuclear power industry. In the face of this expanding peaceful nuclear technology, further progress must be made to expand and implement international safeguards. It has been estimated, for example, that by 1985 the world's peaceful nuclear power stations alone will be turning out enough plutonium for the production of some 20 nuclear bombs every day. The safeguards capabilities of the International Atomic Energy Agency will have to be expanded to meet the need. Its staff of trained inspectors will have to be increased.

The IAEA is an existing organization with much experience to build on. We believe it capable of handling the job better than any new organization which might be set up.

Paragraphs 6 and 7 deal with the principle of sharing the benefits of peaceful applications of nuclear energy, and of making technological byproducts of work on nuclear explosives available for peaceful purposes.

Paragraphs 8 through 11 express the urgent need for further progress toward disarmament and limitations on the nuclear arms race.

The last preambular pararaph reaffirms the principles of the United Nations Charter regarding the use of force and threats of force in international relations.

Related to this last paragraph is the concern expressed by a number of nonaligned countries that, should they adhere to a nonproliferation treaty and forego the option of developing nuclear weapons, they would subject themselves to possible nuclear blackmail. There is no provision on this subject in the treaty beyond this preambular paragraph. To deal with the problem, on March 7, the United States, Soviet Union, and United Kingdom representatives joined at the 18-Nation Disarmament Committee in introducing a draft U.N. Security

Council resolution on security assurances. It was adopted by the Security Council on June 19 by a vote of 10 to 0 with five abstentions.

The resolution is intended to reassure nonaligned Nations of their security should they become parties to the treaty. The resolution does not involve the United States in any new commitment, but recognizes that "aggression with nuclear weapons or the threat of such aggression against a non-nuclear-weapon state would create a situation in which the Security Council, and above all its nuclear-weapon state permanent members, would have to act immediately in accordance with their obligations under the United Nations Charter."

ARTICLES I AND II—OPERATIVE PARTS

Articles I and II contain the basic undertakings of the parties to prevent the proliferation of nuclear weapons. As Secretary Rusk has pointed out, these articles deal with what is prohibited, not with what is permitted.

Article I deals with the obligations of parties that are nuclear-weapon states.

First, such states undertake not to transfer nuclear weapons, or control over them, to any recipient whatsoever.

Second, nuclear-weapon states must not assist non-nuclear-weapon states to manufacture or otherwise acquire nuclear weapons.

Third, these prohibitions apply not only to nuclear weapons but also to other nuclear explosive devices. Inclusion of the latter was necessary because a nuclear explosive device intended for peaceful purposes can be used as a weapon or can be easily adapted for such use, and because the technology for making such devices is essentially indistinguishable from that of making nuclear weapons.

Article II deals with the obligations of all parties that are not nuclear-weapon states. Such non-nuclear-weapon states undertake first, not to receive the transfer of nuclear weapons or other nuclear explosive devices, or control over them, from any transferor whatsoever. Second, they must not manufacture or otherwise acquire such weapons or devices or seek or receive assistance in such manufacture.

ARTICLE III—SAFEGUARDS

Article III provides for verification by means of international safeguards of compliance with the obligations assumed by non-nuclear-weapon parties to the treaty to insure that nuclear energy is not diverted from peaceful uses to nuclear weapons or other nuclear explosive devices. I understand Chairman Seaborg of the Atomic Energy Commission is prepared to address the subject of safeguards, so I will restrict my comments to what the article provides in the context of its negotiating background.

Paragraph 1 provides that such safeguards shall be applied on all source or special fissionable material in all peaceful nuclear activities within the territory, jurisdiction or control of non-nuclear-weapon parties. Source or special fissionable materials include all the nuclear materials which are essential to the manufacture of nuclear explosives. Non-nuclear-weapon parties undertake to accept safeguards on such material for the exclusive purpose of verification of the fulfillment of their obligations under the treaty not to divert fissionable materials to weapons use. The safeguards are to be as set forth in agreements to be negotiated and concluded with the International Atomic Energy Agency (IAEA) in accordance with the statute of the IAEA and the IAEA safeguards system.

Paragraph 2 prohibits the provision by any of the parties of (*a*) source or special fissionable material or (*b*) equipment or material especially designed or prepared for the processing, use or production of special fissionable material, to any non-nuclear-weapon state for peaceful purposes, unless the source or special fissionable material shall be subject to the safeguards required by article III.

Paragraph 3 prescribes that the safeguards be implemented so as to comply with article IV of the treaty—which deals with furthering the peaceful uses of nuclear energy—and to avoid hampering either the economic and technological development of the parties or international cooperation in the field of peaceful nuclear activities.

Paragraph 4 of the safeguards article concerns the manner in which the agreements called for in paragraph 1 shall be concluded. Non-nuclear parties may conclude such agreements either individually or together with other states in accordance with the statute of the IAEA. Euratom states, for example, could, therefore, work out safeguards arrangements as a group. Paragraph 4 also provides that negotiations of safeguards agreements shall commence within 180 days after the treaty's entry into force and shall be concluded within 18 months after the date of initiation of negotiations. This provides for a transition period during which the arrangements for treaty safeguards can be worked out and put into operation.

GUIDING PRINCIPLES

In negotiating the safeguards article. the United States was guided by certain principles worked out in the course of extensive and detailed discussions of safeguards with our NATO and Euratom allies. I request that the principles be inserted in the record at this point.

(The material referred to follows:)

GUIDING PRINCIPLES RE ARTICLE III ENUNCIATED BY U.S. REPRESENTATIVE AT THE 18-NATION DISARMAMENT CONFERENCE ON JANUARY 18, 1968

1. There should be safeguards for all non-nuclear-weapon parties of such a nature that all parties can have confidence in their effectiveness. Therefore safeguards established by an agreement negotiated and concluded with the IAEA in accordance with the Statute of the IAEA and the Agency's safeguards system must enable the IAEA to carry out its responsibility of providing assurance that no diversion is taking place.

2. In discharging their obligations under article III. non-nuclear-weapon parties may negotiate safeguards agreements with the IAEA individually or together with other parties; and, specifically, an agreement covering such obligations may be entered into between the IAEA and another international organization the work of which is related to the IAEA and the membership of which includes the parties concerned.

3. In order to avoid unnecessary duplication. the IAEA should make appropriate use of existing records and safeguards, provided that under such mutually-agreed arrangements IAEA can satisfy itself that nuclear material is not diverted to nuclear weapons or other nuclear explosive devices.

Mr. Chairman, if you should want those read later I will be happy, of course, to do so.

Mr. FOSTER. Article III does not require safeguards on the peaceful nuclear activities of nuclear-weapon parties. This factor was noted by many States at the ENDC, in the U.N. and in the consultations in the North Atlantic Council. It proved impossible to negotiate those arrangements within the treaty itself. Therefore, and to remove the grounds for claim that safeguards would unfairly place industrial, economic, or other burdens on nonnuclear parties, President Johnson, on December 2, 1967, stated that the United States is not asking any country to accept safeguards that we are unwilling to accept ourselves. He announced that "when such safeguards are applied under the treaty, the United States will permit the International Atomic Energy Agency to apply its safeguards to all nuclear activities in the United States—excluding only those with direct national security significance."

The United Kingdom has made a parallel offer.

ARTICLES IV AND V—PEACEFUL USES OF NUCLEAR ENERGY

Articles IV and V of the treaty encourage the peaceful uses of nuclear energy. They thus serve to further goals of the United States such as those enunciated by President Eisenhower in his "Atoms for Peace" plan.

Earlier drafts of the Nonproliferation Treaty contained several preambular paragraphs encouraging the peaceful uses of nuclear energy under international safeguards. During the course of negotiations, some states believed that these positive aspects of the treaty should be further emphasized through substantive provisions in the body of the treaty in order to gain wider support for it. New articles setting forth undertakings with regard to the peaceful uses of nuclear energy were developed at the ENDC and strengthened in later drafts at the United Nations.

Paragraph 1 of article IV insures that nothing in the treaty will be interpreted as affecting the right of all parties, without discrimination, to use nuclear energy for peaceful purposes in conformity with articles I and II.

Paragraph 2 contains an undertaking by all parties to facilitate, and affirms their right to participate in, the fullest possible exchange of equipment, materials and scientific and technological information for the peaceful uses of nuclear energy. Finally it requires those parties in a position to do so to cooperate in contributing to the further development of peaceful applications of nuclear energy, especially in the territories of non-nuclear-weapon states and with due consideration for the needs of the developing areas of the world.

Article V is designed to compensate for the undertaking by non-nuclear-weapon parties to article II not to acquire nuclear explosive devices even for peaceful purposes. It provides assurance to such parties that they will not lose, by such renunciation, the potential benefits from peaceful applications of nuclear explosions. It is also designed to make it completely clear that there would be no economic incentive for them to try to develop their own nuclear explosive devices for such purposes. Specifically, the parties to the treaty undertake to take appropriate measures to insure that the potential benefits of such peaceful applications will be made available to non-nuclear-weapon parties on a nondiscriminatory basis and that the charge to such parties for the explosive devices used will be as low as possible and exclude any charge for research and development. The article requires that such benefits shall be made available in accordance with the treaty—which would preclude non-nuclear-weapon states from acquiring the nuclear explosive devices themselves or control over them. Thus the devices would remain under the custody and control of a nuclear-weapon state, which would, in effect, provide a nuclear explosion service.

The article speaks of making such services available "through appropriate procedures" and "under appropriate international observation." It contemplates that non-nuclear-weapon states will be able to obtain such services pursuant to a special international agreement or agreements, through an appropriate international body with adequate representation of non-nuclear-weapon states. It provides that negotiations on this subject shall commence as soon as possible after the treaty enters into force. But it preserves the option to meet requests for such services on a bilateral basis without the need to await multilateral agreement or action concerning the provision of such services through an international body.

This article is in accord with the five general principles that I proposed in Geneva on March 21, 1967, which spell out in somewhat greater detail our thinking on this subject. I request, Mr. Chairman, that these principles be inserted in the record at this point.

Senator SPARKMAN. Without objection that insertion and the previous one that you requested will be made a part of the record.

Mr. FOSTER. Thank you, sir.

(The material referred to follows:)

PRINCIPLES RELATING TO NUCLEAR EXPLOSION SERVICES SUGGESTED BY U.S. REPRESENTATIVE TO ENDC, MARCH 21, 1967

First, if and when peaceful applications of nuclear explosives which are permissible under the test-ban treaty prove technically and economically feasible, nuclear-weapon-states should make available to other states nuclear explosive services for peaceful applications. Such a service would consist of performing the desired nuclear detonation under appropriate international observation with the nuclear device remaining under the custody and control of the state which performed the service.

Second, there should be a means provided for non-nuclear-weapon states wishing to do so to request nuclear explosive services from the nuclear-weapon-states through an international body in which the non-nuclear-weapon states would participate. The purpose of these arrangements would be to make clear that, once the participating nuclear powers are prepared to undertake practical applications of peaceful nuclear explosives, they will not withhold nuclear detonation services to others because of extraneous considerations.

Third, costs to non-nuclear-weapon states for peaceful-purpose detonations by nuclear states would be kept as low as possible. They should not, for example, include the costs of research and development.

Fourth, there should be full consultation among nuclear and non-nuclear parties to the limited test-ban treaty about any amendment of that treaty required in order to carry out feasible projects.

And fifth, the conditions and procedures for international collaboration in accomplishing peaceful nuclear explosive projects would be developed in full consultation with the non-nuclear-weapon states.

ARTICLE VI—PURSUE NEGOTIATIONS

Mr. FOSTER. Article VI is an undertaking by all parties to pursue negotiations in good faith on effective measures relating to cessation of the nuclear arms race at an early date and to nuclear disarmament, and on a treaty on general and complete disarmament under strict and effective international control.

OTHER TREATY PROVISIONS

The remaining articles of the treaty (arts. VII through XI) are described in the Executive message transmitting the treaty to the Senate.

Of these articles, two of them are worthy of your particular attention.

Article VIII establishes the procedures for amending the treaty.

Paragraph 1 of that article is derived from the Limited Nuclear Test Ban Treaty. It requires the depositary Governments to convene a conference to consider a proposed amendment if requested to do so by one-third or more of the parties to the treaty.

Paragraph 2 provides that for an amendment to enter into force it must be ratified by a majority of all parties to the treaty, including all nuclear-weapon parties and all other parties which, on the date the amendment is circulated, are members of the Board of Governors of the IAEA. No amendment will enter into force for any party that does not ratify it.

Article VIII also provides for a conference, 5 years after the treaty enters into force, to review the operation of the treaty. Further review conferences, at 5-year intervals thereafter, will be held if requested by a majority of the parties.

The other important article is article X.

Paragraph 1 of that article provides a right of withdrawal upon 3 months' notice if a party finds that extraordinary events related to the subject matter of the treaty have jeopardized its supreme interests. This provision is the same as the withdrawal provision in the Nuclear Test Ban Treaty except that it requires notice of such withdrawal to be given to the United Nations Security Council as well as to the other treaty parties and requires the notice to include a statement of the extraordinary events involved.

Paragraph 2 of article X provides for a conference, to be held 25 years after the treaty enters into force, at which a majority of the parties will decide whether the treaty shall continue in force indefinitely, or be extended for an additional fixed period or periods.

That concludes my statement, Mr. Chairman. I think this treaty is very much in our national interest. I join the President and Secretary Rusk in recommending your consent to its ratification and I would, of course, be glad to answer any questions you may have.

Thank you very much.

Senator SPARKMAN. Thank you very much, Mr. Foster.

I shall be very brief in my questioning.

14

SAFEGUARDS ARRANGEMENTS NOT YET DEFINITE

Do I understand correctly from the two statements that safeguards are not yet definite?

Secretary Rusk. The safeguards arrangements—in the first place there are a number of safeguards arrangements that are already in effect. The International Atomic Energy Agency applies safeguards, Euratom applies safeguards, we ourselves apply safeguards on a national basis to facilities and plants in our own country. We ourselves have inspectors who look at safeguards in certain other countries. So there are a good many safeguards already in operation.

But under this treaty, it is anticipated that what is required are safeguards in which everyone can have confidence and, therefore, we contemplate that there would be agreements worked out with the International Atomic Energy Agency, which would take into account the nature of the safeguards required, the nature of the facilities being safeguarded and all the special circumstances that might exist in particular countries in order to achieve an international safeguards system in which all can have confidence. So we would anticipate there would be a considerable number of negotiations with the International Atomic Energy Agency, one of the most important of which would be the one between the Euratom countries and the IAEA.

Senator Sparkman. As I recall from one of your statements Russia objected to using the Euratom formula, but was willing to use the International Atomic Energy Agency system.

Secretary Rusk. The objection raised by the Soviet Union was, if you relied solely upon the Euratom arrangements this would be tantamount to having allies inspecting themselves. They insisted that it would be necessary to have an international system in which all countries could have confidence.

Now, as a matter of fact, the safeguards of the sort that are applied by Euratom are very similar to the safeguards applied by the International Atomic Energy Agency, and we see no special problem in meshing those safeguards, in relating them to each other, in such a way that there is confidence in the nature of the safeguards, but that Euratom safeguards and the Euratom system of peaceful cooperation in the use of nuclear energy can proceed without interruption in the light of an agreement to be worked out between Euratom and the IAEA.

Senator Sparkman. Then the purport of the treaty is that while they recognize the various safeguards that you have mentioned there will be continuing negotiations seeking a uniform application, is that right?

Secretary Rusk. Yes.

And I think one could illustrate the way in which these would be meshed in another way. As Chairman Seaborg can spell out for you in any detail you wish, we have our own safeguard system inside the United States with respect to our own peaceful facilities.

Now, in working out our arrangements with the International Atomic Energy Agency for safeguarding the plants that the President announced would be put under safeguards, of course, these internal safeguards of ours will be directly related to the safeguards that the

15

IAEA might wish, in such a way as not to intrude or interfere with the normal operations of the plants.

IS THE UNITED STATES COMMITTED TO ADDITIONAL RESPONSIBILITIES?

Senator SPARKMAN. Let me ask you this question: Does the Security Council resolution and the U.S. declaration commit the United States to any additional responsibilities other than those already assumed under the United Nations Charter?

Secretary RUSK. I would think not, Mr. Chairman, both as a matter of law and as a matter of policy.

This is a reflection of the basic concept upon which the charter itself was originally conceived. Article 24 of the charter states that its members, the United Nations members, "confer on the Security Council primary responsibility for the maintenance of international peace and security, and agree that in carrying out its duties under this responsibility the Security Council acts on their behalf."

It was further anticipated, as a basic premise of the United Nations Charter, that action by the Security Council would require agreement among the permanent members. It was assumed that, unless the permanent members agreed, the Security Council would not be in position to act under the security arrangements in chapters 6 and 7, for example. That is the so-called veto, a measure which guaranties that it would act only on the basis of agreement among the permanent members.

I think if you will read the charter it will be seen also that the permanent members do have a special responsibility under the charter. The five permanent members, for example, constitute the Military Staff Committee. Now, we regret that the arrangements that were contemplated in the charter for the organization of United Nations Forces available to the Security Council never came into being. As a junior officer in the Department of State I participated in those negotiations back in 1946, and those forces were never established as contemplated by chapter 7 of the charter.

But it was assumed that in situations, including the situations discussed in this resolution, it would be the primary responsibility of the Security Council, that it would require the agreement of permanent members, and that the permanent members themselves would have a special responsibility.

Now, this resolution is aimed at aggression by nuclear weapons or the threat of such aggression by nuclear weapons, as determined by the Security Council, including all of its permanent members. It does not—as the declaration itself clearly states—attempt to modify article 51 of the charter, which itself states that "Nothing in the present charter shall impair the inherent right of individual or collective self-defense if an armed attack occurs against a member of the United Nations, until the Security Council has taken the measures necessary to maintain international peace and security."

Now, there are those who minimize the importance of this resolution—a good many of the non-nuclear countries—on the grounds that it would be extremely difficult for the permanent members to be in agreement.

But I think it is politically of very considerable importance that three of the permanent members—the Soviet Union, the United Kingdom and the United States—made identical declarations, and that France at least consented through an abstention rather than through a negative vote, which made it clear that an aggression by nuclear weapons or the threat of such aggression fell squarely within the primary responsibility of the Security Council as delineated in the charter.

So, in a very specific answer to your question, I would say that this does not change the basic obligations which were written into the charter in any event when it was originally drafted and ratified. It is, I think, a welcome step toward the possibility that the permanent members might under certain limited circumstances be prepared to move together, and this itself might have a very important deterrent effect upon those who might frivolously contemplate aggression by means of nuclear weapons.

U.S. USE OF VETO POWER

Senator SPARKMAN. Am I correct then in this assumption, that the United States remains free to use its veto power in the event a future proposal before the Security Council seems incompatible with the interests of the United States?

Secretary RUSK. Oh, yes; there is nothing in this resolution which requires us in advance to vote for resolutions on a hypothetical basis. This would require a major decision by the President of the United States, and I am sure he would be in consultation with the leaders of the Congress in casting a vote on such an important matter, because there would be a very grave situation that would have to be considered under all the circumstances existing at the time.

THREAT OF NUCLEAR AGGRESSION

Senator SPARKMAN. Now, let me ask you this question: What would be a specific illustration of what might be a case of a threat of nuclear aggression as specified in the security guarantee resolution? For instance, could India claim it was threatened by nuclear aggression from China, and, if so, what would be the situation then?

Secretary RUSK. It is, Mr. Chairman, a little delicate to speculate in detail about specific cases—specific but hypothetical cases—involving other nations, so I hope you will understand some caution on my part. But I would think that if there were, for example, a clear instance of an ultimatum or direct threat by a nuclear power against a nonnuclear power which in effect said, "You bow your neck, you submit to what I am demanding of you or I will use nuclear weapons," then it would be for the permanent members of the Security Council especially and for the Security Council as a whole to consider whether that created a situation referred to in this resolution which could be described as an aggression by nuclear weapons, or the threat of such use, that would make operational the responsibilities of the Security Council.

Senator SPARKMAN. Well, thank you very much, Mr. Secretary.

Now, I am going to ask the chairman of the Joint Committee on Atomic Energy to question the witness.

Senator PASTORE. First of all, I should like very much to compliment Bill Foster for the excellent job that he did in reaching an agreement on this treaty. As he has pointed out, he has been in constant consultation with the Foreign Relations Committee and also with the Joint Committee on Atomic Energy, and we have watched this thing develop step by step.

IS UNITED STATES SOLE GUARANTOR AGAINST NUCLEAR BLACKMAIL?

Now, I think it is necessary for us to nail down this question of prevention of blackmail and the responsibility of the United States in this regard. In other words, it must be clear that there is no unilateral commitment on the part of the United States to become the sole guarantor against nuclear blackmail; is that correct?

Secretary RUSK. That is correct.

Mr. FOSTER. That is correct.

Secretary RUSK. That is correct, Senator.

You see, when you ask more than 100 nations to forgo the option of developing nuclear weapons, a great many of them are going to ask themselves the natural question, "Does this enhance our security; does it jeopardize our security?"

Along the way, various ideas were suggested. One was that somehow we ought to take ourselves unilateral responsibility, under what might be called alliances, to those who signed the treaty. Now, that is something that we and the other great powers would not want. It is something that the nonnuclears themselves would not want. I am sure the Senate would not want it. In any event there was the United Nations Security Council which has by charter the primary responsibility for maintaining international peace and stability. So it was agreed it was the Security Council's responsibility. We are a member of that Council and we are a permanent member of that Council. Our vote is essential. If we vote "No" there is no effective action by the Security Council. But in any event that is the way the charter was written. So this does not in any way extend the unilateral obligations of the United States but does make it clear that we think this is the responsibility of the Security Council.

Senator PASTORE. But whatever action the United States decides to take in the future, depending upon what the events might be, would have to be a decision made by the U.S. Government exclusive of this March 7 resolution?

Secretary RUSK. The decision itself would have to be made at the time in terms of the total interests of the United States and the judgment of the President, in consultation with the leaders of the Congress, as to what is required in our own interests at that time.

Senator PASTORE. Insofar as the resolution is concerned that response must be international in character?

Secretary RUSK. It must be international, and it must include the agreement of the permanent members of the Security Council, all of them, because if any one of them votes "No," the resolution could have no practical effect.

EFFECT OF NONSIGNERS ON U.S. RATIFICATION

Senator PASTORE. Should we be discouraged in any way from pursuing the ratification of this treaty because it has not been signed by all the nations of the world?

Secretary RUSK. I think not, Mr. Chairman. Including two who are signing today, there will have been 60 nations that have signed in Washington, and there are certain other nations that have signed in other capitals who have not signed here. There are a good many other nations who now have this before their own governments for decision. Some of them have parliamentary procedures to go through. There is the Euratom Commission considering the compatibility between this treaty and the Treaty of Rome. There is a conference of the nonnuclear countries in August which might affect the attitudes of some.

We think that there will be a very large number of nations still to sign the treaty. We know certain countries have some problems, and they have made this clear in some of their public statements.

But we think that this will obtain the signature of an overwhelming number of countries. There may be a few countries who are going to have to take a little more time to look at the total situation with greater care before they feel their security is enhanced by signing this treaty.

TREATY IS AN IMPROVEMENT OVER PRESENT SITUATION

Senator PASTORE. Until we have reached this day of unanimity which, of course, may be quite distant, the fact still remains that without the treaty we would have the status quo and nations could go along willy-nilly and do anything that they could do today.

Secretary RUSK. That is right.

Senator PASTORE. Yet this treaty even though at the present moment we feel that it needs a little more filling out, is a vast improvement over the present situation?

Secretary RUSK. Yes, indeed, Mr. Chairman. A treaty which has 100 signatories puts the world in a vastly better position than the world would be in if there were no treaty at all, and this itself is a very important element in this situation.

Now, there are those who are concerned about the fact that two nuclear powers are not expected to sign this treaty. But, it still is important that 100 nations or more sign this treaty, because it means that the potential customers of these two who have not signed have undertaken obligations not to receive nuclear weapons.

It also means that 100 nations or more will have accepted an obligation not to develop their own weapons even without the assistance of existing nuclear powers. So that, again, the total situation is greatly enhanced even though the treaty does not achieve perfection in terms of total adherence by every authority or government or state in the world.

Senator PASTORE. That is all, Mr. Chairman.

Senator SPARKMAN. Senator Hickenlooper, who is a member not only of the Foreign Relations Committee but also of the Joint Committee on Atomic Energy.

Senator HICKENLOOPER. Thank you, Mr. Chairman.

I want to join with the chairman, Mr. Sparkman, and with the Chairman of the Joint Committee, Senator Pastore, in appreciation of the work that has been done by Mr. Foster and also by Secretary Rusk in connection with the search for further steps toward solution of these very difficult problems.

U.S. INSPECTION PRIVILEGES

I would like to address a question to Secretary Rusk. Mr. Secretary, it seems that this whole situation which culminates in the proposed treaty was begun with the Baruch plan. Isn't that true?

Secretary RUSK. That is exactly true.

Senator HICKENLOOPER. And step by step the International Atomic Energy Agency was a part of it. All of this was a progressive step operation culminating finally in the Nonproliferation Treaty which admittedly is not perfect but which may—and I am not ready to testify to that yet fully—have some acceptable safeguards in it, perhaps only psychological or emotional.

What are our privileges by way of inspection of the Soviet nuclear plants or those of any other nuclear power in connection with this treaty? Can we send in teams under this treaty to see what they are doing?

Secretary RUSK. This treaty itself, Senator, does not provide for safeguards in the nuclear weapon states themselves. The Soviet Union has refused to accept inspection of its plants, even the plants for peaceful uses.

Senator HICKENLOOPER. That was one of the things that held up the Baruch plan, wasn't it?

Secretary RUSK. Yes, we would have hoped very much that they would do that. Despite this fact we felt it was very important for us to be willing to do that for one very particular reason. Some of the nonnuclear countries were afraid we were trying to find some commercial advantage for ourselves in these arrangements. Some were fearful of what was called, what might be called, industrial espionage. We know very well that safeguards are not involved with industrial secrets. Safeguards can be adequate without getting into the special techniques which industries may develop in the normal course of research and development. The safeguarding has to do with what happens to the dangerous fuel, the dangerous elements.

So we thought we ought to reassure them that these irrelevant factors are not really involved, and so we thought it would be wise for us to demonstrate that by making it clear that we are prepared to accept in our country safeguards of the sort which we wanted in their countries.

Senator HICKENLOOPER. It all adds up to the fact we cannot inspect, is that it?

Secretary RUSK. We cannot inspect inside the Soviet Union, that is correct, sir, until such time as the Soviet Union——

Senator HICKENLOOPER. Can we go into other countries and inspect their nuclear plants?

Secretary RUSK. The International Atomic Energy Agency does that and we ourselves do a certain amount of that, as you know, sir, in connection with some of our own arrangements so that, yes, in that sense there is inspection. We will have personnel who are part of the International Atomic Energy Agency system and our normal safeguard arrangements would continue to operate.

Senator HICKENLOOPER. Can the International Atomic Energy Agency inspectors come in and inspect us?

Secretary RUSK. Arrangements would be made by which they could come in under agreements to be worked out between us and the IAEA, to look at those plants which are made available for such safeguards in the recent declaration made by the President.

RELUCTANCE OF SOVIETS TO ACCEPT INSPECTION

Senator HICKENLOOPER. How about the Soviets?

Secretary RUSK. The Soviets would not accept such inspectors at the present time on the plants in their own country even for peaceful uses.

Senator HICKENLOOPER. So we didn't make any gain on that at all.

Secretary RUSK. On that particular point we did not, sir. And I might just comment in passing that when we look ahead to the unfinished business in the field of disarmament, the problem of inspection, verification safeguards is a major problem, major obstacle, which somehow we have got to find a way through, because the disinclination of the Soviet Union to accept inspection safeguards and verification inside its own territory has proved to be a major obstacle in moving down this path.

Senator HICKENLOOPER. So at least at the moment under this treaty we have to rely on what the Soviets tell us?

Secretary RUSK. That is correct. But, of course, since they are a nuclear power, and do, of course, make many nuclear weapons, the purpose of the treaty, which is nonproliferation, is not directly involved with that particular issue.

SOVIET DECISION TO ENTER NUCLEAR DISCUSSIONS

Senator HICKENLOOPER. Is there any significance to the fact that the Soviets were willing to talk about a test ban treaty a reasonable time after they had completed some very extensive tests on high atmospheric explosions and were theoretically at least able to get the results of those tests? And likewise now that they have an over the horizon atomic weapon, they now say "we are ready to talk to you."

Secretary RUSK. In my 8th year on this job, Senator, I have gotten to be a little careful about trying to explore the minds of our colleagues in the Soviet Union. My guess is that they made a judgment which we made at that time, and that is that they did not consider that the partial test ban treaty represented an injury to their security interests, and in making that judgment they undoubtedly took into account where they considered they were in the development of nuclear weapons. We made the same kind of judgment ourselves actually in terms of whether it was in our interests whether to accept such a treaty.

Senator HICKENLOOPER. Yes, I know we accepted it, but I am not so sure it was in our interests. I have a great question about that.

EFFECT OF TREATY ON NATO AND WARSAW PACT

What effect will this treaty have on NATO and the Warsaw Pact?

Secretary RUSK. In my opening statement I reflected the result of careful consultation between ourselves and our NATO allies on this point, It does not, for example, affect the deployment of U.S.-owned and controlled nuclear weapons on the territory of our allies and the existing arrangements under which those weapons are present. It does not affect the closest consultation in, for example, the Nuclear Committee of NATO on all of the problems of strategy and the decisions which have to be made in that field. It does not, of course, apply to a situation of war. It does not interfere with the development of European unity if that unity moves to a significant unity involving a single control over the defense and foreign policy of the participating countries.

So we feel that this treaty enhances the security of NATO, because they, too, have an interest in the nonproliferation of nuclear weapons.

EFFECT OF TREATY ON MILITARY USE OF NUCLEAR DEVICES

Senator HICKENLOOPER. Does this treaty in any way limit our military use of atomic or nuclear devices or the Soviet military use of nuclear or atomic devices that were not in existence prior to the adoption of this treaty or the resolution by the United Nations?

Secretary RUSK. First, Senator, this treaty does not get into the problem which is generally called the nonuse problem. Along the way efforts were made to include provisions in this treaty that would deal with the problem of nonuse. But this is a special highly complicated and difficult subject which we felt could not be the basis for agreement as a part of this treaty. So when you take into account not only our alliances but also the Charter of the United Nations, this does not change the existing situation with respect to the use of nuclear weapons.

Senator HICKENLOOPER. Either by us or the Russians?

Secretary RUSK. That is right.

I would point out, for example, Senator, there is an implication, of course, a strong implication, in the resolution passed by the Security Council as distinct from the treaty, that we do not contemplate committing aggression by the use of or threat of nuclear weapons. Well, that is an obligation we had already under the Charter of the U.N. But this treaty does not change the existing circumstance with respect to the use of nuclear weapons.

IS PROPOSED TREATY SELF EXECUTING?

Senator HICKENLOOPER. Is this treaty self executing?

Secretary RUSK. I would think, Mr. Chairman, that, subject to safeguards—that is the safeguard feature would make it something less than totally self executing.

Senator HICKENLOOPER. Will we have to have supplementary legislation?

Secretary RUSK. I don't believe that we ourselves would need further legislation on the subject because, primarily the purpose of the treaty and the arrangements under the treaty reflect in large part the provisions of our law that are already there in the McMahon Act as amended by you gentlemen here in the Congress.

EFFECT OF TREATY ON PLOWSHARE-TYPE OPERATIONS

Senator HICKENLOOPER. Does this treaty in anyway prevent our providing atomic or nuclear devices to other countries or making mutual arrangements with those countries concerning such devices for peaceful use such as Plowshare?

Secretary RUSK. On the first point: with regard to weapons, this treaty would prevent our turning over the ownership or control of nuclear weapons to any nonnuclear country or to any recipient whatsoever in that respect.

This treaty itself not only does not prohibit the use of nuclear explosions for such things as Plowshare but clearly encourages such use if opportunities appear where the use of such explosions is feasible from a technical and economic point of view.

As a matter of fact, we, under this treaty, have indicated that we would be prepared to furnish such services of peaceful explosions to other countries if a suitable occasion for the use of such explosives appeared. In that circumstance, Senator, I just might add, because we are, I think, making a record of interpretation here at the same time that we are having our colloquy; if we do provide a nuclear explosion for peaceful purposes the control of the device itself would remain with us. There would be an invitation for international observation for those who wanted to look at the total situation to assure themselves that this was not simply an experiment with a nuclear weapon, that it was in fact a Plowshare exercise.

Senator HICKENLOOPER. We pretty well took care of Plowshare under the Test Ban Treaty, didn't we?

Secretary RUSK. Well, as a matter of fact, Chairman Seaborg can testify more directly to this, but some of the more interesting possibilities in Plowshare are developing with regard to underground explosions. Now, it also is contemplated that in an excavation situation where there might be extraterritorial atmospheric fallout there would be discussions in a suitable international body such as the IAEA in Vienna and conceivably the Security Council. And one can imagine that there would be consent and agreement that a particular type of explosion for peaceful purposes might occur, despite the limitations of the Test Ban Treaty, with the consent of everybody who would be ready to acknowledge that this is in fact a genuine Plowshare operation with a legitimate civilian purpose.

EFFECT ON MANUFACTURE OR STOCKPILING OF NUCLEAR WEAPONS

Senator HICKENLOOPER. Does this treaty in any way incur an obligation on the part of nuclear weapon states to cease manufacture of nuclear weapons, to liquidate stockpiles or to eliminate nuclear weapons for their arsenals?

Secretary RUSK. The treaty itself does not make specific provision for that, but article VI says that each of the parties to the treaty undertakes to pursue negotiations in good faith on effective measures relating to the cessation of the nuclear arms race at an early date and to nuclear disarmament, and so forth.

Now, it is, I think, in direct relation to article VI of this treaty, as well as on broader considerations, that we hope very much that we can soon be seriously engaged with the Soviet Union in responsible discussion of the possibilities of limiting the race in offensive and defensive missiles.

Senator HICKENLOOPER. I have a great many more questions, but in deference to all the members here, I am going to desist. Thank you very much, Mr. Secretary.

Secretary RUSK. Thank you.

Senator HICKENLOOPER. Mr. Foster, I have some questions I will direct to you one of these days.

Mr. FOSTER. Any time, sir.

Senator HICKENLOOPER. I want to make a record.

LIST OF SIGNATORY POWERS

Senator SPARKMAN. Mr. Secretary, by the way, it would be helpful to include in the record the list of the countries that are the signatory powers?

Secretary RUSK. Yes, I will be glad to do so.

Senator SPARKMAN. And keep it up to date before the record is closed.

Secretary RUSK. Yes, sir.

(The material referred to follows:)

DEPARTMENT OF STATE,
Washington, July 10, 1968.

Hon. JOHN J. SPARKMAN,
Acting Chairman, Committee on Foreign Relations, U.S. Senate,
Washington, D.C.

DEAR SENATOR SPARKMAN: In response to your request today for information regarding additional signatories to the Treaty on the Non-Proliferation of Nuclear Weapons, I am glad to inform you that the treaty was signed in Washington on July 9 for Ecuador and Lesotho and on July 10 for Yugoslavia and Jordan.

The following six signed the treaty either in London or Moscow but have not signed it in Washington: Chad, Iraq, Mongolia, Syria, United Arab Republic, and the so-called German Democratic Republic.

Ireland deposited her ratification of the treaty in Washington on July 1, 1968.

The enclosed list of 65 countries and the so-called German Democratic Republic indicates signatories to the treaty in one or more of the three capitals, Washington, London, and Moscow.

I shall be glad to communicate to you any further developments regarding signatures and ratifications of the treaty.

Sincerely yours,

WILLIAM B. MACOMBER, Jr.,
Assistant Secretary for Congressional Relations.

STATUS OF THE TREATY ON THE NON-PROLIFERATION OF NUCLEAR WEAPONS

SIGNATORIES

(All signatures were affixed on July 1, 1968 except as otherwise indicated.)

Legend:

    W—signature in Washington.
    L—signature in London.
    M—signature in Moscow.

United States—W,L,M
Afghanistan—W,L,M
Austria—W,L,M
Barbados—W
Bolivia—W
Botswana—W
Bulgaria—W,L,M
Ceylon—W,L,M
Chad—M
China—W
Colombia—W
Costa Rica—W
Cyprus—W,M
Czechoslovakia—W,L,M
Dahomey—W
Denmark—W,L,M
Dominican Republic—W
Ecuador—W—July 9, 1968
El Salvador—W
Finland—W,L,M
German Democratic Republic—M
Ghana—W,M
Greece—W,M
Haiti—W
Honduras—W
Hungary—W,L,M
Iceland—W,L,M
Iran—W,L,M
Iraq—M
Ireland—W
Ivory Coast—W
Jordan—W—July 10, 1968
Kenya—W

Korea—W
Laos—W,L,M
Lebanon—W,L,M
Lesotho—W—July 9, 1968
Liberia—W
Malaysia—W,M
Mauritius—W
Mongolia—M
Morocco—W,M
Nepal—W,L,M
New Zealand—W,M
Nicaragua—W,L
Nigeria—W,M
Norway—W,L,M
Panama—W
Paraguay—W
Peru—W
Philippines—W
Poland—W,L,M
Romania—W,L,M
San Marino—W
Senegal—W,M
Somalia—W,L,M
Syria—M
Togo—W
Tunisia—W,L,M
USSR—W,L,M
United Arab Republic—L,M
United Kingdom—W,L,M
Uruguay—W
Venezuela—W
Viet-Nam—W
Yugoslavia—W—July 10, 1968

Ratifications deposited: Ireland, July 1, 1968, at Washington.

(The following additional countries have signed as of August 2, 1968:)

Cameroon—W—July 16, 1968
Libya—W—July 19, 1968
Congo (Kinshasa)—W—July 22, 1968

Canada—W—July 23, 1968
Mexico—W—July 26, 1968
Guatemala—W—July 26, 1968

Senator SPARKMAN. Senator Gore?

Senator GORE. Mr. Chairman, I have had the privilege of being a congressional adviser to the Disarmament Conference. I have watched with admiration the conduct of negotiations on the part of the United States, and I wish to congratulate and commend President Johnson, Secretary Rusk, Ambassador Foster, and Ambassador Adrian Fisher who have kept me and my subcommittee so fully and currently informed upon this notable achievement.

Also I wish to congratulate the signatory powers to this treaty. This is a great achievement.

ADHERENCE TO TREATY OF SMALL POWERS

Mr. Secretary, you mentioned a few moments ago that two other nations had signed the treaty today. Would you identify those nations?

Secretary RUSK. Jordan and Yugoslavia are signing today.

Senator GORE. Has Lebanon signed?

Secretary RUSK. Lebanon has signed, yes, sir.

Senator GORE. Has Lesotho signed?

Mr. FOSTER. Yes, it has.

Senator GORE. Today?

Mr. FOSTER. No, not today. It signed it yesterday.

Senator GORE. The adherence to the treaty by these small powers illustrates two things, both of which I think are important: One, the wide support which the conclusion of this treaty has met. Secondly, the inability of Lesotho and Lebanon and Jordan to significantly affect the treaty except as a portion of world public opinion. It illustrates, it seems to me, the importance in the future of not only the United States and Russia, recognizing the mutuality of interest to which you made reference, but also the other great populous nuclear power, and it is about that that I wish to ask one or two questions.

As you may recall, Mr. Secretary, I have repeatedly suggested that instead of some of the things that we are doing, to which I do not wish to make any specific reference, we should be concerning ourselves with what seems to me to be the most overriding and important matter of the future affecting our security, and that is the equation between the three major nuclear powers, the United States, Russia and Red China.

This, it seems to me, is another step in easing relations between the United States and Russia, which I applaud. I hope there will be others.

MAINLAND CHINA AND THE TREATY

But the great challenge to Western civilization is to find a way to bring Red China, one-fourth of the human race, and a burgeoning nuclear power, into responsible membership in the family of nations.

Now with this brief background—I apologize, but I seem to find it necessary to lay a foundation for the question—what are the plans, what are the hopes, of the administration, yourself and President Johnson, Ambassador Foster and his agency, for putting China into cooperation with and possible adherence to the treaty.

Secretary RUSK. Senator, first, in regard to this treaty and issues directly related to it. We would be glad to see Mainland China adhere to this treaty.

The Secretary General of the United Nations, with our knowledge and ready consent, invited the authorities of Mainland China to attend the conference of the nonnuclear powers which is to convene in August. There the nuclear powers are being invited as, I think, observers.

The authorities in Peking indicated they could not even receive, would not even receive, that communication from the Secretary General.

There are some very difficult problems in the way of, relating to your question, first in terms of our own bilateral situation. We run into the single simple proposition over and over again, in our discussions with Peking, that there is nothing really to discuss unless we are prepared to surrender Taiwan.

We have tried in a good many ways to establish certain contacts, to begin to draw them into the family of nations somewhat more. I think the same issue relates to the United Nations question: that they would not consider the United Nations except that the Republic of China on Taiwan be expelled from the United Nations.

So there are some serious obstacles on this question. But in the field of arms limitation and control of arms, I think that we would hope that even the present authorities in Peking, which have what seem to us to be very difficult attitudes, could get themselves involved in these very serious issues.

To come back to a point made by Senator Hickenlooper a moment ago—that these issues really started with the Baruch plan in 1946—if we strip away all ideology, if we strip away what might be called passing disputes, however difficult or dangerous, and just look at ourselves as a human race for a moment, it was a great tragedy in the story of mankind that the Baruch proposals of 1946 failed to achieve agreement, because the basis for those agreements, of that proposal, was that one nuclear power is too many.

Now, they failed, and for as long as the human race endures, its No. 1 problem therefore must be to try to find a way to keep this nuclear beast in its cage.

Now, this has little to do with ideology. It has little to do with the passing disputes. This has to do with whether the human race is going to try to be reasonable and sane in terms of handling a capacity to destroy itself. So we are not going to interpose any obstacles of frivolous objections. We are trying to bring the authorities of Peking into a serious discussion of these great issues of arms limitations and arms reduction.

Senator GORE. This is encouraging. By using the term "responsible membership in the family of nations" I was not making the narrow reference to membership in the United Nations.

Secretary RUSK. I understand.

CHINA'S NUCLEAR CAPABILITY

Senator GORE. I was referring to it in a broader way. I realize China has been thoroughly intractable and not only does not wish to be a member of the United Nations, or has not so indicated, but sets up conditions which are intolerable for membership. I was not referring to one narrow sense, but to the broader, from which membership in the United Nations ultimately might flow. The broader question involves a mutuality of interests in avoiding a nuclear war.

Obviously the threat to the United States from nuclear development in Mainland China, as you referred to that nation, is a real one. Former Secretary of Defense McNamara said that she would have a capacity, a significant capacity, to place nuclear weapons on American cities by 1975. That is 8 years away.

Secretary RUSK. Right.

Senator GORE. The action of the United States with respect to the ABM limited deployment has been premised on the threat of China.

What are the plans of the administration to take the initiative in involving China in discussions on the mutuality of interest in avoiding a nuclear war?

Secretary RUSK. We have tried in public statements to deal with this matter. It has been raised in private conversations on occasion.

Senator Gore. With China's representatives?

Secretary Rusk. That is correct, sir, in terms of the general problem of disarmament matters.

Senator Gore. Congratulations, sir.

Secretary Rusk. But I cannot really say that I have much basis for optimism that they will in the near future take up these questions seriously themselves.

I would hope, Senator, and I think you would understand the basis for this hope, that now that they have had a chance to see these weapons, now that they have some direct firsthand knowledge of what such a nuclear conflict could mean, that this itself would have a sobering effect.

I have the impression that the other nuclear powers are pretty sober about this question of nuclear war—they have every reason to be sober about it. And we would hope that perhaps this could begin to work its way in the minds of the authorities in Mainland China, because it is a problem that goes beyond and outside ideology. It has to do with the human race.

Senator Sparkman. Senator Carlson.

Senator Carlson. Mr. Secretary, I want to state that I appreciate the splendid work you have done as Secretary of State, and the fine work that Mr. Foster has done toward the nonproliferation of nuclear weapons. It was my privilege to attend some of the meetings in Geneva and I am delighted that you are here this morning and the treaty is as far along as it is.

STATUS OF TREATY IN CONDITION OF WAR

I have only one or two questions. I notice in your statement, Mr. Secretary, and I will just quote this one sentence:

It (the treaty) does not deal with arrangements for deployment of nuclear weapons within allied territory as these do not involve any transfer of nuclear weapons or control over them unless and until a decision were made to go to war, at which time the Treaty would no longer be controlling.

What do I get from that sentence?

Secretary Rusk. I think, sir, that this was simply a recognition of what today is almost an element of nature; and that is that, in a condition of general war involving the nuclear powers, treaty structures of this kind that were formerly interposed between the parties would be terminated or suspended.

Senator Carlson. In other words, if as a result of a provocation or for some other reason a nation determines to go to war with its neighbors, it would be in a position, I assume, of getting this type of material anywhere it could get it?

Secretary Rusk. The Treaty itself is a major effort to prevent such a war and you are speaking of trying to regulate such a war after it occurs.

Senator Carlson. In other words, let's assume that a nation would decide it was necessary that it become involved in a war, could it, for instance, go to France if France were not a signatory and get not only weapons but warheads and materials to transmit them?

Secretary RUSK. Well, I think, sir, that there would be inhibitions in the treaty against the notion that any kind of a conflict or a dispute would automatically relieve that particular country or disputant from the obligations of the treaty. There have been a good many armed clashes since the end of World War II.

Senator CARLSON. There will be some more, I am sure.

Secretary RUSK. I am sure there will be some more. It is not intended here that the mere fact there is an armed clash would operate to relieve a party of its obligations under the treaty. But such party might invoke the withdrawal article, give formal notice—excuse me, I just wanted to look at this—if "Extraordinary events related to the subject matter of this treaty have jeopardized the supreme interests of its country." Now, that withdrawal article is there, and each signatory to the treaty has access to it under the provisions of the treaty.

Senator CARLSON. In other words, you use the term "supreme interests?"

Secretary RUSK. Yes; supreme interests.

Senator CARLSON. It is your thought it would take more than just a provocation to result in a local conflict?

Secretary RUSK. That is correct, sir.

Senator CARLSON. I was interested in that because I can see where it might be very easy to withdraw even though you were a signatory to this treaty, provided you decided that it was necessary to get into a conflict with another country. I wanted some clarification on that if I can get it.

Secretary RUSK. Senator, let me review the record and see whether I ought to make a small extension of my remarks on this point. But the great objective of this treaty is to make nuclear war less likely by preventing the spread of nuclear weapons to additional countries.

Again, looking back toward the dozens and dozens of armed engagements that have occurred since the end of World War II, some small scale, others large scale, we would not expect that each one of these engagements should be translated into a nuclear engagement by causal action on the part either of a nuclear power or nonnuclear powers.

Senator CARLSON. I shall not press it further, but it is rather easy to get into a nuclear situation when you use nuclear warheads, is it not; they need not be very large?

Secretary RUSK. That is correct, sir.

Senator CARLSON. That is all, Mr. Chairman.

Senator SPARKMAN. Senator Lausche.

Senator LAUSCHE. Yes, thanks, Mr. Chairman.

I want to join with my colleagues in expressing profound gratitude to the President, to the Secretary of State, Mr. Rusk, and to Mr. William Foster, for the excellent work that has been done on this matter. It is a delightful feeling, Mr. Secretary, to be present at a meeting of the Foreign Relations Committee where the general attitude is of a most friendly nature and is indicative of triumph at one time at least in our international relations.

Secretary RUSK. May I associate myself with your statement, Senator? [Laughter.]

Senator GORE. With some enthusiasm. [Laughter.]

ABSENCE OF PUNITIVE PROVISIONS

Senator LAUSCHE. Articles I and II in substance provide that the signatory nations, especially the nuclear nations, shall not transfer or receive directly or indirectly nuclear weapons or other nuclear explosive devices; is that correct?

Secretary RUSK. That is correct, sir.

Senator LAUSCHE. These are declarations and promises made by the nuclear powers that they will not transfer or help nonnuclear nations to acquire nuclear devices and explosives?

Secretary RUSK. That is correct, sir.

Senator LAUSCHE. There are no punitive provisions in the treaty that would become applicable to any nation that would violate this undertaking?

Secretary RUSK. That is correct, Senator.

The treaty itself does not attempt to deal with the question of sanctions in the event of violation. The great overriding sanction is that the treaty reflects very important underlying national interests, national security interest considerations, for the signatories, and this is true of the nuclear countries. So that the treaty itself would collapse if there were serious violation.

Senator LAUSCHE. I can understand that quite thoroughly, that the most that can be expected is that there will be a declaration and an undertaking and that in the end the signatory nuclear power nations will have the honor and dignity to carry into effect their commitments?

Secretary RUSK. Yes, sir; I would say that a treaty which is solemnly entered into by more than 100 nations on as important a matter as this, which begins by being based upon consideration of national security interests, is a pretty solemn and formidable treaty, and I would think that no signatory would take lightly the idea of violating the treaty.

POTENTIAL NUCLEAR POWER NATIONS

Senator LAUSCHE. Mr. Secretary, there are now five nuclear power nations that we definitely know about; is that correct?

Secretary RUSK. That is correct, sir.

Senator LAUSCHE. Three of the five are signatories to the treaty?

Secretary RUSK. That is correct.

Senator LAUSCHE. France and China are not?

Secretary RUSK. That is correct, sir.

Senator LAUSCHE. How many potential nuclear power nations are there that are now on the threshold or have the capability of breaking through?

Secretary RUSK. I should think that, depending upon who is making the estimate, this number might be somewhere between say, 12 and 20, if you look ahead for the next 5 to 10 years.

Senator LAUSCHE. Has India signed?

Secretary RUSK. No, sir; it has not signed.

Senator LAUSCHE. India, Japan, West Germany, France have not signed. That is correct?

Secretary RUSK. That is correct, sir, as of the present time.

Now, some of these governments are still considering the matter and some of them must go through a parliamentary phase before they feel that they should sign. In the case of India, they have indicated they do not expect to sign. We understand they also are indicating that they have not made a decision to go nuclear. They are, of course, impressed by the problem which they face of a nuclear China across the mountains, and so for them to forego a nuclear option under the terms of this treaty is a very serious problem. We hope that after they have given it the fullest consideration, they would feel that it is in their security interests to join the rest of the world in this matter. But this is something that they will have to decide themselves as they see their own problem.

Senator LAUSCHE. Does the declination to sign grow primarily out of the belief that these particular nations do not want to place their security, not having the nuclear bomb, under the protection of the nuclear nations that have signed?

Secretary RUSK. Well, first, I would not wish to gereralize in any way about those who have not yet signed, Senator, because we know that a great many of them have this under their own constitutional procedures and that a great many who have not yet signed will, in fact, sign.

Senator LAUSCHE. Has Italy signed?

Secretary RUSK. The members of Euratom have not yet signed because they are expecting the Commission to give them a study of the relation between the Nonproliferation Treaty and the Treaty of Rome, and my guess is that most of them will sign in the late summer or early fall.

STATES NEAREST A NUCLEAR CAPABILITY

Senator LAUSCHE. Please name those states that are nearest to a nuclear capability.

Secretary RUSK. Well, Senator, this would involve a complete judgment with respect to the industrial and the scientific state of development of a particular country. I would be glad to submit a list for the record. I would give you an example or two now. I think the industrial capabilities and technical and scientific capabilities of a country like India would be an example of one that is, whose capabilities are, moving ahead in this general field, quite apart from whether they have made a decision to go nuclear. But I suspect that I perhaps ought to consult with Chairman Seaborg and some of my colleagues before putting in a specific list.

(The following material was subsequently supplied for the record by the Atomic Energy Commission:)

MEMORANDUM ON NUCLEAR WEAPON MANUFACTURING CAPABILITIES

In considering the prospects for the manufacture of nuclear weapons or other nuclear explosives by additional nations without special external assistance, one must consider several factors. One such factor—and a very important one—is the question of intention or national decision to undertake such a program. No government beyond the present five nuclear weapons states has declared such an intention or decision. The remarks which follow should therefore not be considered as imputing such a present intention to any government. In discussing the capability of a nation to undertake the manufacture of nuclear weapons, one must also be careful to relate its capability to possible objectives. The possible objectives, in turn, must be related to the type of proliferation problem with which one is concerned.

One type of proliferation problem concerns the likelihood that additional nations may manufacture even a few rudimentary nuclear explosive devices—perhaps only one—which might be intended, for example, to intimidate an antagonist. Means of delivery of a single weapon to a target could, in such a situation, be of secondary importance and might also be quite unsophisticated since the objective would appear to be largely psychological or political.

The resources necessary for the manufacture of a few rudimentary nuclear weapons are within the means of many nations. The essentials are a cadre of trained personnel, uranium, and an industrial base adequate to permit the construction of a nuclear reactor and auxiliary facilities large enough to provide the necessary quantities of plutonium. Thus many nations possess resources sufficient to undertake, without special outside assistance, to manufacture a few rudimentary nuclear weapons, given the national will to do so and the readiness, in some cases, to forego the benefits from the endeavors to which those resources might otherwise be applied. The time required would vary among the group of countries, and for those which have only the minimum resources, the time might be ten years or more.

At the upper end of the scale, highly industrialized nations, with substantial national income, large numbers of trained scientific, technical and managerial personnel and a reasonably available source of uranium could become capable of manufacturing a few rudimentary nuclear weapons within a few years or less. Depending upon the military objectives upon which the national decision is justified, some of these countries might seek to acquire a variety of sophisticated nuclear weapons or systems including means of delivery. The independent development and manufacture of an arsenal of sophisticated nuclear weapons and delivery systems would be quite costly. The equivalent of at least hundreds of millions and, more likely, billions of dollars of resources could be expended over a period of five or ten years on such a program. Expenditures of this magnitude could be sustained by a number of countries, if a national decision were made to do so.

Recognizing that there are many countries which could, if they wished, undertake to manufacture a few rudimentary nuclear weapons and that countries have varying levels of resources which could be devoted to the acquisition of nuclear weapons and delivery systems of greater sophistication, the question of the independent capabilities of various countries can be considered. It is emphasized that, in doing so, one must take into account the state of the development of industry in general, experience in advanced technology, the availability of skilled and trained personnel, and other general indices. Specific experience in non-military atomic energy activities such as nuclear research or operation of a nuclear reactor is a factor, but in general is not likely to be a controlling one.

Among those non-nuclear-weapon countries whose industrial economies are probably adequate to support a program for the manufacture of a sizable number of reasonably sophisticated nuclear weapons and systems for their delivery, within five to ten years from a national decision to do so, are those such as Australia, Canada, the Federal Republic of Germany, India, Italy, Japan and Sweden. Those states whose resources are somewhat more limited, and might therefore take somewhat longer to reach that level of numbers or types of weapons systems, could include Argentina, Austria, Belgium, Brazil, Chile, Czechoslovakia, Hungary, Israel, Netherlands, Pakistan, South Africa, Spain, Switzerland, United Arab Republic, and Yugoslavia.

It is emphasized that the foregoing groupings are not definitive and, in any event, are subject to change. It should be noted that a particular country may, by design or otherwise, take steps to put itself in a position to expedite the manufacture of nuclear weapons if and when a decision is made to do so. Thus, by concentrating its resources to that end, a country could advance its nuclear weapon manufacturing capabilities beyond those attributable to its level of general industrial activity.

RATIFICATION URGED

Senator LAUSCHE. Do I understand it to be your position that while this treaty does not embrace all that you hoped it would, it nevertheless has adequate provisions which overpower the weaknesses that it might contain, and that, therefore, the Senate of the United States ought to approve it.

Secretary RUSK. I do, Senator, very much. Obviously we would be glad to see every nuclear power sign it. We would be glad to see every nonnuclear power or authority sign it. Whether or not we recognize them politically, we would like to see it total and complete.

Now, it isn't likely to be total and complete, but we think that a treaty of this sort with more than 100 signatories will put us far ahead of where we would be without a treaty.

Senator LAUSCHE. I subscribe fully to the statement made by Secretary of State Herter, which you quoted, that the greater number of nations that have the bomb, the greater the potential of involvement in a nuclear war. And it looks to me, though there may be weaknesses in this treaty, that the ultimate result is that the good that will come from it by far exceeds the evils that might arise in its absence. That is all.

Secretary RUSK. Thank you, Senator.

Senator SPARKMAN. Senator Williams?

EFFECT OF ABSENCE OF FRANCE AND RED CHINA PARTICIPATION

Senator WILLIAMS. Mr. Secretary, we all recognize that this treaty may well be a milestone in the progress of international diplomacy and I want to join with my colleagues in congratulating you in reaching this point. But to what extent do you think that the failure of France and Communist China to participate in this may have an adverse effect on the treaty?

Secretary RUSK. I think, Senator, I would have to say honestly that we think that the situation would be greatly improved if both Mainland China and France were to sign the treaty. We have regretted the fact, for example, that France, for reasons best known to its own Government, has not taken its seat at the Geneva Disarmanent Conference. We regretted that because we need the talents of France in working on these very complex and difficult issues. But they have elected not to take part.

I do think, sir, that we must keep in mind two points. I think I alluded to them briefly earlier. One is that if you get an overwhelming majority of the world to sign the treaty, many of the potential customers will themselves have undertaken an obligation not to receive such weapons even from those nuclear powers who have not signed the treaty.

And secondly, the fact that two nuclear powers have not signed the treaty may not affect the possibility that some presently nonnuclear powers might develop the capability to proceed to nuclear weapons with their own knowledge and talents, without any direct assistance from any existing nuclear power. So that we feel that, because of those factors, the treaty, despite the regrettable absence of two nuclear powers as signatories, is a very valuable step forward.

Senator WILLIAMS. Do you think that there is any thought that perhaps since France and Communist China might not sign it that they will become arsenals for nuclear weapons for these nations?

Secretary Rusk. I would think not, sir, if we get the signatories to the treaty which we are now contemplating, because the customers will have indicated they are not buying, you see. So I think that this puts us a long way ahead, even though Mainland China and France do not sign.

There is another factor on which I speak with perhaps less absolute confidence, but it seems almost in the very nature of these weapons that those who have them understand the implications and are not interested in having a general spread of these weapons among other nations.

SHARING KNOWLEDGE OF NUCLEAR POWER FOR PEACEFUL PURPOSES

Senator Williams. One feature of this is that we will share knowledge of nuclear power for peaceful purposes with other nations without any regard to the cost of development, and so forth. Does that mean that we are going to make it available in unlimited amounts, and if so, is Russia likewise sharing her knowledge on the same basis?

Secretary Rusk. The Soviet Union and we undertake the same obligation under this treaty on that particular point. We would anticipate that the cost of the provision of a peaceful explosive service would be borne by the recipient country, but that, in assessing such a cost, we would not apply to that the pro rata share of the very large research and development expenditures which we have made since World War II in this field, but that the operational cost will be a part of the cost actually assigned to this explosion.

Senator Williams. And this sharing of knowledge could be applicable equally to all signatories?

Secretary Rusk. That is correct, sir, as the treaty puts it without discrimination. We have no doubt that, in terms of peaceful uses, it would be much simpler and easier for us to work out these arrangements with some countries and that the Soviet Union might have arrangements with other countries. It is possible that both of us might be involved in peaceful uses in a particular country.

PROBLEM OF INSPECTION

Senator Williams. You mentioned the problem of inspection and the reluctance of the Soviet Union to open their plants for inspection. We understand that.

Now, we have opened ours for inspection, have we not?

Secretary Rusk. We have indicated that when the treaty comes into force we would make arrangements for that, and that would involve arrangements between us and the International Atomic Energy Agency with regard to safeguards. Chairman Seaborg will be here and can go into that in considerable detail in terms of exactly what types of plants we have in mind, and those related to national security which will not be included.

Senator Williams. That was going to be my next question. To what extent will that handicap us in view of the fact that apparently Russia could inspect our plants where we would not be able to inspect the extent of development of hers?

Secretary RUSK. Well, our security, our installations which have a security importance, would not be included.

Senator WILLIAMS. Not included?

Secretary RUSK. Then, too, under the arrangements now in force by the International Atomic Energy Agency, the International Atomic Energy Agency arranges for inspectors that are acceptable and agreeable to the country that is going to be inspected in terms of—as you know, sir, we have opened certain of our facilities to these arrangements and we have not detected any handicaps arising from these arrangements.

Senator WILLIAMS. I understand. And you do not feel this would expand that beyond the present arrangement?

Secretary RUSK. That is correct, in any damaging or negative way.

Senator WILLIAMS. That is all, Mr. Chairman.

Senator SPARKMAN. Senator Anderson?

Senator ANDERSON. I don't think I have any questions. I would want to commend the Secretary of State for the fine work he has done, and Ambassador Foster for the fine work he has done.

Secretary RUSK. Thank you, Senator.

Senator SPARKMAN. Senator Bennett?

EFFECT OF TREATY ON U.S. BILATERAL DEFENSE TREATIES

Senator BENNETT. Thank you, Mr. Chairman. I have just one or two questions. I have been out in my State and there is a fear out there that this is opening or widening our obligation to go to the defense of countries that might be subject to nuclear blackmail.

Does this in any extent, to any extent, expand our existing treaty obligations to go to the defense of any nations with which we have bilateral defense treaties?

Secretary RUSK. No, sir.

The President, at the time of signing this treaty, did reaffirm our bilateral mutual security treaties, but this does not extend those in any way. It does not affect those in any way.

Now, those treaties are not limited with respect to the nature of the weapons that might be involved in carrying those treaties into effect.

Furthermore, as I indicated earlier, Senator, the assertion by the Security Council of the United Nations of its responsibility in this field—in the event of nuclear aggression or nuclear blackmail—is simply a reassertion of what the Charter of the United Nations gave it, namely a primary responsibility for the maintenance of international peace and security, and as it was originally written, that contemplated agreement among the permanent members. And the resolution of the Security Council which is before you also necessarily contemplates agreement among the permanent members.

It is our hope if I may elaborate this just for a second, it is our hope, that anyone who might be flirting with the possibility of aggression by nuclear weapons would be very sober indeed about the prospect that the nuclear powers who are permanent members of the Security Council will take a common view of the threat to the peace that is involved in such a situation, and that this would have a great deterrent effect.

U.S. UNILATERAL OBLIGATION QUESTIONED

Senator BENNETT. But failing that, are we under any obligation to step in unilaterally to give aid, special aid, to a friend that might be subject to nuclear blackmail when he realizes that the Security Council is not going to act?

Secretary RUSK. This resolution itself, in the Security Council, does not contemplate unilateral action, so we can eliminate that from consideration.

Now, we have certain mutual security treaties and some of them are multilateral, some of them are bilateral. Those treaties would remain in effect. So it does not change in any way the obligations of those treaties.

Senator BENNETT. So it is very far-fetched but theoretically it is possible then that failing an action by the Security Council, at least a demand might be made upon us by another country with which we had a mutual security treaty asking for our assistance in defending them against a threat of nuclear attack.

Secretary RUSK. Yes, Senator, and that has been true since about 1950 when we have had mutual security treaties with the possibility of antagonists who had nuclear weapons at their disposal.

Senator BENNETT. This treaty, this agreement, does not change that.

Secretary RUSK. Does not affect that in any way.

Senator BENNETT. In any way. I think it is well to get that on the record because there is a great deal of misunderstanding about that in the country outside. I wanted to discuss the question of the makeup of IAEA teams but the record is already clear on that. I understand then we could prevent the presence of a Soviet inspector in the team that might come to this country to inspect?

Secretary RUSK. We could do so under International Atomic Energy Agency practice.

Senator BENNETT. Thank you.

Senator SPARKMAN. Senator Symington?

Senator SYMINGTON. Thank you, Mr. Chairman.

Mr. Secretary, and Mr. Director, I apologize for not being here earlier, but was at another hearing on military research and development.

Let me congratulate you on this treaty.

Secretary RUSK. Thank you, Senator.

SOVIET OFFER TO DISCUSS ARMS LIMITATIONS

Senator SYMINGTON. I would ask Mr. Foster, if I may, about this suggestion on the part of the Soviets to discuss limitation and control of nuclear weapons. Do you believe that a sincere gesture on their part, or just a political move?

Mr. FOSTER. No, Senator, I think that it is a sincere offer. We, of course, have been attempting to develop these talks for some years now with the Soviet Union, believing that this area is the most important one in which, if we could make progress, it would be much better for the world.

They have agreed, in accepting this treaty, under article VI, to negotiate in good faith toward this sort of limitation and reduction.

Following the signing of the treaty last week, they have immediately, as you know, through Mr. Gromyko's announcement in the Supreme Soviet, and with the agreement of Mr. Kosygin, asked for talks in the nearest future toward this end.

Now, this is a very complicated, complex problem. I am sure this will not come to a successful conclusion overnight, but I do believe they mean this, I do believe they recognize that only if we are able to make progress in this direction will we really build on this nonproliferation treaty in a way to really achieve the basic objectives we have in mind.

So we are very hopeful that it is a sincere gesture. We have no plan yet for the particular place and time, but we are moving to study this aggressively with the hope that these talks will start in the nearest future.

NECESSITY FOR A U.S. ABM SYSTEM

Senator SYMINGTON. Last January, Secretary McNamara described to us the Tallinn system, and detailed it was a defense against bomber attack. He also described the Galosh system around Moscow, an antiballistic missile defense system. Inasmuch as we now know they are not carrying on with the Galosh system around Moscow to the extent and degree we previously thought they would, why is it so necessary for us to now create an ABM system of our own?

Secretary RUSK. Senator, may I comment briefly on that, sir?

Senator SYMINGTON. I would appreciate the Director's comment first and then I would appreciate yours, also.

Mr. FOSTER. These, of course, would be part of any discussions that take place on the subject of limitations and possible reductions of both offensive and defensive missiles, and pending the beginning of those talks I think it would be unwise to comment directly on what the effect might be.

Senator SYMINGTON. So in effect you say you do not want to comment?

Mr. FOSTER. Except to say obviously this would be included in such talks.

Senator SYMINGTON. What would be included?

Mr. FOSTER. The question of limitations on both offensive and defensive missiles and subsequent reductions thereof.

Senator SYMINGTON. Thank you, Mr. Director.

Mr. Secretary, I would appreciate your thoughts.

Secretary RUSK. Senator, I have only a very brief comment to add to that.

As I think few people know better than you, any such negotiation in this field is going to be extremely complicated. We feel that, until we get an understanding and agreement it would be important for us to maintain the preliminary work that is now being done of ABMs. One of the questions, I suppose, that we and the Soviets are going to have to take into account what the result would be in our own discussions of the possibility that there would be another nuclear power who would not be willing to get into, and try to resolve these same issues because both they and we would face the fact that we are not the only ones who have at our disposal offensive and defensive missiles.

Senator SYMINGTON. I think we will agree the Communist Chinese threat is a little theoretical. It has to be theoretical until it is an entity. But with that promise, if it is true that the Soviets are not pursuing their ABM activities as we thought they would, do you feel it wise for us to pursue ours to this extent?

Secretary RUSK. Well, I would hope you would put that same question to my colleague, the Secretary of Defense, because my understanding is that in the arrangements that are presently before us, they are fairly modest developments in process on our own side. I would hope that we could get agreement with the Soviet Union that would cut through some of this because——

Senator SYMINGTON. Fairly modest? Only about a billion dollars this year. Incidentally, I put in the record yesterday that the research and development cost to the Federal Government is $17 billion this year; has tripled in the last decade.

The past Secretary of Defense was emphatic up until last fall that we did not need this ABM system. He then changed and said we needed a system, not against the Soviets, but against the Chinese, which I could not work out in my mind.

Are we trying for real substance in this effort for mutual arms control or are we trying for just form instead of substance.

Secretary RUSK. Not in any sense a matter of form or gesture. For example, President Johnson himself has worked very hard personally trying to bring this treaty to fruition. We will approach these talks with the Soviet Union with the utmost seriousness.

I would draw your attention to the use of the word "mutual". This is important in terms of the total security throughout the world, and I hope very much we can reach an understanding with the Soviet Union about mutual measures in this field.

ESTIMATING SECURITY NEEDS

Senator SYMINGTON. I have one more observation. We put our money you might say, on assured entry in case we were attacked; and that has cost the American people a great many billion dollars, this effort to be sure, regardless of what an enemy might do that we could retaliate effectively, gives them punishment they could not afford to take; which is the essence of deterrence.

After spending those tens of billions for assured entry, and with our current fiscal and monetary problems, I am regretful of the fact apparently we now plan to spend many additional billions on defense entry, especially as I do not think the latter technically possible.

Secretary RUSK. Senator, you put your finger on the driving motivation behind the effort to reach an understanding with the Soviet Union on offensive and defensive missiles.

Mr. Foster commented on your question about their seriousness of purpose. We would hope that both sides could understand that we are now in a situation where each can inflict massive destruction upon the other. We could go, both go, to tens of billions of additional dollars of expenditure in a further——in moves to a new plateau of scientific and technical development, without changing the underlying fact that both sides are in a position to inflict massive damage upon the other.

Therefore, if a man from Mars should suddenly visit among us, he would look at both sides and say, "Are you people crazy? Can't you find some way to stop this?"

And that is what we are going to try to do.

Senator SYMINGTON. Well, I remember the thousands of bombers we were told that the Soviets were going to build, in the early 1950s. They didn't. Then I remember in the late 1950s the CIA reducing the number of ICBMs they had on launching pads $97\frac{1}{2}$ percent, in four separate reductions. So I hope this time we don't jump off into a gigantic new program which we later find was not essential to our security.

Mr. Secretary, may I congratulate you and the Director for the superb work you both have done in this arms control field.

Secretary RUSK. Thank you very much, Senator.

Senator SYMINGTON. It is our hope for the future to develop this dialog. I am glad you have been partially successful already.

Secretary RUSK. Thank you, Senator, and may I say we very much appreciate your encouragement along the way on this, and that you are also a cosponsor of the Pastore resolution.

Senator SYMINGTON. Thank you, Mr. Chairman.

Senator SPARKMAN. Senator Case?

Senator CASE. Thank you, Mr. Chairman.

Mr. Secretary, may I join my colleagues and express appreciation and admiration for the job you have done and which Ambassador Foster and Ambassador Fisher have done. I share that admiration and I congratulate you.

Secretary RUSK. Thank you, sir.

Senator CASE. I also want to make it clear that for its value, and I am sure it will have value, in moving the world to a safer posture, I support this treaty fully.

I am concerned to bring out certain questions to eliminate, if possible, some ambiguities and doubts that have existed in my mind. My questions relate not so much to specific terms of the treaty itself. I do have one question on that as to clarification.

DISTINCTION BETWEEN NUCLEAR EXPLOSIVE DEVICES

Where do you draw the line between a nuclear explosive device and something on which a nonnuclear nation may work in research and development under another provision of the treaty?

Secretary RUSK. Well, I have a layman's understanding of that difference, but perhaps——

Senator CASE. That is much better for me.

Secretary RUSK. Well, it seems to me that, for example, the distinction is in that type of chain reaction which leads to a major explosion and other and controlled uses of nuclear energy such as are involved in propulsion, power reactors, and experimental reactors and things of that sort.

Now, Chairman Seaborg or perhaps Ambassador Foster, can give you a little more expert distinction, but I think this is a distinction that is generally understood and recognized.

Senator CASE. It is, of course, true that one thing may lead to another.

Secretary RUSK. Yes, and, therefore, safeguards.

Senator CASE. If there is anything anybody else wants to add to this either now or later, I would be glad to have it.

Mr. FOSTER. I think the Secretary, Senator Case, has covered this. It is an uncontrolled fission or fusion and is instantaneous as contrasted with a somewhat slower—we are talking about microseconds, I guess, microseconds of the fusion or fission as contrasted with even a run away power reactor, that might be milliseconds. And an uncontrolled nuclear reaction can be used as a weapon. What we want to prevent is to have such an uncontrolled nuclear reaction available to nonnuclear weapon states since it can be used, as was dramatically expressed, either to move a million tons of earth or to kill a million people.

Senator CASE. Thank you very much.

(The following information was provided:)

EXTENSION OF REMARKS BY MR. FOSTER IN RESPONSE TO QUESTION REGARDING NUCLEAR EXPLOSIVE DEVICES

The treaty articles in question are Article II, in which non-nuclear-weapon parties undertake "not to manufacture or otherwise acquire nuclear weapons or other nuclear explosive devices," and Article IV, which provides that nothing in the Treaty is to be interpreted as affecting the right of all Parties to the Treaty "to develop research, production and use of nuclear energy for peaceful purposes . . . in conformity with Articles I and II of this Treaty." In the course of the negotiation of the Treaty, United States representatives were asked their views on what would constitute the "manufacture" of a nuclear weapon or other nuclear explosive device under Article II of the draft treaty. Our reply was as follows:

"While the general intent of this provision seems clear, and its application to cases such as those discussed below should present little difficulty, the United States believe it is not possible at this time to formulate a comprehensive definition or interpretation. There are many hypothetical situations which might be imagined and it is doubtful that any general definition or interpretation, unrelated to specific fact situations could satisfactorily deal with all such situations."

"Some general observations can be made with respect to the question of whether or not a specific activity constitutes prohibited manufacture under the proposed treaty. For example, facts indicating that the purpose of a particular activity was the acquisition of a nuclear explosive device would tend to show non-compliance. (Thus, the construction of an experimental or prototype nuclear explosive device would be covered by the term "manufacture" as would be the production of components which could only have relevance to a nuclear explosive device.) Again, while the placing of a particular activity under safeguards would not, in and of itself, settle the question of whether that activity was in compliance with the treaty, it would of course be helpful in allaying any suspicion of non-compliance."

"It may be useful to point out, for illustrative purposes, several activities which the United States would not consider per se to be violations of the prohibitions in Article II. Neither uranium enrichment nor the stockpiling of fissionable material in connection with a peaceful program would violate Article II so long as these activities were safeguarded under Article III. Also clearly permitted would be the development, under safeguards, of plutonium fueled power reactors, including research on the properties of metallic plutonium, nor would Article II interfere with the development or use of fast breeder reactors under safeguards."

PRESIDENTIAL AUTHORITY AND OBLIGATION UNDER TREATY

Senator CASE. Now, my other questions relate chiefly to this matter of the protection of nonnuclear nations against aggression. This is a matter apart from safeguards which relates to performance by nuclear countries and nonnuclear countries, too, of obligations with regard to the handling of fissionable material and experiments. You have, I think, taken the position that the United States as a state does not assume any additional obligations to go to the defense of a country which is subject to aggression beyond those it already has under existing treaties as a member of the United Nations.

Secretary RUSK. That is correct, sir.

Senator CASE. Now I want to draw a distinction between the obligation that the United States has as a state to go to the defense of the nation subject to aggression and the power of the President to move the armed forces without decision by Congress in the event he determines, without formal action by Congress, that an aggression exists and that the interests of the United States and its obligations under this and other treaties or as a member of the United Nations require action by the armed forces of the United States, my distinction being between our obligation as a country and who exercises that obligation.

Is it the President alone, or the President after consultation which is just advice and not involving a sharing of power, or the Congress with the President making formal decisions?

Would you please develop that for me?

Secretary RUSK. Well, Senator, this is a question that involves the basic structure of our Constitution, on which there is, has been, a great deal of discussion over the decades and a great deal of law and history.

The President, as Chief Executive and Commander in Chief, has important powers under the Constitution and important obligations under the Constitution, and so does the Congress, and the problem then is how these two relate to each other in particular situations. This has varied over the years.

Looking back historically, on some occasions it has been necessary for the President to act immediately without formal action by the Congress. In other situations, there have been resolutions by the Congress declaring the policy of the Congress. In some other situations, there has been consultation between the President and the leadership of the Congress and they have reached a common conclusion as to whether or not, and, if so, how, the Congress should be directly involved in a particular decision.

In some of the lesser decisions, it has been done on the basis of informal consultation with certain Members of the Congress.

I think that the best thing for me to say now, Senator, is that one can recognize that this is a major feature in our Constitution, that there perhaps are some edges which are not completely delineated with absolute clarity in the great variety of situations that are constantly arising in the world.

But whatever the answer is, I would suppose that the answer remains whatever it was before we convened this morning. In other words, I would not want by my testimony to attempt to try to change that in any way.

Senator CASE. You are most disarming, Mr. Secretary, but we really haven't come to grips with it.

COMMITMENT INVOLVED IN SENATE ADVICE AND CONSENT TO RATIFICATION

Are you going to come back here next year or 10 years from now, if you are still Secretary of State [laughter], and charge Congress with having taken an action which amounted to a functional declaration of war by giving the President authority to move in certain situations?

Secretary RUSK. No, no.

Senator CASE. By reason of our ratification of this treaty?

Secretary RUSK. No; this treaty does not bear upon it.

Senator CASE. This treaty does not. But does our action in ratifying this treaty in these circumstances amount to giving authority to the President to take action which he would not otherwise have had?

Secretary RUSK. No. This treaty does not bear upon that subject in any way.

Senator CASE. But would our action in ratification do that, in your judgment?

Secretary RUSK. No, I don't think so. This is not a subject matter of this treaty. It does not affect this problem.

Senator CASE. This would not be one of those things that might be cited to us on a later occasion as having given rise to a commitment of the United States?

Secretary RUSK. No, sir; and since we are talking about assurances, Senator, I can assure you that I will not be back here next year or 10 years from now to attempt to impose anything upon you as Secretary of State.

Senator CASE. Well, we could do much worse.

Secretary RUSK. Thank you, Senator.

Senator CASE. And we have. [Laughter.]

But I wanted to give you the chance to make that remark.

EFFECT OF TREATY ON CONSTITUTIONAL PROCESSES

Let me get back to the serious question which I do have and does concern me and, as you know, has affected our relations over the past several years.

Secretary RUSK. Right.

Senator CASE. I just wanted to be sure that we were not now taking an action which would eliminate the necessity for a hearing to whatever constitutional processes may be applicable in the event the question arises as to the use of the armed forces of the United States in the future.

Secretary RUSK. That is correct, sir. This treaty has nothing whatever to do with that point.

Senator CASE. And those requirements of constitutional process would not be affected by our action or by the action of the United States in becoming a signatory and ratifying this treaty?

Secretary RUSK. That is correct, sir.

Senator CASE. May I say, Mr. Chairman, at the conclusion of my own questions which will not be much longer, I would like to present several questions that Senator Cooper, who is in the hospital and unable to be here, wished to present to the Secretary and ask for the right to submit additional questions for answer in the record later.

Senator SPARKMAN. That will be done.

EXPECTATIONS OF WEST GERMAN GOVERNMENT

Senator CASE. Now, Mr. Secretary, for the remainder of my questions, I have here what seems to be a wire service report of a story from the West German papers dated July 4 making several points.

One is, and I quote this now:

The Federal Government—

That is, the Government of West Germany—

expects the United States to make a binding public statement in one or two months. In such a statement the United States would undertake the nuclear protection of present NATO territory as it does now even if the NATO Treaty should end prematurely.

I am sure, Mr. Secretary, you have seen this particular report. I don't want to delay all of us by reading it in detail, but I wonder if you could comment on that proposition.

There are several other statements in here, further prerequisites of adherence by the West German Government to this treaty. One would be "a statement by the European commission in Brussels as to whether signing the treaty accords with obligations resulting from the Euratom Treaty." Another, "The proposition here that the U.S. Government will presumably disclose during the ratification debate in the U.S. Senate four important American interpretations of the treaty text as discussed with Bonn. They will thus become binding for the United States."

"Third, if the Soviet Union objects to these interpretations," it says, "the situation of the Federal Government will change."

"During the visit to Bonn in June, Secretary Rusk asserted this would hold true for the United States as well."

I wonder if you would make such comment as you can on, first, this matter of the binding public statement the Federal Government of Germany expects us to make in 1 or 2 months, and whether our action here would widen the President's authority to make binding commitments of any nature to other countries as an inducement to their adherence to the treaty.

Secretary RUSK. Senator, I do not wish to impugn any particular report, but I understand that the particular report that you referred to is not in every respect accurate.

We understand that the Chancellor said that these questions are on the agenda of the nonnuclear conference. One of these undoubtedly is a clear definition of the future role of the North Atlantic Alliance, which we expect will be continued, and naturally also the role of the United States as the first nuclear power in the West.

Now, we do not contemplate attempting by executive action to amend the NATO treaty. If there is an amendment to the NATO treaty, it would be submitted to the Senate as an amendment.

Now, it is also true that nonnuclear countries concerned about their own security are interested in the status of these alliances, because some of those who are allied with us look upon the alliance as their principal protection against nuclear attack and nuclear blackmail.

I think that if NATO were to dissolve, this might well be interpreted by some countries as one of those events affecting their vital interests which could raise the question of the withdrawal clause under the treaty, if their judgment at that time was that their own national security required it.

But, in regard to your specific question, we do not contemplate attempting to amend the NATO treaty.

Senator CASE. May I just carry that a little further though.

Secretary RUSK. Yes.

EXTENT OF U.S. ASSURANCES TOWARD OTHER COUNTRIES

Senator CASE. Supposing NATO dissolves, and I think this is what the concern that is raised here, does our Government intend, in the case of Germany or any other NATO power, or outside of NATO, to give assurances against aggression beyond those contained in our action in the United Nations Security Council and our adherence to the treaty itself.

In this connection, may I ask if you would comment upon a statement made in the Security Council resolution approving indications of intention by us, among other nations. What are they talking about there, if I may ask? What statement of intention is referred to?

Secretary RUSK. I might put into the record, Mr. Chairman, the identical declarations by the United States, United Kingdom, and the Soviet Union in the Security Council on this point.

(The material referred to follows:)

DECLARATIONS MADE AT THE MEETING OF THE UNITED NATIONS SECURITY COUNCIL HELD ON JUNE 17, 1968

(See page 264 for United States declaration.)

DECLARATION OF THE UNITED KINGDOM

The Government of the United Kingdom notes with appreciation the desire expressed by a large number of States to subscribe to the treaty on the nonproliferation of nuclear weapons.

We welcome the willingness of these States to undertake not to receive the transfer from any transferor whatsoever of nuclear weapons or other nuclear explosive devices or of control over such weapons or explosive devices directly or indirectly; not to manufacture or otherwise acquire nuclear weapons or other nuclear explosive devices; and not to seek or receive any assistance in the manufacture of nuclear weapons or other nuclear explosive devices.

The United Kingdom also notes the concern of certain of these States that, in conjunction with their adherence to the Treaty on the non-proliferation of nuclear weapons, appropriate measures be undertaken to safeguard their security. Any aggression accompanied by the use of nuclear weapons would endanger the peace and security of all States.

Bearing these considerations in mind, the United Kingdom declares the following:

Aggression with nuclear weapons, or the threat of such aggression, against a non-nuclear-weapon State would create a qualitatively new situation in which the nuclear-weapon States which are permanent members of the United Nations Security Council would have to act immediately through the Security Council to take the measures necessary to counter such aggression or remove the threat of aggression in accordance with the United Nations Charter, which calls for taking "effective collective measures for the prevention and removal of threats to the peace, and for the suppression of acts of aggression or other breaches of the peace . . .". Therefore, any State which commits aggression accompanied by the use of nuclear weapons or which threatens such aggression must be aware that its actions are to be countered effectively by measures to be taken in accordance with the United Nations Charter to suppress the aggression or remove the threat of aggression.

The United Kingdom affirms its intention, as a permanent member of the United Nations Security Council, to seek immediate Security Council action to provide assistance, in accordance with the Charter, to any non-nuclear-weapon State, party to the Treaty on the nonproliferation of nuclear weapons, that is a victim of an act of aggression or an object of a threat of aggression in which nuclear weapons are used.

The United Kingdom reaffirms in particular the inherent right, recognized under Article 51 of the Charter, of individual and collective self-defence if an armed attack, including a nuclear attack, occurs against a Member of the United Nations, until the Security Council has taken measures necessary to maintain international peace and security.

The United Kingdom vote for the draft resolution before us and this statement of the way in which the United Kingdom intends to act in accordance with the Charter of the United Nations are based upon the fact that the draft resolution is supported by other permanent members of the Security Council which are nuclear-weapon States and are also proposing to sign the treaty on the nonproliferation of nuclear weapons, and that these States have made similar statements as to the way in which they intend to act in accordance with the Charter.

DECLARATION OF THE UNION OF SOVIET SOCIALIST REPUBLICS

The Government of the Union of Soviet Socialist Republics notes with appreciation the desire expressed by a large number of States to subscribe to the treaty on the nonproliferation of nuclear weapons.

We welcome the willingness of these States to undertake not to receive the transfer from any transferor whatsoever of nuclear weapons or other nuclear explosive devices or of control over such weapons or explosive devices directly or indirectly; not to manufacture or otherwise acquire nuclear weapons or other nuclear explosive devices; and not to seek or receive any assistance in the manufacture of nuclear weapons or other nuclear explosive devices.

The Union of Soviet Socialist Republics also notes the concern of certain of these States that, in conjunction with their adherence to the treaty on the non-proliferation of nuclear weapons, appropriate measures should be undertaken to safeguard their security. Any act of aggression accompanied by the use of nuclear weapons would endanger the peace and security of all States.

Bearing these considerations in mind, the Soviet Union declares the following:

Aggression with nuclear weapons, or the threat of such aggression, against a non-nuclear-weapon State would create a qualitatively new situation in which the nuclear-weapon States which are permanent members of the United Nations Security Council would have to act immediately through the Security Council to take the measures necessary to counter such aggression or to remove the threat of aggression in accordance with the United Nations Charter, which calls for taking ". . . effective collective measures for the prevention and removal of threats to the peace, and for the suppression of acts of aggression or other breaches of the peace . . .".

Therefore, any State which commits aggression accompanied by the use of nuclear weapons or which threatens such aggression must be aware that its actions are to be countered effectively by measures to be taken in accordance with the United Nations Charter to suppress aggression or remove the threat of aggression.

The Soviet Union affirms its intention, as a permanent member of the United Nations Security Council, to seek immediate Security Council action to provide assistance, in accordance wth the Charter, to any non-nuclear-weapon State party to the treaty on the non-proliferation of nuclear weapons that is a victim of an act of aggression or an object of a threat of aggression in which nuclear weapons are used.

The Soviet Union reaffirms in particular the inherent right, recognized under Article 51 of the Charter, of individual and collective self-defense if an armed attack, including a nuclear attack, occurs against a Member of the United Nations, until the Security Council has taken measures necessary to maintain international peace and security.

The vote of the Soviet Union for the draft resolution before us and this statement of the way in which the Soviet Union intends to act in accordance with the Charter of the United Nations are based upon the fact that the draft resolution is supported by other permanent members of the Security Council which are nuclear-weapon States and are also proposing to sign the treaty on the non-proliferation of nuclear weapons, and that these States have made similar statements as to the way in which they intend to act in accordance with the Charter.

Secretary RUSK. Those refer to the identical declarations made by the three permanent members, nuclear powers.

SUMMARY OF DECLARATIONS

Senator CASE. Would you just summarize, just very quickly, their effect? This includes the United States, of course.

Secretary RUSK. I think you might want that declaration in the record, Mr. Chairman, at this point. (See above.) The operational part of the declaration, the key paragraph in this regard, is that aggression with nuclear weapons or the threat of such aggression against a non-nuclear-weapon state would create a qualitatively new situation in which the nuclear weapon states, which are permanent members of the U.N. Security Council, would have to act immediately through the Security Council or take the measures necessary to counter such aggression or to remove the threat of aggression in accordance with the United Nations Charter, which calls for taking "effective collective measures for the prevention and removal of threats to the peace and for the suppression of acts of aggression or other breaches of the peace."

Now, that is based upon the underlying assumption of the charter that the permanent members would act in agreement in such a situation and, of course, it is limited to the question of aggression with nuclear weapons or the threat of such aggression, which would be the preliminary conclusion that the Security Council would have to reach; that is, that there is an aggression or threat of such an aggression with nuclear weapons against a non-nuclear-weapon state.

Senator CASE. That declaration and also the reference to it in the Security Council resolution, paragraph 2 (see page 264), does not in any way deal with what would happen if the procedures of the charter fail?

Secretary RUSK. That is correct, sir.

Senator CASE. We are assuming no individual obligation beyond that which we have as a member of the Security Council.

Secretary RUSK. That is correct, sir. We have made it very clear in this matter we are not directly or indirectly making ourselves a bilateral ally with every nonnuclear state. We are simply expressing our responsibility as a permanent member in the Security Council in accordance with the charter which has been part of the law of the land since the United Nations was organized.

Senator CASE. Now, Mr. Secretary, not only the West German paper but the New York Times and I am sure other papers in this country carried stories a day or two ago. Here is the July 6 story in the New York Times, "Bonn Seeks United States Guarantee Against Soviet Atom War."

This question then is not just one of a German newspaper's interpretation of its Government's concern. It is apparently something quite real, and my question is again in no hostile vein at all.

Secretary RUSK. I understand, sir.

Senator CASE. But if anything substantial beyond what is already contained in the treaty, the Security Council resolution and this declaration of intention is intended to be given by our Government, am I correct in assuming that it will not be done without consultation with the Senate of the United States?

Secretary RUSK. In the President's statement at the time of the signing of the Nonproliferation Treaty on July 1 he made the following statement, which I think is a part of the legislative history of this treaty——

Senator CASE. This is the President's statement?

Secretary RUSK. The President states:

> In welcoming the treaty that prevents the spread of nuclear weapons, I should like to repeat the U.S. commitment to honor all our obligations under existing treaties of mutual security. Such agreements have added greatly, we think, to the security of our Nation and the nations with which such agreements exist. They have created a degree of stability in a sometimes unstable world.

That was the statement that was made at the time of the signing of the Nonproliferation Treaty.

Senator CASE. You know, I wish in a way you hadn't brought that up, because it raises a question as to whether we are by approving any treaty now accepting the administration's position in regard to the President's authority to act without reference to specific action and authorization by the Congress. This is a very troublesome thing for me, and I would like to make it very clear that I have this reservation if I vote for this, and I hope I can, that I am not accepting your previous testimony in these matters, or Secretary Katzenbach's rather notorious statement up here. I do not accept them, and if I vote, and I hope to, expect to, ratify this, I am not adopting the administration's position in regard to its powers and the powers of the President. I just want to make that clear for the record, Mr. Secretary.

Secretary RUSK. Senator, with respect, I would suggest that the President did not in any way get into that question by stating that the United States has a commitment to honor all our obligations under existing treaties of mutual security because those treaties of mutual security have been approved by overwhelming votes in the Senate.

Senator CASE. Yes; and it is just a question of interpretation as to what those obligations are. Of course we understand what we are talking about.

Secretary RUSK. Yes, exactly.

Senator CASE. And whether other matters such as foreign aid and whatnot give rise to commitments which are beyond recall by this body.

EXTENT OF U.S. PROMISES TO PROTECT AGAINST AGGRESSION

Now, did you—I don't think you did—give us any indication of how far you intend to go in regard to the request for assurances by non-nuclear powers as a condition to their signing?

Secretary RUSK. I referred to the——

Senator CASE. You referred to a statement that——

Secretary RUSK. The statement of the President in this respect which is our——

Senator CASE. What was the date of that statement?

Secretary RUSK. July 1.

Senator CASE. Well, that was earlier than this statement by Mr. Kiesinger, who apparently didn't indicate that that was enough to satisfy him. He wants more. Now, what more are we going to give him?

Secretary RUSK. I don't think I can deal with that on the basis of press reports because we have not——

Senator CASE. Let's just do it on questions by me. Are we going to commit, to promise any kind of action on the part of this country to any nations in the way of protection to them in the event of aggression?

Secretary RUSK. We don't contemplate the dissolution of NATO.

Now, if NATO were to dissolve, that would raise new and fresh questions for everybody, and I am not in any position to even speculate about that situation because we have not even discussed it.

The President on July 1 repeated the U.S. commitment to honor all our obligations under existing treaties of mutual security. That does not amend in any way the existing security treaties.

To speculate beyond that as to what would happen if NATO dissolves is something that I, for one, could not say very much about, because we haven't thought about it in those terms.

Senator CASE. Mr. Secretary, suppose it isn't me asking this or the Senate asking you about what you will or will not speculate about, would you say to the Chancellor of the German Government, "We are not going to speculate about what is going to happen if NATO is dissolved," when he comes to you and wants protection against aggression in that event?

Secretary RUSK. Of course, I think there is very definitely in his mind, and perhaps properly so, a relationship about the conditions and circumstances of NATO. And I would suppose, if there was any change in the situation in NATO, which we do not see on the horizon, that that very well may raise very serious questions for the Chancellor or his successors in terms of the Non-Proliferation Treaty and the withdrawal clause and other matters of that sort.

But those are, it seems to me, far in the future as problems, Senator, and I just don't know——

EXTENT OF U.S. COMMITMENTS TO INDUCE COUNTRIES TO ADHERE TO TREATY

Senator CASE. May I take it, then, Mr. Secretary, that you do not plan any kind of commitments beyond those already existing in order to induce countries to adhere in the first instance to the treaty?

I take it that you are saying that to us.

Secretary Rusk. That is right. Adherence to this treaty does not change the treaty structure of the United States in terms of mutual security treaties.

Senator Case. Nor will promises be made to countries in order to get them to adhere to the treaty in the first instance. If I understand you, when you are saying that if West Germany adheres and NATO dissolves, this will present her with a serious problem, and that if they should want to withdraw from the treaty, that is not the same thing as saying——

Secretary Rusk. No; I would not wish to suggest a conclusion on the question, except to say it would raise the question as to what they might do.

Senator Case. It would invite a conclusion on their part that it might justify their withdrawing. It would not necessarily be an unreasonable one and I fully agree with that. That is not fully answering the question.

Are we intending to make commitments beyond those that we already are bound by in order to induce adherence of any country to this treaty?

Secretary Rusk. We have no intention of changing the treaty structure of the United States with respect to such.

Senator Case. And that includes adding any commitments? We are not intending to add any commitments?

Secretary Rusk. Beyond those which we are already involved in: the treaties which the Senate has approved.

Senator Case. The answer is correct?

Secretary Rusk. That is right.

Senator Case. Thank you, Mr. Chairman.

Senator Sparkman. May I suggest to Senator Case that in the Washington Post article yesterday morning, Mr. Kiesinger was quoted as saying he was going to follow very carefully the debates in the Senate, so perhaps some of the burden is on us.

Senator Case. You don't suppose it was an attempt to butter up the Senate? It is very flattering to be so regarded.

QUESTIONS OF SENATOR COOPER

Mr. Chairman, if I may briefly just present Senator Cooper's questions.

Senator Sparkman. I wonder if I may make this suggestion. I know that more than one of us have appointments coming up pretty soon. I wonder if you would submit them to the Secretary and let him reply in writing, a copy to be sent to Senator Cooper and a copy to this committee, and, if you desire, a copy to you.

Senator Case. Well, I think the Senator's questions are always cogent and important, and I regard these as that. I am sure the Secretary would, too. I should be happy to present the questions to the Secretary and in accordance with our previous understanding reserve for Senator Cooper the right to ask additional questions in writing also.

Secretary Rusk. Thank you, sir. We would be delighted to do that because we have great respect for the interest and concern Senator Cooper has taken in this matter.

Senator SPARKMAN. And the questions and answers both would be a part of the record.

Senator CASE. If it is convenient, I would like to have a copy sent to Senator Cooper.

Senator SPARKMAN. Yes, indeed.

(The questions and answers referred to follow:)

QUESTIONS POSED BY SENATOR COOPER, TOGETHER WITH ANSWERS SUBMITTED BY THE DEPARTMENT OF STATE

1. *Considering the urgent and hopeful intents expressed in the Preamble for lessening the dangers of war and the promise of the parties in Article VI to take effective measures to cease the nuclear arms race, how do you relate the decision of the Administration, authorized thus far by the Senate, to proceed with the deployment of the ABM system? Is it not now possible to show good faith by deferring deployment of an ABM system at least until the outcome of talks is known?*

We agree with Secretary Clifford on the relationship between the decision to deploy the Sentinel system and the proposed talks. As he said:

"I believe our deployment decision is consistent with our continuing desire for arms control and arms limitation. The Soviets are at the present time deploying a ballistic missile defense around Moscow. We will continue our efforts to negotiate limitations of both strategic offensive and defensive weapons systems, but in the absence of agreement we must not suspend taking actions in our own defense."

2. *Concerning the Resolution and Declaration of the U.S. in the Security Council, do you believe this Resolution has any effectiveness? If so, can you illustrate?*

As the Secretary said in answer to similar questions from Senators Sparkman and Bennett: "I think it is politically of very considerable importance that three of the permanent members—the Soviet Union, the United Kingdom and the United States—made identical declarations, and that France at least consented through an abstention rather than through a negative vote [to the Resolution], which made it clear that an aggression by nuclear weapons or the threat of such aggression fell squarely within the primary responsibility of the Security Council as delineated in the Charter."

"It is our hope . . . that anyone who might be flirting with the possibility of aggression by nuclear weapons would be very sober indeed about the prospect that the nuclear powers who are permanent members of the Security Council will take a common view of the threat to the peace that is involved in such a situation and that this would have a great deterrent effect."

As an illustration, he said: "I would think that if there were, for example, a clear instance of an ultimatum or direct threat by a nuclear power against a non-nuclear power which in effect said 'you bow your neck, you submit to what I am demanding of you or I will use nuclear weapons' then it would be for the permanent members of the Security Council especially and for the Security Council as a whole to consider whether that created a situation referred to in this resolution which could be described as an aggression by nuclear weapons or the threat of such use that would make operational the responsibilities of the Security Council."

3. *Article III, Section 1 (Safeguards). Can you explain how the agreement with IAEA regarding safeguards would be negotiated?*

It is contemplated that not later than 180 days after the treaty enters into force, each non-nuclear weapon party, either individually or together with other states, will commence negotiations with the IAEA on a safeguards agreement that meets the requirements of the treaty. It is also contemplated that such negotiations will be in accordance with the Statute of the IAEA, the Agency's safeguards system and the three guiding principles set forth in the Secretary's report to the President, which is attached to the President's Message to the Senate on this treaty. The treaty provides that the negotiations are to be concluded within 18 months after they commence, which should prove sufficient in light of the experience which the IAEA has had in negotiating many earlier safeguards agreements. I understand that IAEA and a number of prospective parties are already preparing for such negotiations.

4. *Article III, Section 2. If West Germany, France, India, Israel, Japan or other countries do not sign the Treaty, would the U.S. be prevented from transferring material and equipment to such states for peaceful purposes?*

The treaty would not prevent the transfer of nuclear material or equipment to non-parties if the nuclear material, or that used or produced in such equipment, would be made subject to the safeguards required by Article III.

5. *Article III, Section 3 of the Preamble of the Treaty provides the principle for safeguards to be followed by the Parties.*

(a) *Does this refer to the systems of safeguards used by IAEA?*

The reference in section 3 of Article III to "the principle of safeguarding set forth in the Preamble of the Treaty" is to the following language in the fifth preambular paragraph:

"the application, within the framework of the International Atomic Energy Agency safeguards system, of *the principle of safeguarding effectively the flow of source and special fissionable materials by use of instruments and other techniques at certain strategic points.*"

This principle reflects the recognition by the parties that further efforts should be made to make technical improvements in safeguards techniques in the direction of greater automation without loss of effectiveness.

(b) *Would you describe these safeguards?*

A description is attached.

(c) *Has any question been raised by the U.S. or other countries concerning the effectiveness of such safeguards?*

No such question was raised in the course of the negotiations.

(d) *What are they?*

Inapplicable.

DESCRIPTION OF SAFEGUARDS

Safeguards are those measures designed to guard against the diversion of material, such as source and special nuclear material, from uses permitted by law or international agreement, and to give timely indication of possible diversion or assurance that diversion has not occurred.

In application, all safeguard systems depend on two principal elements. First, the maintenance and review of records showing the receipt, production, consumption, transfer and present location of all nuclear material. Secondly, the undertaking of actual on-site inspections designed to determine the validity of these records and therefore the compliance with the commitment to peaceful uses. In carrying out inspections an inspector verifies the amount of safeguarded material actually on hand. His activities include making measurements and, in appropriate cases, taking samples to be sent to his home laboratory for analysis. At a reactor this includes piece counts of the fuel elements on hand at the spent fuel storage pool and making non-destructive tests where possible to determine the U–235 content of the fresh fuel elements. Other steps, such as the use of locks and seals, may be used to verify that the material is not being used for purposes other than those intended.

The IAEA safeguards system incorporates these elements and is described in a set of documents formally approved by the Board of Governors of that Agency. Those documents are subject to review and modification by the Board of Governors in light of experience and new developments.

6. *Article V—Peaceful Explosions*

(a) *What provisions are there or plans for concluding the "special international agreement" and establishing the "Appropriate international body"?*

Article V provides that "Non-nuclear-weapon States Party to the Treaty shall be able to obtain such benefits, pursuant to a special agreement or agreements, through an appropriate international body with adequate representation of non-nuclear-weapon States. Negotiations on this subject shall commence as soon as possible after the Treaty enters into force."

We have been giving the most serious consideration to the general subject of appropriate international procedures for some time. As early as March 21, 1967 Mr. Foster suggested five principles relating to nuclear explosion services, which have been placed in the record of these hearings. We believe that we already have, in the International Atomic Energy Agency, an international body that would be suitable for the role envisaged in the treaty, and we believe the IAEA would be the appropriate forum for developing the necessary details of the multilateral procedures for implementing the Article.

(b) *If no agreement is concluded, could the U.S. or the U.S.S.R. conduct a peaceful explosion in a non-nuclear state under the authority provided in the last sentence to enter into bilateral agreements?*

Yes. As explained in Mr. Foster's opening statement, that last sentence "preserves the option to meet requests for such services on a bilateral basis without the need to await multilateral agreement or action concerning the provision of such services through an international body." But, as Chairman Seaborg stated, even in such cases "an opportunity shall be provided for appropriate international observation of the actual detonation."

(c) *Does this Article present any problems in connection with Article X?*
No.

7. *Was Article X opposed by the U.S. or the U.S.S.R.? If so, what were their objections?*

The United States and the Soviet Union each originally contemplated that the treaty would be of unlimited duration, but there would be a right of withdrawal if a party found that extraordinary events related to the subject matter of the treaty had jeopardized its supreme interests. This was reflected in the U.S. draft treaty of August 17, 1965, the Soviet draft treaty of September 24, 1965 and the identical U.S. and Soviets drafts of August 24, 1967.

The second paragraph of Article X first appeared in the identical revised drafts presented to the Eighteen Nation Disarmament Committee by the U.S. and Soviet Co-Chairmen on January 18, 1968. In commenting to the Committee on this new provision, the United States representative said:

"While remaining mindful of the strength of the arguments for a treaty of unlimited duration, the Co-Chairmen have carefully considered the comments of those members of the Committee who have expressed concern about a treaty of this type having no limit in time. As a consequence we have included a provision for a conference to meet twenty-five years after the treaty has entered into force to decide how much longer the treaty should continue. In recommending this change, the Co-Chairmen have also recognized the widespread desire that the treaty be assured a life-span adequate to enable it to serve effectively as a stable foundation upon which other vitally needed measures of nuclear disarmament can be built."

8. *During the debates and discussions, were there any illustrations of the kind of "extraordinary" events to authorize a party to withdraw?*

Generally, during the debate and discussions we pointed out that the decision as to whether "extraordinary events, related to the subject matter of this treaty, have jeopardized the supreme interests of its country," would be made by each party for itself, although we think it should not be made without compelling reasons. We have presumed that the U.N. Security Council would wish to consider the consequences of such a decision.

In response to a question from Senator Case, the Secretary gave a possible illustration, when we said:

"I think that, if NATO were to dissolve, this might well be interpreted by some countries as one of those events affecting their vital interests which could raise the question of the withdrawal clause under the treaty, if their judgment at that time was that their own national security required it."

Senator SPARKMAN. Senator Pell?

Senator PELL. Thank you, Mr. Chairman.

I think it was Premier Khrushchev who once said that in the event of nuclear war the living would envy the dead.

I congratulate you, Mr. Secretary, for the work you have done, and you, Mr. Foster, the Director of the Disarmament Agency for its whole life, for all that you both have done to try to avoid this eventuality.

STATUS OF A FEDERATION OF STATES

I have a couple of specific questions here. First, if the Western European nations, including France, decide to organize a political federation, could the nonnuclear signatories under this treaty receive nuclear weapons from the federation? In other words, if France moved into a federation under this treaty, could, for the sake of argument, West Germany as part of the federation, or Sweden, receive weapons?

Secretary RUSK. In my opening statement, Senator, I tried to deal with that question rather specifically as a matter of interpretation.

This treaty does not deal, I say, with the problem of European unity and would not bar succession by a new federated European state to the nuclear status of one of its former components.

So a new federated European state would have to control all of its external security functions including defense and all foreign policy matters relating to external security, but would not have to be so centralized as to assume all governmental functions. So that we are thinking here in terms of what now appears to be a somewhat deferred possibility, of a genuine federation which would have a unified control of defense and security related foreign policy matters. In that case, this treaty does not require a nuclear country to become nonnuclear in order to enter into such a federation.

Therefore, the federation would necessarily succeed as a nuclear entity to the status of its former nuclear components.

Senator PELL. I thank you for spelling that out that way.

EXTENT OF IAEA INSPECTION

Another question: Will the International Atomic Energy Agency inspection be restricted only to the declared peaceful nuclear facilities or will they also apply to the undeclared or clandestine facilities? How will they be sought out?

Secretary RUSK. The undeclared and clandestine?

Mr. FOSTER. The IAEA inspection would only be as to declared. If there were undeclared, if they were found, this would be a breach of the treaty.

Senator PELL. But under the treaty there is no provision for searching out the clandestine?

Mr. FOSTER. No, sir.

Senator PELL. Just as there is no sanction?

Mr. FOSTER. But there would be great alertness on the part of many, including ourselves, on that latter point, Senator.

SAFEGUARDS

Senator PELL. In connection with article III, paragraph 2, where it says that "Each State Party to the Treaty undertakes not to provide: source or fissionable material," et cetera, "to any non-nuclear-weapon State for peaceful purposes, unless the source or special fissionable material shall be subject to the safeguards required by this article," does this mean that the United States should cut off all nuclear aid to West Germany if it will not adhere to the treaty?

Secretary RUSK. This article is more general than that. The question is whether they have accepted safeguards, not whether they are party to the treaty.

Senator PELL. Right.

Secretary RUSK. So this would apply both to parties to the treaty and nonparties to the treaty.

Senator PELL. And she would presumably accept the safeguards and she has already?

Secretary RUSK. We have every reason to believe that there should be no underlying difficulty about an agreement between Euratom and the IAEA on safeguards. The purpose of both systems of safeguards is the same.

MASS DESTRUCTION WEAPONS ON THE OCEAN FLOOR

Senator PELL. Finally, while this treaty applies to all the signatory powers, there is 70 percent of the earth which is covered by the oceans. As I understand it, this treaty would in no way affect the very difficult problem of the possible emplacement of weapons of mass destruction on the ocean floor, is that correct?

Secretary RUSK. This treaty does not bear upon that question as it relates to nuclear powers, of course, it has a good deal to do with presently nonnuclear powers. Will they develop nuclear devices on the ocean floor? It does not deal with that question. That question is now under discussion at the U.N., and our distinguished legal adviser, Mr. Leonard Meeker, has been engaged in those discussions.

Senator PELL. Am I correct in saying discussions on this matter are being moved to Geneva, and being taken out of the U.N. in New York? Am I correct?

Secretary RUSK. We have proposed that this matter be discussed in the 18-Nation Disarmament Conference in Geneva which reconvenes shortly. Mr. Foster is leaving tomorrow morning for preliminary discussions with his fellow cochairman, Mr. Roshchin, and we think that would be a suitable forum to pursue this matter further on the limitation of disarmaments aspects of it.

Senator PELL. Exactly. And maybe achieving disarmament in the ocean space.

Mr. FOSTER. We know of your interest and we will be discussing those.

Senator PELL. Will this be discussed in the coming weeks in Geneva?

Mr. FOSTER. We would hope so.

Senator PELL. Would it be our intention to raise the subject?

Mr. FOSTER. We have suggested it at New York.

The Soviet Union has suggested it also be discussed at the 18-Nation Disarmament Committee.

Therefore, we both of us as cochairmen are suggesting that; it would seem it would be discussed.

Senator PELL. Thank you very much.

Senator SPARKMAN. Thank you both very much, Mr. Secretary, and Mr. Director.

This will conclude the hearings this morning. This committee stands in recess until 10 a.m. tomorrow, at which time we will hear the representatives of the Defense Department.

Secretary RUSK. Thank you very much, Senator.

(Whereupon, at 12:45 p.m., the committee recessed, to reconvene at 10 a.m., Thursday, July 11, 1968.)

NONPROLIFERATION TREATY

UNITED STATES SENATE,
COMMITTEE ON FOREIGN RELATIONS,
Washington, D.C.

The committee met, pursuant to recess, at 10:05 a.m., in room 318, Old Senate Office Building, Senator John Sparkman presiding.

Present: Senators Sparkman, Gore, Symington, Clark, Pell, Hickenlooper, Aiken, Carlson, Case, and Cooper.

Also present: Senator Pastore from the Joint Committee on Atomic Energy.

Senator SPARKMAN. Let the committee come to order, please.

We are very pleased to have with us this morning the distinguished Deputy Secretary of Defense, Paul H. Nitze, and the Chairman of the Joint Chiefs of Staff, Gen. Earle G. Wheeler.

Mr. Secretary, we have statements from both of you. You may proceed as you see fit.

STATEMENT OF HON. PAUL H. NITZE, DEPUTY SECRETARY OF DEFENSE

Mr. NITZE. Mr. Chairman and members of the committee, I am happy to present the views of the Department of Defense on the Nuclear Nonproliferation Treaty. I fully support the statements of Secretary Rusk and Mr. Foster. Consequently my statement on this treaty will be brief.

Since we began to consider the subject of an international agreement to prevent the spread of nuclear weapons, the Department of Defense has worked closely with the Department of State, the Arms Control and Disarmament Agency, and others in the development of U.S. positions on the many important questions which arose. At each step of the way, the pros and cons of every major issue were staffed throughout the Department, and the comments and advice of all participants were fully considered. The views of the Joint Chiefs of Staff particularly were sought. Their advice was most helpful on all issues and was of paramount importance in formulating certain provisions of the treaty, in such a way as to insure that our current and projected mutual defense arrangements were not adversely affected. General Wheeler is with me today and will present the views of the Joint Chiefs of Staff.

EFFECT ON CURRENT MUTUAL DEFENSE OBLIGATIONS

All of us in the Defense Department were concerned with the difficulties encountered in negotiating an effective treaty while, at the same time, assuring that it would not adversely affect our ability to meet our current mutual defense obligations. The treaty you are now considering meets this criterion. In this connection I would like to repeat a statement that Secretary Clifford made to the NATO Nuclear Planning Group ministerial meeting at The Hague last April. You may recall that the Nuclear Planning Group is that organ of NATO established at the Defense Minister level to provide our allies an opportunity to work with us in planning their own defense, and I quote:

The U.S. Government holds the view that the entry into force of the Nonproliferation Treaty will not interfere with the work of the Nuclear Planning Group. The U.S. Government intends to continue to pursue actively the work of the Nuclear Planning Group and to seek to find solutions satisfactory to its nonnuclear partners in NATO. It also is the view of the U.S. Government that the Nonproliferation Treaty will not hinder the further development of nuclear defense arrangements within the alliance compatible with articles I and II of the Nonproliferation Treaty.

We have also assured our NATO and other allies that the treaty would not interfere with any existing nuclear arrangements.

The views and special problems of our NATO allies have been fully considered throughout the treaty negotiations. Early in 1967 several of these allies raised questions about our interpretation of some of the treaty provisions. In early April of that year we circulated these questions, together with our answers, to all the NATO partners. Secretary Rusk has quoted these answers for the committee. We believe they describe arrangements fully compatible with our security requirements.

U.N. SECURITY ASSURANCES RESOLUTION

I would like to say just a few words about the security assurances resolution adopted by the United Nations Security Council in connection with the U.N. debate on this treaty.

The Defense Department worked closely with the State Department and ACDA in working out the provisions of the resolution and the statement. We believe that the adoption of this resolution, sponsored by the United States, the United Kingdom, and the U.S.S.R., adds significantly to the security of those nonnuclear weapon states adhering to the Nonproliferation Treaty. It does so, not by increasing security commitments but by giving evidence to all nations that both the United States and the Soviet Union share the utmost concern in preventing any act or threat of aggression with nuclear weapons.

I wish the committee clearly to understand that the Department of Defense is under no illusion that we need no longer worry about the proliferation of nuclear weapons. We recognize that the consummation of this treaty will not, of itself, guarantee against any possibility of another nation acquiring nuclear weapons. I do believe, however, that this treaty is the best that can be negotiated in the present world order, that it will gain wide adherence, and that the security of all nations will be increased proportionately with the signature and ratification of each new party.

As others have done in previous statements before this committee, I would also like to take note of President Johnson's remark that this treaty is "the most important international agreement since the beginning of the nuclear age." The acceptance of this treaty by a large number of states will do much to lessen the fears and to enhance the security of all peoples. Moreover, the fact the United States and the Soviet Union have been able to work together in the negotiation of this treaty gives us cautious encouragement that we may also be able to work together in other areas of mutual interest.

In conclusion, the treaty before you is an important step forward toward new forms of security, and I am pleased to have an opportunity in urging that the Senate advise and consent to ratification. Thank you, Mr. Chairman.

Senator SPARKMAN. Thank you, Mr. Secretary.

Now, General Wheeler, we will be very glad to hear from you, sir.

STATEMENT OF GEN. EARLE G. WHEELER, CHAIRMAN, JOINT CHIEFS OF STAFF

General WHEELER. Thank you, Mr. Chairman.

Mr. Chairman and members of the committee, I welcome the opportunity of appearing before your committee to discuss the military aspects of the Treaty on the Nonproliferation of Nuclear Weapons. In support of the treaty, I would like to present for your consideration the basis for the military judgments of the Joint Chiefs of Staff.

We have kept in close contact with the U.S. negotiating team throughout the development of the treaty. There was a JCS representative at each session of the 18-Nation Disarmament Committee in Geneva and at many of the discussions at the United Nations in New York. The Joint Chiefs of Staff have enjoyed also a constant exchange of information concerning progress on the treaty with the other agencies of the Government here in Washington. Frequently, Joint Chiefs of Staff opinions on various aspects of the treaty were requested; on other occasions, opinions were volunteered.

JOINT CHIEFS' PRINCIPLES RELATING TO NATIONAL SECURITY

The Joint Chiefs of Staff have long been on record as supporting balanced, phased, safeguarded, and verifiable arms control measures. However, empirical evidence from man's historical attempts at arms control leads us to view such measures with circumspection. Consequently, at the initiation of treaty discussions, the Joint Chiefs of Staff formulated certain principles relating to national security that should not be violated by such a treaty. First, we believe that any international agreement on the control of nuclear weapons must not operate to the disadvantage of the United States and our allies. Secondly, it must not disrupt any existing defense alliances in which the United States is pledged to assist in protecting the political independence and territorial integrity of other nations. These principles have been observed. Additionally, the Joint Chiefs of Staff consider that any arms control agreement must contain provision for effective safeguards and reliable verification procedures. Article III of the treaty provides for the establishment of these safeguards under the monitorship of the International Atomic Energy Agency.

In summary, the Joint Chiefs of Staff are in agreement with the expressed objectives of this treaty and support ratification of the treaty as not inimical to U.S. security interests.

58

Thank you, Mr. Chairman.

Senator Sparkman. Thank you very much, General Wheeler.

TREATY A STEP IN CONTROL OF NUCLEAR WEAPONS

Now, the purport of both your papers is one of, shall I say, complete support of this treaty; is that correct?

Mr. Nitze. That is correct, Mr. Chairman.

General Wheeler. That is correct, Mr. Chairman.

Senator Sparkman. And you believe it does not in any way endanger or weaken our own national security?

General Wheeler. That is correct, sir.

Mr. Nitze. That is correct.

Senator Sparkman. You also feel, and you made it clear in your statements, that this is not to be considered as an ultimate solution of the nuclear weapons problem? That it is a step in that direction?

Mr. Nitze. That is correct.

General Wheeler. That is correct, sir.

Senator Sparkman. And while this may be recognized now as the greatest treaty since the start of nuclear weapons, it does not mean that it closes the book. There is a lot of negotiating yet to be required?

Mr. Nitze. Yes, sir.

General Wheeler. Yes, Mr. Chairman.

Senator Sparkman. Let me ask you just these few questions, please.

IS COMPLETE DISARMAMENT IN U.S. SECURITY INTERESTS?

In article VI of the treaty, reference is made to "the cessation of the manufacture of nuclear weapons, the liquidation of * * * existing stockpiles, and the elimination of nuclear weapons and the means of their delivery pursuant to a treaty on general and complete disarmament under strict and effective international control." Under what circumstances could you foresee that the U.S. security interests would be served by the cessation of the manufacture of nuclear weapons and the destruction of nuclear stockpiles?

Mr. Nitze. Mr. Chairman, the negotiations with respect to universal and complete disarmament have been going on for many years, as you know, and the principal concern that we in the Defense Department have had is with respect to the question of verification, because it has been our view that it would be imprudent to undertake action such as would be implied by the general and complete disarmament without full and complete verification. I believe that is also the view of the Joint Chiefs of Staff.

General Wheeler. That is the view of the Joint Chiefs of Staff also, Mr. Chairman.

Senator Sparkman. Certainly, we would never enter into a program of destruction of existing stockpiles or cessation of manufacturing nuclear weapons unless we felt absolutely assured that our security interests would be protected.

General Wheeler. That is correct, sir.

Senator Sparkman. In the view of both of you gentlemen, as was expressed yesterday, any such program, any further treaty or agreement looking to this, would be subject to ratification by the Senate of the United States?

Mr. NITZE. That is correct, sir.

General WHEELER. That is correct, sir.

DEPARTMENT VIEW ON OFFENSIVE AND DEFENSIVE MISSILE SYSTEMS

Senator SPARKMAN. The nonnuclear weapons signatories to this treaty expect that the major powers will make important progress in nuclear disarmament. What steps do you recommend that the United States take in order to fulfill this expectation? I will name three possibilities: A comprehensive test ban, a freeze on offensive and defensive strategic weapons, and a moratorium on ABM deployment.

Mr. NITZE. Mr. Chairman, it would seem to me that the most hopeful development now is the possibility for discussions with the Soviet Union on the offensive and defense missile systems. Now, exactly how those talks might go and what items might come up first and what the interrelationship of them might be, I think it is too early to comment on.

Senator SPARKMAN. Perhaps too early even to consider whether we should do anything about holding up the ABM deployment.

Mr. NITZE. Well, it is my view, and I am sure it is Mr. Clifford's view, that it would be a mistake to hold up the deployment of the ABM.

I think pertinent to that might be a paragraph from Mr. Clifford's letter to Senator Russell, in which he addressed himself to the Sentinel system. The next to last paragraph of that letter says:

I believe our deployment decision is consistent with our continuing desire for arms control and arms limitation. The Soviets are at the present time deploying a ballistic missile defense around Moscow. We will continue our efforts to negotiate limitations of both strategic offensive and defensive weapons systems, but in the absence of agreement, we must not suspend taking actions in our own defense.

Senator SPARKMAN. I wonder, Mr. Secretary, if you might submit that letter for the record. I think it would be very good to have it in.

Mr. NITZE. I would be delighted to, Mr. Chairman.

(The letter referred to follows:)

THE SECRETARY OF DEFENSE,
Washington, June 18, 1968.

Hon. RICHARD B. RUSSELL,
Chairman, Committee on Armed Services,
U.S. Senate,
Washington, D.C.

DEAR SENATOR RUSSELL: You asked that I give you my personal views with respect to proceeding with the deployment of the Sentinel Antiballistic Missile System.

During the three and a half months since I became Secretary of Defense, I have had an opportunity to go into the merits of the System in considerable depth. As a result of that review I have come to the conclusion that it would be a serious mistake to eliminate construction and procurement funds in fiscal year 1969 for the deployment of the Sentinel System.

The reasons for that view are the following. The program represents twelve years of intense research and development effort. During those years we have devoted a substantial portion of our best scientific technological abilities to its development at a cost of some $3 billion. As long as seven years ago we demonstrated that we could with confidence destroy single incoming missiles. Since that time we have demonstrated that we can reliably track substantial numbers of incoming objects and defend the U.S. from relatively simple missile attacks. I believe that the time has arrived when we can no longer rely merely on continued research and development but should proceed with actual deployment of an operating system.

The Director of Defense Research and Engineering, Dr. John Foster, has prepared the following statement of the purposes of the Sentinel System, which I have approved on the recommendation of the Joint Chiefs of Staff and the Secretaries of the Army, Navy and the Air Force.

"The Sentinel missile defense system is designed to (a) prevent a successful missile attack from China through the late 1970's (with the capability to continue to deny or at least substantially reduce damage from threats in later years) ; (b) limit damage from an accidental launch from any source ; and (c) provide the option for increased defense of our Minuteman force, if necessary in the future.

"The ability to protect ourselves from unacceptable damage from a numerically large and technically advanced missile force such as that of the Soviet Union is not yet technically feasible. However the Sentinel system will complicate any attack on the United States.

"We will continue an intensive R&D program in an attempt to provide increasingly effective means to limit damage from both the advancing Chinese and the Soviet missile threats."

I understand that a proposal may be introduced in the Senate to eliminate funds for deployment of the Sentinel System in fiscal year 1969 and restrict the program to continued research and development. Approval of such a proposal would disrupt the work currently underway and, more seriously, would lose some two years in the availability of an operating system which in my judgment is important to the security of the United States.

I believe that our deployment decision is consistent with our continuing desire for arms control and arms limitation. The Soviets are, at the present time, deploying a ballistic missile defense around Moscow. We will continue our efforts to negotiate limitation of both strategic offensive and defensive weapons systems, but, in the absence of agreement, we must not suspend taking action in our own defense.

I have discussed the above views with the President, who shares my concern.

CLARK M. CLIFFORD.

Senator SPARKMAN. Do you hold that same view, General Wheeler?

General WHEELER. I do, Mr. Chairman.

Senator SPARKMAN. Under article VI of the treaty, the United States would undertake, among other things, and I quote, "to pursue negotiations in good faith on effective measures relating to nuclear disarmament."

Would you say that nuclear disarmament would advance the security interests of the United States or can you foresee the day when we can disarm our nuclear forces? I presume the answer you just gave fits that, too, that it is dependent upon future development in negotiations, talks to see what progress can be made on the broad front instead of any unilateral action.

Mr. NITZE. That is correct, Mr. Chairman.

General WHEELER. I agree, Mr. Chairman.

Senator SPARKMAN. Thank you very much.

Senator Pastore?

BILATERAL AGREEMENT WITH RUSSIA FAVORED

Senator PASTORE. As a matter of fact, do you see any advantage to the security of America in initiating steps on a unilateral basis which might cut down the military power or the posture of the

United States without having a bilateral agreement with Russia?

Mr. NITZE. That is not our view, Senator. Our view is that, as is expressed in that paragraph which I read, we think in the absence of actual agreement we should continue those matters, those actions, which are necessary for the continued defense of the United States.

Senator PASTORE. Russia is going to be bent on doing what she cares to do for her national security and it is our responsibility for our own security to do what we must do; is that correct?

Mr. NITZE. That is correct.

Senator PASTORE. Unless we reach an understanding on a bilateral basis, that is quid pro quo, it would be rather dangerous for our military posture to enter into any unilateral action?

Mr. NITZE. That is correct.

IS THERE MILITARY DISADVANTAGE TO U.S.?

Senator PASTORE. The one impression that I get is this: In these hearings we seem to accentuate the negative and not emphasize the positive enough.

I am referring to General Wheeler's statement. He said "First, we believe that any international agreement on the control of nuclear weapons must not operate to the disadvantage of the United States and our Allies."

Now, there is absolutely nothing in this treaty that is of a disadvantage to us in a military sense; is that true?

General WHEELER. That is my belief, sir.

Senator PASTORE. As a matter of fact, all that the military, all that the nuclear powers, are being asked to do is not to pass the control of these weapons to other countries.

General WHEELER. That is correct, sir.

Senator PASTORE. And we are doing it, in other words, we bind ourselves not to do it and, at the same time, Russia binds itself not to do it as well?

General WHEELER. That is correct, sir.

EFFECT ON U.S. COMMITMENT IN EUROPE

Senator PASTORE. Now, referring to our NATO allies, and coming back to the positive rather than the negative, what are the advantages, as you envision them, in this nuclear nonproliferation treaty, which might relieve us of some of our responsibility in Western Europe? I am not talking about today or tomorrow, but here we are, we have the two military titans of the world, Russia and the United States of America, who have negotiated and consummated an agreement whereby each of them has bound itself not to proliferate these weapons, which in a sense is more or less an understanding between the two military giants of the world. What are the advantages that you see in this in the future insofar as America's commitment in Europe?

General WHEELER. I think in this sense, Senator Pastore, and that is that I do not believe that the proliferation of nuclear weapons would do other than increase world tensions. I believe nonproliferation is the desire of all of us, and I believe that this is the positive rather than the negative which you mentioned a while ago; I believe that it is in our best interests, and in the best interests of everyone, that tensions be dampened rather than increased. Therefore, in the long term, I believe that this treaty, if followed out, if adhered to, by the majority of the nations of the world, will serve to create a better atmosphere in Europe and elsewhere which will serve the interests of all countries.

NATO MEMBERS AS SIGNATORIES

Senator PASTORE. Now, how many of our NATO allies have signed this treaty? Are you prepared to tell us that?

Mr. NITZE. I think I have the list here, Senator Pastore. Those that have signed are the United States, United Kingdom, Denmark, Greece, Iceland, and Norway. But in addition to those, there are those who voted for the U.N. resolution, and they are Canada, Turkey, Belgium, Italy, Luxembourg, and the Netherlands, and, in fact, Canada, Belgium, Italy, and the Netherlands were cosponsors of the U.N. resolution, and we have every anticipation that they will sign.

Those who abstained in the U.N. resolution were France and Portugal. The FRG was not involved in the U.N. resolution, and we hope that they will sign this fall.

Senator PASTORE. That is all.

Senator SPARKMAN. Senator Hickenlooper.

Senator HICKENLOOPER. Thank you, Mr. Chairman.

EFFECT ON U.S. SELF DEFENSE

Secretary Nitze, I want to ask a question I asked yesterday. I want your view on this: Does this treaty create any inhibitions on our own national defense—and perhaps I should direct this also to General Wheeler—over and above those which existed before the resolution was adopted or before the treaty was brought to consummation?

Mr. NITZE. It does not, Senator.

General WHEELER. That is my view also, Senator.

Senator HICKENLOOPER. As I understand it, we have the same right to the preparation of self defense, and the means of self defense after this treaty is signed as we had before, with the exception that we agree not to proliferate these weapons to nonnuclear countries or——

Mr. NITZE. Which it was not our intention to do prior to the treaty.

Senator HICKENLOOPER. I don't understand your answer.

Mr. NITZE. I say—you say except that it prohibits us from proliferating or transferring the control over nuclear weapons to other countries, and I say it was not our intention to do this prior to the negotiations.

Senator HICKENLOOPER. Not only was it not our intention, but we could do it prior to this.

Mr. NITZE. We could do it prior to the time it was adopted.

Senator HICKENLOOPER. Yes, in accordance with our statutes. I don't think the administration can transfer nuclear weapons willynilly. It would take a statute, I realize, to transfer material. But I am just trying to see, if we adopt the treaty, if it would inhibit us in any way beyond the restrictions which we had or assumed prior to the adoption of this treaty.

VIEWS OF JOINT CHIEFS OF STAFF

Mr. Nitze, I notice you say, referring to the Joint Chiefs of Staff, about the middle of that second paragraph:

The views of the Joint Chiefs of Staff particularly were sought. Their advice was most helpful on all issues, and was of paramount importance in formulating certain provisions of the Treaty in such a way as to insure that our current and projected mutual defense arrangements were not adversely affected.

What were the views of the Joint Chiefs of Staff? Did they agree with all the provisions of this treaty?

Mr. NITZE. I think General Wheeler should answer.

Senator HICKENLOOPER. Were there any objections, and if so, what were they, and from what sources?

General WHEELER. Senator, as the treaty was negotiated there were put forward from many sources many proposals upon which our advice was sought; we pointed out that certain of the proposals were, we thought, improper and were not in the interests of the security of the United States or of our treaty commitments; we made these views known to the Secretary of Defense and to others engaged in formulating the treaty, and our views were honored in each case. We do support the provisions of this treaty.

Senator HICKENLOOPER. You mean the objectionable provisions were eliminated?

General WHEELER. That is correct, sir.

Senator HICKENLOOPER. The objections which the Joint Chiefs of Staff raised?

General WHEELER. That is correct, sir.

Senator HICKENLOOPER. In the final analysis were the Joint Chiefs of Staff unanimous in their position?

General WHEELER. They were, Senator.

Senator HICKENLOOPER. Did you make any provisions or did you make any recommendations, as the Joint Chiefs of Staff, which were considered by the Joint Chiefs to be in the national interest to safeguard our interests which were not incorporated in this treaty?

General WHEELER. No, sir.

I think that every proposal that we made and every proposal that we opposed, our views were honored.

RELIABLE VERIFICATION PROCEDURES

Senator HICKENLOOPER. General Wheeler, in your statement you say:

Additionally, the Joint Chiefs of Staff consider that any arms control agreement must contain provisions for effective safeguards and reliable verification procedures.

I am especially interested in that term "reliable verification procedures." What do you consider to be reliable verification procedures in this treaty?

General WHEELER. The one which provides for the parties to the treaty negotiating with the International Atomic Energy Agency for the inspection of facilities. Now, of course, this is a follow on provision in this particular treaty, but we believe that these safeguards will be adequate for purposes of vertification in this kind of treaty.

Senator HICKENLOOPER. It will require a substantial increase in the personnel of the International Atomic Energy Agency; won't it?

General WHEELER. It probably will, sir. I am not aware of the details. I imagine Chairman Seaborg is probably the best witness on that, but I would think they will need an increase; yes, sir.

Senator HICKENLOOPER. At the present time they don't have enough competent inspectors to man an operation of this kind, I believe.

General WHEELER. I wouldn't think they would, sir.

DEFINITION OF "SOURCE OR SPECIAL FISSIONABLE MATERIAL"

Senator HICKENLOOPER. Let me ask this: I don't know whether I should direct this to Secretary Nitze or to General Wheeler, but in the last sentence of paragraph 1 of article III the treaty says:

The safeguards required by this article shall be applied on all source or special fissionable material in all peaceful nuclear activities within the territory of such state, under its jurisdiction, or carried out under its control anywhere.

Now, where do you define the term "source or special fissionable materials"? I believe those terms are terms in the Atomic Energy Act. Is that defined in this treaty, do you know?

Mr. NITZE. I believe not specifically. There is no definition.

General WHEELER. There is no definition, sir.

Senator HICKENLOOPER. What do you mean then by "source or special fissionable material"? It is well defined in the Atomic Energy Act.

Mr. NITZE. We believe it means exactly the same as it does in the Atomic Energy Act.

Senator HICKENLOOPER. I see.

Does this mean that military nuclear activities that are not directly related to the production of warheads or missiles are exempt from safeguards?

Mr. NITZE. That is correct—wait a minute. I am not sure I understood the question correctly. Could you repeat the question, Senator Hickenlooper?

Senator HICKENLOOPER. Again, this last sentence starting: "The safeguards required by this article," does that mean that military nuclear activities that are not directly related to the production of warheads or missiles are exempt from safeguards?

Mr. NITZE. That is correct.

Senator HICKENLOOPER. Which?

Mr. NITZE. That they are exempt.

Senator HICKENLOOPER. They are exempt?

MILITARY NUCLEAR PROGRAMS NOT CONNECTED WITH
WARHEADS OR MISSILES

Then may I ask you this: Is there any prohibition in this treaty of nuclear programs that are military in nature but have nothing to do with the research and production of warheads and missiles? For example, research and development of nuclear submarines. Could Sweden, for example, which is a neutral country, develop a nuclear submarine without violating the treaty?

Mr. NITZE. Yes.

Senator Pastore. Will the Senator yield at that point?

Under the atomic energy law a nuclear sub is not defined as a weapon; unless you put a bomb in it, it is not a weapon.

Mr. Nitze. That is correct.

General Wheeler. That is correct, Senator.

Senator Hickenlooper. There is no question that that definition is in the Atomic Energy Act, but what does it mean here?

Senator Pastore. The same thing.

Senator Hickenlooper. This is not the same law and we have specialized definitions in the Atomic Energy Act. If they apply here that is different.

Senator Pastore. The point that the Senator from Rhode Island is making is that the mere fact that another nation builds a sub, a nuclear sub, it is not building a weapon. It can be used, of course, to convey a weapon, but in itself it is not a weapon and, therefore, it is not included in this treaty.

OPINION OF THE ATOMIC ENERGY COMMISSION

Senator Hickenlooper. I want to read here from the Atomic Energy Act of 1954. Chapter 2, Definitions, section 11 (aa) which says:

The term "special nuclear material" means, (1) plutonium, uranium enriched in the isotope 233 or in the isotope 235, and any other material which the Commission—

Now that puts the definition in the Commission's hands—

pursuant to the provision of section 51, determines to be special nuclear material, but does not include source material; or (2) any material artificially enriched by any of the foregoing, but does not include source material.

Now, the difficulty we may be up against here is, suppose these other countries say they won't accept the arbitrary or whimsical opinion of the Atomic Energy Commission of the United States on some of these definitions. They are not defined in the treaty. I can envision the possibility of the Commission doing some things at some time in the future that we don't necessarily consider now.

Mr. Nitze. Might I submit a considered answer to that question, Senator, for the record, because it is an important question.

Senator Hickenlooper. Yes, because it is an extremely important point. The importance of this treaty has been emphasized and reemphasized. It is one of the greatest treaties that has ever been drawn involving atomic energy, and I think it is highly significant myself. But I don't think we should necessarily gloss over anything of this kind which might be subject to a different interpretation. It may be perfectly safeguarded. But it is something that ought to be clarified.

Mr. Nitze. We will submit a considered response, Senator.

Senator Hickenlooper. Good.

I wouldn't expect you necessarily under the circumstances to answer right off the top of your head at the moment. But if you will submit an opinion going specifically to this point I would appreciate it.

Mr. Nitze. Thank you.

(The information referred to follows:)

DEFENSE DEPARTMENT MEMORANDUM ON DEFINITION OF TERMS

The terms "source material" and "special fissionable material" are defined in the Statute of the International Atomic Energy Agency, a treaty to which the United States is a party. These definitions, which were patterned after U.S. atomic energy legislation, will be applicable under the Non-Proliferation Treaty by virtue of the role to be played by the International Atomic Energy Agency with respect to safeguards under that treaty. The definitions are as follows:

"Article XX. Definitions.

"As used in this Statute:

1. The term "special fissionable material" means plutonium-239; uranium-233; uranium enriched in the isotopes 235 or 233; any material containing one or more of the foregoing; and such other fissionable material as the Board of Governors shall from time to time determine; but the term "special fissionable material" does not include source material.

2. The term "uranium enriched in the isotopes 235 or 233" means uranium containing the isotopes 235 or 233 or both in an amount such that the abundance ratio of the sum of these isotopes to the isotope 238 is greater than the ratio of the isotope 235 to the isotope 238 occurring in nature.

3. The term "source material" means uranium containing the mixture of isotopes occurring in nature; uranium depleted in the isotope 235; thorium; any of the foregoing in the form of metal, alloy, chemical compound, or concentrate; any other material containing one or more of the foregoing in such concentration as the Board of Governors shall from time to time determine; and such other material as the Board of Governors shall from time to time determine."

The Board of Governors has never made any determination as to the inclusion of other material in the definition of either "source material" or "special fissionable material".

With reference to another point raised by Senator Hickenlooper in the same colloquy, the negotiating history of the Non-Proliferation Treaty fully supports the response by Senator Pastore to the effect that a nuclear submarine (as distinguished from a nuclear bomb that might be carried in such a submarine) is not considered to be a "nuclear weapon" within the meaning of this treaty.

Senator SPARKMAN. Senator Clark?

Senator CLARK. Gentlemen, as you know, I am not one of the Members of the Senate who is frightened of this treaty. I think it has been long overdue. I am delighted it has been negotiated and I want to congratulate both of you and the Secretary of Defense and everybody else over at the Department of Defense for the strong support you have given this treaty. I think you have rendered a very real public service and I am sure it was not easy to come to the courageous conclusion which you did come to. I think it was a courageous conclusion. This treaty is in the national interests, and you don't always have to say no to everything which has to do with the advancement of peace. I congratulate you.

PURSUIT OF DISARMAMENT NEGOTIATIONS

I would like to read to you a couple of clauses from the preamble and from the treaty and then ask you to express the attitude of the Department of Defense with respect to the implementation of these clauses in the treaty.

First, from the preamble, and I will be skipping around a bit:

Considering the devastation that would be visited upon all mankind by a nuclear war and the consequent need to make every effort to avert the danger of such a war and to take measures to safeguard the security of peoples,

And then further down—

Declaring their intention to achieve at the earliest possible date the cessation of the nuclear arms race and to undertake effective measures in the direction of nuclear disarmament, note the word "disarmament" and not the words "arms control."

Desiring to further the easing of international tension and the strengthening of trust between States in order to facilitate the cessation of the manufacture of nuclear weapons, the liquidation of all their existing stockpiles, and the elimination from national arsenals of nuclear weapons and the means of their delivery pursuant to a treaty on general and complete disarmament under strict and effective international control.

Recalling that, in accordance with the Charter of the United Nations, States must refrain in their international relations from the threat or use of force against the territorial integrity or political independence of any State, or in any other manner inconsistent with the purposes of the United Nations, and that the establishment and maintenance of international peace and security are to be promoted with the least diversion for armaments of the world's human and economic forces:

That is all in the preamble, and now I turn to article VI and read.

Each of the parties to the treaty undertakes to pursue negotiations in good faith on effective measures relating to cessation of the nuclear arms race at an early date and to nuclear disarmament, again not arms control, disarmament and on a treaty on general and complete disarmament under strict and effective international control.

Then skipping to the third subsection of article VIII.

Five years after the entry into force of this treaty, a conference of parties to the treaty shall be held in Geneva, Switzerland, in order to review the operation of this treaty with a view to assuring that the purposes of the Preamble and the provisions of the treaty are being realized.

Now, gentlemen, I assume, in view of your support of the treaty given in your testimony here, that you also support those clauses of the treaty, is that correct?

Mr. NITZE. That is correct, Mr. Senator.

ROLES OF DEFENSE DEPARTMENT AND OTHER AGENCIES

Senator CLARK. What would be the respective roles of the Department of Defense, the Department of State, and the Arms Control and Disarmament Agency in working within this 5-year period to achieve the objectives of the treaty as you now see them? I appreciate full well that your statement will have to be general and cannot be particularly specific; but I nonetheless think it important to get it on the record as to what DOD considers its mission to be as opposed to ACDA and State.

Mr. NITZE. In the first place, the State Department, ACDA, and the Department of Defense and the Joint Chiefs of Staff worked very closely together, as we have in connection with the NPT, with the nonproliferation treaty.

You asked a question as to the differentiation of the roles: We rather look to the State Department for the leadership in negotiations. We look to the Joint Chiefs of Staff particularly for concern with respect to our continuing defense and our commitments.

Senator CLARK. In other words, would it be fair to say that State takes the initiative in attempting to achieve these objectives, and the role of Defense is to assure that none of the negotiations instituted by State might result in a violation of the security interests of the United States?

Mr. NITZE. No; that is not what I am trying to say. What I am trying to say is that all of us try to work together toward the support of the interests of the United States. But that there are certain differentiations obviously due to the nature of our responsibilities in the contribution we make but all of us work together toward the common objective.

Senator CLARK. I have been concerned that the Arms Control and Disarmament Agency since it was created by the Congress has been downgraded in connection with its activities under the statute which created it, which was to take the initiative in this area of arms control and disarmament. I wonder if you would comment on that?

Mr. NITZE. I wouldn't share the view, Senator.

Senator CLARK. We can't agree about everything, can we?

SENATOR M'CARTHY'S POSITION PAPER ON ARMS CONTROL

Yesterday morning there was issued by our colleague, Senator McCarthy, what is called a position paper on arms control.

Mr. Chairman, with your permission, I would like to have this paper inserted in the record at this point.

Senator SPARKMAN. Without objection it will be done.

(The paper referred to follows:)

POSITION PAPER ON ARMS CONTROL, SENATOR EUGENE J. McCARTHY, JULY 10, 1968

THE PROBLEM

In 1959 the Antarctic Treaty barred nuclear weapons from the Antarctic continent and provided for free and open inspection of Antarctic bases. The test-ban treaty of 1963 prohibited nuclear explosions in the atmosphere, in the seas and in outer space. The 1967 treaty governed the exploration and use of outer space. And just recently, after years of negotiation, the Non-Proliferation Treaty was aimed at preventing the spread of nuclear weapons.

These have been necessary steps toward a more peaceful world. But we will have to do better in the future. There is today special urgency for sustained progress.

First, broader arms control measures among the great powers may be essential to convince other nations to sign the Nuclear Non-Proliferation Treaty.

Second, we are at a particularly critical period in terms of technological development. At present there exists a strategic stability which results from the presence, on both sides of invulnerable deterrent forces capable of inflicting substantial damage in a retaliatory attack. But the introduction of sophisticated anti-ballistic missile systems and new missiles equipped with multiple warheads threaten to make the situation unstable. With the deployment of such weapons systems, each side will become concerned as to whether in the event of a preemptive attack it will be able to inflict sufficient damage in retaliation—if not, its deterrent will not be credible. The arms race will thus be impelled to a new intensity. In crises, there could be an incentive to launch a first strike—an incentive which does not now exist because each side can have confidence in its deterrent.

Further progress, then, is particularly urgent today. There is also reason to believe it is possible. Agreement on the Nuclear Non-Proliferation Treaty, Soviet ratification of the consular agreement, implementation of direct airline routes between the United States and the U.S.S.R., the Soviet proposals to discuss other specific measures at the Eighteen Nation Disarmament Conference, and most importantly the Soviet acceptance of our offer to conduct discussions on the control of strategic offensive and defensive weapons, all suggest that much more significant steps might be taken.

It is imperative that we exploit the momentum of these events. Highest priority should be given to the achievement of international agreements. We must invite China to participate in all disarmament and arms control discussions. This makes a change in our overall diplomatic policy desirable—by recognizing

China, by opening up trade and cultural exchange, and by revising our general military policy in Asia. In the meantime, important arms control agreements can be safely reached without the participation of China.

INTERNATIONAL AGREEMENTS

Implementation of a comprehensive arms control and disarmament program will require the following initial steps:

(1) We must seek an immediate international moratorium—a freeze—on the number and characteristics of strategic weapons, both offensive and defensive. Such a moratorium would prevent ABM deployments by the United States and the Soviet Union. It would mean there would be no deployment by the United States of new offensive missiles, for example in the multiple warhead missiles, Minuteman III and Poseidon. The Soviet Union in turn would terminate the very considerable expansion of its offensive strategic program that is now underway. It is particularly important that this moratorium come into effect before there is any major ABM deployment by the United States and before the Soviet ABM is extended.

So long as the moratorium is effective there should also be an agreement that there shall be no flight testing of new ICBM's, or new submarine-launched missiles. Fortunately it appears feasible to verify compliance with all these prohibitions—on ABM deployment, on significant new offensive missile deployment and on flight testing of new offensive missiles—without there being any need for intrusive verification procedures. Both sides now have other verification capabilities, including observation satellites, which are sufficiently dependable to minimize the risks of significant undetected evasions even in the absence of specific inspection agreements.

As an initial step toward reaching agreements to limit strategic armaments we should announce that we are delaying deployment of the Sentinel ABM system and the Poseidon and Minuteman III ICBM pending speedy agreement with the U.S.S.R. We can do this without putting our security in jeopardy, since neither the Chinese nuclear threat against which we are deploying Sentinel, nor the Soviet ABM which is the rationale for the Poseidon and Minuteman III developments, are moving ahead perceptibly. At the very least we would be deferring expenditures in a year when our economy is seriously strained; and if our restraint should promote an agreement on strategic forces we would have gained greatly from our unilateral initiatives in this area.

(2) As part of a freeze on strategic offensive and defensive systems, we should also seek an international agreement to prohibit both development and deployment of new intercontinental bombers. Compliance in this case too could be easily verified.

(3) Following a freeze on strategic offensive systems and ABM's, there should be an agreement to reduce the number of strategic weapons. Reaching agreement on this point may be more difficult because of the problems of establishing the levels to be retained, and balancing dissimilar weapons systems. Reductions of strategic systems to very low levels will be extremely difficult and we should not make the mistake of believing otherwise. It will be necessary but not easy to persuade all countries having nuclear weapon capabilities to accede to such agreements. It will also be difficult to secure agreement on the intrusive inspection procedures that will be necessary when the retained levels are so low that small evasions could affect the strategic balance. These problems, however, are not beyond solution if they are not beyond political will.

(4) A freeze on strategic delivery systems and ABM's should significantly reduce the military demand for production of additional nuclear warheads, and encourage the Soviets to agree finally to prohibit further production of fissionable material for military purposes. Such an agreement too could be verified without intrusive inspection. It would require merely the same International Atomic Energy Agency controls on reactors and on the facilities that are used for peaceful purposes.

With a reduction or elimination of the production of fissionable materials, there could also be a program wherein both sides would transfer specified amounts of fissionable material to stockpiles to be used for peaceful purposes under International Atomic Energy Agency controls.

(5) The time has come for a renewed effort to achieve a Comprehensive Nuclear Test Ban Treaty. There is now only a marginal need for testing nuclear warheads. If we secure a moratorium on deployment of new strategic systems, virtually all

need for testing will have been eliminated. Capabilities for detecting underground tests and for discriminating between tests and earthquakes have greatly improved in recent years. Both factors suggest that agreement can now be more easily achieved.

We have almost certainly reached the point where any clandestine explosions that could escape detection and identification would be militarily insignificant. However, an agreement with provision for two or three on-site inspections (a number at one time acceptable to the Soviet Union) or some system of inspection by challenge, would be more viable, because means would be available for resolving doubts about the origin of some unidentified seismic events.

(6) Unrestricted use of chemical and biological weapons could lead to the development of devices which would be at least as great a threat to life as thermonuclear bombs. It is therefore vital to implement all measures which would inhibit the initiation of chemical and biological warfare. The United States is the only major power which is not at this time a party to the 1925 Geneva Protocol which prohibits the use of chemical and biological weapons. We should be prepared to accede to an updated version of the Protocol. Under the auspices of the Eighteen Nation Disarmament Conference, a meeting of technical experts should be convened immediately to establish the criteria which specify chemical and biological weapons and thereby make it possible to update the 1925 protocol consistent with more recent developments.

(7) We should support the establishment of a technical committee of members of the Eighteen Nation Disarmament Conference as a forum where parties to arms control agreements may raise questions concerning the activities of other parties in areas where the treaty is applicable. This would be particularly important in the case of a comprehensive test ban treaty verified only by unilateral means.

(8) A conscientious and vigorous effort should be made to strengthen the role of the United Nations in peace keeping operations.

All these measures are made more possible by a confluence of interest now developing between the United States and the Soviet Union which may well express itself in the area of arms control and disarmament. In view of this confluence, the initial steps suggested above are far more feasible than is generally acknowledged. There is no question that they can be taken without affecting our national security adversely.

UNILATERAL ACTIONS

While we are attempting to reach agreements to limit armaments through international agreements, it is important to recognize that there is a great deal we can achieve simply by having the courage to exercise self-restraint on our own military activities. We must recognize that if we continue to equate security with ever growing weaponry we may be marching toward disaster.

We should also recognize that our decisions to procure certain weapon systems will normally provoke equivalent responses by our potential adversaries which, if one judges by the past record, negate our own efforts. We must consider military expenditures as critically as we do those for non-military programs. There are indications that the Congress is at long last beginning to do this. It should continue to do so.

With respect to our commitments abroad there are also important opportunities for us to profit by restraining our military activities unilaterally.

First, there is our military presence in Europe. To adjust to the change of Soviet strategy we must seek to reduce tensions further. In addition to dealing with the problems of men and conventional armaments in Europe, we must attend to the problem of tactical nuclear weapons. The situation could be improved considerably by our withdrawing from Europe large quantities of unneeded nuclear weapons.

Second, there are our activities in the developing nations of Asia, Latin America and Africa. In these countries we have competed with both our allies and our adversaries in the sale and supply of arms. An alarming increase has taken place, particularly within the past few years, in the number and sophistication of arms we supply to the developing countries. Across the globe, wars are being fought with American weapons—often on both sides. We have become the principal weapon suppliers of the world. And that policy must change.

We have often in the past acceded to requests for military aid simply because a military clique desired to maintain its influence and position. We have too often been motivated by our desire to buy or maintain influence in recipient countries, to secure military bases, or to generate sales to help our balance of payments problems. None of these reasons can justify our arms sales program.

Ideally, this problem should be dealt with by international agreements. The United States should again become the leader in the search persuade other major suppliers to agree to some sort of arms moratorium. In any case, the United States must unilaterally limit its arms sales abroad.

CONCLUSION

We seek, finally, a new era for arms control and disarmament. The United States should again become the leader in the search for a rational world security system. There is good reason for optimism. Many of the obstacles in the past have been the product of the Cold War between the U.S. and the Soviet Union. The detente between the two great powers, interrupted by the war in Vietnam, can be renewed with peace in Southeast Asia. If each of the powers is willing to enter accords in a spirit of conciliation, arms control agreements can be the principal expression of a renewed detente. An end to the war in Vietnam must occasion a complete reappraisal of our diplomacy and a new thrust toward peace.

DEPLOYMENT OF AN ABM SYSTEM

Senator CLARK. Has either of you gentlemen had an opportunity to look at it?

Mr. NITZE. I have not, Senator.

Senator CLARK. General Wheeler?

General WHEELER. I only had a chance to scan a report in the newspaper this morning, Senator Clark. I did not read it carefully.

Senator CLARK. I would commend it to both of you.

I would like to ask you a couple of questions which are based on Senator McCarthy's paper.

As you know, according to the newspapers he was aided in the preparation of this paper by two very distinguished scientists, Jerome Wiesner and George Kistiakowsky who, I am sure, are well known to both of you. He makes this point:

We are at a particularly critical period in terms of technological development. At present there exists a strategic stability which results from the presence, on both sides, of invulnerable deterrent forces capable of inflicting substantial damage in retaliatory attack. But the introduction of sophisticated antiballistic missile systems and new missiles equipped with multiple warheads threaten to make the situation unstable. With the deployment of such weapons systems, each side will become concerned as to whether in the event of a preemptive attack it will be able to inflect sufficient damage in retaliation—if not, its deterrent will not be credible. The arms race will thus be impelled to renewed intensity. In crises, there could be an incentive to launch a first strike—an incentive which does not now exist because each side can have confidence in its deterrent.

It is largely for those reasons that I have been so largely opposed to the deployment of the antiballistic missile system which I understand you gentlemen support. I wonder if either or both of you would comment on Senator McCarthy's statement?

Mr. NITZE. I would rather make a considered reply.

Senator CLARK. Let me interrupt to say I think that would be wiser, too, unless you would like to volunteer something now.

Mr. NITZE. I think maybe I had better supply a reply for the record.

Senator CLARK. You say you would like to reply now or later?

Mr. Chairman, I would like to have permission to have General Wheeler and Deputy Secretary Nitze file with the committee a considered statement of their reaction to the suggestions made by Senator McCarthy, which I personally, as a member of this committee, concur in.

Senator SPARKMAN. I am sure you would be glad to do that, wouldn't you?

Mr. NITZE. Yes.

(The material referred to follows:)

COMMENTS OF THE DEPUTY SECRETARY OF DEFENSE CONCERNING SENATOR McCARTHY'S POSITION PAPER ON ARMS CONTROL

The position paper on arms control issued by Senator McCarthy reflects a desire for progress in limiting the nuclear arms race and for negotiating measures to deal with conventional arms races which are fully consistent with objectives stated by all of the post-war Presidents of the United States.

The difficulty has been and continues to be that of defining and securing agreement to proposals which are in the security interests of the countries concerned and which can be adequately verified. The United States Government has put forward a number of proposals in the areas raised by Senator McCarthy's memorandum and our representatives in Geneva and elsewhere are actively seeking agreement on adequately verified arrangements.

I cannot accept the suggestion that the United States on a unilateral basis should suspend existing programs. The programs approved are those essential to maintain the security of the United States in the absence of an agreement and must be carried forward until and unless we can negotiate an acceptable agreement.

COMMENTS OF THE CHAIRMAN OF THE JOINT CHIEFS OF STAFF CONCERNING SENATOR McCARTHY'S POSITION PAPER ON ARMS CONTROL

I have been asked to give my views on Senator McCarthy's position paper of 10 July 1968 concerning an arms moratorium on strategic offensive and defensive weapons.

The Sentinel System is being developed and deployed to provide: protection to U.S. cities against an initial capability of Chinese communist ICBM attack; the option to protect selected Minuteman ICBM fields against Soviet attack; and a guard against an accidental or unauthorized missile launch by any foreign country.

In this configuration, it does not constitute an effective defense against the USSR ballistic missile threat. Thus, a decision to postpone deployment of the system would likely have no significant effect on arms control discussions with the Soviets but would leave the United States vulnerable to an attack by the Chinese People's Republic.

Concerning Poseidon and Minuteman III deployment, the quantitative and qualitative increase in Soviet offensive capabilities, the uncertainties resulting from their defensive deployments, and the relative decline in U.S. capabilities show clearly the essential requirement for improvements in the programmed force.

In the absence of continued U.S. improvements in strategic capabilities, Soviet offensive and defensive systems could attain, in the course of their development, significant counterforce and defensive damage-limiting capability against the United States. It is necessary, therefore, for the United States to make timely improvements in its strategic offensive and defensive capabilities in order to preserve a credible deterrent and effective force to convince the Soviets that they cannot achieve a viable first-strike option.

REMARKS OF PREMIER KOSYGIN

Senator CLARK. Mr. Chairman, in view of your desire for them to make a more careful appraisal I will not read further but call your attention to paragraphs 5 and 6 which I believe to be of considerable importance. Finally, gentlemen, I imagine that you have had an opportunity, have you not, to read the statement by the President of the

United States on missile talks with Moscow, and excerpts from the remarks of Mr. Kosygin of the U.S.S.R. and the arms memorandum which followed his remarks which appeared in the New York Times on Tuesday, July 2?

Mr. NITZE. I have read them but I am not sure that I have them all firmly in mind.

Senator CLARK. Because these are really desperately serious matters, I think it would be highly preferable if you gentlemen would be willing to furnish the committee, with the approval of the Chairman, with a detailed comment to the eighth, the ninth, specific suggestions for further progress in the area of arms control and disarmament made by Premier Kosygin. I assume you are in accord with the statement of our President in that connection?

Mr. NITZE. We are.

General WHEELER. Yes, sir.

Senator CLARK. May we have that for the record?

Senator SPARKMAN. Very well, we will be very glad if you will comment on that.

Senator CLARK. Thank you, Mr. Chairman.

(The remarks of Mr. Kosygin, excerpts from the arms memo, and the comments of Mr. Nitze and General Wheeler follow:)

[From the New York Times, July 2, 1968]

KOSYGIN REMARKS AND EXCERPTS FROM ARMS MEMO

Following are remarks by Premier Aleksei N. Kosygin and excerpts from a Soviet memorandum on steps to reduce the arms race, as made public in English by Tass, Soviet press agency:

(By Premier Kosygin)

Permit me on the instructions of the Soviet Government to express profound satisfaction over the fact that today commences the signing of the treaty on the nonproliferation of nuclear weapons which is an important international document commended by the overwhelming majority of the United Nations members.

The conclusion of a treaty on the nonproliferation of nuclear weapons is a major success of the cause of peace. Since the very emergence of nuclear weapons, the Soviet Union has firmly and consistently come out for delivering mankind from the nuclear threat. The treaty is an important step toward this goal since it bars further proliferation of nuclear weapons, thus reducing the danger of an outbreak of a nuclear war.

The participation of a great number of states in the signing of the treaty today is a convincing proof that states are capable of finding mutually acceptance solutions of complicated international problems of vital importance for the whole of mankind.

The preparation of the treaty required great efforts and prolonged negotiations, taking part in which were nuclear and non-nuclear, big and small, developed and developing nations, countries belonging to different social systems.

NUMEROUS VIEWS REFLECTED

The treaty reflects numerous wishes and proposals expressed by states, takes into account various points of view on the solution of the nonproliferation problem; under these circumstances, all the states approving it have agreed about the main thing: the necessity of barring further proliferation of nuclear weapons.

A significant supplement to the treaty is furnished by the Security Council decision on security assurances for non-nuclear weapon countries, party to the treaty, adopted quite recently. As was stated in the Security Council, the Soviet Government intends to comply with this decision unswervingly.

Five years ago here in Moscow we signed the treaty barring nuclear weapon tests in three environments. After that the treaty prohibiting the use of outer space for military purposes was concluded. Alongside with the treaty on the non-proliferation of nuclear weapons, there are practical steps towards limiting the arms race which creates more favorable conditions for progress in disarmament.

The Soviet Government, assigning great significance to the provisions of the treaty on the nonproliferation of nuclear weapons, whereby its parties undertake to pursue negotiations in good faith on effective measures relating to cessation of the nuclear race and to nuclear disarmament, decided and sent to all governments a memorandum on some urgent measures for stopping the arms race and for disarmament, which lists such measures as prohibition of the use of nuclear weapons, cessation of the manufacture of nuclear weapons, and reduction and destruction of their stockpiles, limitation and subsequent reduction of means of delivery of strategic weapons, and others.

The Soviet Government attaches exclusively great importance to the memorandum as it is aimed at the strengthening of peace. Simultaneous or stage-by-stage implementation of the measures for disarmament proposed by the Soviet Union would be a serious contribution to the struggle for the cessation of the arms race and for a radical solution of the disarmament problem.

May I express a hope that the memorandum will receive due consideration from the governments of the world nations, that it will be a subject of comprehensive discussion in the 18-nation committee on disarmament which is going to resume its work shortly, and that this will make it possible to achieve specific results in the field of disarmament, which peoples of the whole world are longing for.

SOVIET MEMORANDUM

Following the conclusion of the treaty on the nonproliferation of nuclear weapons, the Soviet Government proposes that an understanding be reached on the implementation of the following urgent measures on an end to the arms race and on disarmament in the near future.

1. A ban on the use of nuclear weapons

An important advance towards a solution of this problem, towards the elimination of the threat of nuclear war, would be the conclusion of an international agreement, banning the use of nuclear weapons.

With the object of facilitating the earliest possible solution of this problem, the Government of the U.S.S.R. submitted to the 22nd session of the United Nations General Assembly a draft convention on a ban on the use of nuclear weapons.

The Assembly urged all states to study the draft convention on a ban on the use of nuclear weapons, submitted by the Soviet Union, and also other proposals, which may be made on this question, and to hold talks concerning the conclusion of an appropriate convention through convocation of an international conference, in the 18-nations Disarmament Committee or directly between states.

With the object of a practical solution to the problem of banning the use of nuclear weapons, the Soviet Government proposes that the 18-nation committee should discuss as a priority item the draft convention on banning the use of such weapons and exchange opinions on the convocation of an international conference for its signing.

2. Measures on ending the manufacture of nuclear weapons, reducing and liquidating their stockpiles

The Soviet Government proposes that all nuclear powers immediately open talks on an end to the manufacture of nuclear weapons, the reduction of its stockpiles and the subsequent total ban on and liquidation of nuclear weapons under appropriate international control.

The Soviet Government expresses its readiness to open such talks with all other nuclear powers at any time.

3. Limitation and subsequent reduction of means of delivery of strategic weapons

The Soviet Government proposes that an understanding be reached on concrete steps in the limitation and subsequent reduction of strategic means of delivery of strategic nuclear weapons. In doing so the Soviet Government proceeds from the assumption that the destruction of the entire arsenal of means of strategic delivery and, in any case, the reduction of this arsenal to the absolute minimum, with the retention, and this only temporarily, of only a strictly limited quantity of such means, would be a measure leading to the elimination of the threat of nuclear war.

The Soviet Government expresses its readiness to hold an exchange of opinion with concerned states on mutual limitation and subsequent reduction of strategic means of delivery of nuclear weapons.

4. Ban on flights of bombers, carrying nuclear weapons, beyond national frontiers. Limitation of zones of voyages of submarines carrying missiles

The Soviet Government has more than once drawn the attention of the governments of other states and world opinion to the danger of flights of bombers, carrying nuclear weapons, beyond the boundaries of national frontiers. The increasing crashes of American bombers, carrying nuclear weapons beyond the territory of the United States, arouse the legitimate anxiety of various countries.

From a military point of view, these flights of bombers are devoid of sense in conditions of the existence of nuclear rocket weapons.

The Soviet Government proposes that flights of bombers, carrying nuclear weapons, beyond the boundaries of national frontiers be banned without delay.

In order to reduce the risk of the outbreak of a nuclear war, the Soviet Government also proposes that an agreement be reached on an end to the patroling by submarines, carrying nuclear missiles, within missile-striking range of the borders of the contracting sides.

5. Ban on underground tests of nuclear weapons

The Soviet Government is prepared to reach an immediate understanding on the banning of underground tests of nuclear weapons on the basis of using national means of detection to control this ban.

6. Ban on the use of chemical and bacteriological weapons

The Soviet Government has more than once drawn the attention of states to the threat for mankind from the use of chemical and bacteriological weapons.

Reflecting the common anxiety of the peoples in view of such a threat, the 21st session of the United Nations General Assembly passed a resolution, calling for strict observance by all states of the principles of the Geneva protocol of 1925 on a ban on the use of chemical and bacteriological weapons, denouncing all actions contradicting this aim, and proposing that all states accede to the Geneva protocol.

However, this important decision of the General Assembly, is not fulfilled by some countries, first and foremost the United States. The United States uses chemical weapons in its aggressive war in Vietnam.

In view of this, the Soviet Government proposes that the 18-nation committee examine ways and means of securing observance by all states of the Geneva Protocol on a ban on the use of chemical and bacteriological weapons.

7. Liquidation of foreign military bases

Foreign military bases on alien territories create a serious threat to the peace. Such bases serve as a source of outbreak of military conflicts, threaten the freedom and independence of the peoples. This is convincingly borne out by the continuing aggressive war of the United States in Vietnam, by the tension and conflicts in other parts of the world, where foreign bases are located.

The Soviet Government proposes that, in conformity with instructions of the 21st session of the United Nations General Assembly, the 18-nation Disarmament Committee urgently examine the question of the liquidation of foreign military bases.

8. Measures on regional disarmament

The Soviet Government supports the setting up of denuclearized zones in various parts of the world.

The Soviet Government believes that not only groups of states, embracing whole continents or major geographic regions, but also more limited groups of states or even individual countries, may assume commitments for the establishment of denuclearized zones.

The Soviet Government also supports proposals concerning the implementation of measures for regional disarmament and for the reduction of armaments in various regions of the world, including the Middle East. The question of such measures for slackening the arms race in the Middle East, of course, could be considered only in conditions of elimination of the consequences of the Israeli aggression against the Arab countries, and, above all, the full evacuation of the Israeli forces from the territories of Arab countries occupied by them.

9. *Peaceful uses of the sea bed and ocean floor*

The progress of research and the prospect for the development of the sea bed and the ocean floor make it possible to raise the question of the timely recording in a proper form of conditions that would insure the utilization of the sea bed beyond the limits of existing territorial waters exclusively for peaceful purposes.

This would ban, specifically, the establishment of fixed military installations on the sea bed and also any other military activity.

The Soviet Government proposes that the 18-nation committee open talks on the use of the sea bed beyond the limits of existing territorial waters exclusively for peaceful purposes.

———

COMMENTS OF THE DEPUTY SECRETARY OF DEFENSE CONCERNING THE SOVIET MEMORANDUM ON DISARMAMENT

The memorandum on disarmament issued by the Soviet Union on July 1, 1968 is being studied with interest by the Department of Defense. Our initial reaction is that, of the nine disarmament items listed in the paper, only two reflect any significant change from previous Soviet positions. We are, of course, encouraged by these two changes, one of which concerns the discussion of limitations of strategic delivery vehicles and the other concerns measures to limit arms in the Near East.

We will be discussing strategic limitations with the Soviets in the near future, and are again assessing our positions on the other topics of the Soviet memorandum in preparation for the upcoming session of the Eighteen Nation Disarmament Committee.

I feel that the Soviet proposal for a convention prohibiting the use of nuclear weapons would not enhance the security of any nation. First of all, it would be ineffective in preventing the use of nuclear weapons in time of war. It might also raise false hopes that the danger of nuclear war had been eliminated, and would undermine the deterrent effect of our nuclear forces.

The Soviets have proposed negotiations on the cessation of the production of nuclear weapons, the reduction of their stocks and the subsequent complete banning and liquidation of nuclear weapons under appropriate international control. The United States has previously proposed negotiations toward these goals.

I have already mentioned our upcoming talks with the Soviets regarding both offensive and defensive strategic delivery vehicles, which is the subject of item number three of the Soviet memorandum.

The question of limitations on bomber flights and submarine patrols with nuclear weapons aboard is receiving careful study within the Department. However, the problems of verifying any agreement on this subject appear formidable.

Since negotiations began on the Limited Test Ban Treaty, the United States has consistently made clear its position on an extension of that treaty to the underground environment.

We are giving careful consideration to the Soviet proposal concerning chemical and bacteriological weapons. Although the United States is not a party to the Geneva Protocol of 1925, we have consistently supported the worthy objectives which it seeks to achieve and believe that all states should do likewise. The U.S. voted affirmatively for the 1966 UNGA Resolution concerning these issues.

I believe that the Soviet proposal for the elimination of all foreign military bases would not further the goals of international peace and security. The United States maintains military bases on foreign soil only to assist in maintaining peace. Only in consultation with our Allies and after substantial progress in the reduction of armaments and armed forces could elimination of our overseas bases be contemplated.

The memorandum states that the Soviet Government supports the creation of nuclear free zones in various areas of the world. I welcome this statement: I would welcome even more Soviet signature to Protocol II of the Treaty of Tlatelolco as evidence of their support. The United States has signed this Protocol, but the Soviet Union has not yet signed. This eighth item of the Soviet memorandum also states that the Soviet Government supports proposals for the implementation of measures for regional disarmament and the decrease of armaments in the various regions of the world, including the Near East. I would point out that President Johnson made a concrete proposal to the members of the United Nations in June of 1967 for the registration of all arms shipments to the Near East and for other measures to limit the flow of such arms. The United States has acted with the utmost restraint in the supply of armaments to all areas, but most particularly to the Near East, whereas the Soviet Union has shipped vast quantities of arms to this area in the past year.

The United States would welcome any serious Soviet proposal for a limitation of arms in the Middle East. The present Soviet memorandum requires complete withdrawal of Israeli forces from the territories of the Arab countries as a precondition for consideration of this subject. The question of withdrawal cannot be separated from the vast number of other very complex issues.

In item number nine of the memorandum, the Soviet Government proposes starting, in the ENDC, talks on the question of utilization of the seabed beyond existing territorial waters for peaceful purposes only.

The U.S. Government has been discussing this subject with the Soviets and others in the U.N. Ad Hoc Committee on seabeds in New York, and has made the following statement.

"The United States is dedicated to workable Arms Control measures that will enhance the peace and security of all nations and bring the world nearer to general and complete disarmament. We propose that the ENDC be asked to take up the question of arms control on the seabed with a view to defining those factors vital to a workable, verifiable and effective international agreement which would prevent the use of this new environment for the emplacement of weapons of mass destruction."

We will continue our discussions of these issues both in New York and Geneva in an effort to find areas of agreement on this important subject.

COMMENTS OF THE CHAIRMAN OF THE JOINT CHIEFS OF STAFF CONCERNING PREMIER KOSYGIN'S MEMORANDUM ON DISARMAMENT

Before responding to the inquiry as to my opinion of the nine specific proposals of Premier Kosygin for curbing the arms race and on disarmament, I would like to reaffirm that the Joint Chiefs of Staff are in favor of any arms control negotiations which enhance national security through balanced, phased, and safeguarded arms control agreements limiting the military capabilities of nations in a manner conducive to the achievement of a secure, free, and peaceful world.

Of the nine proposals made by the Soviet Union on 1 July 1968, the one deserving most attention is that which appears to respond to President Johnson's statement at the United Nations General Assembly on 12 June 1968 in which he stated the urgent desire of the United States to begin early discussions on the limitation of strategic offensive and defensive nuclear weapons systems. The United States and the Soviet Union are now negotiating a time and place for beginning bilateral talks in the immediate future.

As to the proposal for banning the use of nuclear weapons, I could support such an agreement only if it were a part of a balanced, phased, and safeguarded agreement on general and complete disarmament by all militarily significant states with assurance that no undue advantage would accrue to any state during the general disarmament process.

The proposal concerning the cessation of the production of nuclear weapons and reducing stockpiles is roughly similar to that proposed by President Johnson in 1966.

I would consider any proposal to prohibit the flights of bombers carrying nuclear weapons beyond national borders to be inimical to the national interest. It is not, in my view, a serious disarmament proposal.

The United States missile-armed submarine force is an important part of its overall nuclear deterrent capability. The Soviet proposal is impractical since it is unverifiable. The United States should continue to deploy its submarine force in waters where it has the right to do so in accordance with the rules of international law.

While considerable progress has been made in technology for detecting underground tests, the state of the art has not reached the point where the United States should rely solely on national means of detection for verification of such a prohibition as proposed by the Soviets.

The proposal that the Eighteen-Nation Disarmament Committee review the paths and means of ensuring the fulfillment by all nations of the Geneva Protocol of 1925 on the prohibition of the use of asphyxiating, poisonous gases and bacteriological methods of warfare is obviously designed for other than serious negotiations. I base this observation on the fact that the proposal was accompanied by an accusation that the United States is involved in a war of aggression in Vietnam.

The only reason the United States maintains military bases on foreign soil is to assist in maintaining peace. Only in consultation with our allies and after substantial progress in the reduction of armaments and armed forces would elimination of United States overseas military bases contribute towards world peace.

The United States has long advocated effective regional arms control measures. President Johnson suggested in his message to the Eighteen-Nation Disarmament Committee on 22 January 1966 "that countries, on a regional basis, explore ways to limit competition among themselves for costly weapons often sought for reasons of illusory prestige. The initiative for arrangements of this kind should, of course, come from the regions concerned."

On 19 June 1967, President Johnson proposed that the United Nations immediately call upon all of its members to report all shipments of all military arms into Israel and the Arab States.

Further, the United States has signed Protocol II of the Treaty of Tlatelolco, or Latin American Nuclear Free Zone Treaty, which the Soviet Union has yet to do.

The United States has proposed in the United Nations that the Eighteen-Nation Disarmament Committee take up the question of arms limitations on the seabed with a view to defining those factors vital to a workable, verifiable, and effective international agreement which would prevent the use of this new environment for the emplacement of weapons of mass destruction.

Senator SPARKMAN. Senator Aiken!

"EXTRAORDINARY EVENT" LEADING TO WITHDRAWAL FROM TREATY

Senator AIKEN. General Wheeler, article X of the treaty, first line, is that "Each Party shall in exercising its national sovereignty have the right to withdraw from the Treaty if it decides that extraordinary events, related to the subject matter of this Treaty, have jeopardized the supreme interests of its country."

Will you give us an illustration of an extraordinary event short of general war which would cause you, as Chairman of the Joint Chiefs of Staff, to recommend withdrawal from the treaty? What would be an extraordinary event?

General WHEELER. Well, of course, in the case of a war, Senator Aiken, the treaty, as I believe Secretary Rusk pointed out yesterday, immediately becomes inoperative.

I would think that if we detected serious violations of the treaty provisions, that is, regarding the proliferation of nuclear weapons to nonnuclear states that would be hostile to us, we would be justified in examining our position and perhaps recommending to the President that we withdraw from the treaty.

Senator AIKEN. Then you would say either war itself or the threat of an impending war, existence of conditions which appear to be heading for war?

General WHEELER. And which would find us at a substantial disadvantage in the strategic nuclear field.

U.S. MAINTENANCE OF NUCLEAR WEAPONS IN OTHER COUNTRIES

Senator AIKEN. Is there anything in this treaty which would prohibit the United States from maintaining nuclear weapons in any other country so long as they were owned and controlled by our own Government?

General WHEELER. No, sir.

Senator AIKEN. And that would apply to Russia in the same manner?

General WHEELER. That is correct, sir.

Senator AIKEN. I think that is all the questions for you, General Wheeler.

NUCLEAR TEST BAN TREATY

Secretary Nitze, I noticed you put some stress on the President's statement and I quote: "This treaty is the most important international agreement since the beginning of the nuclear age." You consider it more important than the Test Ban Treaty of 1963?

Mr. NITZE. That is correct.

Senator AIKEN. Would this treaty have been possible had it not been for the existence of the Test Ban Treaty?

Mr. NITZE. I doubt that it would have. At that time we anticipated that the Test Ban Treaty would have benefits in itself, and that it might lead to the possibility of further agreements thereafter. This would seem to me to be a notable carrying on of that hope.

Senator AIKEN. Then if we were withdrawing from either treaty you would say it would be to our advantage to withdraw from the Test Ban Treaty rather than the Nonproliferation Treaty?

Mr. NITZE. I would hope it would not be necessary to withdraw from either, Mr. Senator.

Senator AIKEN. I had one other question, but in view of the recent colloquy I don't think I will ask it, but I was going to ask why does it happen that Mr. Kosygin and other members of the Russian Government have suddenly become much more cooperative with our own Government, but I am not asking that. Don't try to answer. That is all.

Senator SPARKMAN. Senator Pell.

Senator PELL. I would like to defer, if I may, until I have had a chance to read the testimony.

Senator SPARKMAN. Senator Carlson.

NATO NUCLEAR PLANNING GROUP

Senator CARLSON. Mr. Secretary, I have been glancing through your statement, and I find some words here that I think ought to be clarified before we go too far with this treaty.

The U.S. Government holds the view that the entry into force of one nonproliferation treaty will not interfere with the work of the nuclear planning group. The U.S. Government intends to continue to pursue actively the work of the nuclear planning group and to seek to find solutions satisfactory to its nonnuclear partners in NATO.

First, who composes the Nuclear Planning Group?

Mr. NITZE. This is a group within the NATO organizational structure which is subordinate to the Defense Minister's group, and it has certain permanent members, the United States, the United Kingdom,

Germany, and Italy, and then it has rotating members from the other members of NATO, and I think the current membership of those rotating spots is, let me just say, I think——

General WHEELER. I think it is Greece at the present time, Belgium and Denmark. So that there are seven members at the present time, sir.

Senator CARLSON. The reason I bring this up, Mr. Secretary, is simply this: Of course this nonproliferation treaty was signed by 56 other nations, including the Soviet Union and the United Kingdom on July 1, but here in your statement you say the "U.S. Government." Now do you have additional obligations or are we accepting something here outside of the treaty?

Mr. NITZE. No, not at all.

Senator CARLSON. We are not, all right.

U.S. COMMITMENT TO WEST GERMANY QUESTIONED

I notice that Mr. Kiesinger on July 5 had a news conference in which he stressed West Germany's great interest in this treaty, and I shall quote one or two statements, one that appears in a recent issue of the Christian Science Monitor. I shall place the entire article in the record so there will be no question about it. I quote this sentence:

"Bonn in particular reportedly wants an American guaranty to defend West Germany against nuclear attack, even if NATO should be dissolved." Are we making that commitment?

Mr. NITZE. No, we are not, Mr. Senator.

Senator CARLSON. The answer is "We are not?"

Mr. NITZE. We are not.

Senator CARLSON. Has the West German Government then, for instance, implied in any way that the continued stationing at any particular level of American troops in Europe is related to their attitude toward ratification of this treaty?

Mr. NITZE. No; they have not indicated that to us.

Senator CARLSON. We definitely understand then on the basis of even these commitments and statements from Mr. Kiesinger that say, and I quote, this time from the New York Times, "His call implied a lack of confidence in the survival of the Atlantic Alliance, from which member nations may withdraw beginning in 1970," that we have made no commitments as to the United States unilaterally on the nuclear proliferation of material and the American troops situation.

Mr. NITZE. We have not, Mr. Senator.

Senator CARLSON. I think it is a point that ought to be clarified because if there is any behind the scenes trading on this in regard to the defense of nations who might be outside NATO, it is important to this Nation that we have that very definite assurance. You say we have not.

Mr. NITZE. We have not, Mr. Senator.

Senator CARLSON. That is all, Mr. Chairman.

Senator SPARKMAN. Senator Carlson did you offer the article for insertion in the record?

Senator CARLSON. I would like to offer both the article and the editorial.

81

Senator SPARKMAN. Without objection they will be inserted in the record.

(The material referred to follows:)

[From the New York Times, July 8, 1968]

BONN'S NUCLEAR PACT BLUFF

If there is one Government on earth that cannot long refuse to sign the treaty to prevent the spread of nuclear weapons it is that of West Germany. The Soviet Union would have a propaganda field day using a Bonn refusal to restoke fears in Europe of German aggression.

Chancellor Kiesinger is fully aware of this, but in stalling temporarily on the treaty he evidently hopes to achieve two things: a unilateral guarantee from the United States against nuclear aggression, and pacification of the more nationalistic elements in his Christian Democratic Union and its Bavarian sister, the Christian Social Union. which oppose the pact.

Dr. Kiesinger surely knew he would embarrass Washington by practically demanding such an American guarantee at his recent press conference. His call implied a lack of confidence in the survival of the Atlantic Alliance, from which member nations may withdraw beginning in 1970, and in the guarantee of aid to any non-nuclear country facing nuclear attack, which the United States, Britain and Russia have made to the United Nations Security Council.

The Chancellor says there is "no direct link" between Bonn's delay and the new East Germany pressures against West Berlin. He may, however, hope at least that in conjunction with other West German and allied moves, the stalling on the treaty will help persuade Moscow to restrain East Germany from further curbs on Berlin access. The United States, Britain and France recently sent notes to the Kremlin charging that the new restrictions violate four-power agreements; but the allies were almost immediately rebuffed by Soviet Communist leader Leonid Brezhnev, who said East Germany had a "right to protect its territory."

The Berlin problem is serious enough, but it will not be resolved by ritualistic allied notes or by Bonn's threat to stay out of the nonproliferation treaty, which Moscow will recognize for the bluff it is. But Moscow in turn should realize that in supporting threats against free West Berlin it only encourages those ultranationalist and "revanchist" forces in Germany it professes so much to fear.

[From the Christian Science Monitor, July 8, 1968]

BONN STRESSES A-POLICY ROLE FOR HAVE-NOTS

Chancellor Kurt Georg Kiesinger lays great stress on the efforts of major non-nuclear powers to hammer out a joint approach to the nuclear nonproliferation treaty.

He told a news conference July 5 that West Germany would be neither a "gang leader" nor a passive bystander when the world's nonnuclear states meet in Geneva next month.

West Germany. Japan, India, and other important nations are deeply concerned, lest the American-Soviet treaty deprive them of security and of full access to nuclear fuel for peaceful uses.

Bonn in particular reportedly wants an American guaranty to defend West Germany against nuclear attack, even if NATO should be dissolved.

Dr. Kiesinger also declared Germany would take the lead in trying to give "new impulse" to the Common Market, perhaps through a summit conference of the Six.

PLUG FOR 'OLD POLITICIANS'

Europe's "restless youth," the Chancellor added, should be shown that "old politicians" still had the energy and vision to unite the Continent.

Dr. Kiesinger regretted that nothing had come of his earlier call in Rome in May, 1967, for a summit conference. The Chancellor implied he would discuss the issue with President de Gaulle in September.

Speaking of Czechoslovakia, Dr. Kiesinger indicated his government was leaning over backward not to give the Soviets an excuse to apply new pressure on the Czech regime in Prague.

Thus a visit to Prague at this time by West German Foreign Minister Willy Brandt, Dr. Kiesinger said, could be misunderstood in Eastern Europe.

With goodwill on both sides, the Chancellor saw no reason why Czechoslovakia and West Germany could not iron out the problems which still keep them from diplomatic relations.

Dr. Kiesinger refused to comment on the presence of Soviet troops in Czechoslovakia. His government, he said, operated from the principle of noninterference in the internal affairs of other countries and would like to see this principle universally followed.

The Chancellor spoke less than 24 hours after he had testified in a war-crimes trial in Bonn. Dr. Kiesinger acknowledged that he had become a Nazi Party member in 1933 and rose eventually to become deputy chief of the radio propaganda section of Hitler's Foreign Ministry.

Dr. Kiesinger testified that, despite his position, he had not known until late in World War II that Jews were being systematically killed by the Nazis. He said he had dismissed allied reports to that effect as "atrocity propaganda."

On trial was a former German diplomat, accused of complicity in the slaying of more than 11,000 Jews. Defense lawyers called Dr. Kiesinger as a witness to prove that a relatively high-ranking official might not have known of the Jewish program.

Senator SPARKMAN. Senator Symington?

Senator SYMINGTON. Thank you, Mr. Chairman.

CHANGE OF DOD POSITION ON DEPLOYMENT OF ABM SYSTEM

Mr. Secretary and General Wheeler, this appears a move forward. I would ask questions about the ABM. For some years the Department of Defense felt such a system was not needed, and we went ahead to spend many billions of dollars to assure we would counterattack any country with our retaliatory capacity if we were attacked. Mr. Secretary, when was this position changed by the Department of Defense?

Mr. NITZE. I think the announcement of the change was made by Secretary McNamara in a speech in San Francisco in September of last year, as I recall it.

Senator SYMINGTON. 1967?

Mr. NITZE. That is correct.

Senator SYMINGTON. At that time it was stated the new proposed ABM system was to protect us against the Chinese, but not against the Soviets?

Mr. NITZE. My recollection is that Secretary McNamara made three points about the purposes of the Sentinel system. One of them was that it would give an absolute protection against the foreseeable Chinese threat for some period of years. The second one was that it offered the possibility of increasing the survivability of our Minuteman sites.

Senator SYMINGTON. He said that when?

Mr. NITZE. He said that in his San Francisco speech. And the third one was that it could contribute to the diminution of the possibility of a small scale or accidental kind of war, I think he used the words "accidental war."

Senator SYMINGTON. At that time he felt it was not a building block to a larger system, did he not?

Mr. NITZE. I think the way he put it was that the technology of today and that involved in the Sentinel system could not give the prospect for the defense of our cities against a large scale Soviet attack, and he did not view this system as being a building block toward such a defense.

Senator SYMINGTON. That was the position taken by Dr. Foster before the Joint Committee in a dialog he had with Congressman Hosmer.

In his declassified statement in January 1968, Secretary McNamara discussed the Tallinn system and also the Galosh system. It is my understanding the Tallinn system is a system for protection against incoming bombers?

Mr. NITZE. The best opinion is that the purpose for which it is now deployed is for a defense against air rather than space vehicles.

Senator SYMINGTON. The nature of the Tallinn locations could have something to do with opinions along those lines, could they not?

Mr. NITZE. That is correct.

Senator SYMINGTON. It is also my understanding the so-called Galosh system is around the one city of Moscow and is considered an ABM effort.

Mr. NITZE. That is correct.

Senator SYMINGTON. First, we spend much money to assure entry— now there is this sudden belief that we must have also an ABM system, even though intelligence shows the Soviets are not doing as much in this ABM field today as we thought they would be doing.

Apparently we plan now to start up something which apparently now they are not interested in proceeding with. Intelligence says the Soviets built the Tallinn system because we said we were going to build a lot of bombers, but we didn't build them; and I don't think that a mistake. They built the Tallinn system against what we said we were going to do, but we didn't do.

It is hard for me to understand the reasons for this sudden switch. I know we like full employment, but I know also we have gigantic Federal expenditures. It seems this, our latest action, is directly contrary to the spirit, if not the letter, of possible future detente; and that could be the most important single thing diplomatically for this country.

Would you comment?

Mr. NITZE. I am not sure I can comment on all the points I would really like to comment on but just to take a few——

Senator SYMINGTON. Comment on whatever you wish.

DECISION TO DEPLOY ABM SYSTEM

Mr. NITZE. You suggest it was a sudden decision. It was not a sudden decision. I think if you will go back to Mr. McNamara's testimony in January of 1967 and in January of 1966, he analyzed this problem and the necessity for an ABM defense in great detail. At that time he said he didn't think that the time had yet come when we had to make the decision. But by the summer of last year he felt that the time had come to make the decision.

Senator SYMINGTON. Why did he change his opinion? That is my point.

Mr. NITZE. He changed his opinion on two grounds. One was that the Sentinel system had come to technical maturity.

Senator Symington. Our system?

Mr. Nitze. Yes. The second one was that the time when the Chinese might be estimated to have their capability was such that we ought to get cracking at it.

Senator Symington. So the second point did not have to do with anything the Soviets did?

Mr. Nitze. That is correct.

I would like to point out, however, that on this question of whether or not our decision to go forward with the ABM system in any way is a deterrent to talks with the Soviet Union, it would seem to me to be in conflict with what actually happened after the Senate took its vote, and there was some concern that this might be inhibitory to talks with the Soviet Union. Three days later the Soviets did say that they were prepared for talks. I really don't think there is an inconsistency between going forward with the Sentinel system and the prospect for serious and productive talks which would result, come out with results both in the Soviet Union's interest and in ours without a diminution in our own security.

Senator Symington. Are you saying you believe the Senate vote was the reason for Mr. Gromyko's speech?

Mr. Nitze. I didn't say that, no.

Senator Symington. Then, do you say it could have been the reason for his speech?

Mr. Nitze. No, I didn't say that. But what it was was it seemed to demonstrate there was not an inconsistency between our going forward with the Sentinel system and serious conversations with the Soviet Union.

U.S. SERIOUS FINANCIAL SITUATION

Senator Symington. I was reading this morning a statement made by the president of the world's largest bank who said we are in serious financial trouble, and added we must establish priorities. He also said the year 1965 was the year that got us into this trouble, because it was the year in which we decided to go ahead with the Vietnam war and also the Great Society—all the guns and all the butter at the same time.

It could be that the Soviets, after building something they now don't think they need based their decision on some of our decisions including abandonment of the B-70, or because they now know the degree of success necessary to have in an ABM system to make it in any true sense effective. It might be because they now know the tremendous cost involved. Maybe they now want to consider the necessity for a better living standard and put more money into their country. Would this decision to go ahead with an ABM system make it necessary for the Soviets to say "Well, if the United States is going ahead with an ABM system maybe we had better go ahead with ours." What would be your thoughts on that?

Mr. Nitze. It would have seemed to me that the whole purpose of the conversations with the Soviet Union and ourselves is to explore whether or not we can avoid that kind of increase in expenditures and, on the contrary, improve our mutual security through other measures.

Senator Symington. Thank you, Mr. Secretary.

General Wheeler, have you any comments, sir, that you would care to make on this all important subject?

General WHEELER. No, sir. I think Secretary Nitze answered adequately from my point of view.

Senator SYMINGTON. Thank you.

Thank you, Mr. Chairman.

Senator SPARKMAN. Thank you.

Senator Case?

Senator CASE. Thank you, Mr. Chairman.

CONCERN EXPRESSED ABOUT ABM DEPLOYMENT

First, since the matter has been brought up by two of my colleagues, I wanted to express my own complete agreement with the concern about proceeding with the deployment of the so-called thin antiballistic missile system for reasons that all of us have made clear on other occasions, Senator Cooper of this committee very notably, a leader on two occassions on the Senate floor. I am not persuaded by everything you said, I am sure sincerely, General, and by you, Mr. Secretary, in support of this deployment or by Secretary McNamara. The inconsistency with his recommendation and splendid arguments against fullscale antiballistic missile system seem to me to be still obvious to everyone and I do not want to have my silence indicate any lessened interest in our withdrawing from this project.

More directly on the matter before us, Mr. Secretary, I think it is terribly important that whatever we do we do with a complete understanding and that the public have an understanding of what we are doing, as to the meaning of the treaty insofar as we can lay it out.

STATUS OF A FEDERATED EUROPEAN STATE UNDER TREATY

Now the President in his message says the treaty would not bar succession by a new federated European state to the nuclear status of one of its former components. But the treaty would bar transfer of nuclear weapons, including ownership or control over them, to any country by any nuclear power including ourselves, and that would include a bar against transfer of anything to a multilateral entity as pointed out by the answer of our Government.

I take it this means that we would not transfer any nuclear materials to any nonnuclear party under the treaty and such a state could not acquire them other than by succession to the nuclear status of one of its components. Is that your understanding?

Mr. NITZE. I think the last part of your statement is the important part that if you did have a federated Europe which was in fact a union, and it did involve a successor state then, it could become a nuclear power.

Senator CASE. Well, I wonder. Suppose it is made up of states which are now nonnuclear and some which are nuclear, which status would it succeed to?

Mr. NITZE. If amongst the states which are absorbed, one of them, if it is a real state, and one of the states which is absorbed is a nuclear power, a nuclear state, then I think the successor state becomes one under the terms of the treaty.

Senator CASE. Even though composed also of nonnuclear powers?

Mr. NITZE. That is correct.

Senator CASE. But this is the only way in which a federated state could acquire nuclear capacity.

Mr. NITZE. That is correct.

Senator CASE. And so we are obligating ourselves, just to be sure of what we are doing, not to give nuclear weapons to any other state or federation at all, regardless of what we conceive to be our national interests at the time, and this would include, of course, friendly countries as well as hostile countries?

Mr. NITZE. That is correct.

Senator CASE. And whatever the status of danger to them at a time, as the General pointed out, short of an actual state of war? I just want to be very clear about that.

U.S. OBLIGATIONS TO OTHER COUNTRIES

Just one other matter, Mr. Secretary. In your response to questions by Senator Carlson as to the absence of any commitment already made or any intention to make commitments to Germany, for example, or any other state which adhered to this treaty, your negative answer was very clear and in accord with my understanding of the Secretary's position stated yesterday, especially in response to questions which I asked on that point. I want to emphasize this, for I think it is terribly important for a number of reasons.

One of them is a statement by the President that this is the most important international agreement since the beginning of the nuclear age. I think this is a significant treaty, useful, a step, but I don't think it justifies quite that kind of statement. But apart from that, what bothers me is if the President really believes this, are we likely to want adherence by Germany and others so much as to start making commitments in order to get that? In this connection it has been stated, I don't know whether by responsible authority or not, that Russia would not be willing to complete adherence to this treaty unless Germany did. This sort of thing does concern me very much and that is why I am very happy to have reiterated today the assurance we got yesterday that there was nothing beyond present obligations under existing treaties that was contemplated. Also, and on this point, too, I want your agreement or disagreement, that the action by the Senate in ratification of this treaty, should it take that action, would not be regarded as authorization to make any such commitments.

Mr. NITZE. That is correct.

Senator CASE. Thank you very much.

General, do you agree?

Mr. NITZE. I would just like to add to this, Mr. Case, I do think that this treaty is important.

Senator CASE. I understand, you said so.

Mr. NITZE. And I do think it is important that Germany adhere. But I want to repeat that we have no obligation to Germany, we have made no special arrangements with Germany and have no such intention.

Senator CASE. And further, if I may say so, you specifically agree with my suggestion that our ratification involves no authorization to the President to make any such commitment?

Mr. Nitze. That is correct.
General Wheeler. That is correct, sir.
Senator Case. Thank you very much.
Senator Sparkman. Senator Pell?
Senator Pell. Thank you, Mr. Chairman.

DIFFERENCE BETWEEN LIMITED AND UNLIMITED NUCLEAR WAR

Mr. Secretary, I have one general question and a couple of specific ones. From the viewpoint of general philosophy what is the difference between a limited and an unlimited nuclear war? Is there any such thing as a limited nuclear war in fact? I realize it is not directly related to the subject at hand, but it is related to the viewpoint of the escape clause and it has always concerned me because I realize the military's use of the term "tactical nuclear weapons." A nuclear war could require all-out escalation, it could not be contained. I would be interested in your view in this matter.

Mr. Nitze. Clearly any use of nuclear weapons contains in it a very great threat that it would spread to higher and higher levels. But I would not have the view that this is inevitable. It is very difficult to foresee, but not inevitable.

Senator Pell. Would you have any comments on that, General Wheeler?

General Wheeler. Well, you made two points, I believe, sir; that is, the difference between limited and unlimited nuclear war——

Senator Pell. No, I said what is the difference?

General Wheeler. That is right, I was going to respond to that point.

Senator Pell. Thank you.

General Wheeler. An unlimited nuclear war is commonly understood to be a general nuclear exchange involving strikes at strategic targets. A limited nuclear war would be one which would be limited in the geography where the weapons were employed, perhaps the size of the weapons that were used, and the targets that were attacked. Generally speaking, when we talk of a limited nuclear war we are thinking of the use of smaller nuclear weapons against military targets rather than strategic or industrial targets and things of that kind.

I would agree also that use of nuclear weapons, even in a limited sense, of course, does carry with it a danger of escalation to a higher and larger, more extensive use of nuclear weapons. But I would agree with Secretary Nitze that this is, by no means, inevitable. It would depend, in my thinking, upon the geographic locale of the enemy, the circumstances of use.

Senator Pell. Isn't what you are really saying that the use of nuclear weapons by a nuclear power against a nonnuclear power might be considered a limited nuclear war? Can you conceive of war between two nuclear powers conducted with limited nuclear weapons?

General Wheeler. Yes. However, I would say that the dangers of escalation to a higher level of nuclear use would be greater. But I could still conceive of it as being a rational possibility. In other words, I think that rational men looking at a military situation would regard as being the worst form of war the general nuclear exchange that I spoke of. And there could be a nuclear exchange between two small nuclear powers as well as between the two superpowers. These things are all relative, I think, Senator.

Senator PELL. I appreciate your viewpoint. To me it would be inconceivable but I realize that you have good grounds for your views in this matter.

NUCLEAR WEAPONS AVAILABLE TO THE U.N.

Under the Nonproliferation Treaty could nuclear weapons be made available to a United Nations force if it was ever decided that a U.N. peacekeeping force in accordance with articles 43, 44, and 45 of the charter were set up or would the Nonproliferation Treaty prevent turning over of such weapons to such a force?

Mr. NITZE. In my view it would prevent it.

Senator PELL. It would prevent it?

Mr. NITZE. I don't believe we could turn over control. It says "to any recipient whatsoever," and I think this would include a U.N. peacekeeping force.

Senator PELL. I see, thank you.

NUCLEAR WEAPONS ON THE OCEAN FLOOR

Am I correct in saying that while the Nonproliferation Treaty is concerned with all the countries of the world, in geographic areas it has no bearing on ocean space, which is 70 percent of our globe. In other words, the Nonproliferation Treaty does not cover the implantation of nuclear weapons on the ocean floor, ocean bed?

Mr. NITZE. It doesn't cover the deployment of weapons any place. It just covers transfer of ownership or control.

Senator PELL. So, in other words, even the passage of this treaty does not take away from the urgency of reaching some sort of agreement with regard to the determination as to the uses of the ocean bed?

Mr. NITZE. It doesn't bear on that question.

Senator PELL. Right.

CONTROVERSY OVER TREATY AMONG EASTERN EUROPEAN COUNTRIES

Finally, do we have any evidence of the controversy behind the Iron Curtain with regard to signing of this treaty?

I notice that most of the Warsaw Pact countries with the exception of Albania have signed it. Was there any controversy so far as you know within the Soviet Union or within the Warsaw Pact countries or did they all sign it fairly readily?

Mr. NITZE. Not to my knowledge, Senator Pell.

Senator PELL. Thank you very much.

Senator SPARKMAN. Senator Cooper.

Senator COOPER. Thank you, Mr. Chairman.

TRANSFER OF WEAPONS

I was unable to be here yesterday and it may be that I will ask some questions that have been asked before. I believe there is general approval of this treaty. But it is important that we secure as best we can the interpretation and understanding of our own Government respecting the treaty.

Am I correct that article I would prohibit the transfer of nuclear weapons or their control to any country, including England with whom we are said to have a special relationship?

Mr. NITZE. That is correct.

Senator COOPER. Would it prohibit the interchange of scientific information or scientists assisting each other?

Mr. NITZE. No; it would not.

Senator COOPER. You have said that this treaty would not prohibit emplacement of nuclear weapons on the territory of any country, nuclear or nonnuclear. Is that correct?

Mr. NITZE. That is correct.

Senator COOPER. Article II states that each nonnuclear-weapon state party would undertake not to receive the transfer of nuclear weapons or other nuclear explosive devices. But that section would not prohibit the emplacement on the soil of our nuclear weapons as long as we retained control?

Mr. NITZE. That is correct.

NEGOTIATIONS ABOUT SAFEGUARDS

Senator COOPER. I know General Wheeler particularly has spoken, and I thought with some concern, about safeguards. I believe article III is ambiguous. It provides that each nonnuclear weapon state shall agree to accept safeguards which have been negotiated in accordance with the statute of IAEA. There is nothing in that article that states how these negotiations are to be undertaken, by whom, with whom. Can you give us any information about that?

General WHEELER. I think paragraph 4 of the same article, Senator Cooper, addresses this particular issue. It says:

Nonnuclear weapon states party to the treaty shall conclude agreements with the International Atomic Energy Agency to meet the requirements of this article either individually or together with other states in accordance with the statute of the International Atomic Energy Agency. Negotiation of such agreements shall commence within 180 days from the original entry into force of this treaty. For states depositing their instruments of ratification or accession after the 180-day period, negotiation of such agreements shall commence not later than the date of such deposit. Such agreements shall enter into force not later than 18 months after the date of initiation of negotiations.

Senator COOPER. I remember that. Then the effect of this article, with all its paragraphs, is that the nonnuclear states will accept the statute.

General WHEELER. That is right, sir.

Senator COOPER. That is all it means; doesn't it?

General WHEELER. There is not much negotiation about it, sir.

Senator COOPER. In the event that Germany, Japan, Italy, Israel, do not accept the statute, then the United States would be precluded from transferring to one or any of those states materials for peaceful purposes.

General WHEELER. It could. Interestingly enough, Senator Cooper, there is no punitive article in the treaty that I am aware of. However, I would think that as a matter of procedure, that under these circumstances the nuclear nations party to the agreement would not make such transfer.

Senator COOPER. As I read article III with all of its provisions, it is that unless a nonnuclear state agrees with the safeguards of IAEA they are prohibited from accepting, and the United States would be prohibiting from transferring to them, nuclear materials for peaceful purposes.

General WHEELER. I think you are correct. I see paragraph 2, here, Senator, which I had not gone through carefully.

Senator COOPER. So it is a lever upon these countries to accept the statute, the safeguards of the IAEA? It has some weight?

General WHEELER. As I read paragraph 2 of article III, it says that each state party to the treaty undertakes not to provide these materials unless special fissionable material shall be subject to the safeguards required by the article.

ADEQUACY OF SAFEGUARDS QUESTIONED

Senator COOPER. Now, I want to speak about the safeguards for a moment. Has there been any doubt at all in our Government, in the military, the Joint Chiefs of Staff, that these safeguards of IAEA are not adequate?

Mr. NITZE. No; I believe it has been everybody's view——

Senator COOPER. I know there has been a change in the viewpoint of the Government and the military as was noted in the Outer Space Treaty. You don't require or ask for the kind of inspection that you did at one time. But I am asking, has any question been raised about the adequacy of the safeguards of the IAEA which would be, of course, the ones required?

Mr. NITZE. No; we have not had a question about that. We have looked in part to the AEC, Dr. Seaborg and his group, because they are the great experts in this field, but we have been satisfied from our conversations with them that these safeguards are adequate.

Senator COOPER. This is the view of your Department that they are adequate? General Wheeler, is this the opinion of the Joint Chiefs?

General WHEELER. The Joint Chiefs of Staff view also is that they are adequate.

PROCEDURES TO PROVIDE BENEFITS TO NONNUCLEAR STATES

Senator COOPER. Now, article V enables countries to be benefited from a nuclear explosion provided by a nuclear state. It provides that such benefits shall be under an international agreement and through an appropriate international body. Have any procedures been developed to establish international agreements or an international body to supervise benefits to a nonnuclear state? Would it be under IAEA?

Mr. NITZE. I am not sure on that.

Senator COOPER. Will you find out?

Mr. NITZE. I will find out and submit an answer for the record.

(The answer referred to as item 6 is on page 50.)

SAFEGUARDS IN CASE OF SHARING PEACEFUL NUCLEAR DEVICES

Senator COOPER. I note in the same article, in the last sentence, it provides:

Nonnuclear weapon states party to the treaty so desiring may also obtain such benefits pursuant to bilateral agreements.

My question is: Under that last sentence would the United States be able to enter into an agreement, say, with Brazil to conduct nuclear explosions in Brazil for peaceful purposes and would the U.S.S.R. be able to conduct peaceful explosions in Egypt under this last sentence?

Mr. NITZE. That is correct.

Senator COOPER. What would be the safeguards in such a case?

Mr. NITZE. Under those circumstances the nuclear device which was being exploded would stay under the control of the nuclear power. It would never leave the control of the nuclear power.

Senator COOPER. This kind of situation would be one where there would be the greatest possibility of a breach in the transfer of nuclear weapons to nonnuclear states, and there is nothing in this article that prescribes the kind of safeguards which would be in effect in such a case just discussed and——

Mr. NITZE. I think the important point here is that the only people who could explode these nuclear devices are the nuclear powers, and under the treaty; and those are to date three, the U.S.S.R., the United States, and the United Kingdom.

Senator COOPER. I understand that.

Mr. NITZE. And they would be responsible for seeing to it——

Senator COOPER. But my question is: What would be the safeguards exercised by IAEA? Would you let the committee know what safeguards would then be provided by the IAEA in such a case?

Mr. NITZE. Well, there would be appropriate international observation of the explosion. But, isn't the real question we are talking about here the possibility of the diversion of nuclear material?

Senator COOPER. Yes.

Mr. NITZE. Then it would seem to me that primary reliance is to be put upon the fact that it is a nuclear power which would be the one who did not lose control over its device and, therefore, there would be no interest——

Senator COOPER. That is the premise of the first article. My question goes to cases where explosions were made for peaceful purposes and when this international agreement and international body had not been constituted—whether or not there would be safeguards provided under the authority of the IAEA.

Mr. NITZE. I think not necessarily, Senator.

Senator COOPER. Then the consequence would be that the United States could enter into an agreement with Brazil, the U.S.S.R. could enter into an agreement with Egypt and conduct peaceful explosions, and there would be no safeguards as to transfer except the good faith of the parties?

Mr. NITZE. There has to be appropriate international observation. The IAEA safeguards are with respect to the diversion of nuclear material. But here I don't see that that is a matter of concern because that material never goes from the possession and control of the nuclear power involved.

Senator COOPER. I am pointing out that it is not so spelled out in article V.

92

INSPECTIONS OF TRANSFERS OF NUCLEAR MATERIAL

One other question on the subject of safeguards. In article III it is
provided:

> Procedures for the safeguards required by this article shall be followed with
> respect to source or special fissionable material whether it is being produced,
> processed or used in any principal nuclear facility or is outside any such facility.

I know this article deals with nonnuclear weapon states but my
question is: Would the sentence which I have read, would it permit
the IAEA to apply inspection as to source or special fissionable
material which is being produced and processed in the United States
for transfer to a nonnuclear state?

Mr. NITZE. This is not called for by the treaty but it is something
we have declared that we are prepared to do.

Senator COOPER. Will you explain?

Mr. NITZE. It is not called for by the treaty but it is something that
we have said that we are prepared to do—to have the IAEA safeguards apply to our peacetime uses in the United States.

Senator SPARKMAN. Senator Cooper, would you yield to me for
just a moment?

Senator COOPER. Yes.

Senator SPARKMAN. We had a great deal of discussion on the question of safeguards yesterday. The IAEA safeguards that they have
at the present time would not necessarily be the safeguards applied
here nor would those of Euratom nor would the safeguards that
the United States has written into its law. But the idea would be that
there would be negotiations to see if they would work out a uniform
system of safeguards. I think that is what we have to look for rather
than to the IAEA or any other country or agency.

Senator COOPER. I understand that, particularly in view of the preamble to the paragraph which says we should support safeguards
provided by IAEA. Ultimately the safeguards will be the safeguards
prescribed in IAEA through negotiations. What I am asking is a
specific question. I ask under article III if the United States enters
into an agreement with Germany or Italy or other nonnuclear country
to provide them with material for peaceful purposes, would the inspection be required in the United States as well as in Germany?

Mr. NITZE. It is not required by the treaty. It is required——

Senator COOPER. It might be required under the agreement.

Mr. NITZE. No; we have made an offer that we would permit the
application of the International Atomic Energy Agency safeguards to
our peacetime facilities in the United States. But that is not required
by the treaty. This was merely offered in order to make it clear to the
nonnuclear powers that they were not being asked to have safeguards
imposed that we were not prepared to have imposed on the United
States.

Senator PASTORE. Will the Senator yield to me for just a moment?

Senator COOPER. Yes.

IAEA INSPECTIONS IN THE UNITED STATES

Senator PASTORE. The question touches upon a very sensitive area
which has been before the Joint Committee for years. Any time we

transfer any special nuclear material that could result in the manufacture of a weapon, we have had a bilateral agreement with the receiving country that the United States would inspect it, and these bilateral agreements have come before the Senate many, many times, and have been approved.

Now, we have, after the establishment of the International Agency, transferred this responsibility to the International Agency because it is the policy of the United States of America to put as much of this inspection under international control as we possibly can.

Now, there always has been the feeling on the part of the receiving countries that this might have been an impingement upon their sovereignty, and they have resisted this. We have found that in the case of India, and we have found it in other cases as well, and that has been, a reluctance, of course, that can be understood.

Now, in order to prove to these people that there is no impingement upon sovereignty or that there might be a revelation of technological advantage on a competitive business basis we have opened up some of our plants to international inspection, but we have done this merely as an encouragement to other nations to do likewise, and we have always been hopeful that Russia would agree with us.

However, insofar as the International Agency is concerned we are a party to it. There are about 102 nations that belong to it. It has worked well. They have developed certain standards. These standards, of course, are not adequate for this new responsibility, but when this responsibility comes to the International Agency, of course, they will have to expand their endeavor and that activity and they will have to improve it just like we have improved our safeguards with reference to the nuclear Test Ban Treaty. That is all to come. And I say this, without the treaty there will be little encouragement for the creation of adequate inspection standards. With the treaty this will not only be an inspiration for it but there will be a need for it and that is the story.

Senator COOPER. Thank you, Senator Pastore. I have just a few more questions.

I would assume that the preamble to the treaty expresses worthy objectives, but if there is failure to agree, to make agreements in the worthy objects expressed in the preamble, it would not itself be a breach of the treaty?

Mr. NITZE. I think that is correct. I think the operative articles are articles I and II, et cetera.

Senator COOPER. But we do enter into the treaty in good faith to achieve the objectives?

Mr. NITZE. That is right.

DEPLOYMENT OF AN ABM SYSTEM

Senator COOPER. One of the questions of greatest importance and one which is very much in the news today because of the statements of the President and the statements of the representatives of the U.S.S.R. deals with the control of offensive and defensive nuclear weapons. I noted your comments about the ABM with Senator Symington and Senator Case. Isn't it the view of the military as well as of the State Department that it would be better if neither the United States nor the U.S.S.R. deployed an ABM system?

Mr. NITZE. That is certainly something we would want to discuss with the Soviet Union. We have agreed we would discuss both offensive and defensive systems together with the Soviet Union.

Senator COOPER. Put it another way then. Assume that you might discuss with the U.S.S.R. the thin system about China. Would you say it would be the view of the United States that it would be better for our countries, better for the world, if neither of us deployed an ABM system which would be related to the defense against the other?

Mr. NITZE. I think that is correct. But that still avoids the question of the nth country problem.

Senator COOPER. My reason for asking this question is if this is the view of our Government would you consider that if we want to start negotiations with talks with Russia that it might be better if we didn't deploy even a limited ABM system?

Mr. NITZE. I don't agree with that.

SENATE VOTE ON ABM SYSTEM

Senator COOPER. I recall your statement that you thought the vote of the Senate might have had an effect upon the decision of the U.S.S.R., and I suppose no one can say definitely whether that was so or not?

Mr. NITZE. I didn't say that, Mr. Senator.

Senator COOPER. I beg your pardon; I thought you did.

Mr. NITZE. All I said was I thought the vote of the Senate was not inconsistent with it.

Senator COOPER. I see.

But isn't it correct that long before the vote was taken the United States and the U.S.S.R. had been discussing this question?

Mr. NITZE. That is correct.

Senator COOPER. With your wide knowledge, long knowledge of the Soviet bureaucratic system, you don't think such decisions are made lightly, do you, in a day or two?

Mr. NITZE. No; not in a day or two, but I think the timing of this may have been made in a short period of time.

Senator COOPER. I want to ask, and I will ask the State Department at the proper time, whether or not our Government did not know that the statements of the U.S.S.R. were to be made before the vote in the Senate.

Thank you, I have no further questions.

Senator SPARKMAN. Senator Pastore.

Senator PASTORE. I merely want to get my two cents worth in on the ABM because I think the record is rather cloudy in regard to that. It is anybody's guess as to what happened and what convinced the Russians to come along but all that Pastore knows is this: That President Johnson talked with Kosygin at Glassboro and Kosygin held a press conference at the United Nations immediately after that, and said that he would not discuss a limitation on ABM until we pulled out of Vietnam, and it stayed in that position until 3 days after we took the vote in the Senate, and Pastore thinks that that vote had a lot to do with the decision of the Russians to come along and now talk about it.

Amen!

Senator SPARKMAN. Senator Cooper, I may say before you came in we had discussed to some extent the deployment of the ABM system, and the question was put to Secretary Nitze, and he is going to give a considered reply in full to that question which will be printed in the record. (See letter on page 59.)

Anything else?

Thank you very much, gentlemen.

The committee will meet again tomorrow morning at 10 a.m. in this room, at which time we will hear from Dr. Seaborg and Professor Strausz-Hupé. The committee stands adjourned.

(Whereupon, at 11:55 a.m., the hearing was recessed, to reconvene 10 a.m., Friday, July 12, 1968.)

NONPROLIFERATION TREATY

UNITED STATES SENATE,
COMMITTEE ON FOREIGN RELATIONS,
Washington, D.C.

The Committee met, pursuant to recess, at 10:05 a.m., in room 318, Old Senate Office Building, Senator John Sparkman presiding.

Present: Senators Sparkman, Carlson, and Cooper.

Also present: Senators Pastore and Anderson of the Joint Committee on Atomic Energy.

Senator SPARKMAN. Let the committee come to order, please.

This morning the Foreign Relations Committee continues its hearings on the Nonproliferation Treaty. It is my particular pleasure to welcome Dr. Glenn T. Seaborg, Chairman of the Atomic Energy Commission. Dr. Seaborg's knowledge of the intricacies of safeguard arrangements and of the capability of the International Atomic Energy Agency to assume new responsibilities should prove of great assistance to the committee in its consideration of the treaty now before us.

I should also like to welcome Dr. Strausz-Hupé, director of the Foreign Policy Research Institute of the University of Pennsylvania. These will be the two witnesses for today.

Dr. Seaborg, we have a copy of your statement. You may proceed as you see fit.

We are glad to have you.

STATEMENT OF DR. GLENN T. SEABORG, CHAIRMAN OF THE ATOMIC ENERGY COMMISSION; ACCOMPANIED BY JAMES T. RAMEY, DR. GERALD S. TAPE, COMMISSIONERS; ALLAN M. LABOWITZ, SPECIAL ASSISTANT FOR DISARMAMENT; AND MYRON B. KRATZER, ASSISTANT GENERAL MANAGER FOR INTERNATIONAL ACTIVITIES

Dr. SEABORG. I am glad to be here.

Chairman Sparkman, Chairman Pastore, Senator Carlson, I might begin by identifying those with me. To my left is Mr. Allan Labowitz, who is the Special Assistant for Disarmament to the Atomic Energy Commission; and immediately behind me are Commissioners James Ramey and Gerald Tape, and Mr. Myron Kratzer, who is our Assistant General Manager for International Activities.

Senator SPARKMAN. We are glad to have all of them.

Dr. SEABORG. It is a great pleasure for me to appear today to testify in support of the Treaty on the Nonproliferation of Nuclear Weapons.

We are discussing a major milestone in our efforts to bring the atom under control—efforts which the United States began at the birth of the atomic age. I believe that the treaty now before you should permit the nations of the world to intensify their efforts to tap the enormous power of the peaceful atom without fear that this power will be diverted to destructive purposes.

Before turning to the substantive aspects of the treaty, I should like to pay tribute to the skill of the U.S. negotiators, and, above all, to the perseverance and leadership of the President, whose determination to achieve this goal never wavered. The treaty also is a tribute to the foresight that the Congress has displayed in urging positive actions to check the growing threat of nuclear weapon proliferation. The Senate contributed importantly to the achievement of this treaty when it passed Senate Resolution 179, which was sponsored by Senator Pastore and cosponsored by 58 other Senators. We also have enjoyed the strong support of this commitee, as well as the Joint Committee on Atomic Energy, in the efforts we have undertaken over many years to limit the spread of nuclear weapons. We could not have progressed as far as we have without such support from the Congress.

Secretary Rusk and Mr. Foster have described why this treaty is extremely important from the standpoint of peace and security, and how the United States views a number of the provisions. In my remarks, I should like to emphasize the treaty's significant relationship to the enormous worldwide growth in nuclear power which is foreseen for the future, I shall devote some of my attention to the important role that international safeguards, as set forth in this treaty, will play in assuring that the future byproducts of these atomic power stations will not be diverted to the production of nuclear weapons. I also would like to discuss briefly the affirmative responsibilities that this treaty will place on the adhering nuclear powers, including the United States, to share the benefits of their atomic advances with other countries.

PEACEFUL USES OF ATOMIC ENERGY

In the 25 years that have passed since Enrico Fermi and his team produced the first nuclear chain reaction at Chicago, we have seen a remarkable growth in the importance of atomic energy in our everyday lives. Vague hopes for the future have been replaced with impressive realities. Moreover, the dreams we once had about the peaceful atom now seem small when we compare them with our firm expectations for the future. The atom is now helping us to treat and diagnose the sick, to produce and grow better crops, and to run our industries more efficiently. Most dramatically, dozens of nuclear power stations which will produce millions of kilowatts of electricity are now under construction and the prospects for the future are enormous. We also are now looking forward to the day when the energy from large nuclear reactors will produce fresh water, fertilizers, and various industrial chemicals in addition to electricity.

However, the great upsurge in the growth of nuclear power also poses a very serious problem. In several more years the nuclear plants in operation in nonnuclear weapons countries will be producing enough plutonium to make hundreds of bombs each year. The amount of material that will be produced would be sufficient, if diverted to the production of nuclear weapons, to level many cities and destroy much of humanity.

This is a principal reason why this treaty and its safeguard provisions are so important and why many months have been spent to negotiate and produce the document that is now before you.

I think we can take great pride in this treaty. I also think we can take much pride in all of the preparatory work that predated this agreement, and I refer specifically to the work that has gone into establishing the International Atomic Energy Agency, and in developing the safeguards that are administered by that organization.

SAFEGUARDS TO AVOID DIVERSION TO MILITARY PURPOSES

From the outset of the atoms for peace program, the United States has developed arrangements with cooperating countries to insure that our peaceful nuclear assistance will not be diverted to military purposes. For this purpose we have required a system of safeguards which includes actual onsite inspection and the maintenance of records and reports necessary to keep track of materials. Originally, these safeguards were bilateral, in that the recipient country granted rights to the United States to require the submission of information and to obtain access to all data and all places, at all times, for the purpose of determining that materials and equipment supplied by the United States were not being used to further any military purpose. We realized, however, from the start that such bilateral safeguards should be interim in nature and that it would be preferable to transfer this responsibility to a multilateral organization.

Accordingly, we worked diligently in the 1950s to help establish the International Atomic Energy Agency and we have been working diligently since to assist the Agency in establishing an effective safeguards system designed to detect the diversion of atomic energy from peaceful to military purposes. We have been working steadily to transfer to the IAEA the responsibility of applying safeguards to activities covered by our bilateral atomic agreements. Since 1963 we have concluded 19 trilateral agreements transferring this responsibility to the Agency. Six more have been approved or are under negotiation.

IAEA SAFEGUARDS

I am dwelling a bit on this history because it is relevant to the treaty now before you. As a result of steady progress, the IAEA now has in operation an effective safeguards system that is suitable for application to a wide variety of peaceful nuclear activities. Moreover, as a result of steady efforts, a growing acceptance of such international safeguards has developed among various nations of the world. The safeguards which have been administered to date have done more than simply serve their immediate purpose of assuring that particular activities were not being used for military purposes. They have demonstrated that the techniques of international inspection are feasible and effective and are not considered an invasion of national sovereignty. They also have stimulated the development of the institutional framework and a cadre of properly trained people to be used in implementing any broader agreements in the future. In doing so, they have created much of the foundation upon which article III of the NPT has been structured.

As encouraging as this progress has been, however, IAEA safeguards have been applied to date only to projects receiving Agency assistance or to projects voluntarily placed under IAEA controls. They have not covered the entire nuclear programs of the countries concerned. Neither have many nations given up, through treaty commitment, the right or independence to make nuclear weapons. The treaty will serve to fill these gaps and it will represent an unprecedented advance in international, let alone nuclear, affairs. It will represent the first time since the beginning of the nuclear age that many nations throughout the globe will have relinquished the right to make nuclear weapons and will have agreed to submit all of their peaceful nuclear activities to international inspection to help verify that this commitment is being adhered to.

SAFEGUARDS A DIFFICULT NEGOTIATING PROBLEM

Although we have been able, over the years, to engender a growing acceptance of international safeguards, the provisions in this treaty relating to this subject presented some of the most difficult negotiating problems. This is an area of the treaty that also has stimulated much comment in the press and elsewhere.

I would, with your permission, like to make a few observations on certain aspects of this matter. There were concerns expressed by several countries during the negotiations that the application of IAEA safeguards might serve to place the nonnuclear weapon states at a commercial disadvantage by compromising their commercial secrets or by interfering with the operation of the facilities involved. We have felt these fears to be groundless. Agency inspectors are precluded from interfering in plant operations and they normally require access only to information that is not commercially sensitive. Nevertheless, they are barred from transmitting any information that they receive to unauthorized parties and any state has the right to declare a proposed Agency inspector unacceptable.

I am certain that once the safeguards under this treaty are in operation, those states that expressed some reservations will understand why we have been so confident on this matter. They will also understand why President Johnson was prepared and able to state that following the entry into force and the application of safeguards under this treaty, the United States would permit the IAEA to apply its safeguards to all nuclear activities in the United States, excluding only those with direct national security significance. We took this step to demonstrate the sincerity of our convictions that the safeguards to be applied under this treaty would not place the nonnuclear weapon states at any disadvantage. We also wished to demonstrate that we sought no commercial advantage through this treaty and were prepared to submit our own nuclear industry to the same safeguards as will be applied in nonnuclear weapons states.

As confident as we are in international safeguards, we intend to work constantly toward improving their effectiveness on one hand and simplifying them on the other. The preamble to the treaty explicitly recognizes the importance of this point by expressing support for safeguards research and development. The AEC is conducting an active research and development program directed toward improving safeguards techniques and is sharing the results of this effort with the IAEA and other countries.

IAEA RESPONSIBILITIES UNDER TREATY

Some questions have been expressed as to whether the IAEA will be able to muster the requisite number of people to administer the responsibilities called for by this treaty. There also have been assertions that the costs involved will be enormous. I should like to comment briefly on these two points. The present IAEA safeguards staff, while modest in size, is in balance with the size of the workload for which the Agency has responsibility to date. We recognize that a major increase in the size of the Agency's staff will be required to meet the new responsibilities placed upon it by the treaty, and we do not underestimate the difficulty of the problem. However, given the burgeoning growth of the nuclear industry and associated training opportunities, I am confident that the IAEA will be able to recruit the necessary number of people to perform this function. The IAEA's total expenditures for administering these safeguards pursuant to the treaty obviously will go up over the fairly modest amounts that the Agency spends at present. These funds are now being drawn by the IAEA out of the assessed contributions from the various IAEA member states. We believe, however, that these costs will represent no more than a fraction of 1 percent of the cost of the electricity produced in nuclear powerplants. Almost every industrial activity in today's complex society entails certain risks which must be contained by suitable measures. I cannot believe that we will find it difficult to find the necessary funds and an appropriate mechanism to cover the costs of safeguards against the intolerable risk of nuclear proliferation.

SAFEGUARDS AGREEMENT TO BE CONCLUDED

I should like to say a word about the nature of the safeguards agreements to be concluded pursuant to this treaty. Article III permits the necessary agreements with the IAEA to be concluded by individual states or a group of states. As Mr. Foster has indicated, an integral part of the negotiating history of article III is the statement of principles enumerated by the U.S. Cochairman of the Eighteen-Nation Disarmament Committee when this article was first publicly presented on January 18, 1968. These principles already have been presented to this committee and I shall not repeat them now. They were designed to recognize, on the one hand, that the IAEA as well as all parties to the treaty should have confidence in the effectiveness of the safeguards arrangements concluded by the IAEA with every nonnuclear party to the treaty. On the other hand, they recognized that nonnuclear weapon parties to the treaty could negotiate with the IAEA individually or together with other parties; for example, through regional organizations such as Euratom. Moreover, they recognized that in order to avoid unnecessary duplication, the IAEA should make appropriate use of existing records and safeguards, provided that it can satisfy itself that diversions are not taking place.

I believe the IAEA and Euratom will succeed in developing a mutually satisfactory safeguards arrangement. I base this confidence on my belief first, that the IAEA and Euratom safeguards systems are generally compatible, and second, that the IAEA will wish to take advantage of the Euratom procedures wherever it can in developing the arrangements, bearing in mind that the Euratom system has worked effectively for many years.

SHARING IN THE PEACEFUL ATOM

In the course of the negotiations, a number of countries expressed the strong view that neither their renunciation of nuclear weapons nor the concomitant safeguards should prejudice their opportunity to share in the peaceful atom. The Nonproliferation Treaty not only satisfies this condition, but should actually enhance progress in the peaceful uses of nuclear energy by its signatories. This is not only because of the positive provisions concerning atomic cooperation which are found in articles IV and V. It is also due, in large part, to the confidence the treaty will inspire that international cooperation in peaceful uses will not contribute to the acquisition of nuclear weapons.

As President Johnson has indicated, pursuant to the provisions of the treaty, we shall engage in "the fullest possible exchange of equipment, materials, and scientific and technological information for the peaceful uses of atomic energy." Moreover, he noted that pursuant to the treaty, "the needs of the developing nations will be given particular attention."

I believe that the concept that within its capabilities the United States should work toward continued and increased cooperation with the nonnuclear countries who have abjured the acquisition of nuclear weapons is a fair and reasonable one. It is fully consistent with the policy of atomic cooperation which this Nation pioneered, and in which it has been the world leader for 15 years. Cooperation with other countries in fields pertaining to the peaceful uses of atomic energy will thus not represent a new or novel challenge for the United States. Our program has stressed the very activities specified in the treaty—the exchange of equipment, materials, and scientific and technological information for the peaceful uses of atomic energy. Perhaps most importantly, we have already committed ourselves to supply sizable blocks of uranium enriching services to other countries to satisfy their long-term needs for fuel for their nuclear power program.

The NPT should facilitate the continuation and expansion of these programs.

For the United States, it has been axiomatic from the start that our ability to cooperate with others in the peaceful application of nuclear energy is dependent on the assurance that our assistance will not be turned to military purposes. This policy is reflected in the Atomic Energy Act of 1954 itself, which calls for "a program of international cooperation to promote the common defense and security and to make available to cooperating nations the benefits of peaceful applications of atomic energy as widely as expanding technology and consideration of the common defense and security will permit." I believe it follows that since this treaty will enhance our security, as well as the security of many other nations, by strengthened assurances that U.S. cooperation will not contribute to nuclear weapons programs in signatory countries, our cooperation with these countries can and should be intensified.

SHARING BENEFITS FROM PEACEFUL NUCLEAR EXPLOSIONS

In conclusion, I would like to comment on article V of the treaty. This article specifically commits us to take appropriate measures to make available the benefits which can be obtained from peaceful nuclear explosions. This resulted from the recognition, when the treaty was formulated, that nuclear explosive devices intended for use for peaceful purposes could be used as or could be readily adapted for use as weapons. Hence, to avoid a loophole, article I and II were written to preclude the nonnuclear weapons parties from manufacturing or acquiring nuclear explosive devices even for peaceful purposes. At the same time, and within this limitation, it was recognized as essential to provide the nonnuclear parties with the firmest possible assurance that they will be able to derive the full potential benefits from the peaceful applications of nuclear explosions.

Article V, consequently, stipulates that all parties to the treaty will undertake to take appropriate measures to insure that the potential benefits of such peaceful applications will be made available to nonnuclear weapons parties on a nondiscriminatory basis and that the charge to such parties for the explosive devices used will be as low as possible and will exclude any charge for research and development. These services are to be provided either through an international body (which, I believe, should be the IAEA) or bilaterally. In each case, an opportunity shall be provided for appropriate international observation of the actual detonation.

The seriousness with which the United States views its prospective obligations under this section of the proposed treaty was emphasized by President Johnson who said, before the United Nations General Assembly, ". . ., we shall continue our research and development into the use of nuclear explosions for peaceful purposes and we shall make available to the nonnuclear treaty partners without delay and under the treaty's provisions the benefits of such explosions." The importance of this obligation is underscored by the fact that the United States has full intentions to be one of the principal suppliers of such explosion services. We plan to demonstrate these intentions by a series of steps.

We will continue to conduct, within the limitations of available funds, an active program to develop nuclear explosive devices particularly suited for peaceful applications and to develop the technology for using nuclear explosions in a variety of peaceful applications. Let me emphasize that the technology of using nuclear explosions for peaceful purposes is still in a relatively early stage of development. Considerable effort is still required to apply our basic knowledge to specific commercial applications and we have much to learn about the industrialization of operations and the design of supporting equipment. Our domestic research and development program is addressing all of these facets, but it will be several years before optimum nuclear explosive designs and the technology for all applications of nuclear explosions will be developed to the stage of commercial use. However, beginning in the near future, we hope some applications will become economically attractive and will be exploited even as the technology continues to develop.

As our research and development efforts proceed, we will continue to make freely available the information and data obtained, except information relating to the design or manufacture of nuclear explosive devices. Furthermore, we will be prepared to make arrangements whereby we will make available technical advice and assistance, within our capability, to those nonnuclear weapon parties to the treaty which seek assistance in studying specific peaceful applications of nuclear explosions. The knowledge we would gain from assisting in such studies should also permit us to take into account, in our research and development program, various applications in which other countries are interested. We would not rule out the possibility, for which we already have the basic legislative authority, of conducting, within our research and development program, cooperative experiments abroad, under arrangements similar to those for cooperative experiments with U.S. industry.

PROPOSED NUCLEAR EXPLOSION SERVICE

When particular applications are found to be feasible, we plan to make a nuclear explosion service available on a commercial basis to domestic users and to nonnuclear weapon parties to the NPT. Such a service would include the fabrication of the nuclear explosive device, its transportation from the assembly plant to the project site, its emplacement at the prepared site, and its arming and firing. The service would also include appropriate technical reviews of the proposed detonation, such as those relating to health and safety. The users of the service, whether it is furnished domestically or pursuant to article V, will pay for the service in accordance with rates established for its various elements. As I have already noted, the charges for the nuclear explosive devices used in furnishing the service will not include the cost of their research and development.

Arrangement for insuring that the nuclear explosive devices used in furnishing such a service to nonnuclear weapon parties to the NPT remain at all times under the custody and control of the U.S. Government, are necessary in order to be consistent with articles I and II of the treaty. Furthermore, the objectives of the treaty could not permit any observation contemplated by the treaty to include access by the observers to the design or internal operation of nuclear explosive devices. Consequently, there will be no transfer of nuclear explosive devices or control over them; nor will the service, in any way, assist, encourage, or induce any nonnuclear weapon state to manufacture or otherwise acquire nuclear explosive devices.

REQUIREMENTS OF LIMITED TEST BAN TREATY

It has been made clear, in the principles relating to article V which Mr. Foster has placed in the record of these hearings, that article V of this treaty is not intended to modify the provisions of the limited Test Ban Treaty. Therefore, in providing a nuclear explosion service pursuant to article V, the United States will be obligated to observe the requirements of the limited Test Ban Treaty. Meeting those requirements will not be difficult in our research and development of nuclear explosive devices for all peaceful applications or in the development of the technology for application to underground engineering projects. There will be some nuclear excavation projects, however, such as a trans-isthmian canal for which the development of the technology could not be completely carried out or which could not be executed within the present restrictions of the Limited Test Ban Treaty as presently interpreted; modification would be required to permit the United States to provide the nuclear explosion service for those projects.

I am confident that the technology of using nuclear explosions for peaceful purposes will produce enormous civil dividends not only for ourselves, but also for the nonnuclear weapon countries with whom we will cooperate, pursuant to the treaty. Moreover, I think the treaty should facilitate such cooperation to a greater extent than was previously possible.

Mr. Chairman, in summary, I am pleased to give my full support to this important treaty. It will represent a notable landmark in our efforts to control the atom. It also should inaugurate a new and important era in mankind's effort to use the atom for peaceful purposes.

Senator SPARKMAN. Thank you very much, Dr. Seaborg. I think that is a very fine, forceful, and helpful statement.

I know we are all interested in this subject of safeguards, particularly since under this treaty the specifics of the safeguards are left to subsequent negotiations.

EURATOM AND IAEA SAFEGUARDS

Reference has been made from time to time to the fact that IAEA has safeguards, and that Euratom has safeguards and that even the individual countries have certain safeguards. The United States does too under what I think has been legislation very carefully considered by Congress.

Now, I understand from the testimony that we have been given that the Euratom safeguards have been considered adequate by the United States, but are not acceptable to some of the other nuclear nations.

Would we take the position that the Euratom safeguards are adequate during the negotiation between the International Atomic Energy Agency and Euratom as contemplated by the Nonproliferation Treaty? What are the principal differences that exist between the safeguards systems of the IAEA and Euratom? Does Euratom require unanimous consent of its members for any agreement such as the one contemplated by the treaty and, if so, can any agreement be reached if France dissents? Would we accept the reservation of the signatory that it accepts the treaty but will only accept Euratom inspection and procedures?

Now, as I say, that is a compound question but I thought perhaps by presenting it all at once why you could answer it generally.

Dr. SEABORG. I will try to respond to them serially, if I recall them all.

U.S. ATTITUDE TOWARD EURATOM SAFEGUARDS

With respect to the attitude of the United States toward the Euratom safeguards, I think that we do regard them as adequate, if they are applied as contemplated under this Nonproliferation Treaty, that is with the proper involvement of the IAEA to oversee or to verify their application.

You mentioned that there are a number of countries that are not satisfied with the Euratom safeguards. I think that some of that dissatisfaction perhaps has been taken care of in the way that the relationship between the IAEA and Euratom is spelled out in the treaty and pursuant to what these countries expect in the future. We still have the task of working out the details of a satisfactory relationship there.

COMPARISON OF EURATOM AND IAEA SAFEGUARDS

With respect to the differences between the Euratom and the IAEA safeguards, I think that they are generally compatible. There are some differences in detail. We could furnish those for the record. One of the differences that comes to mind is that I believe the IAEA requires resident inspectors in some circumstances where the Euratom safeguard procedures do not yet do so, although that question is still under consideration.

There are differences in detail and, as I have indicated, we could furnish those for the record, but the important point is that they are generally compatible, and the Euratom safeguards have worked and seem to be effective.

Senator SPARKMAN. May I say that I think it would be well if you could give us a statement for the record spelling out the differences, because I know that question will be coming up.

Dr. SEABORG. Yes, I would rather do that because I think that it is important enough to be sure that we have it entirely correct.

(The material referred to appears on page 266.)

UNANIMOUS CONSENT REQUIREMENT ON EURATOM AGREEMENTS

Dr. SEABORG. Now, with respect to the question of whether there must be unanimous consent among the six Euratom members in order to put into effect the NPT and in particular, the safeguards arrangement involving this IAEA-Euratom application, I believe that consideration on the part of the six members, including France, might be required. But I would like to add that there have been no indications at all that France would raise objections. She is not intending to adhere to the treaty herself, but she hasn't given indications of wanting to obstruct the treaty from this point of view. I am not sure whether I responded to all components of your question.

Senator SPARKMAN. Well now, there is one other point I asked: Suppose a signatory power accepted the treaty with a reservation that it accepts the treaty only on condition that Euratom inspection or Euratom procedures are followed? What would be the situation?

Dr. SEABORG. Do you mean, would that constitute a ratification of the treaty by that country?

Senator SPARKMAN. Yes, sir; and what would be our attitude? As I understand, we are satisfied with either IAEA or Euratom standards.

Dr. SEABORG. I don't know whether there is any provision in the treaty for the accession to it of a party with such reservations. I would say that the United States doesn't foresee any situation where it itself would be dissatisfied with the Euratom safeguards.

POSSIBLE RESERVATION REGARDING ACCEPTANCE OF SAFEGUARDS

Senator PASTORE. Will the Senator yield at that point?

Senator SPARKMAN. Yes.

Senator PASTORE. As a matter of fact, such a reservation would be outside the content of the treaty.

Dr. SEABORG. I would think it would be.

Senator PASTORE. Because the treaty itself recognizes the fact that IAEA is the controlling inspecting power but that it has the authority to negotiate with other individuals or groups, and if you made that kind of a reservation you would be precluding yourself from that particular article of the treaty, would you not?

Dr. SEABORG. That would be my judgment.

Senator SPARKMAN. I agree that so far as the execution of the safeguards program, that is to be agreed to by IAEA under the provisions of the treaty. But the safeguards themselves, the substance of the safeguards, is left open for future negotiation.

Senator PASTORE. That is true, but it has to ultimately be to the satisfaction of the IAEA.

If you make that kind of a reservation you might as well not sign the treaty.

Senator SPARKMAN. That is what I was asking, if some nation says "We will accept only Euratom," then what would be our attitude?

Dr. SEABORG. I think that would not be considered an accession to the treaty. I think that such a reservation would go against the guts of the treaty.

Senator SPARKMAN. All right.

Thank you very much Dr. Seaborg.

Senator Pastore?

Senator PASTORE. If France were not a signatory to this treaty it would necessarily mean she would not come under the terms, but if she did give her consent to Euratom in order to constitute the unanimity under the atomic treaty itself, that would mean that while France might be precluded from internal inspection by an international agency, the fact still remains that the other five powers of Euratom would come under the treaty?

Dr. SEABORG. That is correct, and they would be subject to inspection through their Euratom safeguards arm, with this involvement of the IAEA yet to be worked out in detail.

U.S. ATTITUDE TOWARD IAEA STANDARDS

Senator PASTORE. How many nations are member nations of the International Agency?

Dr. SEABORG. Ninety-eight.

Senator PASTORE. Ninety-eight.

And up to this point has there been much work for an inspection agency or under the International Agency to do? What I am getting at is this: We must recognize the fact that we are not wholly satisfied with the standards that are in existence with IAEA today. We are hopeful they will improve them, is that correct?

Dr. SEABORG. Yes. I think that the procedures followed by Euratom have been adequate to date but in order to perform the function that will be required in the future, which is certainly a more extensive one, they will have to be improved.

Senator PASTORE. Would you say that they are comparable to the standards that we adopt and pursue?

Dr. SEABORG. I would say that the standards that the United States adopts and pursues, both domestically and in its bilateral agreements, are probably more stringent than those of Euratom.

Senator PASTORE. More stringent?

Would you say that the same might apply to the International Agency as of now?

Dr. SEABORG. I think it is a little more difficult to make that statement there. I did mention one area in which the International Agency——

Senator PASTORE. You see, I am not raising this as a block, Dr. Seaborg, because I don't think there is any man in the country who knows more about the International Agency than you do. I am raising these questions because some doubts have been raised in previous hearings with regard to the International Agency and, of course, now if this treaty comes into being and I am hopeful that it will, the fact still remains that this is the responsibility that we have been waiting for to give to the International Agency; am I correct in that?

Dr. SEABORG. This is one of the main responsibilities that we have been hoping to give to the International Agency, that is the United States has had this as an objective.

Senator PASTORE. As a matter of fact, the International Agency heretofore has been working on a set of standards, but this more or less has been academic. For all practical purposes they haven't had the instrumentality to apply it to as they would have when this nonproliferation treaty is constituted, is that correct?

Dr. SEABORG. You might say they have been getting ready—for the day when we would have such a function for them.

For example, the IAEA has conducted between July 1, 1966, and April 30, 1968, 67 safeguard inspections. These have been largely, of course, on research reactors, and facilities of that kind. But they have been aided a great deal by the fact that the United States has made four of its reactors available for the IAEA to make inspections on so that they could perfect their methods, and we have also made available a commercial chemical reprocessing plant.

EFFORT TO IMPROVE IAEA'S INSPECTION FORCE

Senator PASTORE. Therefore, it is reasonable to assume that once this treaty comes into being that there will be a concerted effort to improve the adequacy and competency and staffing of the International Agency's inspection force. Is that correct?

Dr. SEABORG. Very definitely.

The staffing would go up, there would be a large increase in the number of professional and support personnel, and there would be an improvement, as they gain experience and gain numbers, in the efficacy of their inspection and their safeguards performance.

Senator PASTORE. Let me put this in the negative. If this treaty did not come into being, it is reasonable to assume that would dampen the whole function of the International Atomic Energy Agency, isn't that correct?

Dr. SEABORG. It certainly would not grow in its importance to the world at anything like the rate that it will grow when this Nonproliferation Treaty comes into effect.

Senator PASTORE. And, therefore, you believe, as Chairman of the Atomic Energy Commission, as a renowned scientist, that safeguards will be adopted that will be commensurate with the protection that we seek under this treaty?

Dr. SEABORG. I do. I think that it is quite within the capability of the International Atomic Energy Agency to take on this responsibility. I am sure they will staff up to the required strength, and that they will discharge this responsibility effectively.

ATOMIC EXPLOSIONS FOR PEACEFUL PURPOSES

Senator PASTORE. Now, there has been a lot of talk here about atomic explosions for peaceful purposes. Since December 1942 when chain reaction was controlled by Enrico Fermi, has there ever been an atomic explosion for peaceful purposes outside of research?

Dr. SEABORG. No.

Senator PASTORE. There has never been?

Dr. SEABORG. There hasn't been.

Senator PASTORE. I mean, we still have a long way to go; that is the point I want to make.

Dr. SEABORG. That is right.

I would rate all of the atomic explosions for peaceful purposes up until today as in the domain of research.

Senator PASTORE. Now, there has been a lot of conjecture about this with relation to, let's say, a substitute for the Panama Canal. How far do you think we are away from that kind of an atomic explosion?

Dr. SEABORG. This, of course, will depend on how fast we go, which in turn depends upon such mundane things as funding. With maximum funding and with an appropriate interpretation of the Limited Test Ban Treaty, I believe that we could be there within 5 to 10 years.

Senator PASTORE. Five or ten years?

Dr. SEABORG. Yes.

NONNUCLEAR NATIONS SUBJECT TO INSPECTION

Senator PASTORE. Now, one further question, but first of all I want to say that, as usual, your statement is very comprehensive. It doesn't leave much room for questioning, but one final question: Once a nation becomes a signatory under this agreement—and I am talking now about a nonnuclear nation—and that nation on its own can build, let's say, a reactor without any outside help of any sort as to hardware and fuel, and that reactor can produce plutonium which can make the bomb, would that nation automatically, because it is a signatory, be subject to inspection in that kind of a unilateral action?

Dr. SEABORG. Yes.

You made the condition that this hypothetical nation was a signatory to the treaty.

Senator PASTORE. Was a signatory.

Dr. SEABORG. Yes.

Senator PASTORE. In other words, even if a nonnuclear power should, on its own, without any outside help, build a reactor, which in all probability could produce weapons material, then by the mere fact of becoming a signatory it automatically is subject to international inspection?

Dr. SEABORG. That is right, and that is one of the most significant parts of the treaty, that it places such a nation under the injunction not to manufacture nuclear weapons, and I would say that articles II and III are applicable here.

Senator PASTORE. And the only ones who are excluded are the nuclear powers?

Dr. SEABORG. Yes; they are excluded from the inspection provision. That is right, nonnuclear weapon parties would be subject to inspection, but the nuclear powers would not be——

Senator PASTORE. Subject to international inspection?

Dr. SEABORG. Subject to inspection.

Senator PASTORE. But we, in order to prove our sincerity, as you have brought out, have agreed to do it voluntarily?

Dr. SEABORG. That is right.

President Johnson, in his statement on December 2, 1967, on the occasion of the 25th anniversary of the first nuclear chain reaction, made the offer to place all the nuclear activities of the United States, including the industrial activities, under IAEA safeguards when a nonproliferation treaty with inspection safeguards was in effect, excepting only activities with national security significance.

(Excerpt from speech referred to follows:)

EXCERPT FROM REMARKS BY PRESIDENT JOHNSON ON THE 25TH ANNIVERSARY OF ATOMIC ENERGY, DECEMBER 2, 1967

And I want to make it clear to the world that we in the United States are not asking any country to accept safeguards that we are unwilling to accept ourselves.

So I am, today, announcing that when such safeguards are applied under the Treaty, the United States will permit the International Atomic Energy Agency to apply its safeguards to all nuclear activities in the United States—excluding only those with direct national security significance.

Under this offer the Agency will be able to inspect a broad range of U.S. nuclear activities, both governmental and private, including the fuel in nuclear power reactors owned by utilities for generating electricity, and the fabrication and chemical reprocessing of such fuel.

This pledge maintains the consistent policy of the United States since the beginning of the nuclear age.

(The following memorandum was supplied by the AEC at the request of the committee staff for an explanation of the President's offer.)

U.S. OFFER CONCERNING IAEA SAFEGUARDS

The President's announcement of December 2, 1967, stated that "when such safeguards are applied under the Treaty, the United States will permit the International Atomic Energy Agency to apply its safeguards to all nuclear activities in the United States—excluding only those with direct national security significance."

The date at which this offer is to take effect cannot be fixed at this time, since neither the date at which the Non-Proliferation Treaty will enter into force nor the time at which the safeguards required by Article III will be applied in non-nuclear weapon parties can be fixed. We will wish to consider the progress being made in gaining adherence to the Treaty and in the negotiation and implementation of the agreements between non-nuclear parties and the IAEA, in determining when the U.S. offer will take effect.

The U.S. offer will be fulfilled by the negotiation of a formal implementing agreement between the IAEA and the U.S. Government. That agreement would identify those activities in which the IAEA could apply its safeguards. In implementing the agreement, the IAEA will determine in which of the activities among those listed safeguards are to be applied. It is doubtful that the IAEA will wish to apply its safeguards to all activities listed, nor do we believe that the purpose of the U.S. offer would require that it do so. It is more likely that the IAEA would elect to apply safeguards to a representative number of U.S. activities, at least initially.

No definite list can be drawn up at this time identifying all the facilities which will meet the objectives of the offer at that time in the future when the IAEA is prepared to accept the offer, since there will be new facilities and some of the present facilities may either shut down or possibly be operated for a different purpose in the future.

With regard to the latter point it may be recalled that the President offered "activities", not "facilities". Therefore, the terms of our agreement with the Agency to implement the offer will recognize that a facility will be safeguarded as long as the activity normally associated with it is not of "direct national security significance". A few facilities, for example some fuel fabricating facilities, may handle both material having direct national security significance and material which does not. Safeguards will be applied at such a facility only with respect to materials it handles which do not have a direct national security significance. This might be accomplished either by sufficient physical separation between the two types of materials to preclude security problems or by handling the two types as separate items on a batch or campaign basis. Such a procedure was followed at the NFS plant in processing IAEA safeguarded fuel from the Yankee nuclear power station.

Attachment "A" is an illustrative list of facilities in various categories which might meet the criteria of the offer. Prior to officially submitting the name of any facility or activity to the IAEA a detailed review will have to be made to assure that it does meet the criteria of the offer.

The list of facilities which would be submitted to the IAEA would exclude: (1) military reactors, (2) Pu production reactors, (3) space propulsion experiments (Rover), (4) auxiliary power reactors (SNAP), (5) facilities concerned at present with military, nuclear explosive device or other classified work and (6) facilities located in an area at a site generally engaged in military, nuclear plosive device or classified work. Attachment "B" is an illustrative list of facilities in these excluded categories.

ATTACHMENT A

Illustrative list of facilities which might meet the criteria of the President's December 2, 1967 Safeguards Offer.
  A. Central-Station Electric Power Reactors:
        1. Dresden Nuclear Power Station No. 1, Morris, Ill., a 200 MWE BWR.
        2. Turkey Point Station No. 3, Turkey Point, Fla., a 651 MWE PWR.
  B. Dual Purpose Plants:
        1. Bolsa Island Nuclear Power & Desalting Plant, Calif., an 800 MWE Plant.
  C. Experimental Electric Power Systems:
        1. Experimental Breeder Reactor No. 2, NRTS Idaho, a 62.5 MWT sodium cooled fast reactor.
  D. Test, Research and University Reactors:
        1. Fast Flux Test Facility, Richland, Washington, a 400 MWT sodium cooled reactor.

2. National Bureau of Standards, Gaithersburg, Md., a 10 MWT D_2O reactor.

3. Industrial Laboratories, Inc., Plainsboro, N.J., a 5 MWT pool reactor.

4. Rhode Island Nuclear Science Center, Ft. Kearney, R.I., a 1 MWT pool reactor.

5. University of Michigan, Ann Arbor, Mich., a 2 MWT pool reactor.

E. Critical Assembly Facilities:

    1. Atomics International Epithermal Critical Experiment Lab., Santa Susana, California.

    2. Lockheed Aircraft Co., critical facility, Dawsonville, Ga.

    3. Plutonium Recycle Critical Facility, Richland, Wash.

F. Fuel Fabrication and Chemical Processing Facilities:

    1. NUMEC, Apollo, Pa. (Fuel Fabrication).

    2. NFS, West Valley, NY (Chemical Processing).

ATTACHMENT B

Illustrative list of facilities which would *not* be included in the President's December 2, 1967 Safeguards Offer.

A. Military Reactors: e.g., PM–1, Sundance, Wyoming, a 1 MWE PWR

B. Production Reactors: e.g., the K Reactor at the Savannah River Plant

C. Auxiliary Power: e.g., SNAP–8 Ground Prototype System, Santa Susana, California, a 600 KW (T) reactor

D. Space Propulsion: e.g., Nuclear Rocket Reactor Experiment, Phoebus 2A, NRDS, Nevada

E. Facilities used for military or classified work: e.g., Engineering Test Reactor, NRTS, Idaho, a 175 MW(T) tank reactor

F. Facilities located in or near a classified site: e.g.., Ultra High Temperature Reactor Experiment; Los Alamos, N. Mex., a 3 MW(T) helium cooled reactor.

FURTHER QUESTIONS AND ANSWERS

Senator PASTORE. Now, Mr. Chairman, there is a set of questions here that has been drafted by members of the staff of the Joint Committee on Atomic Energy. I am not going to take the time of the committee but I would ask unanimous consent that they be submitted to Dr. Seaborg and that the questions and the answers appear in the record.

Senator SPARKMAN. Without objection, so ordered.

(The questions and answers referred to follow:)

AEC ANSWERS TO QUESTIONS PREPARED BY THE JOINT COMMITTEE ON ATOMIC ENERGY STAFF

1. *Q.* Would international observers be given access to sensitive information on the nuclear explosive devices used in an international Plowshare project?

A. No. The peaceful nuclear explosion services contemplated under Article V must be carried out within the provisions of Articles I and II, which prohibit nuclear-weapons Parties from transferring, and non-nuclear-weapon Parties from receiving, either nuclear explosive devices, as such, or assistance in manufacturing or acquiring them.

Accordingly, neither nuclear explosive devices nor information which would constitute assistance in their manufacture could be made available to the international observers contemplated under Article V. Furthermore, the U.S. has made it clear that the nuclear explosive devices used in providing the nuclear explosion service, pursuant to Article V, would be required to remain, at all times, under the custody and control of the nuclear-weapon state performing the service. This, of course, is consistent with the existing requirements of the Atomic Energy Act of 1954, as amended.

2. *Q.* Am I correct then in assuming that the functions of the observers are to assure that a nuclear detonation was conducted and to report on the conditions and purpose of the detonation?

3. *Q.* Is it fair to say, then, that such observers would serve a function similar to that of the observers at our first Plowshare experiment, Project Gnome, in 1960, and at our recent experiment, Project Gasbuggy?

A. In answer to the related questions 2 and 3, we envision that, prior to each nuclear explosion for peaceful purposes carried out by the U.S. in the territory of a non-nuclear-weapon state pursuant to Article V, a reasonable opportunity will be provided for international observation. The principal purpose of such an invitation would appear to be to provide assurance to other Parties to the Treaty, that the nuclear explosive devices used by the U.S. in furnishing the nuclear explosion service, remained under the custody and control of the U.S. at all times, and that the nuclear explosions carried out in the course of furnishing the service were not being used for other than declared purposes.

It will be necessary to work out arrangements for providing an opportunity for such observation and, at the same time, assuring that information inconsistent with U.S. law and Articles I and II of the Treaty, concerning the design and manufacture of the nuclear explosive devices used, is not made available to the observers.

It would appear to us that the IAEA would be the appropriate international organization to be invited to carry out international observation, pursuant to Article V. It is therefore likely that international observation arrangements will be worked out ultimately with the IAEA and the government in whose territory the explosion will be carried out.

We do not expect that those arrangements would interfere with any independent plans by the host government to invite visitors from other countries to witness the nuclear explosion or other aspects of a project.

4. *Q.* In other words, am I correct in stating that observers at peaceful nuclear experiments will be permitted, but not required. In other words, we would not have to hold up a peaceful nuclear explosion service just because some recalcitrant foreign country or organization was opposed to the project and refused to attend?

A. Article V of the Treaty would certainly require that a reasonable opportunity be offered for international observation of explosions conducted pursuant to that Article. In all probability, the IAEA will be the organization or at least one of the organizations invited to observe peaceful nuclear explosions conducted pursuant to Article V. If the invitation is extended in good faith and allows reasonable notice to permit the international observation, then we believe the obligation under this provision would be discharged, even if the IAEA or other international observers did not appear. On the other hand, if the arrangements for the carrying out of the nuclear explosion were such as to make international observation impracticable, then obviously there would not have been compliance with the provision.

5. *Q.* Am I correct in my understanding that, under Article V, the nuclear explosive device would remain at all times under the custody and control of the U.S. or the supplying nation?

A. Yes, that is correct. This is consistent with the Atomic Energy Act of 1954, as amended.

6. *Q.* Also you stated in your testimony, I believe, that there would not be any access by the observers or by the non-nuclear-weapon-state, in which the service was being performed, to the design or internal operation of the nuclear explosive device. Is that correct?

A. Yes, the nuclear explosive devices would remain in the custody and control of the U.S. or other supplier nuclear-weapon government. Neither the international observers or nationals of the recipient nonnuclear-weapon state would be permitted access to that information concerning the design or internal operation of nuclear explosive devices which would be inconsistent with the objectives or the provisions of Articles I and II of the Treaty. No information would be made available by the U.S. which would be contrary to the provisions of the Atomic Energy Act of 1954, as amended.

7. *Q.* Consequently, am I correct in assuming that since there will be no transfer of the nuclear explosive devices or control over them; since the service will not assist, encourage, or induce any non-nuclear-weapon state to manufacture or otherwise acquire nuclear explosive devices; and since the service will not provide source or special fissionable material, or equipment or material especially designed or prepared for the processing, use, or production of special fissionable

material to any non-nuclear-weapon state, the safeguards contemplated by Article III of the Treaty are not considered to apply to the peaceful nuclear explosion service contemplated in Article V?

A. The procedures to be developed for the provision by nuclear-weapon Parties of a peaceful nuclear explosion service to non-nuclear-weapon Parties pursuant to Article V will necessarily include arrangements to assure that the nuclear explosive devices used in providing the service will remain at all times in the custody and control of the nuclear-weapon State providing the service. Moreover, the procedures could not permit the dissemination of that information concerning design and manufacture of the nuclear explosive devices used, such as the quantities of the special fissionable materials contained in the devices, which would be contrary to the objectives of the Treaty and prohibited by Articles I and II.

Accordingly, it will not be possible for an international organization to account for the special fissionable materials involved in providing the peaceful nuclear explosion services to non-nuclear-weapon states pursuant to Article V. It is thus difficult to see how Article III "safeguards", as we might envisage their application to activities such as nuclear reactors or fuel fabrication or reprocessing plants, could be applied to the nuclear explosive devices used in providing the service pursuant to Article V.

At the same time, the arrangements for international observation of nuclear explosions contemplated by Article V would serve the purpose of assuring all the Parties that the nuclear explosive devices used in providing the service do, in fact, remain at all times in the custody and control of the nuclear-weapon state supplying the service and that nuclear explosions are not carried out for other than declared purposes.

8. Q. Dr. Seaborg: If I remember correctly, you conducted two excavation experiments earlier this year. These experiments, I understand, only released very small amounts of radioactivity to the atmosphere and most of this was deposited at or near the crater.

A. That is correct. On January 26 we conducted Project Cabriolet, a 2.5 kiloton detonation in hard rock at the Nevada Test Site and on March 12, we conducted Project Buggy, the first nuclear row charge experiment. Both released only very small amounts of radioactivity, most of which was deposited in, or near, the crater.

9. Q. There was no worldwide fallout as occurs from atmospheric or surface explosions, was there?

A. That is correct. Since those nuclear explosions occurred underground, most of the radioactivity produced was entrapped in the rock and soil which surrounded the explosions. Consequently, most of the radioactivity remained in the explosion region underground. Of the small amount of radioactive material incorporated with dust-like matter which escaped from the crater area, only a small percentage of the lighter, more volatile radioactive material escaped to the lower atmosphere.

10. Q. You also have underway, I believe, a program to develop clean explosives. Do you not anticipate that you will be successful in this development program?

A. The "clean explosive" program you refer to, is actually a program to develop a nuclear explosive which will produce a minimum amount of radioactivity. We have made considerable strides in designing an explosive which has a very low fission yield, but we do not envisage an explosive with no fission yield. We are also developing ways of emplacing explosive which will reduce the amount of radioactivity released in cratering explosions. The progress we have made in these efforts is perhaps best illustrated by the fact that if we did Project Sedan— our 1962, 100 kt cratering experiment in alluvium—with today's technology, the amount of radioactivity released to the atmosphere would be reduced a hundredfold. Even given this progress, because of the unavoidable fission product radioactivity and the induced radioactivity mentioned previously, we will still have to review each proposed excavation explosion very carefully to insure that it meets the requirements of the Limited Nuclear Test Ban Treaty.

11. Q. I assume you plan to continue excavation experiments since one is included in your FY 1969 budget.

A. Yes, we plan to conduct Project Schooner, a cratering experiment of approximately 40 kt. in hard rock, at the Nevada Test Site during FY 1969.

12. *Q.* In view of the task assigned Mr. Robert Anderson and his Atlantic-Pacific Interoceanic Canal Study Commission, I suppose you will carry out enough such experiments to furnish them the information necessary for their study.

A. Yes, we plan a number of single and row charge experiments in different rock types, and at higher yields, on a time frame consistent with the needs of the Canal Commission.

13. *Q.* I believe your statement said that it might not be possible for us to develop nuclear excavation technology for some projects such as the transisthmian canal. Would I be correct then in assuming that you are referring to the complete development of that technology?

A. Yes. It is possible, in order to develop completely the technology for some nuclear excavation projects such as a transisthmian canal, that an experiment might have to be conducted in a particular geological situation, or in a wet environment or some other condition similar to that which might actually be expected in digging a canal, and that the desired condition could only be found near a border. Also, before constructing the canal, we might wish to do a number of experiments in the isthmus region to gain experience in the type of media we would encounter in digging the canal. In those cases, the nearness of the borders could present difficulties in conducting such experiments in view of the Limited Test Ban Treaty; thus complete development of all the technology needed to actually undertake construction of the canal could be precluded.

(The following material was submitted at the request of ACDA:)

Supplementary Material Submitted by ACDA

In the interests of further clarification of the meaning of Article III, the following supplementary information is submitted for the record:

1. The question has been raised as to whether mines and ore processing plants will be subjected to safeguards under the treaty.

IAEA practice does not involve the application of safeguards to uranium mines and ore-processing plants. IAEA safeguards, under present practice, commence with the uranium concentrate produced by ore-processing plants. The Non-Proliferation Treaty requires no change in this practice.

Of course, exports of uranium ore to non-nuclear-weapon States by parties to the treaty would be subject to the condition that the safeguards required by Article III of the Treaty would be applied to the source or special fissionable material derived from this ore in the recipient state.

2. Article III(2)(b) prohibits the provision of "equipment or material especially designed or prepared for the processing, use or production of special fissionable material, to any non-nuclear weapon State for peaceful purposes, unless the source or special fissionable material shall be subject to the safeguards required by this Article". The question has been raised as to whether this would apply to the provision by a party to a non-nuclear-weapon state that was not a party to the treaty of a natural uranium fueled reactor, or equipment or components for such a reactor.

It would, and thus, even if the recipient were to use its own domestic natural uranium in the reactor, Article III safeguards would be required. A natural uranium reactor both produces plutonium (a special fissionable material) and uses the plutonium produced, since some of the plutonium produced in the uranium fuel of the reactor undergoes fission in place. Hence such a reactor (and its equipment or components) would constitute equipment "especially designed or prepared for the processing, use or production of special fissionable material."

Senator Pastore. In conclusion, let me say this and I hope I don't hurt anyone's sensibilities, it strikes me that being against this treaty is like being against the Ten Commandments.

Senator Sparkman. Senator Carlson?

Senator Carlson. I just want to say, first, in view of your background and great experience in this field, you are probably the most important witness we are going to have in regard to this hearing. I do appreciate your appearance here this morning.

I want to follow along a little further the line of questioning of Chairman Pastore. I think we all realize the possible future benefits in this use of nuclear explosive devices for peaceful application. Chairman Pastore brought up the construction of the Panama Canal— I assume he had reference to the Isthmus canal—and I believe you stated that construction depends on research and is probably 5 or 10 years away. Is that right?

Dr. SEABORG. That is a very rough estimate, depending on the rate at which we would be able to proceed in our research and the development of devices and the excavation technology.

EFFECT OF LIMITED TEST BAN TREATY

Senator CARLSON. I noticed an interesting sentence in your own statement and I want for the record to get a little clarification on it:

> There will be some nuclear excavation projects herewith, such as the trans-isthmian canal for which the development of the technology could not be completely carried out or which could not be executed within the present restrictions of the limited test ban treaty.

What are some of these restrictions?

Dr. SEABORG. I added "as presently interpreted" when I made the statement.

Those restrictions have to do with causing radioactive debris to be present beyond the boundaries of the country that is conducting the experiment.

Now, there are various possible degrees of stringency of interpretation of the wording of the limited nuclear Test Ban Treaty. We have been able to conduct excavation experiments under the strictest possible interpretation of the wording of the treaty. We might have to, in in order to develop the excavation technology necessary to apply nuclear explosives to the construction of a sea-level canal across the Isthmus, conduct experiments that would release radioactivity into the air which might later be considered to be used beyond the borders of the United States. That is, the amount of radioactivity might be greater than the strictest possible interpretation would allow, but not greater than that which would be allowed by what I would consider a reasonable interpretation of that treaty.

Therefore, we might be able to carry out all of the experiments required, without a modification of the limited Test Ban Treaty. However, I wouldn't rule out the possibility of an amendment to the limited nuclear Test Ban Treaty in view of the worldwide interest in the use of nuclear explosives for such excavation projects. Then, of course, it would be possible to easily carry out any of the experiments in excavation technology.

However, in order to carry out the project itself—the digging of a canal across the Isthmus with nuclear explosions—it would be necessary to amend the limited nuclear test ban treaty.

I do want to emphasize, however, that in the interpretation of the limited nuclear test ban treaty with respect to radioactive debris being present beyond the borders, I am not speaking, when I speak in terms of various interpretations, of a level of radioactivity that would ever present a health problem. Any interpretation that we would make would never include radioactivity at a level that would be anywhere near a health problem. I am talking about the theoretical detection of infinitesimal amounts of radioactivity when I speak of the strictest interpretation.

EFFECT OF TEST BAN TREATY ON SEA LEVEL CANAL

Senator CARLSON. Doctor, as you well know, the construction of a new canal or improvement of our present facilities at the Panama Canal is a very current issue and one that concerns not only our own Nation but many other nations.

What chance would we have of getting modification of the Test Ban Treaty restriction? Let's assume we were ready to use some of this material to build a sea level canal across the country. Whom would we confer with, all of the countries involved in this treaty? Whose approval would we have to get?

Dr. SEABORG. I think in the case of the limited nuclear Test Ban Treaty, an amendment requires an affirmative vote of a majority of all the parties to this treaty including the votes of all of the original parties.

Senator CARLSON. In other words, we built the Panama Canal, and if it now was decided that we, as a nation, wanted to build it we could not go ahead and build it under this treaty without getting the approval of the majority of the nations in this world?

Dr. SEABORG. It wouldn't be the Nonproliferation Treaty that would be limiting this; it would be the limited Test Ban Treaty.

Senator CARLSON. The limited Test Ban Treaty?

Dr. SEABORG. Yes; the limited Test Ban Treaty would have to be amended in order to build a sea level canal across the Isthmus using nuclear explosives. But I do believe that the atmosphere of interest in such uses, and the increased confidence throughout the world that such a project could be carried out without any menace to the public health and safety is creating the kind of a climate that would make such an amendment to the limited Test Ban Treaty feasible, and I believe that the very act of our engaging in discussions concerning the Nonproliferation Treaty has contributed to that climate. It has become more apparent to more and more nations that we can have the benefits of the peaceful uses of nuclear explosives with essentially no detrimental effects concerning the public health and safety.

Senator PASTORE. Would the Senator yield on that point?

Senator CARLSON. Yes.

AMENDMENT NEEDED ONLY FOR NUCLEAR EXCAVATION

Senator PASTORE. Dr. Seaborg, isn't it a fact if any nuclear explosives were suggested for use that might be in serious violation of the nuclear Test Ban Treaty you wouldn't want to use that explosive?

Dr. SEABORG. We wouldn't consider doing that at all.

Senator PASTORE. If you can fabricate a clean bomb it wouldn't let out any radiation. Looking well down the road if you would be doing that you would not be in violation of the Test Ban Treaty and you wouldn't have to amend it?

Dr. SEABORG. Well, I think that in looking at that realistically, Senator Pastore, since the treaty speaks of the presence of radioactive material—and does not identify it further—beyond the borders of the country where the experiment is performed, even the induced radioactivity created by the neutrons from a completely fusion device that gave no fission products could probably cause enough radioactive debris to be present beyond the confines of the small country where the excavation would be performed to create a treaty problem. So I would say that I believe in order to do the trans-isthmian canal we would have to have an amendment, but I don't regard that as an insuperable step at all. I think that there is an increasing awareness among the nations of the world that this can be done safely.

I might also call your attention to the fact that among the principles relating to nuclear explosion services suggested by the U.S. representative to the 18-Nation Disarmament Conference on March 21, 1967, and which was made part of the record of this hearing (see page 12), the nuclear and nonnuclear parties to the limited test ban treaty about any fourth principle is that "There should be full consultation among amendment of that treaty required in order to carry out feasible projects."

So that principle also, it seems to me, anticipates that we might have reasonable optimism to feel but this step could be carried out affirmatively.

Senator SPARKMAN. Will you yield to me briefly?

EXCERPTS FROM TEST BAN TREATY

I think it will be well to insert in the record at this time the full text from which you read in the limited nuclear Test Ban Treaty. The articles in question are articles I and II, and without objection they will be inserted. I think it might be well also to say at this time that the definition of the term "original parties" is the three nations, the United States of America, the United Kingdom of Great Britain and Northern Ireland, and the Union of Soviet Socialist Republics.

Dr. SEABORG. Yes. As a matter of fact, the way I referred to it was the nuclear powers.

Senator SPARKMAN. Yes, the term used in the treaty, "original parties" might be construed as all of the signatories.

Dr. SEABORG. Yes, I noticed that when I read the full language, but you are right that those terms are synonymous; the original parties, and the three nuclear weapon states adhering to the limited nuclear Test Ban Treaty are the same.

Senator SPARKMAN. Thank you.

(The material referred to follows:)

EXCERPTS FROM "TREATY BANNING NUCLEAR WEAPON TESTS IN THE ATMOSPHERE, IN OUTER SPACE AND UNDER WATER"

"The Governments of the United States of America, the United Kingdom of Great Britain and Northern Ireland, and the Union of Soviet Socialist Republics, hereinafter referred to as the 'Original Parties', . . ."

"ARTICLE I"

"1. Each of the Parties to this Treaty undertakes to prohibit, to prevent, and not to carry out any nuclear weapon test explosion, or any other nuclear explosion, at any place under its jurisdiction or control:

(a) in the atmosphere; beyond its limits, including outer space; or underwater, including territorial waters or high seas; or

(b) in any other environment if such explosion causes radioactive debris to be present outside the territorial limits of the State under whose jurisdiction or control such explosion is conducted. It is understood in this connection that the provisions of this subparagraph are without prejudice to the conclusion of a treaty resulting in the permanent banning of all nuclear test explosions, including all such explosions underground, the conclusion of which, as the Parties have stated in the Preamble to this Treaty, they seek to achieve.

"2. Each of the Parties to this Treaty undertakes furthermore to refrain from causing, encouraging, or in any way participating in, the carrying out of any nuclear weapon test explosion, or any other nuclear explosion, anywhere which would take place in any of the environments described, or have the effect referred to, in paragraph 1 of this Article."

"ARTICLE II"

"1. Any Party may propose amendments to this Treaty. The text of any proposed amendment shall be submitted to the Depositary Governments which shall circulate it to all Parties to this Treaty. Thereafter, if requested to do so by one-third or more of the Parties, the Depositary Governments shall convene a conference, to which they shall invite all the Parties, to consider such amendment.

"2. Any amendment to this Treaty must be approved by a majority of the votes of all the Parties to this Treaty, including the votes of all of the Original Parties. The amendment shall enter into force for all Parties upon the deposit of instruments of ratification by a majority of all the Parties, including the instruments of ratification of all of the Original Parties."

Senator CARLSON. Doctor, I am not pressing this point except for the fact I believe there is great future in this field for using nuclear fissionable material for peaceful purposes. It is agreed we have to get the support of a majority of these other signatory countries to construct a new Panama Canal.

NUCLEAR EXCAVATION IN THE UNITED STATES

Assume that we wanted to do some heavy movement of earth within our own Nation's boundaries, what do we have to do then? What is the limitation?

Dr. SEABORG. I would say that it would have to be looked at. It would depend on the particular project and how strict and stringent an interpretation we made of the limited nuclear Test Ban Treaty. I believe we could do some such projects within the United States without causing amounts of radioactive debris to be present beyond our boundaries that would constitute a health menace.

Senator CARLSON. In other words, to follow your answer to that question, we would not be the nation to determine whether the debris goes beyond our boundaries, that would be up to other countries; is that right?

Dr. SEABORG. Other countries could challenge, yes, whether the debris was of such magnitude as to constitute a violation of the limited nuclear Test Bay Treaty. I believe that consultation under point 4 of these principles might, however, take care of that problem. I believe that is——

Senator CARLSON. I notice in article I, subparagraph (b) which reads:

In any other environment if such explosion causes radioactive debris to be present outside the territorial limits of the State under whose jurisdiction or control such explosion is conducted.

So it seems to me that that statement, while I think it is very plain, it does cause some concern, I think, to many people, as to what might be a limitation of use of one of the most recent discoveries of great value to not only this Nation, but to the world.

Dr. SEABORG. Yes.

Senator CARLSON. And I sincerely hope we are not approving a treaty here that would limit this to the extent that we could not use a great force after we have discovered it.

Dr. SEABORG. No, Senator Carlson, this treaty doesn't change that picture at all. We are discussing a provision of the limited nuclear Test Ban Treaty, and I believe that the ratification of this Nonproliferation Treaty which we have under discussion here, with its article V, would make it easier to amend the limited nuclear Test Ban Treaty.

PRODUCTION AND USES OF PLUTONIUM

Senator CARLSON. In your own statement today you stressed the fact that we are producing great quantities of plutonium. The President's letter transmitting the Nonproliferation Treaty to the Senate states, and I quote:

By 1985 the world's peaceful nuclear power stations will probably be turning out enough byproduct plutonium for the production of tons of nuclear bombs every day.

The safeguards system envisioned by this treaty is directed toward preventing the diversion of plutonium. Now, isn't the real problem the world faces today, not the diversion of plutonium, but the accumulation of it? Isn't it a fact that we are getting so much of it we don't know what we are going to do with it?

Dr. SEABORG. No; we have very good uses for plutonium in the field of peaceful uses of atomic energy. Plutonium is the key fuel for the breeder reactor, which opens up the possibility of using all of the uranium rather than just 1 percent or so of uranium we use in today's reactors. So we have an extraordinarily good use for plutonium in producing electricity, in desalting sea water, and producing fertilizers and making changes in our industrial economy and in our ways of doing many things. It is just that what we are trying to do is prevent the diversion of this same plutonium, that can do all these wonderful things, to weapons, where it can do such destructive things.

Senator CARLSON. Isn't it reasonable to assume if this plutonium keeps increasing in certain countries and they accumulate great quantities of it, there will be a tendency to say "Let's get some of it ready to use for military purposes?"

Dr. SEABORG. Well, of course, this is what the Nonproliferation Treaty would be preventing.

NAMING OF ELEMENT PLUTONIUM

Senator PASTORE. As a matter of fact, Doctor, I never could understand why this plutonium was not called Seaborgium; you discovered it and won the Nobel Prize for it. Where did you get the name plutonium?

Dr. SEABORG. That is one question I believe I can answer. [Laughter.]

The heaviest—you will have to cut me off on this one—the heaviest natural element is No. 92, which is uranium, named after the planet Uranus, the outermost planet at the time that uranium was discovered in 1789. Then, a manmade element, No. 93, was discovered, so it was natural to name it as McMillan and Abelson did, after a planet still farther out that had been discovered in the meantime, Neptune, and so that element was named neptunium.

Then we discovered element 94, the next element, and another planet had been found in the meantime, Pluto, the outermost planet. So we named it after Pluto. And I might say, in that connection, that we debated a long time as to whether we should name it "plutium" or "plutonium." We weren't sure which was the correct use of the base Pluto. We decided that plutonium sounded better and we have been told in the meantime that this was the correct use of the base Pluto.

Another interesting aspect of this is that we traditionally had the privilege as discovers of an element to give it its symbol. The logical symbol might have been Pl, the first two letters of the word plutonium, but we were so struck with the possibilities of using the letters "Pu" to describe this element that we almost, somewhat as a lark, decided that we would give it the symbol Pu. This, of course, was during the wartime, when everything was carried on secretly and the rest of the world didn't know what we were up to. But we wrote reports at that time suggesting the name plutonium and the symbol Pu, expecting a real reaction after it was declassified after the war. We expected that people might object to what we thought they might regard as a misuse of our prerogative, but there weren't any objections whatsoever and it was fully accepted.

One more thing. A little later we discovered the next element, 95, and the astronomers had let us down by that time, they hadn't discovered any planets beyond Pluto, so we had to change to a different system, and that is why we named element 95 after the Americas, americium. Here we had the analogy that it is chemically like the rare earth element europium, which is named after Europe. Thus we went into a different system for naming the several elements beyond plutonium.

Senator CARLSON. I think this is a good place for me to conclude my interrogation. [Laughter.]

I do want to say, Chairman Pastore, that I think after Dr. Seaborg, Seaborgium should have been the name.

Thank you.

Senator SPARKMAN. Senator Cooper.

Senator COOPER. Thank you, I should like to say also I agree with my colleagues that the testimony we hear today from Dr. Seaborg is probably the most authoritative and most expert we will hear on this subject.

I refer to the earlier statement of my colleague, Senator Pastore, that anyone who opposed this treaty would be like opposing the Ten Commandments, and may I say that I support the treaty, but I think also we have to be certain that we at least require everyone who may be signatory to this treaty to proceed within the experience of the Ten Commandments.

While I am a lay person inquiring into scientific and technological problems, I do think it is important that we inquire thoroughly into these problems so not only the Congress but the people will be satisfied with the provisions of this treaty.

SAFEGUARDS DETERMINED BY IAEA

Yesterday, I asked certain questions about safeguards which I know now should have been directed to you, but I would like to proceed to that subject.

Would it be correct to say that in articles III and V that ultimately the decision about safeguards would be determined by the International Atomic Energy Agency, taking into consideration the sixth paragraph of the preamble.

Dr. SEABORG. In the case of article III, yes, I would say so.

Senator COOPER. Finally IAEA would determine in each case whether the safeguards were of sufficient effectiveness.

Dr. SEABORG. That is right, taking into account the provisions of its agreements with parties to the treaty.

Senator COOPER. You said 94 states have subscribed to IAEA. How many members are there of the Board of Governors?

Dr. SEABORG. Twenty-five.

Senator COOPER. Would you supply for the record the states who are members of the Board of Governors?

Dr. SEABORG. Yes; we would be glad to do that.

(The list follows:)

1967–68 BOARD OF GOVERNORS (IAEA)

Algeria	Madagascar
Argentina	Mexico
Brazil	Norway
Bulgaria	Peru
Canada	Philippines
Ceylon	Portugal
Czechoslovak Socialist Republic	South Africa
France	Turkey
Germany, Federal Republic of	Union of Soviet Socialist Republics
India	United Kingdom of Great Britain and
Indonesia	Northern Ireland
Japan	United States of America
Lebanon	

Senator COOPER. Would the decision of the safeguards be made by the Board of Governors?

Dr. SEABORG. I think that, like any organization, the Board of Governors, which is the Board of Directors, effectively would make the decisions but the decisions would, if they are important, be subject to referral to the General Conference of the International Atomic

Energy Agency which meets annually in Vienna, a meeting which, by the way, I have attended each year since 1961. It has been held in Vienna each year except 1965 when it was held in Tokyo. At the General Conference representatives with supporting delegations from each of the member nations, 98 at the present time, convene in plenary session, and there are discussions concerning all of the important moves that have been made by the IAEA, and those that are contemplated.

Senator Cooper. My point is that the IAEA is ultimately to determine the effectiveness of safeguards in each case for each country——

Dr. Seaborg. Yes; and I might again point out that among the guiding principles of article III which were enunciated by the U.S. representatives at the Eighteen-Nation Disarmament Conference on January 18, 1968, and which I believe are part of the legislative record of this treaty (see p. 10) is No. 3, which says that, "In order to avoid unnecessary duplication, the IAEA should make appropriate use of existing records and safeguards, provided that under such mutually agreed arrangements, IAEA can satisfy itself that nuclear material is not diverted to nuclear weapons or other nuclear explosive devices."

PROCEDURES FOLLOWED BY IAEA IN APPROVING SAFEGUARDS SYSTEMS

Senator Cooper. My question is to try to clarify the procedures which IAEA would follow in approving any system of safeguards. So could you provide for the record your judgment as to whether the Board of Governors would approve the safeguards for a particular country?

Dr. Seaborg. Right. I see. Each of the agreements that the IAEA would enter into with each of the participating countries or international organizations like Euratom would be subject to ratification or approval by the Board of Governors of the IAEA.

Senator Cooper. These may seem details but I would like them in the record. Would this be made by a two-thirds vote or a majority vote?

Dr. Seaborg. In the IAEA?

Senator Cooper. Yes.

Dr. Seaborg. I have been told that it is normally made by a majority vote, but that a two-thirds vote can be called for. It would be my judgment that this is so important, that this would be a matter to be finally determined by the IAEA Board of Governors, perhaps with referral to the General Conference of the IAEA. That would be my judgment.

Senator Cooper. Is there any provision for a veto?

Dr. Seaborg. No. There is no provision for a veto.

Senator Cooper. In the agreement on safeguards it would not be required, would it, a set of safeguards for one country which would have to conform to all countries?

Dr. Seaborg. No, these would be individually negotiated but one can imagine, as a matter of practicality, that in the cases of a number of similar countries there would be a sort of form agreement that would be applicable but there would have to be a number of those to cover individual categories of the countries.

APPLICATION OF INSPECTION AUTHORITY

Senator COOPER. Looking at the article which provides for safeguards, there is one section which gives to the Agency the authority to inspect all sources, all material, all production facilities in the recipient country where countries receive materials or equipment for peaceful uses. The authority of the Agency to inspect is limited only to recipient countries.

Dr. SEABORG. It only applies to nonnuclear weapon countries but the right of inspection by the IAEA is not limited to material received in such countries from other countries.

Senator COOPER. I quote for the record article XII of the statute of IAEA, paragraph 6.

To send into the territory of the recipient State or States inspectors, designated by the Agency after consultation with the State or States concerned, who shall have access at all times to all places and data and to any person who by reason of his occupation deals with materials, equipment—

and so forth. My point is, isn't it correct that this right of inspection applies only to the recipient countries of materials or equipment to be used for peaceful purposes? In other words, if the United States supplied materials or equipment to India, for example, does the Agency inspect all sources and facilities in India?

Dr. SEABORG. You mean if India adheres to the NPT?

Senator COOPER. No, I am talking about the peaceful uses.

Dr. SEABORG. Yes.

Senator COOPER. Under the statute of IAEA referring to peaceful uses there is no authority for the inspector to come into the nuclear country which is providing materials or equipment to nonusers?

Dr. SEABORG. No, that is right.

INSPECTION AUTHORITY IN THE UNITED STATES UNDER TREATY

Senator COOPER. I come to my point: Does this treaty give to the IAEA under any agreements they make on safeguards the authority to come into the United States, the U.S.S.R., or the United Kingdom to

Dr. SEABORG. No. The treaty does not, but we have offered that.

The treaty does not, but we have offered that.

Senator COOPER. I realize that. But the United States in the statement of President Johnson has agreed or at least on his part he has stated that we would allow IAEA to inspect our facilities and our sources.

Dr. SEABORG. That is right. He has gone beyond the provisions and the obligations of the treaty in doing that.

Senator COOPER. Under the Atomic Energy Act would that require an amendment by the Congress?

Dr. SEABORG. In order to allow these inspections?

Senator COOPER. Yes.

Dr. SEABORG. I think that it is probably consistent with the Atomic Energy Act and that it wouldn't require an amendment, but this is certainly something that we would look at very carefully with the Joint Committee.

Senator PASTORE. Would the Senator yield?

It would require it if classified information were involved. But if
it is unclassified information, I don't see why you would have to amend
the act at all.

Senator Cooper. All right.

Dr. Seaborg. However; we do expect to proceed under President
Johnson's offer through the voluntary cooperation of all the industrial
concerns involved and we were assured, before President Johnson
made his offer, through a number of reliable representatives that they
would voluntarily cooperate.

Senator Cooper. Now, has the U.S.S.R. similarly made a declaration that they would permit inspection?

Dr. Seaborg. They have not.

Senator Cooper. Has the United Kingdom?

Dr. Seaborg. The United Kingdom has.

Senator Cooper. I assume France has not?

Dr. Seaborg. France has not.

NECESSITY OF U.S. DECLARATION ON INSPECTION

Senator Cooper. Do you think it was necessary for the United
States to make this declaration when the U.S.S.R. did not?

Dr. Seaborg. I think it was very helpful in the attainment of the
agreement by a number of counties to the NPT, that the United
States made this offer. It did prove that we were willing to undergo
the same kind of inspections as the non-nuclear-weapons states, which
we wanted to adhere to the treaty. I believe this went a long way in
proving to them that their fears of industrial espionage and interference with their peaceful activities were unfounded. The very fact
that we were willing to undergo the same regime ourselves, I think,
did a lot to allay these fears.

Senator Cooper. In your judgment does that present any security
problems for the United States?

Dr. Seaborg. No; I don't think so. Because the President exempted
all activities with direct national security significance.

NOTICE OF WITHDRAWAL PROVISION

Senator Cooper. I turn to article X which permits any party to
"withdraw from the treaty if it decides that extraordinary events,
related to the subject matter of this treaty, have jeopardized the
supreme interests of its country. It shall give notice of such withdrawal
to all other parties to the treaty and the United Nations Security
Council three months in advance. Such notice shall include a statement
of extraordinary events which it regards as having jeopardized its
supreme interests."

Do you know whether this provision was proposed by the United
States or by the Soviet Union or was it a matter of general discussion?

Dr. Seaborg. I don't know the origin of it. It is patterned after a
similar article permitting withdrawal from the limited nuclear Test
Ban Treaty, so I suspect that the origin is sort of jointly the United
States and the Soviet Union. But all of this, of course, evolved as
a result of consultations with numerous countries. I believe a total of

124 countries were consulted in the course of finally coming up with this language that we have before us today.

Senator COOPER. I remember a provision in the nuclear Test Ban Treaty, and this is somewhat similar, but it would appear to me if such an event or extraordinary event which threatened the supreme interests of a country, the United States, that I presume in our right of self-defense we would protect the supreme interests of this country. We would not be limited to withdrawal and have to wait for three months. The treaty says that.

Dr. SEABORG. That is what it says. Of course, it depends on what the circumstances are that have led to this extraordinary situation.

ACTION BY SECURITY COUNCIL IN EVENT OF AGGRESSION

Senator COOPER. This is probably a political matter and I don't know whether you would care to answer it or not. A declaration was made by the United States and by the Soviet Union and by the United Kingdom in the United Nations in which they declared in the event of a threat of nuclear aggression or aggression against another country, that the United States, the United Kingdom, the U.S.S.R. would present the matter to the Security Council of the United Nations and would take steps to protect against such aggression. Do you know whether or not there was any promise or any declaration that the right of veto would not be exercised?

Dr. SEABORG. I think there was not.

Senator COOPER. This is beyond the framework of this particular discussion, but suppose China or some other countries threatened nuclear aggression, what could the Security Council do about it practically? How would you meet either the threat of nuclear aggression or, say, limited nuclear aggression?

Dr. SEABORG. Well, I think that I probably should defer to Secretary Rusk for the answer to that question, Senator Cooper.

Senator COOPER. I think so, but I wondered if Red China, for example, threatened nuclear blackmail—there has been a lot of talk here about nuclear blackmail by China not only in connection with this but in connection with the ABM discussion and I wondered, suppose they do threaten some Asian countries with nuclear blackmail—suppose the Chinese threatened to use their nuclear weapons, what would the United States do about it? Would we start a nuclear attack upon China? I am just questioning what the actual value of, the effectiveness of, the declaration made by Ambassador Goldberg and others before the U.N. is. It was a good statement to make, but I just wondered what its true effectiveness would be.

Dr. SEABORG. I would say that there is certainly significance to such declarations in that the three countries, the United States, the Soviet Union, and the United Kingdom made identical declarations.

PEACEFUL NUCLEAR EXPLOSIONS

Senator COOPER. I think that is all, except I think it is clear then so far as article V is concerned it would not come into effect unless there is an amendment to the limited nuclear Test Ban Treaty.

Dr. Seaborg. No, I wouldn't say that. Under article V, it might be possible to do some of the excavation experiments that I have focused on so far without amendment to the limited nuclear Test Ban Treaty, and there are a number of applications of the peaceful uses of nuclear explosives known as "underground engineering" that definitely can be carried out without an amendment to the limited nuclear Test Ban Treaty. These have to do with the explosion of nuclear devices, very deep underground to increase the recovery of gas and oil from light formations, to recover oil from oil shale, to increase the economic recovery of metals from low grade minerals, to create underground storage cavities for gas and for water, and things of that sort. All of these could be carried out within the strictest interpretation of the limited nuclear Test Ban Treaty, and they in their own right, have tremendous potential economic implication for our country and the world. It may be that we will be turning to this method, to this use of underground nuclear explosions to help us recover the energy resources and the mineral resources that we will need in the future as we begin to run out of high grade deposits of gas and oil and minerals. It could be that this use of nuclear explosives might be our salvation in the future.

Senator Cooper. My question was not clear. What I was intending to say was that you said you could not use the explosions for the construction of an Isthmian canal without amendment.

Dr. Seaborg. Yes; there I expressed the personal judgment that I thought we would have to have an amendment to the limited nuclear Test Ban Treaty, but I also expressed the feeling, the optimistic feeling, that this might be quite feasible to obtain in view of the increasing recognition throughout the world of the potential advantages of nuclear explosions for excavation, together with the realization that they can be carried out without undue risk to health or safety.

STEPS TO PURSUE DISARMAMENT NEGOTIATIONS

Senator Cooper. I have just one further question. That is article VI in which, "Each of the parties to the treaty undertakes to pursue negotiations in good faith on effective measures relating to cessation of the nuclear arms race at an early date and to nuclear disarmament, and on a treaty on general and complete disarmament under strict and effective international control."

With your knowledge of the subject what would you consider to be the first step which should be taken under this article?

Dr. Seaborg. Well, I would think that a first step would be the discussions that have been announced by President Johnson and Premier Kosygin, that is, discussions concerning the limitation on the strategic offensive and defensive missile weapons systems.

SOVIET ABM SYSTEMS

Senator Cooper. I don't want to go deeply into the ABM issue, and I am not going to ask you your judgment about the political aspects of this question, but I do want to ask about technological aspects because these are questions which have arisen recently too in connection with the ABM system. If you can answer it properly and without entering into the political implications, do so. There has been a great deal of discussion about the defensive system which the Soviet Union has installed and it has been said again and again the Soviet Union is constructing an anti ballistic missile system. That occurred again and again in the debate we had in the Senate. According to my study of this problem, which is limited, compared to your knowledge, but I understood from what information was available to the Senate that the Leningrad system had been considered by the consensus of our intelligence and by our scientists as an ineffective and outmoded system. Can you state whether or not that is correct?

Dr. SEABORG. Well, I don't know; it certainly has limited capability. It represents a truly first generation of what might be possible there. In other words, they aren't far down the road in developing a sophisticated ABM system as represented by what they have there.

Senator COOPER. Now, it has been said also in certain articles and statements, the consensus of the intelligence community and also by Mr. McNamara that the system which was being installed around Moscow, the so-called Galosh system, was not being expedited, in fact, it was being slowed down. Are you able to state whether or not that is correct?

Dr. SEABORG. No, I don't have information of a first hand kind with which I could add meaningfully to what you have said.

Senator COOPER. Mr. McNamara, in his statement in his San Francisco speech and later in his statement before the Armed Services Committee at the beginning of this year, stated that, notwithstanding all of these efforts by the Soviet Union, the United States had what he called "assured destructive capability" to meet the first strike of any potential enemy.

Dr. SEABORG. Yes.

Senator COOPER. Following that up, is it correct then that the installation of these systems at Leningrad and Moscow and Tallinn have not degraded that assured destructive capability of the United States?

Dr. SEABORG. I think that I would say that they have not, taking into account the improvements that we are making in our offensive delivery vehicles.

Senator COOPER. I won't go any further into a political question. I will save that for Secretary Rusk.

Thank you.

Senator SPARKMAN. Senator Anderson?

Senator ANDERSON. Thank you, Mr. Chairman.

I am always reassured when I hear testimony from Dr. Seaborg and Dr. Tape and Mr. Ramey. I think we have had a fine presentation. I have no questions, except to express my general view of my confidence in their very fine presentation.

Senator SPARKMAN. Thank you, Dr. Seaborg and your associates, it has been a very helpful hearing.

We have one more witness today. Dr. Robert Strausz-Hupé, director of the Foreign Policy Institute of the University of Pennsylvania. Dr. Strausz-Hupé, if you will come around, we will be glad to hear from you. We welcome you back. We have had the privilege of hearing from you on many occasions and we are glad to hear from you again, sir.

We have a copy of your statement which will be printed in full in the record. You may proceed to read it, discuss it, or summarize it, to present it as you see fit.

STATEMENT OF DR. ROBERT STRAUSZ-HUPÉ, DIRECTOR, FOREIGN POLICY RESEARCH INSTITUTE, UNIVERSITY OF PENNSYLVANIA

Dr. STRAUSZ-HUPÉ. In order to set forth my ideas clearly, Mr. Chairman, would you permit me to read my statement?
Senator SPARKMAN. Yes, indeed.
Dr. STRAUSZ-HUPÉ. Thank you, Mr. Chairman.

REASONS FOR OPPOSING RATIFICATION

International measures for barring the spread of destructive nuclear devices should be a concern of every responsible government. If I urge the U.S. Senate to withhold ratification from the present nuclear Nonproliferation Treaty, I do so because I have found that: First, the present treaty does not provide effective safeguards against the spread of nuclear weapons; second, the present treaty, if ratified by the Senate, will have been concluded at a cost to U.S. national security far greater than the worth of any of its foreseeable benefits to the United States; third, the present treaty, if ratified by the Senate, will commit U.S. foreign policy further and, perhaps irrevocably, to a course which will alienate the allies of the United States, encourage Communist adventurism, and lead to the perilous isolation of the United States in world politics.

TESTIMONY ON TEST BAN TREATY

In August 1963, I had the honor to give testimony before your committee on the partial nuclear Test Ban Treaty. (My statements are contained in hearings before the Committee on Foreign Relations, U.S. Senate, 88th Cong., first sess., 1963; pp. 507–526.)
At that occasion, my principal concerns were the political implications of the treaty. Specifically, I tried to project the likely effects of the treaty upon the posture of the United States in the Atlantic Alliance. Then, I suggested that the political fallout of the treaty would damage the cohesiveness of the Alliance and that, hence, the deleterious consequences of the treaty would be more dangerous to the security of the American people than the radioactive fallout from hypothetical future nuclear tests, which, incidentally, could be prevented by measures much simpler than those stipulated by the treaty. I stated explicitly my views on the relevance of arms control and disarmament agreements to world peace: The danger of armed conflict is proportionate to the intensity of unresolved political conflicts and not to the quantity of arms possessed by the parties to those unresolved conflicts.

EFFECT OF TEST BAN TREATY

During the intervening 5 years, I saw no reason to revise my views as stated to your committee. The treaty did not halt the arms race, for the unresolved political issues which then divided the two principal nuclear powers not only have remain unsettled but have also proliferated into several areas of the globe—Southeast Asia, the Middle East, and this hemisphere—which, at the time of the signing of this treaty, were relatively free of conflict.

Certainly, the Atlantic Alliance has not prospered during the last 5 years. For all practical purposes, France has withdrawn from the North Atlantic Treaty Organization. Several other European members have significantly diminished their commitments to the Alliance—and this despite the fact that the Warsaw Pact forces have not been reduced proportionately. My principal objection to the ratification of the partial nuclear test ban was not so much addressed to the treaty itself, unnecessary and unsatisfactory as it was, as to the turn of U.S. foreign policy which the treaty appeared to mark. According to the communique issued by the United States and the Soviet Union at the occasion of the signing ceremonies in Moscow, the treaty was to be followed by "next steps." Indeed, the treaty opened that era of bilateral United States-Soviet negotiations on arms control and disarmament which not only were paced by significant changes in the strategic doctrine and posture of the United States but also engendered growing tensions within the Atlantic Alliance.

EFFECT ON COMMITMENT TO WESTERN EUROPE

Indeed, Mr. William Foster, Director of the Arms Control and Disarmament Agency, Department of State, explicitly declared the grave risk of Alliance crisis worth taking in order to complete that latest "step" which the Senate has now been asked to approve; namely, the nuclear Nonproliferation Treaty. In the July 1965 issue of "Foreign Affairs," Mr. Foster wrote as follows:

A heavier cost could be the erosion of alliances resulting from the high degree of United States-Soviet cooperation which will be required if a nonproliferation program is to be successful. Within NATO, there could be concern that the détente would lead to a weakening of our commitment to Western Europe. The problem will be particularly acute in Germany where there will be the added concern that the amelioration of the East-West confrontation could lead to an increased acceptance of the status quo in Central Europe.

Not so surprisingly, Mr. Foster's estimate of the treaty's cost effectiveness was received with incredulity and consternation by some of our European allies, including some of our most important and avowedly most cherished ones. The present treaty, if ratified, will nail down the lid on the coffin of NATO.

UNITED STATES ROLE IN NATO ALLIANCE

I am far from asserting that NATO is about to perish because of an excess of arms control agreements. For a long time, NATO has suffered from a variety of diseases. By no means, all of these are routed in the ambiguities of U.S. foreign policy. Some of NATO's ills are rooted in the complacency and frivolity of our European allies; some of them are endemic in the West as a whole, incapable, so it seems, of putting collective security ahead of narrow national self-interest. Although the lesser powers of the Western Alliance have contributed their mite to the present disarray of NATO, the United States bears the heaviest share of the responsibility for the incipient lapse of the

Western Alliance. The reason for this is simple: the United States initiated and led the Alliance, and U.S. power is its mainstay. When the leading, the most powerful member of an alliance falters, the lesser members cannot be expected to advance good order by themselves.

THESIS OF REVISIONISM

The thesis of revisionism—the priority in U.S. foreign policy of bilaterally negotiated arms control and security agreements with the Soviet Union over the maintenance of the Western Alliance—has won an ever increasing number of adherents among our academic experts on international politics and opinion makers. Indeed, one has to embrace this thesis in order to live happily with the nuclear Nonproliferation Treaty. In order to clinch the argument and to still residual doubts about the wisdom of reversing priorities, it is necessary and expedient to reappraise, so the word goes, the uses and usefulness of NATO: If the usefulness of NATO now resides in its serviceability as an instrument for building bridges toward the Soviet Union—the most important and visible bridges being, thus far, arms control agreements—then, obviously, the usefulness of the Alliance's military-strategic arrangements has diminished. In brief, there are other ways, so we are told, for insuring national security and world peace, and NATO, if it proves a hindrance to the relaxation of tensions, should be scrapped. With this argument, the Soviets heartily agree. As a matter of fact, they have made it their own for a long time.

SOVIET FOREIGN POLICY OBJECTIVES

Ever since the founding of NATO, the destruction of the Western military alliance has been a principal objective of Soviet policy, next only in importance to the enfeeblement of U.S. power. In the pursuit of this objective, Soviet policy has been admirably patient, consistent, and adroit. Soviet Foreign Minister Gromyko, informing the Supreme Soviet on June 27, 1968, of the successful negotiation of the nuclear nonproliferation pact, called for the "liquidation of foreign military bases," denounced NATO as an obstacle to arms control and disarmament agreements, and singled out the German Federal Republic as the would be disturber of the peace in Central Europe, haven of "the spirit of the cold war," and source of "threats to the peace."

Unfortunately, only excerpts from Mr. Gromyko's speech to the Supreme Soviet, carefully selected by Tass, were published in the American press. One has to read the full text of Mr. Gromyko's statement in order to savor its flavor. This disdainful and menacing statement bears down hard upon the United States, humbled by defeat in Vietnam; upon America's principal ally in continental Europe, West Germany; and upon America's closest friend in the Middle East, Israel. It throws virtually every cliche of Marxist-Leninist ideology into the teeth of monopolist, capitalist imperialism, equated explicitly with the United States.

Only brief passages are addressed to the nuclear Nonproliferation Treaty, and even this scanty reference belittles the United States and contradicts flatly statements made by U.S. officials. The Soviet Union, not the United States—as asserted by a high official of the Arms Control and Disarmament Agency—took the initiative which has led to the drafting of an agreement on a treaty on nuclear nonproliferation. Those parts of this shocking statement of the Soviet Foreign Minister which do not heap vituperation upon us and our own friends, are mainly concerned with general and complete disarmament, under strict international control, the oldest prop of Soviet propaganda. Let us note here in passing that, thus far, the Soviet Union has indignantly rejected all American proposals for the effective control and verification, made in the course of all United States-Soviet negotiations on arms control to date, and that the control provisions of the nuclear Nonproliferation Treaty do not apply to the existing nuclear powers. Consistent with previous practice, the Soviet Foreign Minister urged all states, above all, the nuclear powers, to discontinue immediately underground tests of nuclear weapons and rejected the necessity of some control [as being] unfounded and farfetched.

DISSOLUTION OF WESTERN ALLIANCE

Mr. Gromyko's statement, hailed by some of our news media as a harbinger of the relaxation of tension, need be placed next to that of Chairman Brezhnev, made on April 25, 1967, to the Conference of European Communist and Workers' Parties at Karlovy-Vary, Czechoslovakia. Mr. Brezhnev spoke as follows, and I quote:

In weighing the opportunities opened up by developments in Europe, we cannot bypass the fact that within 2 years the governments of the NATO countries are to decide whether or not the North Atlantic Treaty is to be extended. In our opinion it is very right that Communists and all progressive forces are endeavoring to make use of this circumstance in order to develop on an ever wider scale the struggle against preserving this aggressive bloc.

As the attentive reader will note readily the two statements—that of the chairman of the party and that of his Foreign Minister—make a perfect fit: Their common targets are the dissolution of the Western alliance, the isolation of our key European allies, the removal of American influence from Europe, and the emasculation of American power. Within the context of Soviet foreign policy, the nuclear Nonproliferation Treaty is simply a means to this end.

SOVIET UNION GAINS THROUGH PROPOSED TREATY

The Soviet Union has nothing to lose and much to gain by the ratification of the nuclear Nonproliferation Treaty. The fact is that the United States, but for its collaboration with Britain dating back to World War II, has not shared its nuclear weapon knowledge with anybody. The Soviets have assisted Red China in developing a nuclear arsenal. The Soviets have never had the intention of giving nuclear weapons to any other Communist state—and this for the reason that: (1) Their strategic posture, especially their military presence in Eastern Europe, does not require such largesse; and, (2) Their mistrust of the satellite people rules out nuclear weapons in potentially hostile hands.

PROPOSED MULTILATERAL FORCE

The United States, by contrast, could well afford to place nuclear weapons, especially defensive nuclear weapons, in the hands of some of our allies and friends. If we were to do so we need not fear a nuclear surprise attack by, let us say, Australia, New Zealand, Canada, Israel, the German Federal Republic, and India. Of course, the United States never proposed to make such a distribution. The United States did envisage, however, the possibility of a NATO nuclear force—the modest proposal for a multilateral force (MLF) tried awkwardly to translate this vision into operational reality—and, albeit vaguely, the creation of a European nuclear force. The original American draft of 1965 for the nuclear Nonproliferation Treaty contained the following provisions:

Each of the nuclear States Party to this Treaty undertakes . . . not to take any other action which would cause an increase in the total number of States and other organizations having independent power to use nuclear weapons (and) not to assist any nonnuclear state in the manufacture of nuclear weapons.

Each of the nonnuclear States Party to this Treaty undertakes not to manufacture nuclear weapons . . . not to take any other action which would cause an increase in the total number of States and other organizations having independent power to use nuclear weapons (and) not to seek or to receive assistance in the manufacture of nuclear weapons, or itself to grant such assistance.

Under this provision, the United States could have assisted a united Europe to build a joint nuclear force, for such a development would not increase the "total" number of nuclear weapons states. The Soviet objection prevailed, and the clauses were dropped.

EFFECT OF TREATY ON A UNITED EUROPE

The present nuclear treaty does not allow for the creation of an European defense association and other intermediate steps leading to the creation of a European federal state, possessed of effective nuclear defense. According to press reports, the Government of the United States does not view the treaty as denying a united Europe the right—subject to transfer of all powers over foreign and defense policy to the European federal state—to become a military nuclear power. Even if this interpretation were valid—and nothing in the present treaty says it is—a united Europe would be blocked from all interim solutions leading to the establishment of a full-fledged European federal state. Even if a federal European state would be established, the United States would not be able to offer it any support in developing a collective nuclear deterrent for, according to paragraph 3 of article IX, only states "which had manufactured and exploded a nuclear weapon or other nuclear explosive device prior to January 1, 1967," are to be regarded as being nuclear weapon states. This provision closes the door to the future with considerable finality.

Since the present treaty does not differentiate between defensive and offensive nuclear weapons, the nonnuclear members of NATO will be unable to develop their own antiballistic missile systems. Although it might be possible in the future to set up a purely defensive ABM system, it is highly doubtful that, under the provisions of the treaty, these member states could acquire the needed technology. Some highly qualified experts believe that such a system could be devised. If it can be made operational, it will be as essential to the defense of Western Europe as it would be to the defense of U.S. territory, for 700 Soviet ballistic missiles are zeroed in upon West European targets. Thus, the constraints of the treaty weigh heavily upon the future of Western Europe—all the more heavily because no responsible West ern statesman can now assert categorically that NATO can continue to guarantee the safety of Europe during the next 20 years as it has done during the past 20 years.

If anyone can be relied upon to understand the implications of the present treaty for the security of Western Europe, it is surely the Soviets. More likely than not, Western Europe, during the last few years, has not been in danger of an all-out Soviet armed assault. With a few notable exceptions, the Soviets have always preferred piecemeal conquest to a risky all-out challenge. The nuclear Nonproliferation Treaty, because it hamstrings any European attempt at building a viable system of self-defense, supplies the Soviets with vast oppor- tunities for exercising psychological pressures upon individual Euro- pean states, notably the German Federal Republic.

WEST GERMANY AS KEYSTONE TO DEFENSE OF EUROPE

No one knows better than do the Soviets that the German Federal Republic is the keystone of NATO's defense in Europe. To pry loose this keystone has been the principal objective of Soviet policy in Europe. In order to accomplish this purpose, the Soviet propagan- dists have sought to alienate the other Western democracies from Ger- many and the Germans from the West. In this endeavor the Soviets have tirelessly resorted to one and the same propaganda ploy; namely, the allegation that West Germany wants to develop its own nuclear force and, thus armed, refight the Second World War. The fact is that the German Federal Republic never voiced any desire for a national nuclear deterrent. West German public opinion has overwhelmingly endorsed the case for nuclear continence. And even if the West Ger- mans harbored in their dark hearts the longing for nuclear weapons, the West European Union would make it its business to nip in the bud a West German nuclear deterrent. Under the agreement with the WEU, which ratified the German Federal Republic's access to NATO, West Germany renounced the possession of nuclear, biological, and chemical weapons. The agreement provides for a tight system of on- site inspection, far tighter than any system of inspection contemplated by arms control agreements concluded between the United States and the Soviet Union. It is necessary to expose and to squash the Soviet canard of German nuclear concupiscence. This baseless allega- tion has served the Soviets well in their successful resistance to the inclusion of the so-called European clause in the draft nonprolifera- tion treaty.

I said in my opening remarks that, deeply concerned as I had been about specific provisions of the partial nuclear test ban which I con- sidered adverse to the best interests of the United States, I was even more disturbed by its foreseeable impact upon the overall environment of Western security. Today, I am as much concerned about the package in which the present treaty is being delivered to us as with the treaty itself.

UNRESOLVED POLITICAL ISSUES BETWEEN THE UNITED STATES AND U.S.S.R.

None of the basic political issues of the protracted conflict between the Soviet Union and ourselves have been resolved. New conflicts loom on the horizon. All one needs to do in order to ascertain the true state of the United States-Soviet confrontation, is to read Mr. Gromyko's statement of June 27, 1968. Since then, Mr. Leonid I. Brezhnev, the real boss of the Soviet Union, speaking at a rally honoring the Hungarian Premier Kadar, liquidator of the Hungarian rising in 1956, inveighed against the "rotten, degrading, decaying society" of the United States; denounced American "political gangsterism"—let us forget a myriad of political murders in the Soviet Union—and called for a rising of the "working class" and the "civil rights movement" against "monopolist America." Anxious to eradicate the unpleasant impression which Mr. Brezhnev's remark might have engendered in American public opinion, a metropolitan daily, eager to shield its readers' "good feelings" against the icy blast of Mr. Brezhnev's rhetoric, wrote as follows:

Mr. Brezhnev's denunciation of the United States seems to have the purpose of proclaiming publicly that the Soviet Union was not seeking an accommodation with the United States to the detriment of its basic Communist philosophy.

Of such statements is made the euphoria of American public opinion—the euphoria necessary to mask the true implications of the nuclear Nonproliferation Treaty.

UNITED STATES-U.S.S.R. DISARMAMENT NEGOTIATIONS

Two days before Mr. Brezhnev spoke, President Johnson, at the occasion of the signing of the nuclear Nonproliferation Treaty in Washington, advised the American people that another step toward arms control was now in the offing. The President said:

Now at this moment of achievement and great hope, I am gratified to be able to report and to announce to the world a significant agreement—an agreement that we've actively sought and worked for since January 1964.

Agreement has been reached between the Governments of the Union of Socialist Republics and the United States to enter in the nearest future into discussions on the limitation and the reduction of both offensive strategic nuclear weapons delivery systems and systems of defense against ballistic missiles.

The prehistory of President Johnson's statement of July 1, 1968, bears closer examination. On January 27, 1967, Johnson wrote to Premier Kosygin, suggesting measures to limit the missile competition before the United States would make a final decision to deploy antimissile defenses. Five weeks later, the President announced that Premier Kosygin had confirmed the willingness of the Soviet Government to discuss means of limiting the arms race in offensive and defensive nuclear missiles. Now, 15 months later, the Soviet Union again expresses its readiness to hold an exchange of opinion on the limitation and reduction of strategic delivery system—as one point in a nine-point memorandum on steps to reduce the arms race, linking this offer to proposals which have frequently been rejected by the United States in the past, and which cannot possibly be accepted now or in the fore-seeable future.

If the Soviet Union insists on linking certain arms measures to other measures, as it has usually done in the past nothing can be expected to come from the "significant agreement" announced by President John-son. I, for one, cannot understand what is either new or significant about it. Certainly, it should not be taken as placing a premium on the ratification of the nuclear Nonproliferation Treaty. The treaty should be ratified on its own merit and not because it is supposed to preface some other, yet to be concluded agreement with the Soviets.

EFFECT OF TREATY ON U.S. FOREIGN POLICY

On its own merits, the nuclear Nonproliferation Treaty does not deserve the ratification of the Senate. As I have attempted to show, its provisions hobble U.S. foreign policy, discriminate against Amer-ica's friends, and in no way restrict the Soviet Union's freedom of action in world politics. More important still, the treaty, if ratified, would stand as another monument to the West's fundamental mis-understanding of the difference between a free society and a totali-tarian society.

TOTALITARIAN GOVERNMENT ATTITUDE TOWARD INTERNATIONAL AGREEMENTS

International agreement does not mean to a totalitarian government what it means to a democratic people. An arms control agreement has never meant and does not mean to a militant Communist, steeped in the dialectic of conflict, what it means to a democratic statesman, steeped in the doctrine of international cooperation. There is no mystery as to why the Soviets' negotiators proved relatively pliable as regards the treaty's provisions for control: a democratic, an open society controls itself and a free press can be relied upon to ferret out and to denounce any treaty violations by the national government. A totalitarian gov-ernment need not worry about the disclosure of violations by its own well-muzzled citizens. The democratic government commits itself to an international treaty with considerable finality; the domestic oppo-sition to the incumbent government would put a breach of the treaty, solemnly signed and solemnly ratified, to its own political advantage. A totalitarian government can reverse course without having to bother about public opinion, and make and break treaties with the greatest of ease, as easily as the Soviet Union, in 1939, concluded a treaty of al-liance with its archenemy, Nazi Germany.

A totalitarian government can confront the world and its own people with accomplished facts—and then, at leisure, negotiate with demo-cratic governments which have to abide by the measured pace of constitutional process. The Soviets acceded to the conclusion of the partial nuclear Test Ban Treaty after they had carried out a series of nuclear megaton tests in the atmosphere and before the United States was able to duplicate these tests—incidentally, very "dirty" ones. In the wake of the nuclear Nonproliferation Treaty, the Soviet Union might or might not be willing to discuss a "mutual limitation" on the deployment of antimissile systems. The Soviet Union has deployed an advanced ABM system around several of its major cities; the United States has not as yet deployed its Sentinel system. There seems to be a fudamental asymmetry in negotiating arms control agreements—and for that matter, any agreement—between a representative government like the United States and a dictatorship like the Communist Party in Russia.

BURDENS OF AN ARMS RACE

According to Foreign Minister Gromyko, the Soviet Union is eager to relieve mankind from the burden of the arms race. To be sure, the American taxpayer, too, would like to pay less for arms and, if pay he must, contribute to the cost of domestic welfare rather than to economically unrewarding undertakings. Implicit in the administration's advocacy of the present treaty's ratification is the promise of a reduced defense budget. To put it simply, the American people "want out" of costly international commitments and put their money into pressing domestic business as, for example, a higher standard of living, a better education for all, and the renovation of our cities. These are laudable intentions. The fiscal policies of this administration are supposed to be directed toward this end. To ease the implementation of these policies, it would be opportune to extract savings from the Defense Budget and to allocate funds thus saved to domestic projects. If it were possible to halt what is called the arms race, it would be possible, so the argument runs, to enjoy national security as well as rising prosperity for all.

If the nuclear Nonproliferation Treaty could mark the turning point of the arms race, then the American people could do what they want to do and need to do at home without paying additional taxes. But, at this point, the question needs be asked as to whether we have kept up in the arms race.

The war in Vietnam obscured the most important features of our defense budget: according to the financial summary of our defense budget in 1968, the total defense outlay is $78 billion. Deducting the costs of the war in Vietnam, less than $50 billion remains for the upkeep of our defense establishments. Of this sum, $9.6 billion are allocated to our strategic forces, the heart and center of our defense against a nuclear attack by the Soviet Union. This amount represents a reduction by about 15 percent from the outlay for our strategic forces in 1962. Although inflation has done its work, our gross national product has risen more rapidly than our defense budget, including the cost of the war in Vietnam. In brief, the American people are paying out a smaller share of their national income for national defense than they did in the early sixties—years which, according to official statements, were years of rising national prosperity.

RISE OF U.S.S.R. DEFENSE BUDGET

In the meanwhile, the defense budget of the Soviet Union, in spite of several agricultural crises and the alleged pressures of consumer demands, has been rising at an ever accelerating rate—reflecting, according to former Defense Secretary McNamara, "the continual expansion of the Soviet defense effort." According to reliable estimates, available to your committee, the Soviet defense budget allocated to strategic forces, especially missilry, space vehicles and Navy, equals our own. Who is racing whom? It is reasonable to assume that the Soviet Union will fall voluntarily behind us in defense expenditure and that the nuclear Nonproliferation Treaty will induce the Soviets to declare a moratorium on the "arms race" when they are just about to overtake us in the effectiveness of their strategic forces?

U.S. WORLD AND DOMESTIC COMMITMENTS

It is simply not true that, because we are supporting the commitments of the world's leading power, we cannot do at home what, as a civilized people, we ought to do. A people certain of its purpose and poise in its might has no trouble ordering its priorities and will, if need be, submit itself to austerity in order to achieve those things which must come first. As Mr. Brezhnev's and Mr. Gromyko's fulminations and a series of barefaced provocations from the Bering Strait to the Atlantic Ocean clearly show, the Soviets believe that they have us on the ropes. They believe—there can be no other explanation for their conduct—that the United States, a groggy giant tottering under the burden of Vietnam and the strains of domestic insurrection and mired in the sloth of affluence, cannot stand up to the challenge of political revolution abroad and technical revolution at home. They believe that our Government will sign anything—even the most foolish of treaties— in order to buy a temporary respite from public censure. In brief, the Soviets believe that we cannot act rationally and want to deceive ourselves.

REJECTION OF TREATY URGED

I urge the U.S. Senate to reject the nuclear Nonproliferation Treaty.

The present document is riddled with ambiguities. The treaty, if it were ratified, would tie our hands in world politics, the fact notwithstanding that critical political issues the world over may give rise to now unpredictable situations.

The treaty, if ratified, would discriminate against our friends and, for good, alienate some of the best among them. I urge the Senate not only to reject the present treaty but also the package in which it and other measures of arms control have been offered to its scrutiny.

Just as in the case of the partial nuclear test ban, the avowed purposes of the present treaty could be accomplished more effectively by simpler arrangements than those stipulated by the present treaty. In most real world cases, a bilateral understanding between the United States and the two other nuclear weapons countries, the Soviet Union and the United Kingdom, would suffice to prevent the spread of nuclear weapons.

If France and Red China will not sign the present treaty and if they were to decide upon handing out nuclear weapons, there is nothing that the signatories of the treaty—as signatories—can do about it. Of course, the nuclear weapon states of the present treaty might take unilateral action against the uncommitted proliferators. But is this not where we came in in the first place?

The dangers of nuclear weapons falling into irresponsible or criminal hands is growing, and nowhere is this danger greater than in the world under Communist control or influence. The present treaty does not supply an effective remedy to such a contingency. To the contrary, because of the propagandistic claims made on its behalf, the treaty, if it were ratified, would lull the free peoples of the world into a false sense of security.

This is precisely the reason why the Soviets want the United States to conclude the treaty—and during this critical period of debate, might even refrain from slapping us in the face.

I urge you, Mr. Chairman, and the Senate to reject the present treaty.

Senator SPARKMAN. Thank you very much, Doctor, for a very powerful presentation, I would say.

EFFECT OF TREATY ON WESTERN EUROPE

I shall be very brief in my questions. Let me ask you to comment on this question. General Wheeler, in his testimony, the second day of our hearings, said:

* * * in the long term, I believe that this treaty, if followed out, if adhered to by the majority of the nations of the world, will serve to create a better atmosphere in Europe and elsewhere which will serve the interests of all countries.

It seems to me that is somewhat different from your attitude. I wonder of you would comment on that.

Dr. STRAUSZ-HUPÉ. Mr. Chairman, Lord Keynes said in the long run we are all dead, and in the long run this may well be true if the treaty is signed, implemented, faithfully observed by all parties. If all this happens there might be a general feeling of relaxation of tension in Europe and elsewhere.

My field is international politics and I have learned one thing; namely, not to believe that I can foresee anything beyond the next 18 months or two years, and, if I can foresee something within that period, I think I am very, very good.

So I can only talk about the visible implications of the treaty, the impact of the treaty here and now upon our alliance system, the impact which its negotiation has already had upon our alliance system.

This is not the future; this is the past. And I suggest that the implications of the negotiation of the treaty have been disastrous for NATO.

PROLIFERATION OF NUCLEAR WEAPONS

Senator SPARKMAN. Are you disturbed in your thinking on the problem of the proliferation or threatened proliferation of nuclear weapons?

Dr. STRAUSZ-HUPÉ. I am very much concerned with the proliferation of nuclear weapons. I wish we could think of devices to prevent it.

My argument is that this treaty does not prevent it. As a matter of fact, this treaty opens more doors than it closes, and last, but not least, this treaty does nothing to resolve the fundamental policy differences between its signatories as I sought to advert to in my statement. It is really the package I am concerned with, rather than the treaty itself.

I mean, I will go so far as to say great powers break treaties when they have to.

If it were a matter of life and death for the United States, we would break this treaty. But that is not what I am concerned about. I am not concerned so much with the merits of this treaty, although I think it has many demerits, but what I am concerned with is the place of this treaty within the overall context of U.S. foreign policy, and I do not think that enough attention has been given to this broader context.

BILATERAL AGREEMENTS TO CONTROL PROLIFERATION

Senator SPARKMAN. As I understand it, you would prefer control of the proliferation of nuclear weapons through bilateral agreements between the three great nuclear powers. You did not include France. You named just the three; did you not?

Dr. STRAUSZ-HUPÉ. I mentioned the three powers in the treaty.

Senator SPARKMAN. Yes.

Dr. STRAUSZ-HUPÉ. But that does not necessarily mean that we could not on a purely pragmatic basis, given a specific case, conclude an agreement with anyone we want.

Let us say country X, under an irresponsible government, has on the black market acquired nuclear weapons. Well, in this case, we, the United States, have complete diplomatic freedom of action to make whatever agreements we want to make with the most suitable and most interested countries in order to take these black market nuclear weapons away from that particular country.

Incidentally, this is all that the United Nations' guarantee, to which Senator Cooper adverted, amounts to. I mean, in order to implement this guarantee, we still would have to make bilateral agreements with other countries that would assist us or do it by ourselves alone. We do not need the treaty for that.

SHOULD WEST GERMANY SIGN TREATY?

Senator SPARKMAN. There has come up from time to time at these hearings, the question of the position of West Germany. What would be your thought as to what West Germany should do? Should it become a party to this treaty?

Dr. STRAUSZ-HUPÉ. Well, fortunately, I am not in their shoes, Mr. Chairman. I do not know what I would do if I were a German.

As an American, I would hope that the treaty would either be not ratified or it would be so amended that it would take into consideration the legitimate interests not only of West Germany, but of all members of NATO which, I believe, this treaty does not sufficiently consider.

Now there can be no doubt that there is a change of sentiment in Germany. In many ways, what is happening in Germany today is a self fulfilling prophecy. I mean, to some extent, the Germans feel discriminated against by this treaty. This feeling, of course, works to the advantage of the most nationalistic and reactionary elements in Germany.

Reacting to this feeling of discrimination, these nationalist elements in Germany misbehave. This reaction is then published in our press.

The Americans say, "Well, you see, the Germans," and this is really nothing else but a feedback of what we ourselves have done. Other forces are certainly at play here, but our influence in Germany and over German public opinion is immense.

TREATY MAY BE COUNTERPRODUCTIVE TO NUCLEAR STABILIZATION

Senator SPARKMAN. In an unsigned article in Orbis magazine, dated winter 1968, which I assume you either wrote or approved of, there is a statement from which I want to quote:

While the spread of nuclear weapons may be basically destabilizing, its strategic consequences need not be too severe nor necessarily uncontrollable. Thus the attitude of desperation that has attended the negotiation of the non-proliferation treaty is not merely inaccurate and inappropriate, but may well be counterproductive to the efforts of the United States to achieve stabilization.

If you agree with this statement, would you elaborate on that point?

Dr. STRAUSZ-HUPÉ. I would be very glad to, Mr. Chairman.

It really attaches onto a statement I made and a statement I just read.

I would like to see the United States to be free to make such arrangements with its allies that their local defense, their national defense, could be secured in certain cases without immediately triggering the intervention of the United States.

I have a horror of nuclear weapons, I have a horror of all weapons. I personally think a bayonet is vastly more displeasing than a nuclear bomb.

I loathe weapons, but weapons are used in national defense, and I can well conceive of certain countries finding themselves in a position where they must rely on defensive nuclear weapons, that is, weapons that cannot be used for offensive purposes, for example, nuclear landmines such as those, I understand, were requested by the Turks under international control.

Now, I see nothing heinous in such a defensive arrangement. If the Soviets were to attack Turkey, and Soviet troops would step on these landmines and they would go off, well, the provocation would be the Soviets and not the Turks.

I think in these cases we might well relieve ourselves of some of our excessive burdens as "policemen of the world" by giving more powerful local defense to certain of our allies.

Senator SPARKMAN. Thank you.

Senator Cooper.

Senator COOPER. I want to agree with you, Mr. Chairman, that the Doctor has made a very powerful statement.

You said that you are troubled with this treaty, chiefly because of its adverse relationship to the foreign policy of the United States, I believe.

Dr. STRAUSZ-HUPÉ. Yes, sir.

ALLEGATION THAT U.S. IS CHIEF AGENT IN DETERIORATION OF NATO

Senator COOPER. It would seem to me you have questioned it upon two grounds, among others, but two very strongly: one, the effect it would have upon our European Allies, NATO, the Atlantic Alliance, and, second, the effect it would have upon the security arrangements of the United States.

You make this statement:

Although the lesser powers of the Western Alliance have contributed their mite to the present disarray of NATO, the United States bears the heaviest share of the responsibility for the incipient lapse of the Western Alliance.

Looking back over the years, is it not correct that the United States has kept in Europe approximately 300,000 troops, that it has pledged under the NATO agreement that an attack upon any part of the NATO area is an attack upon the United States; that it has risked war several times in breaking obstructions to passage to Berlin, such as President after President has said that the United States would assure the integrity of Berlin, and that we did not know for a time whether it was a very sound proposition or not to enter into the multilateral nuclear force with Europe, with NATO.

Is it not correct, on the other hand, that no other country of NATO has kept up its promised forces; that France has effectively removed itself from NATO as a military alliance?

On all those grounds, how can you say that the United States is the chief agent contributing to the present situation in NATO?

Dr. STRAUSZ-HUPÉ. Senator, the United States has an enormous investment in Europe. The best part of this investment is the good will of the European peoples. Every item you cited has been put to profitable use and could give us an ample return, a far greater return than we can get from any other area of the globe.

What bothers me, not only about this treaty but about the philosophy from which it is derived, is that this philosophy and this kind of bilateral dealing with the Soviet Union is imperiling that great investment.

We have the peoples of Europe and their majority on our side. This is why I am deeply concerned with the way in which this treaty is playing into the hands of our enemies.

Of course, we have enemies in Europe, especially the Communists. It is playing into their hands, it is creating doubts about the commitments of the United States.

There is a fundamental ambiguity in our policy. On the one hand, we are saying that NATO must be strengthened. We have made this great investment, we have our troops in Europe, the first bulwark of European defense.

Yet, on the other hand, we are negotiating bilaterally over the heads of our allies with the very power against which these security arrangements are made. There is a contradiction in it.

CONSULTATION WITH EUROPEAN ALLIES

Senator COOPER. Secretary Rusk and others have testified that we did not enter into this agreement except after consultation with our allies in Europe.

Dr. STRAUSZ-HUPÉ. Well, I am not privy to the negotiations in the Council of NATO, but it is my understanding that the line between consultation and information is at times very thinly drawn.

EUROPE OR NATO AS A NUCLEAR POWER

Senator Cooper. I would have to agree with you on that from my own experience here. But are you suggesting that there should be leeway outside this treaty, if it were not agreed to, for Europe or NATO, to become a nuclear power, either defensively or offensively?

Dr. Strausz-Hupé. I would like to see the door kept open to such a development, and this is precisely the so-called European clause in our 1965 draft did. That was the right intention and that was the right way to implement it.

Senator Cooper. Do you know of any indication or desire on the part of any European country, particularly our NATO allies, to build an offensive nuclear system or defensive nuclear system? France?

Dr. Strausz-Hupé. I think there are within many circles in Europe, that is, in intellectual circles, and in quite a number of political parties, people who believe that there is only one solution for Europe, and that is the consolidation of European resources in one authority. This would, of course, mean the merger, the consolidation, of the nuclear resources for war and for peace.

As a matter of fact, this is an idea which preoccupies a great many of the leading industrialists of Europe, leading financiers, leading economists, and most certainly, all people in Europe who are still fired by the idea of a united Europe.

There is another school of thought which believes that all that should be done under the roof of NATO, that there should be an independent NATO nuclear force in which the United States, naturally, would have the largest stake and probably also the most important controlling voice.

But the development to both of these goals, I mean, the path to both of these goals, is blocked by this treaty.

ADVANTAGE TO UNITED STATES OF ADDITIONAL NUCLEAR POWERS

Senator Cooper. You spoke in the latter part of your statement that you wanted to discuss this treaty with the Senate of the United States upon its merits. The United States, the Soviet Union, France, and China purportedly have developed nuclear weapons.

What advantage would it be for the United States, for additional countries to develop nuclear weapons?

Dr. Strausz-Hupé. None; none. As a matter of fact, I mean an unlimited proliferation would be disastrous.

Senator Cooper. Doesn't this treaty then have that advantage that it does impose the prohibition upon other countries which have the power and the capabilities of developing nuclear weapons?

Dr. Strausz-Hupé. I do not believe that this treaty really prevents it. I do not think this treaty is really so designed and so armed with inspection and control devices that we could really be sure that this would not happen.

But I have not been speaking about an unlimited, indiscriminate proliferation of weapons. I am talking about a selective policy of nuclear armament.

The creation of a European nuclear force or of a NATO nuclear force, far from engendering proliferation, would actually reduce the present number of nuclear states.

I believe, what I hope is, that U.S. policy will keep open options, will remain flexible enough to deal with now unforeseeable contingencies, and to help in a development which for a long time we have been committed.

President Kennedy on July 4, 1962, at Philadelphia, went as far as any American President has ever gone toward saying that we ought to have an Atlantic convention, we ought to have discussions about how to establish an Atlantic authority.

Well, I cannot conceive of an Atlantic authority or of any kind of Atlantic development that sooner or later is not brought face to face with this problem of the control of nuclear weapons.

CAREFUL EXAMINATION OF TREATY URGED

Senator COOPER. I would say that I think your testimony is valuable in this respect it requires the Congress and the people to examine the merits of this treaty carefully.

I must say that I, in reading the treaty for the first time, was rather unimpressed with the language in the preamble dealing with the problem of disarmament. I noted that it was practically in the same language as the Soviet Union has always used, under strict and effective international control.

I would say also that while the declarations of the Soviet Union and the United States and the United Kingdom to the United Nations are valuable as statements, I hope the policy will be observed. The statement alone I could not view as a very effective sanction to protect this treaty.

I remember also that shortly after we had agreed to the Outer Space Treaty, the Soviet Union announced the development of its FOBS, fractional orbital bombardment system, and I did wonder if the administration at the time of the development of the treaty, in their testimony before the Congress, was frank in telling us about it. They would argue that it is a ballistic missile, but it is also a missile which can be used in outer space. The only thing they said about it was that it did not violate the treaty because it would be orbiting in outer space rather than circling round the earth.

This, it would seem to me, is an unreasonable and misleading statement.

So I think your testimony has value because it will require our committee and the Congress to explore all of the statements that have been made, particularly in light of what we were not told during the hearings on the Outer Space Treaty about FOBS. I thought later statements made to justify not being told about FOBS were weak.

That is all.

Senator SPARKMAN. Thank you very much, Doctor.

We appreciate your appearance and your testimony.

Our next hearing session will be Wednesday, July 17, at 10 a.m., and will be held in room 4221 of the New Senate Office Building, the regular committee hearing room.

At that time we hope to conclude the hearings on this treaty.

The committee is recessed until Wednesday, at 10 a.m.

(Whereupon, at 12:35 p.m., the committee adjourned, to reconvene at 10 a.m., Wednesday, July 17, 1968.)

NONPROLIFERATION TREATY

UNITED STATES SENATE,
COMMITTEE ON FOREIGN RELATIONS,
Washington, D.C.

The committee met, pursuant to recess, at 10 a.m., in room 4221, New Senate Office Building, Senator John Sparkman presiding.

Present: Senators Sparkman, Lausche, Clark, Pell, Hickenlooper, Aiken, Carlson, Case, and Cooper.

Also present: Senators Pastore and Curtis of the Joint Committee on Atomic Energy.

Senator SPARKMAN. Let the committee come to order, please.

This morning the Committee on Foreign Relations continues its hearings on the Nonproliferation Treaty. We are very glad to have the witnesses with us today. We have quite a list, so we shall try to move right along.

Our first witness is Hon. Chet Holifield of California, a man with whom I served many years in the House of Representatives. Congressman Holifield is vice chairman of the Joint Committee on Atomic Energy. Congressman Holifield, we are very glad to have you. We have your statement. You may proceed with it as you see fit.

STATEMENT OF HON. CHET HOLIFIELD, U.S. CONGRESSMAN FROM CALIFORNIA, VICE CHAIRMAN, JOINT COMMITTEE ON ATOMIC ENERGY

Mr. HOLIFIELD. Mr. Chairman, I appear before you this morning in support of the Nonproliferation Treaty and I want to thank you for giving me the opportunity to do so.

Before setting forth the reasons I believe the Nonproliferation Treaty is in the best interests of the United States and the rest of the world, I would like the record to show my background and experience in the atomic energy field. I make this request not because I seek any credit or praise from this committee or others, but because I believe my long association and study in the atomic energy field has given me some knowledge and experience with which to better judge the pros and cons of the dangers of nuclear weapon proliferation than others who have not had the benefit of such experience.

EXPERIENCE IN ATOMIC ENERGY FIELD

My work in the atomic energy field began in the 79th Congress shortly after the public first became aware of the atomic bomb when the House Committee on Military Affairs of which I was a member was given the task of drafting legislation for the best method of controlling this awesome power.

I might say I served with the acting chairman at that time, I believe, on that committee.

Senator SPARKMAN. That is correct.

Mr. HOLIFIELD. Together with a number of my colleagues in the House and in the Senate, I successfully fought for the principles contained in the McMahon-Douglas bill, which placed the control of atomic energy in the hands of civilians rather than under the control of the military as proposed by the original May-Johnson bill. In 1946, when the McMahon Act was passed establishing the Joint Committee on Atomic Energy, I was one of the original appointees to that committee and I have served continuously on that committee for over 22 years. For the past 8 years—since 1961, I have served alternately with Senator John Pastore as chairman and vice chairman.

The Joint Committee on Atomic Energy is unique in many ways. Its greatest strength and effectiveness, I believe, lies in its access to information. The Atomic Energy Commission is required to keep the Joint Committee fully and currently informed of all its activities. The Defense Department is required to keep the committee fully and currently informed with respect to all matters within the Defense Department relating to atomic energy, and all Government agencies are required to furnish any information requested by the Joint Committee with respect to that agency's activities in the field of atomic energy. The committee consequently has access on a continuing and current basis to the most detailed classified information available in the atomic field.

During my 22 years of membership on the Joint Committee on Atomic Energy, I and other members of the committee have participated in a number of major policy decisions involving nuclear weapons. I headed up an ad hoc committee formed in 1949, which was created under the chairmanship of the late Senator Brien McMahon to make a study as to whether or not the United States should make an all out effort to develop a thermonuclear weapon. We concluded and recommended to President Truman that an all out effort should be made to develop the H-bomb despite the fact that the Scientific Advisory Committee, without dissent, opposed the project, and I might add that three out of five of the members of the Atomic Energy Commission also opposed it.

Fortunately, President Truman ordered the project to proceed, and the United States obtained a thermonuclear device less than 10 months ahead of the Soviet Union, although we had been more than 4 years ahead of the Russians in testing the atomic bomb.

INVESTIGATION OF NUCLEAR COOPERATION WITH NATO

In 1960 and 1961, I headed up a special ad hoc committee that made a detailed investigation of our nuclear weapons cooperation arrangements within NATO. This involved onsite inspection of NATO nuclear weapon stockpile sites, custody arrangements, training procedures, and deployment plans as well as detailed war plans.

This study resulted in a top secret report to President Kennedy, unanimously adopted by the Joint Committee, containing a number of recommendations which the President adopted. Some of the recommendations which have been made public by the executive branch included the removal of Jupiter IRBM missiles from Turkey and Italy because of their extreme vulnerability and other related problems; the development and installation of permissive action links (PAL), which are electronic and mechanical locks to prevent the unintentional and unauthorized detonation of nuclear weapons; and the development of greater security procedures in the protection of the NATO nuclear stockpile. In addition, our report had a great deal to do with efforts to increase the conventional weapons capability of NATO and a more realistic understanding of how nuclear weapons would be utilized in time of war.

In 1965, in an effort to develop a better understanding by our NATO allies in the decisionmaking process and the devastating effects of nuclear warfare, I recommended to Harlan Cleveland, the U.S. Ambassador to NATO, that arrangements be made whereby our NATO allies could more actively participate in the decisionmaking process as to when and under what conditions nuclear weapons would be used in the defense of Europe. This resulted in the establishment of the NATO Nuclear Planning Group.

As I indicated in the beginning of my statement, I have recited some of my experience and background in the atomic energy field for the sole purpose of establishing my credentials as one who has some knowledge and experience in this field on which to base my decision to support the Nonproliferation Treaty.

U.S. POLICY NOT TO ENCOURAGE NUCLEAR NATIONS

I believe it is in the best interests of this Nation to be a signatory to the Nonproliferation Treaty because it is a logical sequence in the historical position taken by the United States not, I repeat, to encourage additional nuclear weapon nations—a position we have continuously adhered to from the very beginning. The original McMahon Act in 1946, first by interpretation and then by specific amendment in 1951, prohibited the United States from exchanging weapons design and fabrication information with other nations. The McMahon Act also prohibited the transfer by the United States to other nations of fissionable material. The Atomic Energy Act of 1954 made major changes in the original McMahon Act permitting greater cooperation with the other nations in the peaceful uses of atomic energy. It also permitted under agreements for cooperation and appropriate safeguards the communication to our allies of certain limited atomic weapon information necessary to the development defense plans, the training of personnel and the evaluation of nuclear weapon capabilities of potential enemies. Communication of atomic weapon design and fabrication information was limited to external characteristics, effects, and the system employed in their delivery providing the data did not reveal important information which would assist a nation in developing its own independent nuclear weapon capability.

Subsequent to Sputnik in October 1957, the Eisenhower administration proposed a greater scientific and technical collaboration with our allies and in 1958 proposed some major revisions to the Atomic Energy Act to provide for increased cooperation with our allies in the military uses of atomic energy. Detailed hearings held by the Joint Committee on the proposed amendments revealed that the changes proposed could have made it possible, if fully implemented, for nonweapon nations to obtain an independent nuclear weapon capability. The proposed amendments would have authorized the United States to transfer special nuclear material for use in nuclear weapons, nonnuclear parts of atomic weapons, and design and fabrication information on atomic weapons to our allies. As we characterized it at the time, these, in effect, would be a do-it-yourself kit.

The Department of Defense, the State Department, and the Atomic Energy Commission at that time testified that it was not the intent nor the desire of the executive branch to encourage additional nuclear weapon nations and there was no intention to assist other countries to develop an independent nuclear weapon capability.

Accordingly, the Joint Committee redrafted significant portions of the proposed legislation to assure that any cooperation with our allies in the military uses of atomic energy did not lead to assisting a nonnuclear weapon nation to achieve independent weapon capability. Thus the Atomic Energy Act as originally drafted and as it continues to date has as an objective the nonproliferation of nuclear weapons and it prohibits the transfer of nuclear weapons to any nation except in time of war when under the powers of the Constitution the President may exercise such authority as Commander in Chief.

Several years ago, there was an aborted attempt by a small group within the executive branch to foster the so-called multilateral force concept which in its final state would have permitted the transfer of nuclear weapons and their control to a group of nations. The members of the Joint Committee on Atomic Energy who studied and analyzed the proposed concept concluded that it was neither desirable nor practical, and I think we can take some credit for the demise of the MLF.

I recite this history to demonstrate the attitude and actions of the Joint Committee in their consistent guardianship of nonproliferation of weapons or classified weapon design information. We believe this treaty maintains that policy.

QUESTION OF U.S. FLEXIBILITY TO TRANSFER WEAPONS

Those who oppose this treaty on the basis that we must maintain a flexibility which would allow the United States to transfer weapons to another nation in some hypothetical future situation have not proven their point. The inherent power based in the Commander in Chief to protect our Nation in a state of war would not be changed by the treaty, and this is very important.

In all the testimony we have received over the years from our military leaders and our NATO commanders, at no time has the Joint Committee been informed that it was necessary to transfer ownership and control of nuclear weapons to other nations for their effective assignment within NATO. We have repeatedly been told that the current arrangements whereby nuclear weapons are maintained under U.S. custody and our allies are trained in their use have been effective. I note that General Wheeler, who has had many years of experience in NATO command, in his testimony last week in support of the

Nonproliferation Treaty, testified that the current arrangements are satisfactory. And I might add here that there is no demand on the part of the NATO members for transfer into other independent nations custody of nuclear weapons. In fact, there is a great fear among some of the members of NATO, and their representatives have spoken to me personally, against such a transfer.

In my opinion, those who would oppose the Nonproliferation Treaty because they believe the United States should have the flexibility of transferring ownership and control of nuclear weapons to others fail to recognize the consistent and long history of the United States in its position of nonproliferation. Individual rulers come and go, and the politics within nations change. Nations which may be strong allies at certain points in history may alter their alliances in years to come. Weapons and weapons systems transferred to other nations could be used for purposes contrary to the original intent and agreement of the United States.

We have seen conventional weapons which were furnished to Pakistan as an aid in its defense against Red China turned upon and used against India. One recalls that the U.S. military planes furnished to France as a defense against Communist expansion within Europe were used against Egypt in the Suez crisis and also in Algeria. If the Joint Committee on Atomic Energy and others in the Congress had not over the years taken a strong position against the transfer of nuclear weapons to other nations, what might have been the situation in the recent crisis between our two allies, Greece and Turkey? What if one or both of our allies in that situation had independent control of nuclear weapons, whether they be for offensive or defensive use? And I might depart from my script at this moment to say that this is a very difficult line to draw between defensive and offensive weapons. This is a technical question. I know that there will be claims made in support of transferring defensive weapons only, weapons to blow up bridges, weapons perhaps to use in interception of incoming ballistic missiles, and other types of weapons. But let us beware of this type of philosophy because, remember, that the first use of an atomic weapon, whether it be for defense or offense, opens the gate to a nuclear, possible nuclear holocaust. We have tripped the trigger when we pass the boundary of restraining ourselves from entering into nuclear warfare. So let us be very wary of that argument.

I suggest to you that the situation, dangerous as it was, would have been far more precarious. Political control in many nations is not static. For this reason, our security could be jeopardized by shifting political and military leadership in nations whose stability is much weaker than the traditional older nations.

The Nonproliferation Treaty presently before you in no way changes the present arrangements we have with our allies and in no way prohibits us from entering into similar agreements for cooperation in the military uses of atomic energy with other nations. It continues the basic policy of this country not to encourage additional independent nuclear weapon capability among the nations of the world.

INSPECTION CAPABILITIES OF IAEA

There are those who claim that the inspection capabilities of the International Atomic Energy Agency are not sufficiently developed to assure against diversion of special nuclear material or that it will cost too much money to support an inspection system sufficiently capable of doing the job. There are various studies based upon different assumptions as to what the total annual cost will be although no one can be certain at this time. However costly it may be, it will be far more costly if we do not have a Nonproliferation Treaty and if we do not have a proper International Atomic Energy Agency safeguards system, and I would say that this is a method of development and improvement. No one claims that we have perfect systems of safeguards at this time. We have advanced a long way and we are advancing every day, and we will continue to advance in this field, and we must advance in this field, because the diversion of nuclear material for weapons purposes is one of the greatest dangers that we face in the control of the proliferation of nuclear weapons.

We are spending billions of dollars a year in our space program, not to mention the approximately $2½ billion a month it is costing us in Vietnam. Surely we and the world can afford to support the International Atomic Energy Agency in the development and operation of a safeguards system to assure that fissionable materials for peaceful uses of atomic energy are not being diverted for nuclear weapons purposes.

NONSIGNATORIES OF TREATY

There are those who argue against this treaty because two present nuclear weapon countries—France and Communist China—will not sign the treaty and because some nonweapon nations such as India may not become signatories. I deplore the fact that we will not succeed in having all nations of the world parties to the treaty, but I do not believe this should be a bar to the United States signing. We must not minimize the advantages which will result in having an overwhelming number of nations, including the two super powers—the United States and the U.S.S.R.—formally committed against further proliferation of nuclear weapons. If we had been successful in getting the U.S.S.R. and the rest of the world to accept the Baruch plan in 1946 when the United States was the sole possessor of atomic bombs, we all would have been much better off today. If we could have limited the number of nuclear weapon nations to the first three to attain the capability, it would have been to our advantage. I submit to you that each additional nation to join the nuclear weapon club will add to world instability and to the danger of nuclear war. Hopefully, we can succeed in limiting the nuclear weapon club to the present five nations while we continue to explore ways and means to bring these awesome weapons under some type of international control. Practically any nation in the world today which decides to develop nuclear weapon capability—and I speak of industrial nations rather than the backward nations—and is willing to devote its resources to that objective, can within varying periods of time, attain its objective. If a handful of nations including France, India, and Red China refuse to sign this treaty and the rest of the nations of the world willingly commit themselves to its restrictions, it is by far a much better situation than if no restraints exist and all nations are free to proceed down the nuclear weapon path.

I believe it is in the best interest of the United States and the rest of the world for our Nation to accept this treaty, and I commend President Johnson for his leadership and Ambassador Foster and the others who negotiated it for their diligence and capability.

Thank you, Mr. Chairman.

PROPOSED TREATY IN ACCORD WITH U.S. POLICIES

Senator SPARKMAN. Thank you very much. It is a very fine statement. Let me ask you just this one question. As I gather, the thrust of your statement is that the proposed Nonproliferation Treaty is in full accord with the laws, practices, and policies of our country already?

Mr. HOLIFIELD. It is.

Senator SPARKMAN. Senator Pastore?

Senator PASTORE. Well, I join with the chairman in complimenting you for a fine statement. Of course, I am somewhat prejudiced because I agree with every word you say.

FLEXIBILITY IS A TWO-WAY STREET

Now, on the question of flexibility, that argument has been advanced several times. Would you not say that this question of flexibility is not a one-way street? It is a two-way street. If you maintain flexibility yourself you must expect that your adversaries will have the same flexibility, and where do you go from there?

Mr. HOLIFIELD. That is my fear, that independent control of nuclear weapons by flexibility transfer would bring about a condition such as you have described of the sovereign nations receiving those weapons, possibly using those weapons in what they consider to be their primary national interests. Also the other point that I made in my prepared speech or testimony that changes through colonels' coups in many nations of the world are so frequent that there are very few nations that have a stability of continuance such as the United States and England, let's say. Many of these nations change drastically and when they do change people with different philosophies are or could come into power.

The same sovereignty would remain with the new government as was exercised by the old, and that sovereignty might be issued recklessly or as a blackmail weapon to further the interests of the nation then in charge.

IS THERE A MILITARY ADVANTAGE TO THE U.S.S.R.?

Senator PASTORE. One further question, Mr. Holifield. The two primary nations in the consummation of this treaty were the United States and Russia. Do you see in this treaty anything that would give military advantage to Russia because of the treaty as against the United States having a disadvantage because of the treaty?

Mr. HOLIFIELD. I do not. The purpose is to prevent proliferation, and I believe that if either the United States or the U.S.S.R. chose to instruct other nations how to make weapons or to deploy them, that it would be a threat to world peace, and I know the United States does not want to do that. I am very pleased that the Soviet Union has publicly and openly dedicated itself to the same philosophy of nonproliferation of nuclear weapons.

Senator PASTORE. Now, one final question: Would you say that the genie is already out of the bottle and that the concern of our time is to see to it that steps are taken to put it back in the bottle?

Mr. HOLIFIELD. Well, if the Senator speaks of putting the genie of atomic weapons back into the bottle, I am sorry to say that I don't think it can be done. It is out. I think if we can find the possessors of those weapons at this time and the knowledge to make those weapons and the dedication not to spread the knowledge or the weapons to other nations, if he means by that the curtailment of the effect of the genie getting out of the bottle, I would go along with him 100 percent.

Senator PASTORE. I am referring now to that article of the treaty which has to do with the pledge of both the nuclear powers to begin discussions with reference to limitation of weapons. That is what I am talking about.

Mr. HOLIFIELD. I would look hopefully and cautiously toward that. I would say that here again the hope of the world is, and I think the primary responsibility of the leadership of the nations of the world, is to prevent a nuclear holocaust, and I would say that every step, however feeble it might be or seem to some people, is a step in the right direction, a step toward security of peoples, and a step away from destruction of peoples.

Senator PASTORE. That is all.

Senator SPARKMAN. Senator Hickenlooper suggests we pass over to Senator Carlson, since he has just come in.

Senator CARLSON. Mr. Chairman, I appreciate very much your appearance, because I know you have had many years of experience, work, and study in this field. Your testimony is very valuable. I have one question which is aroused by your statement regarding the inspection safeguards of the International Atomic Energy Agency, if we could establish them.

No one among the witnesses has produced any estimate of costs of this inspection program. Can you give us an estimate on that?

Mr. HOLIFIELD. We have some estimates, I believe, that will be supplied by another witness from our committee on that matter. I do not have the figures here, but let me speak to the principle. We are spending $50, $60 billion a year in our military costs at this time. Let me assure you—and we are spending many millions, $16 or $17 million, in research and development. We are spending $4 billion a year in our efforts in space, and I can say to this distinguished group of Senators that the element of cost should not enter into any type of weighted consideration of the adoption of this treaty. It would not be a cost which could not be borne, and the bearing of that cost would bring a security far in excess of many times the billions that we are spending in armaments. That is my sincere belief.

Senator CARLSON. Congressman, I noticed you make that statement in your text here. It says, "However costly it may be, it will be far more costly if we do not have a nonproliferation treaty and if we do not have a proper International Atomic Energy Agency safeguards system."

Mr. HOLIFIELD. Yes.

Senator CARLSON. I would have to agree with you essentially. But at the same time as a Member of the Congress and the Senate and as a member of this committee, I think we ought to explore all phases of it. I think we ought to have some costs.

Mr. HOLIFIELD. Yes, I agree. I think our estimates will show that it would be in the neighborhood of a 1-percent addition to the cost of the production of electricity by nuclear power, and so it would be a percentage cost that would be easily absorbed by the power users.

Senator CARLSON. That is all, Mr. Chairman.

(The Atomic Energy Commission subsequently submitted the following material:)

AEC MEMORANDUM ON IAEA SAFEGUARDS COSTS

Q. What are present costs of IAEA safeguards? What is the amount of the US assessed contribution to the IAEA budget? What is the amount of the US voluntary contribution to the IAEA? What are the projections for each of the foregoing items for 3, 5 and 10 years hence?

A. The budget of the IAEA for CY 1968 includes an estimated amount for safeguards activities of $634,300; the estimated amount for safeguards activities included in the CY 1969 budget is $928,000.

All costs related to safeguards activities of the IAEA are included in the "Regular Budget" of the Agency, which is funded by assessed contributions of the member states. The principles adopted by the United Nations in assessing contributions of Member States to its regular budget are required to be used by the IAEA as a guide for apportioning contributions to the IAEA "Regular Budget". The US assessed contribution to the IAEA "Regular Budget" has averaged about 32 per cent of such budget since the inception of the Agency. The "Regular Budget" for CY 1968 is $10,477,000, of which the US assessed contribution is 31.86% or $3,238,092.

The Agency also maintains an "Operational Budget" which is funded almost entirely by voluntary contributions. The "Operational Budget", which provides for support for the IAEA laboratories and for technical assistance to developing member states, has averaged about $1.3 million for the past ten years. In CY 1967, voluntary contributions totaled $1,441,021, of which the US contribution was $540,383; for CY 1968, voluntary contributions are estimated to be about $1,400,000, of which the US contribution is estimated to be about $480,000.

The IAEA has not published estimated costs of safeguards activities for future years, when it will be carrying out responsibilities under the Non-Proliferation Treaty. The AEC's safeguards Technical Support Organization (TSO) at the Brookhaven National Laboratory has made an estimate of future safeguards costs. In preparing such an estimate it is necessary to make assumptions of (1) the rate at which the demand for electricity will grow in various countries, (2) the portion of such future demands which will be met by installation of generating plants utilizing nuclear reactors, (3) the sizes and geographic distribution of individual nuclear power stations, and (4) the sizes and geographic distribution of other types of plants necessary to manufacture fuel for and to process irradiated fuel from nuclear power stations. Assumptions must also be made concerning the safeguards procedures which will be followed by the IAEA throughout the period covered by the estimate and the salaries and other costs of safeguards inspectors and supporting personnel, as well as the cost of equipment required by the Agency for the safeguards operations.

In preparing its estimate of the costs of future IAEA safeguards activities, the TSO made assumptions, which it considered to be reasonable, for the elements noted above. In order to provide a "maximum" estimated cost, based upon those assumptions, the TSO estimate assumed that the Agency would apply its safeguards, in accordance with its present procedures, to the special fissionable material in all nuclear power stations projected for the generation of electricity and in plants for the manufacture and processing of fuel for such stations throughout the world. Those nuclear power stations and related fuel plants foreseen in the U.S., the UK, and the USSR have been included, even though the Non-Proliferation Treaty (as distinguished from the related offers by the U.S. and the UK) does not call for safeguards in the territory of nuclear-weapon states. The TSO estimate did not, however include in its projections any large nuclear reactors for the desalinization of sea water or other industrial purposes, aside from the generation of electricity. Nor did it attempt to forecast economies or simplifications in IAEA safeguards procedure which might result from research and development already in progress.

The projection of installed electricity generating capacity of nuclear power stations throughout the world, utilized by the TSO in its estimate, and the value of the electricity produced annually, at 5 mills per kilowatt-hour are shown below:

Year	Installed capacity, MWE	Value of electricity produced
1971	37,000	$1,000,000,000
1975	115,000	3,900,000,000
1980	300,000	11,200,000,000
1985	620,000	23,100,000,000
1990	1,050,000	39,100,000,000

The number of safeguards personnel estimated by the TSO to be required by the IAEA to safeguard all the projected nuclear power stations of the world, based upon present IAEA safeguards criteria and procedures, and the total resulting cost of the Agency's safeguards operations estimated by the TSO are:

Year	Manpower	Cost [1]
1971	775	$29,800,000
1975	956	40,100,000
1980	1,302	60,600,000
1985	1,766	93,500,000
1990	2,374	143,400,000

[1] 3 percent annual escalation in individual personnel cost included.

A comparison of the estimated cost of IAEA safeguards activities with the value of the electricity produced from the nuclear power stations involved, and the cost of safeguards in mills per kwh of electricity, is shown below:

Year	Safeguards costs / Value of electricity ×100 (percent)	Safeguards costs, mills per kilowatt-hour
1971	3.0	0.16
1975	1.0	.05
1980	.5	.03
1985	.4	.02
1990	.4	.02

As noted, safeguards costs of the IAEA are presently financed within the "Regular Budget" funded by assessed contributions of the members. We believe this method is the proper one for financing the Agency's safeguards costs, since safeguards benefit the entire world community rather than the country in which they are applied. Other members have, in the past, proposed other means of financing the IAEA's safeguards activities and the membership may be expected to review this matter from time to time as circumstances evolve. To date the average annual growth rate of the Regular Budget has been about 9%. The Agency is currently studying the increased demands the NPT will place on its safeguards activities.

It is difficult to predict future "Operational Budgets" of the IAEA, since they are based upon voluntary contributions. In any event, however, future "Operational Budgets" are not expected to include any of the costs associated with the Agency's safeguards activities.

Senator SPARKMAN. Senator Lausche?
Senator LAUSCHE. I will yield to Senator Cooper.
Senator SPARKMAN. Senator Cooper?
Senator COOPER. Congressman Holifield, I, too, think we are very fortunate in having your testimony because of your long experience in this field?

EFFECT OF TREATY ON U.S. SECURITY

You have said, and it is obvious, that any measure which would inhibit the spread of nuclear weapons is important to the world, and important to the security of the United States. This question has been asked in part by Senator Pastore. Is there any aspect of this treaty that comes to your mind which would in any way adversely affect the security of the United States?

Mr. HOLIFIELD. Not to my knowledge and not to my judgment. We have explored every word of this treaty in hearings by the Joint Committee as it was being developed step by step. Words were changed and I believe, as near as I can understand, that this treaty would help the security of the United States and not be a detriment to it.

EFFECTIVENESS OF IAEA SAFEGUARDS

Senator COOPER. Because of your long experience, I know you are familiar with the safeguards which have been developed by the IAEA. In your judgment, is there any question of the effectiveness of those safeguards?

Mr. HOLIFIELD. My answer would have to be honestly, yes, that the safeguards have not as yet been developed to the point that I am satisfied. A great effort is being made along that line. It will be some time before the material itself in the international reactors will be available for nuclear weapons use, and I believe that within the time that lies before us we can vastly improve the scientific and technical capabilities to prevent diversion.

Senator COOPER. You have reached agreement with these countries?
Mr. HOLIFIELD. I might say that applies to our own reactors right here in the United States, because we have that same problem here although we hope without the same malevolent intent that might occur elsewhere.

Senator COOPER. But under these agreements the United States and U.S.S.R. agree not to transfer nuclear materials without sufficient safeguards as are now available and will be developed.

Mr. HOLIFIELD. A vast improvement and it will be a step forward, in my opinion, the acceleration of the necessary scientific experimental and developmental work which will further strengthen our present capacity to safeguard.

Senator COOPER. As I understand the treaty, it provides that the inspection can be made in the nonnuclear countries as to their use of the source materials that are transferred to them.

Mr. HOLIFIELD. That is right. And at the present time we, in our bilateral agreements with other nations, are enforcing as part of that agreement the right of inspection in every case of bilateral agreements for assistance in building nuclear power type reactors.

Senator COOPER. It does not require that inspection be made of the donor, either the United States or the U.S.S.R.?

Mr. HOLIFIELD. No, it does not. We have opened up, as you know, some of our reactors, our nonmilitary reactors, for inspection of other nations as a gesture of our confidence that it can be done, and that it is not inimical to the security of the United States to have that right or privilege, I might say, of checking.

EFFECT OF INSPECTIONS ON U.S. SECURITY INTERESTS

Senator COOPER. President Johnson in his statement said that the United States would open up its sources and facilities for peaceful use of atomic energy to these same inspections.

Mr. HOLIFIELD. I think that is correct.

Senator COOPER. The U.S.S.R. has not agreed to do that.

Mr. HOLIFIELD. I think that is correct.

Senator COOPER. Do you think if this procedure is carried out that that would in any way be adverse to our security interests?

Mr. HOLIFIELD. I do not think that it is adverse. I think it would be desirable for the U.S.S.R. I think the example that we set in making such a volunteer offer is a good example, and I cannot see any danger to our national interests in allowing a checking of our commercial reactors, the egress of material which might be refined into weapons material. The material that comes out of the reactor, of course, is contaminated material, and it has to go through a very difficult separation process before the material which is used in weapons in extracted. It is not a very difficult matter, I think, to count the number of spent fuel rods that comes out of a reactor and to see that it goes to the separation facility. It is what happens to it, of course, after the separation facility acts upon it that is of primary importance.

WITHDRAWAL NOTICE

Senator Cooper. Another question: This treaty does not in itself affect or change the relative positions of the United States and the U.S.S.R.?

Mr. Holifield. No, it does not.

Senator Cooper. So any progress made in that direction will have to come about because of the faithful and rigorous exercise of procedures and efforts under the article which deals with further disarmament, further steps to reduce——

Mr. Holifield. That is right. I think it will help to create an atmosphere where other progress can be made and, of course, as the Senator knows if at any time the United States believes that its national interest is involved, it has the right of withdrawal from the treaty arrangement.

Senator Cooper. You don't have to wait, even though the treaty says 90 days, if our national interests were jeopardized. You don't think we would have to wait for 90 days, do you?

Mr. Holifield. No, I do not. I think from a practical standpoint it could be considered on the moment, and the announcement of withdrawal formally and legally within 90 days would take effect immediately from a practical standpoint.

Senator Cooper. Thank you.

Senator Sparkman. Senator Hickenlooper, do you wish to ask any questions?

Senator Hickenlooper. I don't want to continue this colloquy. Congressman Holifield has presented a very knowledgeable and informative statement based upon his continuous service on the Joint Committee since it was established. I think we ought to proceed to other witnesses. I may ask just one question of Congressman Holifield.

AMOUNT OF ARMS REDUCTION RESULTING FROM TREATY

Is there anything in this treaty that reduces the atomic arms or weapons race between the United States and Russia over and above what it was just before the treaty was initially signed?

Mr. Holifield. In my opinion, there is nothing in the treaty that affects the armament race between the United States and the Soviet Union unless the mutuality of interest between the United States and the Soviet Union indicates a lessening of armament production.

Senator Hickenlooper. But that is only hopeful; isn't it?

Mr. Holifield. That is a matter of hope. It is a matter of hope and negotiation. It is not a matter of reality in the treaty.

Senator Hickenlooper. So as I understand you, in your opinion, this treaty doesn't accomplish very much except to say that we are not going to give atomic weapons to Mali or some other country and they are not going to give atomic weapons to us. That example is a little facetious, I will admit, but I am trying to find out what this treaty accomplishes.

Mr. HOLIFIELD. I think that in addition to the nonproliferation of weapons, this is the point of agreement of a signatory nation not to build weapons on their own.

Senator HICKENLOOPER. Yes, that is true. Most of them haven't got the money anyway and won't have for a long time.

Mr. HOLIFIELD. Many of them do not have the technical knowledge and when I hpoke in part of my testimony regarding other nations that might build, I modified the text to say industrial, and I would like to elaborate and say industrial nations with industrial capability and scientific technological capability because it is obviously absurd to think that the underdeveloped nations of the world could within themselves do this.

WILL THIS TREATY SAVE THE WORLD?

Senator HICKENLOOPER. Now, this may be on unfair question, but do you view this treaty as a light of peace dawning on the world—as has been put out in propaganda—that it is almost a savior of world peace?

Mr. HOLIFIELD. I only think that it is a step on the long and arduous path toward peace. I do not believe that it solves the problems of a world in which nuclear weapons have been born and invented.

Senator HICKENLOOPER. Thank you. We appreciate your coming here because your background and your devotion to this subject makes your testimony extremely valuable to the committee. I know your dedication to this subject and your sincerity in your views. Thank you.

Mr. HOLIFIELD. Thank you, Senator.

TRIBUTE TO SENATOR HICKENLOOPER

Mr. Chairman, may I at this point make a personal comment? Four members of the original Joint Committee on Atomic Energy are the charter members. Senator Russell, Senator Hickenlooper, Mr. Price of Illinois, and myself. We have served together for 22 years, and I want to at this time, and it may be my last time publicly at least before, certainly before, a Senate committee, to pay my personal tribute to the long years of constructive work which Senator Hickenlooper has given, his dedicated service to this great problem of atomic energy both in the peaceful aspects and in the national security aspects, and I regret very much that he is leaving the Senate of the United States and our committee.

Senator HICKENLOOPER. Well, I thank you, Mr. Holifield.

Senator SPARKMAN. Thank you.

We share that feeling.

Senator PASTORE. I should like to join in that.

Senator SPARKMAN. Senator Lausche.

OFFENSIVE AND DEFENSIVE NUCLEAR DEVICES

Senator LAUSCHE. Mr. Holifield, I want to explore the provisions of articles I and II of the treaty. In article I the parties agree not to give away or transfer nuclear weapons; article II, the signatory parties agree not to accept them.

Now, the pertinent parts of these two articles, I understand to be, are that each nuclear weapon state party to the treaty undertakes not to transfer to any recipient whatsoever nuclear weapons. I now punctuate nuclear weapons or nuclear explosive devices or control over such weapons or explosive devices directly or indirectly.

What do you understand to be the meaning as contemplated in this treaty of nuclear weapons or nuclear explosive devices? As a preface to that question, what if the scientists of the Nation developed an antiballistic missile that was effective and certain in its operation, so as to intercept offensive missiles. Would this treaty prohibit the parties to transfer an effective defensive nuclear device to a nation that was wanting to achieve peace and remain free from attack?

Mr. HOLIFIELD. It would not prohibit the United States from deploying within that nation such a device on a bilateral agreement such as we now deploy nuclear weapons. It would not change the present Atomic Energy Act which prohibits the transfer into sovereign custody of that weapon. But if we develop it, and I know you speak of the future as I do, if we do develop that type of a weapon, it can be deployed in the nations of any of our allies by bilateral agreements, but the custody and control of that device would remain in the hands of the President of the United States through delegates, and would not go to the sovereign nation whose territory was enslaved.

Senator LAUSCHE. Then, you interpret this language to mean that effective defensive antiballistic devices could be transferred but offensive devices cannot?

Mr. HOLIFIELD. No; I do not—I make no such interpretation.

Senator LAUSCHE. All right.

Then do you mean that both defensive and offensive devices would be prohibited?

Mr. HOLIFIELD. No; I do not.

Senator LAUSCHE. Which would be permitted and which would not be permitted?

Mr. HOLIFIELD. Both would be permitted under a bilateral agreement, the same as offensive weapons and other types of weapons such as demolition weapons and that sort of thing are permitted now under a bilateral military agreement, always with the custody remaining in the hands of a representative of the President.

Senator LAUSCHE. But this article I states each nuclear weapon state party to the treaty undertakes not to transfer to any recipient whatsoever nuclear weapons or nuclear explosive devices or control over such weapons or explosive devices. Doesn't the treaty specifically prohibit the transfer of explosive nuclear devices and if it does, doesn't that cover both offensive and defensive devices?

Mr. HOLIFIELD. The point of the gentleman's inquiry rests upon the word "transfer." The word "transfer" is modified by the deployment of weapons on another country but with the maintenance of custody and control in the hands of the United States. So the word "transfer" is a word of art when considered with the other prohibitions of the Atomic Energy Act, and of the State Department's own testimony on page 6 of its publication where the question asked is, "Does the draft treaty prohibit arrangements for the deployment of nuclear weapons owned and controlled by the United States within the territory of nonnuclear area to members?" And the answer, "It does not deal with arrangements for deployment of nuclear weapons within allied territory as these do not involve any transfer of nuclear weapons or control over them unless and until a decision were made to go to war, at which time the treaty would no longer be controlling."

Senator LAUSCHE. Yes, I understand that.

Mr. HOLIFIELD. That is the publication, by the way, of the Foreign Relations Committee, Executive H.

STATUS OF U.S. BILATERAL ARRANGEMENTS

Senator LAUSCHE. Is it your interpreation, Mr. Holifield, that by bilateral agreement, in spite of the treaty, we can install nuclear devices in nonnuclear nations, providing we retain control of the device?

Mr. HOLIFIELD. Providing we retain control and custody, we can.

Senator LAUSCHE. All right.

Mr. HOLIFIELD. As we do now. It does not change the present arrangement. We are doing that now.

Senator LAUSCHE. That is what I want to get clear. It is your interpretation that under the treaty the situation, which allows us to place offensive weapons in foreign nations providing we retain control, remains.

Mr. HOLIFIELD. And custody.

Senator LAUSCHE. Of the trigger?

Mr. HOLIFIELD. That is right.

And custody; control and custody.

Senator LAUSCHE. Isn't that a weakness?

Mr. HOLIFIELD. No.

Senator LAUSCHE. Will Russia be permitted to do the same thing?

Mr. HOLIFIELD. Russia does it now.

STATUS OF CUSTODY OR CONTROL OF PRESENTLY OWNED NUCLEAR WEAPONS

Senator LAUSCHE. Would that not mean then that proliferation would be granted to Russia and to the United States, and the other nuclear powers of the present day, but barred to all other nations?

Mr. HOLIFIELD. No, as the State Department testified, and it is my personal belief, the deployment of nuclear weapons within allied territories of the United States or within the allied territories of the Soviet Union occurs today, it will continue to occur notwithstanding this treaty. This treaty does not change the custody and control of presently owned nuclear weapons as long as they are retained within the custody and control of that nation. But it does, in my opinion, obligate the signatories of the nuclear weapons owning nations not to relinquish custody and control to a sovereign nation upon which their weapons have been placed.

TRANSFER OF A DEFENSIVE NUCLEAR WEAPON

Senator LAUSCHE. This further question: You would subscribe to the idea that if an effective defensive nuclear explosive weapon were devised by the scientists, that that would be an instrumentality for peace rather than for war?

Mr. HOLIFIELD. Well, I would rather state it in my own words, Senator, if you would permit me. Insasmuch as offensive weapons and defensive weapons are instruments of peace my answer would be "Yes."

Senator LAUSCHE. And if it is an instrument of peace, shouldn't we in some way, in the treaty, indicate that a defensive weapon may be transferred by the participating nations, especially if that defensive weapon is equipped with devices that will prevent the use of it offensively?

Mr. HOLIFIELD. It is my considered opinion, Senator, that the transfer of any kind of a nuclear weapon to the sovereign custody of a nonnuclear nation, whether it be in the guise of peace or any other guise, would be a mistake. It would increase the mathematical probability of unauthorized use. It would not be a step toward peace. I believe that any step toward peace which can be obtained by the deployment of offensive or defensive weapons can be exercised more safely by having them remain in the control and custody of the United States, and that the President's finger upon that trigger of possible use is a safer finger than the finger of any nation other than the United States, because our selfish interest is involved in seeing that a nuclear holocaust is not started.

Senator LAUSCHE. I think I have made the point I want and I am glad to have your views, but I thought it was a subject worthy of exploration.

Now, then, what will be the situation if Brazil, Sweden, Australia, Italy, Japan, West Germany, Israel, and India or a major portion of these countries do not sign the treaty?

Mr. HOLIFIELD. It will not be as good a treaty as I would like to see it, but there are many thing in this world that are not as good as I would like to see them. And I think that to take half a loaf or three-quarters of a loaf is better than taking none, and I would say sooner or later world opinion, I believe, will force many of these nations who are now hesitant, to sign this treaty, to come into the treaty orbit.

Senator LAUSCHE. I concur with you that the initial step has to be made by the leading nations, and then the hope that all nations will subscribe, and that world opinion will have some influence upon those nations that don't subscribe.

I think, Mr. Chairman, that is all.

Senator SPARKMAN. Thank you very much, Congressman. We appreciate it.

Mr. HOLIFIELD. Thank you.

Senator SPARKMAN. Before we call the next witness, I want to mention the fact to my colleagues here and also to the witnesses that we have eight witnesses on the list. We have used 54 minutes on the first one, and we, of course, can't go along like that.

So I do ask for the cooperation of my colleagues and the witnesses to move right along.

Next, we will hear from the Honorable Craig Hosmer of California, U.S. Congressman.

Mr. HOSMER. Thank you, Mr. Chairman.

Senator SPARKMAN. We are very glad to have you here. If you move right along, we will appreciate it.

STATEMENT OF HON. CRAIG HOSMER, U.S. CONGRESSMAN FROM CALIFORNIA

Mr. HOSMER. I have a written statement and I would like it placed in the record and I will brief it down.

Senator SPARKMAN. It will be printed in full in the record.

Mr. HOSMER. Mr. Chairman, and Senators, I have shared the last 10 years experience with the previous witness on the Joint Atomic Committee and since about 1946 have had various experience in this general area. The purpose of an arms control treaty is to make a nation more secure with it than without it. The administration witnesses have offered you opinions on this issue in relation to the Nonproliferation Treaty. I respectfully suggest that the validity of their opinions be tested against facts not yet in the record before this body hastens to render its advise and consent.

For example, is nonproliferation good and proliferation bad? As to the British, it was benign. Not so in varying degrees as to the French, the Soviets, and the Red Chinese. So whether proliferation is good or bad depends on whether the proliferee plays a "good guy" or a "bad guy" role in the international scenario, and since that scenario is constantly changing and article X of the treaty allows withdrawal on 3 months notice I recommend that the following safeguards be adopted.

Namely, that a continuing and independent study group be established to assess advantages and disadvantages of proliferation in relation to the changing international situation, and that the group's findings be submitted annually to the Congress.

WILL THE NPT PREVENT PROLIFERATION?

Another question of fact is whether the NPT will effectively prevent proliferation. This treaty recognizes two routes to nuclear club membership. One, where a have-not gets weapons from a nuclear power and the other where a have-not develops its own nuclear capability. The three nuclear powers who will sign the treaty are not about to spread nuclear weapons recklessly. So the treaty will be useless as to them and also as to France and Red China who will not sign.

Most nuclear "have-nots" "cannot be" anyway due to a lack of technical and financial resources, so the treaty will be useless as to them.

As to the few who "can be," most "won't go," but a few will if it ever involves their survival, treaty or no treaty.

Thus, the NPT will be essentially useless to restrain either more or less than the degree of proliferation which is inevitable.

With or without the treaty the probability of proliferation is the same and far from zero.

Therefore, I recommend another safeguard:

That the study group I previously recommend also constantly monitor proliferation potentialities, identify possible proliferees, develop contingency plans for the event of proliferation, and submit its findings annually to the Congress.

WILL THE NPT DISADVANTAGE THE UNITED STATES?

Next, there is an issue of whether the NPT will disadvantage the United States and its allies or disrupt defensive alliances.

General Wheeler's testimony on this point was carefully terse. You will note that he did not tell you that the NPT is a good thing or that it serves the defense interests of the United States. The most he gave you was an opinion that it is "not inimical to United States' interests."

The committee should be aware of certain data which have not been supplied by administration witnesses which is pertinent to the NPT's national security cost-benefit ratio, and amongst which is the fact that the NPT does surrender a valuable U.S. option to selectively proliferate defensive nuclear systems to allies in situations less than actual war if it ever becomes vital to our national security to do so. This option is available merely by amending the Atomic Energy Act and offers considerable opportunity for keeping the U.S. forces out of future Vietnams. Surrendering it is a high price to pay for a treaty which does not clearly stand out from the euphoric ballyhoo in which it has been packaged. And, that price is further escalated by the fact that with NPT's blanket ban on defensive nuclear weapons transfers, hardpressed countries may have to go nuclear on their own and in the process acquire an offensive as well as a defensive capability. In short, the treaty bars a kind of proliferation which might be advantageous and encourages a kind which is not.

So I recommend the following additional safeguards:

That the Senate reserve its consent to the treaty pending a full and complete examination of the document made independently and impartially to assess its cost and effectiveness in relation to national security. And, that such examinations continue to be made annually and reported to the Congress.

ADEQUACY OF TREATY SAFEGUARDS QUESTIONED

The next query: Are the treaty's article III safeguards adequate?

As a matter of fact the treaty contains absolutely no safeguards relating to the process not to give or receive nuclear weapons. I imagine this statement comes as a surprise to some of you. I assure you that it is quite accurate. You may wonder, as I do, why Secretary Rusk, and others, did not bother to point this out to you.

The treaty's other promises by the havenots not to go nuclear are supposed to be policed by separate agreements with the International Atomic Energy Agency. This places squarely in issue the adequacy of IAEA safeguards and their financing. I invite the committee to look into this before it advises and consents.

For an example, the entire IAEA safeguards staff for worldwide operations consist of less than 19 people, fewer people than the Senators who are members of this committee.

It spends only about a half a million annually on safeguards and from my own observation I can state categorically that IAEA's knowledge, techniques, and skills in the art of inspection are rudimentary and its research toward improvement is essentially nil.

Neither the IAEA nor anyone else has the remotest notion what constitutes a normal loss of uranium or plutonium in the peaceful industrial process. Therefore, there is not the slightest possibility of any inspectors spotting illegal diversions because they can't even be told when their suspicions should be aroused.

And even should a suspicion arise for other reasons, IAEA procedures need never bring them to anyones' attention. The Inspector General is not obliged to tell the Director General about it, and if he does, the latter is under no obligation to tip off anybody else.

Then there are technological possibilities to "end run" the IAEA inspectors by obtaining fissionable materials for weapons clandestinely. These involve small and easily hidden plants to obtain U^{235} by either the centrifuge or the nozzle processes or by the development of pure fusion explosives which do not require fissionable material and seem not to be banned by the treaty. Work is underway on all of these approaches in various countries at this very moment.

Then like any other international organization IAEA has trouble collecting its assessments and rocks along on voluntary contributions, half of which come from the United States. Its entire effective budget is around $12 million annually. But note that the first year, 1970, safeguards cost will run over $28 million and escalate from there. Unless and until this committee—or someone—takes an initiative toward establishing an adequate financing system, IAEA safeguards are a sham and a delusion.

165

ANALYSES OF IAEA SAFEGUARDS COSTS

I offer this committee three analysis of IAEA safeguards costs under the treaty, one by Dr. T. B. Taylor, one by myself, one by the Brookhaven National Laboratory, together with a comparison of the assumptions of all three analyses made by Raymond R. Edwards. I respectfully suggest, Senator Cooper, that these are the data which you were seeking previously. Insofar as I know these are the only existing analyses that anybody in any country has ever made, and I offer them for the record at this point.

Senator SPARKMAN. It will be included in the record.

(The analyses referred to begin on page 277.)

Mr. HOSMER. The obvious safeguard which I recommend in light of all this is that the Senate reserve its consent to the treaty pending establishments of IAEA safeguards in which treaty signatories may have confidence and the establishment of a sound system for financing the same on a continuing basis, and that the determination therefore be updated annually and reported to the Congress.

WILL U.S. ROLE AS POLICEMAN BE ENLARGED?

The next query: Will the security assurances given to non-nuclear nations enlarge the U.S. world policeman's role? President Johnson has declared that the nations who do not seek nuclear weapons will have our strong support against nuclear blackmail. His statement has been echoed by Secretaries McNamara, Rusk, and others. Yet Secretary Nitze told you last week that the U.S.-U.S.S.R. assurances are just expressions of utmost concern.

Now, I submit that they are either meaningful or meaningless, and if they are meaningful and if Secretary Rusk's hopes of around a hundred nuclear signers are realistic, there is a measure by which the added U.S. nuclear Sir Galahad burden can be measured.

It is this: Presently we have security arrangements with about 40 countries. The NPT will extend it to about 60 more. It will thus increase our opportunities to get involved in someone else's troubles by 250 percent.

As a safeguard I suggest:

The Senate advise the President and the rest of the world that the security assurance is meaningful to the extent that we will be "concerned to the utmost" if some country becomes the victim of nuclear aggression or blackmail, but that it is meaningless insofar as rushing to its rescue is concerned, And we apologize to anybody who got the wrong idea from what administration spokesmen have said.

FURTHER ARMS CONTROL NEGOTIATIONS

The last query: Is it good that the NPT encourages further arms control negotiations? The answer is good if it leads to a treaty enhancing national security and bad if it leads to a treaty that does not, and also bad if the U.S. strategic position deteriorates vis-a-vis the Soviet Union while negotiations limp along.

You must all be well aware that during the protracted negotiations on this treaty the Soviets quadrupled their IBM force and submarine launched missiles and tripled their deliverable strategic megatonnage. This strategic balance upsetting momentum continues and accelerates.

Therefore, as a further safeguard, I recommend that the Senate take all necessary measures to assure that future negotiating periods are not utilized by the Soviet Union to upset the strategic balance and achieve superiority. This will require enchancement of both our assured destruction systems and our damage limitation systems.

Mr. Chairman, I respectfully suggest that the opinions and conclusions regarding this treaty expressed to you by the administration witnesses come from the very people who sponsored and negotiated the treaty and who are, therefore, unlikely to supply your body with dispassionate testimony. As a matter of deep concern to your body should be the fact that these witnesses largely have limited their testimony to opinion and thus your record today is exceedingly sterile of factual data supporting the treaty and absent the latter I fail to see how you can safely consent to it..

(The full statement of Congressman Hosmer follows:)

STATEMENT OF REPRESENTATIVE CRAIG HOSMER

Mr. Chairman and Senators, the purpose of an arms control treaty is to make a nation more secure with it than without it. If it does this, it should be accepted. If it makes the nation less secure, it should be rejected. In relation to the Nonproliferation Treaty various Administration witnesses have offered the Committee opinions and conclusions on this issue, but have given you essentially no factual data to support them. They have concluded that:

"Nonproliferation of nuclear weapons is good and their spread is bad.

"The NPT will prevent spread.

"The Treaty will not disadvantage us militarily or disrupt our alliances.

"The NPT contains effective safeguards and reliable verification procedures

"Security assurances given won't be burdensome.

"The NPT encourages further arms control negotiations, and that is good."

I respectfully suggest that the validity of these opinions and conclusions be tested by a comprehensive examination of the facts and circumstances surrounding the Treaty and related matters before this body hastens to render its advice or give its consent.

Query. Is preventing Spread of Nuclear Weapons a Good Thing and Their Spread a Bad Thing?

This issue is not absolute. It's one of degree. How good is nonproliferation How bad is proliferation? And, to whose hands?

Since Manhattan District days the U.S. has adhered to a nonproliferation policy and attempted to enforce it by secrecy and suppression of technology. The policy has failed in the case of the British, the French and the Red Chinese. Now it is to be written into a treaty, to be enforced by pledges, and by such verification machinery as the Treaty provides.

As to the British, failure of the policy was benign. Not so as to the Soviets and Red Chinese which has created trouble. French capabilities have disrupted NATO and other consequences remain a question mark.

To date, proliferation has not been good, but it has not been as bad as pessimists estimated. There has not been a nuclear war and some observers believe the nuclear umbrella also has functioned as a deterrent to conventional war between the major powers. If so, and limited to this context, proliferation has not been all bad.

It appears, then, that whether proliferation is good or bad depends on whether a new Nuclear Club member plays a "good guy" or a "bad guy" role in today's scenario of international events. Since the scenario constantly changes and since Article X provides for withdrawal upon a three months' notice, I recommend that the following safeguard be adopted:

A continuing and *independent* study group be established to assess advantages and disadvantages of proliferation in relation to constantly changing international situations. And, that its findings be submitted annually to the Congress.

Query. Will the NPT Prevent Proliferation of Nuclear Weapons?

This Treaty recognizes two routes to Nuclear Club membership, one where a nuclear "have-not" nation gets nuclear weapons from a nuclear power and the other where a "have-not" develops its own nuclear capability.

In the first case, neither the U.S., the U.K. nor the U.S.S.R. are likely to spread nuclear weapons to others in violation of their own self-interest. These are the only nuclear "haves" who will sign the Treaty. Since they will not be spreading nuclear weapons recklessly, the NPT gains nothing as to them. France, who won't sign probably won't proliferate either. But the same cannot be said of Red China to whom circumstances of world instability are highly beneficial. The NPT will be useless as to the two nonsigners as well. And, if it is useless as to them, it is also useless as to "have-nots" who choose to receive give-away weapons.

Insofar as restraining in excess of 100 nuclear "have-nots" from going nuclear "on their own" the NPT will be useless as to the 90% who are not only "have-not" but also are "can never be" countries due to lack of technical and financial resources to go nuclear on their own.

So, what about the 10% of "have-nots" who are "can-be's"? Some are "never-be's" for a variety of good reasons. The remainder "will-be" if ever they calculate survival depends upon it, since treaty promises or not, nations tend to do what they must to avoid extinction. So, whether they sign or not, the Treaty also will be useless as to this category of nations.

It appears, then, that the NPT will be essentially useless to restrain either more or less than the degree of nuclear proliferation which is inevitable. Thus one wonders at the extravagant praise accorded this document. We seem to be addressing the wrong problem. We should be calculating what the world will look like with a somewhat larger Nuclear Club and devising ways to live with it. With or without the Treaty, the probability of continued proliferation is far from zero, therefore I recommend another safeguard:

That the study group heretofore suggested constantly monitor proliferation potentialities, identify possible proliferees, and develop contingency plans for the event of proliferation. And, that its findings be submitted annually to the Congress.

Query: Will the NPT Disadvantage the U.S. and Its Allies or Disrupt Defensive Alliances?

General Wheeler's testimony on this point was carefully terse. You will note that he did *not* tell you the NPT is a good thing or that it serves the defense interests of the United States. The most he gave you was an opinion that it is "not inimical to United States security interests." In contradiction, Dr. Robert Strausz-Hupé, who does not owe his position to an appointment from the President, stated that the Treaty's national security costs far exceed its benefits and that it will alienate our allies. Unlike Wheeler, Strausz-Hupé furnished you compelling facts to back up his statements and I refer you to them.

Further, the Committee should be aware of certain data which has not been supplied by Administration witnesses, but is pertinent to the NPT's national security cost/benefit ratio:

The Soviets realize that nuclear weapons proliferated to the third world might offer a small but independent deterrent to communist instigated wars of national liberation. For example, Cuba or North Vietnam might be less enthusiastic about stirring up trouble in neighboring countries if their intended victims possessed a nuclear deterrent of their own. It is to Soviet advantage that such wars not be deterred, but continue.

As to regional nuclear wars, RAND Corporation's James R. Schlessinger has pointed out that the achievable nuclear capabilities of the powers involved are limited and pose no direct threat to either the U.S. or the U.S.S.R. Nor can one foresee a greater likelihood of the superpowers and others becoming involved in a worldwide holocaust if fighting is done with primitive nuclear weapons rather than with conventional arms. Those who worry about the possible catalytic effect of regional wars should ponder conditions of instability which increase their frequency rather than weapons with which they may be conducted.

The possible stabilizing effect of independent nuclear deterrents in certain tinderbox areas should not go unweighed. For example, an Indian capability to threaten atomic retaliation against Red China might have sobering and stabilizing effects in that region. A nuclear capable Japan could be the focus for a stabilizing Far Eastern regional alliance against Red aggression. Filling these power vacuums would considerably ease the overseas over-commitments of the United States.

The NPT surrenders a valuable U.S. option to selectively proliferate defensive nuclear systems to allies if ever it becomes vital to the common security to do so. Integrated into the weapons would be control devices which permit them to fire in a defensive environment, prohibit offensive firing against another country and which would destroy them in the event of tampering. Such control devices are within the present state of technology. This option is available merely by amending the Atomic Energy Act and offers considerable opportunity for keeping U.S. forces out of future Vietnams. Surrendering it is a high price to pay for a treaty which does not clearly stand out from the euphoric ballyhoo in which it is packaged. And, the price is further escalated by the fact that with the NPT's blanket ban on nuclear weapon transfers hard pressed countries may have to go nuclear on their own and in the process acquire *offensive* as well as *defensive* nuclear arsenals. In short, the Treaty bars a kind of proliferation which might be advantageous and encourages a kind which is not.

It is to be noted that the Administration asks you to surrender this valuable option to proliferate selectively and defensively without ever having subjected the proposition to scrutiny by the Pentagon's vaunted systems analysis procedures to determine cost effectiveness. Therefore I recommend the following additional safeguard:

That the Senate reserve its consent to the Treaty pending a full and complete examination of the document made *independently* and *impartially* to assess its cost and effectiveness in relation to the national security. And, if the Senate nevertheless consents, that such examination be made and updated annually and reported to the Congress.

Query. Are the Treaty's Article III Safeguards Adequate?

Thus far this Committee's record is totally barren of any support for the assertions that this Treaty contains "effective safeguards and reliable verification procedures." As a matter of fact, the Treaty contains absolutely no safeguards or verification procedures relating to the promises not to give or to receive nuclear weapons. I imagine this statement comes as a surprise to many of you. I assure you it is quite accurate. You may wonder, as I do, why Secretary Rusk or Mr. Foster or Dr. Seaborg or Gen. Wheeler or other Administration witnesses have not bothered to point this out to you.

The Treaty's other promises, by the "have-nots" not to go nuclear, are supposed to be policed by separate agreements with the International Atomic Energy Agency for the inspection of peaceful nuclear activities to assure that fissionable material is not being diverted to military channels. This places in issue the adequacy of the IAEA's safeguards system and its financing. Despite Gen. Wheeler's happy conclusion that IAEA will provide "effective safeguards and reliable verification procedures" and Dr. Seaborg's conclusion that IAEA has "effective safeguards" in operation and his optimism that it will not be "difficult to find the necessary funds" to finance them, there are some disturbing facts from which much different and less rosy conclusions may be drawn. I invite this Committee to look into them before it advises and consents. For example:

The entire IAEA safeguards staff for worldwide operations consists of less than 19 people—fewer people than the Senators who are members of this Committee.

Less than $1 million, closer to $1½ million, annually is spent by the IAEA on safeguards—and from my own observation I can state categorically that IAEA's knowledge, skills and techniques in the art of inspection are rudimentary and its research toward improvements is essentially nil.

Neither the IAEA inspection staff, nor anyone else, for that matter, has the remotest notion of what constitutes a normal loss of uranium or plutonium in the industrial process—therefore there is not the slightest possibility of any inspector spotting illegal diversions because he can't even be told when his suspicion should be aroused.

Even should a suspicion be aroused for other reasons, IAEA procedures need never bring it to any one's attention. IAEA's Inspector-General is not obliged to tell IAEA's Director-General about it, and if he does, the latter is under no obligation to tip off anyone else.

There are technological possibilities to "end run" the IAEA inspectors and obtain fissionable material for weapons clandestinely. [These involve small and easily hidden plants to obtain U^{235} by either the centrifuge or the nozzle processes or by the development of pure fusion explosives which do not require fissionable material and seem not to be banned by the Treaty. Work is underway on all of these approaches in various countries at this very moment.]

Like most other international organizations IAEA is chronically and woefully underfinanced. It has trouble collecting its member assessments and rocks along on voluntary contributions, half of which come from the U.S. Its entire effective budget is around $12 million annually. Yet first year (1970) safeguards costs will run over $28 million and escalate from there. [Unless and until this Committee—or someone—takes an initiative toward establishing an adequate financing system, IAEA safeguards are a sham and a delusion.] To assure this Committee otherwise is either wittingly or unwittingly misleading.

I offer this Committee three recent analyses of IAEA safeguards costs under the Treaty, one by Dr. Theodore B. Taylor, one by myself, one by the Technical Support Organization of Brookhaven National Laboratory, together with a comparison of the assumptions of all three analyses by Raymond R. Edwards of TSO and respectfully suggest that they be made a part of the Record.

The obvious safeguard which I recommend in light of the foregoing is:

That the Senate reserve its consent to the Treaty pending establishment of IAEA safeguards procedures in which Treaty signatories may have reasonable confidence and the establishment of a sound system for financing same on a continuing basis. And, that determination thereof be updated annually and reported to the Congress.

Query. Do the "Security Assurances" Given Non-Nuclear Nations Enlarge the United States' "World Policeman" Role?

You will note that Gen. Wheeler's direct testimony carefully skirted this question as did the testimony of Secretary Rusk, Mr. Foster, Chairman Seaborg, et al. Only Under Secretary Nitze touched it lightly, saying essentially that it is meaningless except to evidence that both the U.S. and the U.S.S.R. "share the utmost concern in preventing any act or threat of aggression with nuclear weapons"—whatever that means. Perhaps it is meaningless to the extent that a nuclear victim could not reasonably expect much concern, let alone help, from the Kremlin, and therefore it should expect no more from the co-declarer in this case. If this be so it is a far cry from what was promised by these ringing declarations:

President Johnson: "The nations that do not seek national nuclear weapons can be sure that if they need our strong support against some threat of nuclear blackmail then they will have it." (TV address, Oct. 18, 1964.) "* * * they will have our strong support against threats of nuclear blackmail." (Message to 18-Nation Disarmament Committee, Jan. 27. 1966.)

Secretary McNamara: "* * * they will have our strong support * * * In case of a nuclear attack by country A on country B, the very survival of country B would be immediately at issue and it might well require military intervention by one of the great powers immediately, without time for the negotiation and discussion in international forums that would otherwise take place." (Testimony to Joint Committee on Atomic Energy, March 7, 1966, p. 78 and p. 88.)

Secretary Rusk: Reaffirms President Johnson's declaration. (JCAE Hearings, Feb. 23, 1966, p. 7.)

Wm. C. Foster: Reaffirms President's declaration (JCAE Hearings, March 1, 1966, pp. 36–37.)

If the security assurance is not meaningless—and either it is or it is not—and Secretary Rusk's hopes for some 100 non-nuclear signers are realistic, there is a measure by which the added U.S. nuclear Sir Gallahad burden can be measured: *Presently we have security arrangements with about 40 countries. The NPT will extend it to about 60 more. It will thus increase our opportunities to get involved in someone else's troubles by 250%.*

As a safeguard I suggest:

The Senate advise the President and the rest of the world that the security assurance is meaningful to the extent that we will be "concerned to the utmost" if some country becomes the victim of nuclear aggression or blackmail, but that it is meaningless insofar as rushing to its rescue is concerned and we apologize to anybody who got the wrong idea from what administration spokesmen have said.

Query. The NPT will encourage further arms control negotiations—Is that good?

The answer is good if it leads to a treaty enhancing the national security. The answer is bad if it leads to a treaty which does not. The answer *also is bad* if the U.S. strategic position is permitted to deteriorate via-a-vis the Soviet Union while protracted negotiations limp along.

You will recall that the Soviet Union used the Limited Test Ban Treaty negoations as a stall while it upgraded its nuclear capabilities by a long series of tests, then quickly agreed to the LTB before we could catch up.

You must also be well aware that during the protracted negotiations on the NPT the Soviets quadrupled their ICBM force and submarine launched missiles and tripled their deliverable amount of strategic megatonnage. They vastly improved the quality of their nuclear submarine fleet and achieved an astounding building rate for new submarines. They initiated the Fractional Orbital Ballistic System and began the installation of an Anti-Ballistic Missile defense effective against us whereas our own embryonic system is not even planned to cope with a Soviet surprise attack. This strategic balance-upsetting Soviet momentum continues and accelerates while the number of our ICBMs remains static at 1054, our SAC bomber fleet has been cut back, the lid on Polaris submarines is still 41, and our attack submarine building program is geared to a snail's pace. Also during this interim the Soviet Union picked up a nasty little war in the Mideast and has been supplying North Vietnam with military aid at the rate of $1 billion annually.

Therefore, as a further safeguard I recommend:

That the Senate take all necessary measures to insure that future negotiation periods are not utilized by the Soviet Union first to achieve strategic nuclear parity and second to achieve superiority. This will require enhancement of both our "assured destruction" systems and our "damage limitation" systems.

CONCLUSION

I respectfully suggest to the members of your honorable body that the opinions and conclusions regarding this Treaty expressed to you by the Administration witnesses come from the very people who sponsored and negotiated it and who are therefore unlikely to supply you truly dispassionate testimony. A matter of deep concern to your body should be the fact that these witnesses largely have limited their testimony to opinion and thus your record to date is exceedingly sterile of factual data supporting the Treaty. And, absent the latter, I fail to see how you can safely give your consent to the document.

Senator SPARKMAN. Thank you very much, Congressman Hosmer. Senator Pastore?

Senator Hickenlooper?

Senator HICKENLOOPER. I want to say that Congressman Hosmer is really quite professionally competent in this field. He has been a meticulous worker in the details and the scientific end of atomic energy on the Joint Committee. I would suggest that his testimony and his views, which are well considered, be given the weight to which they are entitled.

Mr. HOSMER. Thank you, Senator.

Senator HICKENLOOPER. I am not going to cross swords with you on this, Mr. Hosmer. I will turn you over to somebody else for that purpose.

Senator SPARKMAN. Senator Lausche?

IAEA SAFEGUARDS SYSTEM UNDETERMINED

Senator LAUSCHE. It is your position that the treaty should not be approved in its present form?

Mr. HOSMER. At this point, yes, sir; until, and particularly until, this matter of the adequacy of IAEA safeguards is worked out.

Senator LAUSCHE. What is your understanding about the present requirements and powers of the IAEA in going into countries for the purpose of inspecting the existence or nonexistence of the the development of nuclear weapons?

Mr. Hosmer. Well, that is a hard question to answer because all this treaty does is establish an agreement to make an agreement later, a side agreement with the IAEA, for the inspection of nonnuclear signatories so-called peaceful industrial nuclear processes. What it is going to amount to nobody knows.

Senator Lausche. All that the treaty does is contain an agreement to enter into negotiations to effectuate an agreement about proper verification, is that correct?

Mr. Hosmer. That is right.

You can't tell whether an actual agreement will come along or not. And you don't know whether you are going to cover just part of the industrial processes, just the fabrication of the fuel elements and taking them out of the reactor, or with it go to the whole fuel reprocessing cycle. IAEA doesn't know anything about all this as yet. So it is just difficult to say how you could depend on that body to adequately safeguard these promises that are to be made.

Senator Lausche. What would you interpret the situation to be if at the end of 18 months, as provided in the treaty, no agreement was reached concerning verification and inspection?

Mr. Hosmer. Well, I suppose that ACDA and State Department people would come here and tell you, "Well, we really don't need inspection. You know, we have all signed up and we are all good guys and so let's not push anybody too hard. The United States is going to obey this treaty and set an example and we hope everybody else will." That is what it will be.

Senator Lausche. You do concur with the idea that we should take whatever effective steps we can to prevent proliferation?

Mr. Hosmer. I certainly do, sir. I don't think proliferation is good, and I am not speaking for it. I am speaking for retaining the option defensively and selectively to proliferate, but not for exercising the option. Certainly I am not advising that it be exercised at this particular moment. But it is a valuable defense option. Ever since McNamara came to the Defense Department almost every vital defense decision has been wrung through the systems analysis procedure, and analyzed right down to the last nut and bolt. This has never been done in connection with the surrender of this option, and certainly it should be done, and the Senate should have the advice of the systems analysts, and know the cost effective equation before it renders consent on this. This has never been done at the Disarmament Agency.

TRANSFER OF DEFENSIVE WEAPONS

Senator Lausche. One final question: Based on your understanding of the treaty, would the transfer of defensive antiballistic missiles equipped with safeguards that would prevent them from being used offensively be permitted?

Mr. Hosmer. Only if the U.S. personnel followed right along with them and nonetheless kept custody and control of the warhead, so there is no change, no change in that connection from the present situation as I see it. You couldn't use your permissive action link devices to send them away without U.S. personnel along in custody and control of them. That would violate the treaty.

Senator LAUSCHE. Where is language in the treaty that would permit the delivery of a defensive system or a defensive atomic device to a nonnuclear nation? Where is the language in the treaty?

Mr. HOSMER. We have to go back to the alliances and the Atomic Energy Act if you are talking about the system by which we now physically place weapons in another country, but keep them there under our own custody and control.

If you are talking about sending them away without our own custody and control, there is a provision in the Atomic Energy Act that prevents that.

Senator LAUSCHE. What becomes of this language then that each nuclear weapon state party to the treaty undertakes not to transfer to any recipient whatsoever nuclear weapons or nuclear explosive devices or control over such weapons either directly or indirectly? Is this language meaningful or is is nullified by other laws that we have?

Mr. HOSMER. No. I don't think that the language has been interpreted in any way to interfere with this custody and control type of thing we are doing now, so far as the U.S. view is concerned. But I can assure you, Senator Lausche, that once this treaty is ratified, that the Soviet Union will, as they did at the beginning of the 18-Nation Disarmament Conference where this was negotiated, get right on that point, claim a violation and propagandize the world on it and again take an opportunity to slice at NATO and our other defensive alliances using that treaty to claim we can't place weapons in other countries even under our own custody and control.

Senator SPARKMAN. Senator Case?

Senator CASE. I will reserve my questions.

Senator SPARKMAN. Senator Cooper?

Senator COOPER. I will be brief.

On this question of safeguards, I did ask Secretary Nitze, Dr. Seaborg and others about their views as to the effectiveness of these safeguards, and all testified that they considered them effective. Your statement is, you do not consider them effective?

Mr. HOSMER. Yes, and I suppose perhaps you didn't ask them the detailed factual questions that would have enabled you to evaluate the conclusions that they gave you that they were effective. This is a matter of opinion, I suppose, and my opinion is that they are not effective. I tried to give you some facts to support that opinion.

Senator COOPER. This is a new field for me and I would suggest that the committee secure from the Secretary of Defense and also from Dr. Seaborg more detailed and specific information about these safeguards and why they consider them effective.

Mr. HOSMER. As a matter of fact, the IAEA Inspector General, a fellow from Australia was fired, he is quitting, and they can't even get a replacement for him. That is how well the organization is functioning.

INCREASE IN U.S. COMMITMENTS

Senator COOPER. Just one other point. You have stated you believe we have undertaken 60 additional commitments or possible commitments to signatories to this treaty in the event they are threatened with nuclear aggression. How do you describe that method?

Mr. Hosmer. I think I am in the same quandary that the committee is, whether this security assurance given at the U.N. is meaningful or isn't meaningful, and I simply said if it is meaningful it is a 250-percent increase in the number of safeguards we are committed to. If they are not meaningful there isn't any increase. Nobody knows, the conflicting statements of the President and Secretary Rusk and so on certainly should cause some alarm. A part of my statement I didn't read was a view given by Secretary McNamara to the Joint Atomic Committee in which he pooh-poohed the idea of anything going through the U.N. He said if country A strikes country B, the reaction would have to be so fast by one of the super powers that you couldn't go through an international organization. I think that view should be run up a great big red flag in front of anybody's mind when they are trying to evaluate this particular point of whether the world policeman burden is being increased.

Senator Cooper. Secretary Nitze said he didn't consider it a part of the operative sections of the treaty because it is in the preamble, but I must say I question how we could go to the assistance of any country that is threatened by nuclear weapons unless we are prepared to use nuclear weapons ourselves. I don't see much substance in the preamble.

Mr. Hosmer. Well, these administration statements are quite contradictory and certainly something should be done to nail down how they interpret the assurance and certainly, how other countries regard it as well.

Senator Sparkman. Senator Case, do you want to ask any questions?

Senator Case. Only that when I was questioning the Secretary of State and other witnesses this matter was very much on my mind, this matter of whether we had or had not increased the commitments in order to induce other nations to adhere to this treaty. It took a long while but I think I got very definite assurance that the Secretary of State did not regard anything in this treaty or in connection with it as any plan for future assurances as adding at all to the commitments of this country. I think that it is probably desirable for our committee in acting upon it, should it act favorably, to make it very clear it is doing so in the light of these assurances and is not in any way either ratifying past commitments or authorizing new ones.

Mr. Hosmer. That is certainly in line with the recommendation I made that it be spelled our clearly for the world to see and understand where there is a commitment or isn't a commitment.

Senator Case. I thank you, Mr. Chairman.

Senator Sparkman. Thank you very much, Congressman Hosmer. Next is Congressman Findley of Illinois.

STATEMENT OF HON. PAUL FINDLEY, U.S. CONGRESSMAN FROM ILLINOIS

Mr. Findley. Senator, I will be very brief and I do appreciate this chance to be with you.

I take this time and your trouble out of my concern with the treaty and my concern arises from three times being a delegate to the North Atlantic Assembly, formerly the NATO Parliamentarians' Conference, an opportunity there to talk to many European leaders privately as well as in the hearing of others in 1965. I gained other impressions when I had the privilege of going on what was known as the Republican sponsored fact finding mission to Paris where a group of Republican House Members had a chance to talk at some length with French leaders. As we consider this treaty and the desirability from the American viewpoint of nonproliferation, I think we could wisely put ourselves in the other fellow's shoes once in a while.

I recall talking with Pierre Messmer who is still the Defense Minister of France and asked him what he thought of nonproliferation of weapons and his answer was "now that France has nuclear weapons we agree with you they should not be proliferated."

But I wonder what our view would be if we were a citizen of Turkey or of Italy or of West Germany, would we have this same view and throw up our hands with horror at the possibility that our government might some day acquire nuclear weapons for its own defense. I think our viewpoint would be quite different.

EFFECT OF TREATY ON ATLANTIC ALLIANCE

I believe that this treaty, if it is approved by the Senate without modification or reservation, will have the effect of seriously weakening and perhaps even destroying the effectiveness of the Atlantic Alliance, and its impact upon the alliance should certainly be of great concern to every American because the alliance is so important politically and militarily to us. Although relations have improved somewhat with the Soviet Union, I think it is easy for any of us to detail some items which would assure that Moscow has not always, in all respects, adopted a more reasonable viewpoint.

I believe that there has been a conscious policy on the part of the present administration to sacrifice the cohesion of the Atlantic Alliance on political, economic, and military affairs in order to achieve bipolarization cooperation with the Soviet Union, and I think the statement of Mr. Foster in the celebrated article of 1965 in "Foreign Affairs" attests to this.

There certainly is a genuine concern in Western Europe regarding U.S. commitment. The treaty is certainly a factor in causing this apprehension, and as evidence, I point out to the committee that of the other 14 members of NATO only 5 up to the present time have signed the treaty, 5 out of 14 others. Among those who have not signed, of course, are France, the Federal Republic of West Germany, Italy, and Turkey.

There are several reasons why this treaty will weaken the alliance. The first is psychological, because since 1961 the United States has undertaken a series of unilateral actions without consultation with our NATO allies which would have affected their security and national interest. Naturally the European countries would view with some concern this treaty because it is essentially a bilateral arrangement between the Soviet Union and the United States.

For these reasons I have sketched briefly, Mr. Chairman, I hope the text of my remarks will be printed in full.

Senator SPARKMAN. It will be printed in full.

175

RESERVATION TO TREATY RECOMMENDED

Mr. FINDLEY. For these reasons, I feel that a reservation to the treaty preserving the option to establish an Atlantic Alliance nuclear defensive system should be made. A reservation for that purpose, and this retention of the NATO option in the treaty was included in all of the proposals on disarmament, proliferation of weapons, made by Presidents Eisenhower and Kennedy, and initially by President Johnson. This has been a consistent policy up to October of 1966, on the part of every U.S. President to retain, protect, and preserve the possibility that some form of nuclear NATO defense might be established, owned, and controlled by NATO as an organization and perhaps not subject to veto of any single nation.

Without such a reservation, I fear that we will see a continuation of two very unfortunate trends which are now clearly evident in Europe. These trends result from the U.S. policy of unilaterally changing its posture regarding Western defenses without consultation or taking into consideration the wishes, the national interests of our allies. Both trends heighten the dangers of the United States becoming isolated in Western Europe.

The first trend is toward the development of national nuclear defenses which I am sure we all don't want to see happen. But it is a curious fact, nevertheless true, that American arms negotiations with the Soviets and other secret negotiations have actually had the effect of proliferating nuclear weapons because they have encouraged the French in one instance to develop their own program, and to pull out of NATO's integrated command structure. I am sure that our negotiations in this field were one of the major considerations there. The second unfortunate trend is one toward accommodation with the Soviet Union over the heads of our allies and placing the objective of arrangements with the Soviet center as more important than strengthening and establishing a greater cohesion within the Atlantic Alliance.

The dangers of war will be reduced, in my view, only in an atmosphere and reality of cohesion within the Atlantic Alliance, one of continued Western nuclear superiority and hopeful changes in the Soviet Union's power structure, and anything that lessens our nuclear superiority or weakens the Atlantic Alliance increases the danger of war.

The treaty's inspection features, as Mr. Hosmer has so very plainly said, are meaningless. Its guarantees against nuclear blackmail are empty. It weakens the military position of the United States and without the NATO reservation, which I have mentioned, I feel it will encourage the nations of Europe to develop their own nuclear forces bringing us closer to the hour of midnight, as the Journal of Atomic Scientists has so often referred to the nuclear dooms day. I thank you, Mr. Chairman.

(The full statement of Mr. Findley follows:)

STATEMENT BY REP. PAUL FINDLEY

Mr. Chairman, I appear before the committee today to propose a reservation to the Nuclear Non-proliferation Treaty. I believe this treaty, if approved by the Senate without modification or reservation will have the effect of seriously weakening and perhaps even destroying the effectiveness of the Atlantic Alliance. Its impact upon the Alliance should be of prime concern to this committee, for I believe that the cohesion of the Alliance is important militarily, politically, and economically to the United States' national interest.

In the last several years there has been less tension between the United States and the Soviet Union. Although it would be misleading to speak of this development as a true detente, there nevertheless has been a more cordial relationship between the two super powers. Four factors are responsible for this turn of events:

 (1) the continued military—especially nuclear—power of the United States;

 (2) the Sino Soviet split;

 (3) the changes in Soviet leadership since the death of Stalin;

 (4) the cohesion of the Atlantic Alliance.

Two of these four factors are beyond the direct influence of the United States, i.e. the Sino Soviet spilt and changes in Soviet leadership. The quarrel between Moscow and Peking could perhaps be patched up with a modification of the position of both sides and the departure of Chairman Mao. Certainly a Sino Soviet rapprochement is not entirely out of the question. Likewise, it is entirely possible that the most reactionary and doctrinaire of Communist leaders could again occupy the seat of power in the Soviet ruling elite. Recent trends in domestic affairs in the Soviet Union show these doctrinaire forces to be much stronger than originally believed in the West. It should be obvious to most that among Soviet goals—as Chairman Kosygin stated only two weeks ago—is (1) achievement of nuclear parity with the U.S. and (2) the disruption of NATO.

Although relations have eased somewhat between Moscow and Washington we should not assume that everywhere else in the world Moscow has adopted a more reasonable position, for it has not. For instance:

 (1) the Soviet Union is now sending arms to Pakistan, thereby endangering Indian security

 (2) the Soviet Union continues to play a very dangerous game in the Middle East, putting on one mask at the UN and quite another with the radical Arabs

 (3) the East German regime—a client state of the Soviet Union—is again putting the squeeze play on Allied rights in West Berlin

 (4) the Soviet Union has reached a high degree of involvement in the Yemen Civil War.

More examples could be cited, but these will perhaps at least show that Soviet intentions are still far from peaceful.

For some time the United States has been confronted with a basic dilemma. In the words of the *Economist*—

 The U.S. does have two conceivable policies. It can be leader of the united West and deal with Russia from there. Or it can lead towards an *entente cordiale* of the two great powers who could have the hope to control everybody else, including the Europeans.

I believe it has been a conscious policy of the Johnson Administration to sacrifice cohesion in the Atlantic Alliance on political and military matters in order to achieve bipolar cooperation with the Soviet Union. This was conceded by Mr. William Foster, Director of the Arms Control and Disarmament Agency, in his article in the July, 1965 issue of *Foreign Affairs*. At that time Mr. Foster wrote regarding the non-proliferation treaty:

 A heavier cost could be the erosion of alliances resulting from the high degree of U.S.-Soviet cooperation, which will be required if a non-proliferation program is to be successful. Within NATO there could be concern that the detente would lead to a weakening of our commitment to Western Europe. The problem will be particularly acute in Germany, where there will be the added concern of the amelioration of the East-West confrontation which could lead to increased acceptance of the status quo in Central Europe.

Ambassador Foster's conjecture is a masterpiece of understatement. There is genuine concern in Western Europe regarding the U.S. commitment. The NNPT is a factor causing this apprehension. As evidence of this I would point out to the committee that of the 14 members of NATO only six have signed the treaty. Among those who have not signed are France, the Federal Republic (Germany), Italy, and Turkey.

There are several reasons why this treaty will weaken the alliance. The first is psychological. Since 1961 the U.S. has undertaken a series of unilateral actions—without consultation with our NATO allies—which have affected their security and national interest. Most of the allies believe that these decisions weakened their security, not increased it. For example, it took five and a half years for the U.S. to persuade the NATO Council to adopt officially the defense posture of "flexible response" for "massive retaliation."

Among the steps taken unilaterally by the U.S. were:

(1) "flexible response" substituted for "massive retaliation" in event of Soviet aggression

(2) secret correspondence between President Kennedy and Chairman Khrushchev regarding matters of security directly affecting Western Europe

(3) placing U.S. troops in Europe on the highest state of alert during the Cuban crisis without consulting European governments who obviously would be affected in the event of an outbreak between U.S. and S.U. in the Caribbean.

(4) decision in 1967 to deploy thin "ABM" system in the U.S. but foreclosing an "ABM" system for Europe

(5) unilaterally withdrawing NATO option in discussions regarding the non-proliferation treaty.

In the military area, the nuclear non-proliferation treaty does two things that genuinely alarm many West Europeans. First, it prevents a purely defensive ABM system under either NATO or national control. Second, it precludes other NATO nuclear defenses.

For these two reasons a reservation should be attached to the treaty preserving the option to establish Atlantic Alliance nuclear defenses. This retention of the NATO option in the NNPT was included in all proposals made by Presidents Eisenhower, Kennedy and, initially at least, by Johnson.

Without such a reservation we will see a continuation of two trends which are now clearly evident in Europe. These two trends result from the United States policy of unilaterally changing its posture regarding Western defenses without consultation or taking into consideration the wishes and national interests of our allies. Both heighten the dangers of the U.S. becoming isolated in Western Europe.

The first trend—that is, to develop national nuclear defenses—is most clearly evident in France although there is a growing element in West Germany and Italy that advocates this position. The French believe the U.S. commitment to defend Europe cannot be taken seriously. They further believe the U.S. and the Soviet Union will try to reach an agreement—a sort of an international condominium—in which the final European settlement will be made over the heads of the Europeans, East and West. Consequently, French strategy is to develop its own defenses and be independent of any integrated command structure. It obviously follows that once a nation is convinced that its Alliance partner will not defend it, it will prepare its own defenses. The French have done this by becoming the fourth nuclear power. They pulled out of the integrated command of NATO because: (1) they fear the U.S. will involve Europe in a war without consulting their allies, as in the Cuban alert of 1962, and (2) the integrated command under American control will make the defense of France dependent upon Washington.

It is a curious fact—but nevertheless true—that American arms negotiations with the Soviet Union and other secret negotiations have had the effect of proliferating nuclear weapons by encouraging the French to develop their own program and to pull out of NATO's command structure.

The second trend in Europe is the opposite of the first and is most noticeable among the smaller European countries, although there is some support for it in Germany because of Germany's exposed position. This trend is one towards accommodation with the Soviet Union. Here it is entirely possible to envision a series of Rappallo-like treaties which will effectively destroy NATO and render Western Europe a continent of Finlands. The ultimate effect of this will be to shift the balance of power to the Soviet state because all of Europe will be under its political suzerainty.

Both of these trends should be alarming for the U.S. I believe that if one more NATO nation acquires nuclear weapons most of the others will be forced to follow because of an atmosphere of mutual fear and distrust will have been generated.

In less than 100 years three major wars have started in Europe because of the jealousies, hates and fears of the European states. Whatever the faults of NATO and the Warsaw Pact they have at least had the effect of restraining the old European jealousies which ignited the sparks of war.

For a period of time it was hoped that a European federation would preclude another war in Europe. Today the trend towards federation has been halted, perhaps even aborted.

A group of European states each having individual nuclear weapons could be a dangerous development for the U.S. Curiously, however, this treaty will not prevent such proliferation; in fact it does just the opposite, it encourages it. No treaty will prevent a nation from acting in its own national self-interest. Those who question this need only look at the fate of the Kellogg-Briand Pact, the League of Nations, the Naval Limitation Conferences of the 1920s and all the rest. Peace is not assured by treaties. The Non-proliferation Treaty will not prevent the spread of nuclear weapons anymore than the Kellogg-Briand Pact prevented war or the Washington Naval Conference limited the construction of capital naval ships in the Pacific.

The dangers of war will be reduced only in an atmosphere and reality of cohesion in the Atlantic Alliance, continued Western nuclear superiority and hopeful changes in the Soviet Union's power structure. Anything that lessens our nuclear superiority or loosens the Atlantic Alliance increases the dangers of war. As Jan Triska wrote in his book "Soviet Foreign Policy" the stronger the Soviet weapons position vis-a-vis the West and the more fragmented the West, the lower the Soviet perception of risk in actual East-West conflicts.

The *Bulletin of Atomic Scientists* has consistently displayed on its front cover a clock. The Bulletin's clock measures the closeness of the world to midnight—a nuclear war. It was originally set at a quarter to twelve. It has moved forward three times and back twice. There are those who believe that the clock will be moved back further with the signing of this treaty. If such is the case, I question the accuracy of this judgment. Because, you see, the clock is not a gauge to register the ups and downs of the international power struggle; it is intended to reflect basic changes in the level of continuous danger in which mankind lives in the nuclear age. Since this treaty seriously weakens and may completely destroy NATO—which I maintain has been a principal cause of any unreasonableness in Soviet behavior—then I would set the clock forward, not backwards.

This is so because the treaty does not effectively prevent the spread of nuclear weapons. Its inspection features are meaningless. Its guarantees against nuclear blackmail are empty. It weakens the relative military position of the United States. Without the NATO reservation, it will encourage the nations of Europe to develop their own independent nuclear forces bringing the world closer to the hour of midnight, the nuclear doomsday.

SUMMARY OF DEVELOPMENTS RELATING TO RETREAT OF U.S. NEGOTIATING POSITION REGARDING NATO OPTION IN NUCLEAR NON-PROLIFERATION TREATY

On August 29, 1957, the U.S. in co-operation with three other powers (France, Canada, and the United Kingdom) proposed a scheme that would restrict nuclear proliferation but at the same time require nuclear nations to cease their production of fissionable material for weapon purposes. A caveat to the non-proliferation proposal was that nuclear weapons could be transferred for individual or collective self-defense.

Initially U.S. position envisioned some nuclear sharing arrangement within the framework of multi-national alliances like NATO but it sought to reduce nuclear weapon production as well as proliferation. The Soviet Union on September 20, 1957, rejected these proposals, especially the collective sharing of nuclear weapons. In 1959, the United Nations adopted a general resolution urging efforts to be undertaken to prevent nuclear proliferation.

In 1961, the United States undertook its first significant change in its position. It abandoned the transfer of nuclear weapons for defense purposes to individual nations. But it still retained collective sharing under an alliance as a part of its policy.

From 1962 to August 17, 1965, the main issue at the Geneva Conference on nuclear proliferation was whether such an agreement would prevent nuclear sharing arrangements within a collective defense organization like NATO. The Soviet Union was anxious to make sure it did, whereas the U.S. did not want to close the door on possible arrangements within NATO.

On August 17, 1965, the U.S. made the second major change in its position. It retained the concept of nuclear sharing, but only if the total number of nuclear states did not increase. Ambassador Foster stated that this U.S. position would not preclude the establishment of nuclear arrangements within NATO so long as the arrangement did not constitute an additional entity having the power to use nuclear weapons independent of existing nuclear nations. In other words, if the U.S. independently surrendered its control over all its own nuclear weapons to a NATO arrangement then a sharing arrangement would be possible. This proposal, in light of the 1964 presidential campaign in which the President re-iterated that U.S. would never surrender control of nuclear weapons was a farce. Since the S.U. realized that the U.S. was not about to turn over voluntarily its entire stockpile of nuclear weapons to a new organization and renounce its right to veto over them, Moscow could see light at the end of the tunnel in their efforts to prohibit any sharing arrangement. On September 24, 1965, the Soviet Union insisted again that any sharing arrangement within a military alliance was out of the question.

Objective evidence indicates that the Soviet Union's patience was rewarded on October 10, 1966, when President Johnson and Secretary Rusk met Soviet Foreign Minister Gromyko at the White House. The New York Times reported on August 25, 1967:

It has since become clear that in their talks that day President Johnson and Mr. Rusk gave Mr. Gromyko strong indication that the previous United States reservations, aimed at accommodating some nuclear sharing device in the North Atlantic Treaty Organization had been withdrawn.

After that time the Geneva Conference marked time waiting for the U.S. to finish "consultation" with its allies. Within less than a year, on August 24, 1967, the U.S. and the S.U. came to an agreement on all particulars except the inspection provision which was soon remedied by absurdly "agreeing to agree" at some later date.

In the ten-year period from 1957 through 1967, the United States changed its position on three major points. It no longer suggested that the nuclear powers reduce their own stockpiles at the same time non-proliferation measures were taken. It no longer insisted upon some arrangement for individual self-defense. Most important, it dropped the requirement that nuclear sharing within NATO be protected.

The advisability of U.S. reducing its nuclear stockpiles is questionable, but it is imperative, for reasons I shall outline below, that the U.S. insist upon some provision for establishing nuclear defense within its regional defense organizations, principally NATO. To facilitate that result I have prepared an amendment to this bill. My amendment reads:

Provided that no funds authorized by this Act may be spent for salaries or other expenses connected with advancing proposals which preclude the provision of weapons or other materials for the establishment of nuclear defenses to regional organizations established under Article 52 of the UN Charter.

In this respect my amendment—which retains the NATO option, so to speak—reflects the position of the U.S. on the non-proliferation treaty up till October, 1966. I believe that the policy of nuclear sharing within regional defense alliances as subscribed to and supported by Presidents Eisenhower and Kennedy, and initially by President Johnson, is wise. Nothing has changed which has altered the basic soundness of their initial judgments.

Senator SPARKMAN. Thank you, Congressman.

Senator Pastore?

Senator PASTORE. No questions.

Senator SPARKMAN. Senator Hickenlooper.

Senator HICKENLOOPER. No questions.

Senator SPARKMAN. Senator Lausche?

Senator LAUSCHE. No questions.

Senator SPARKMAN. Senator Case.

DOES TREATY PRECLUDE NATO NUCLEAR FORCE?

Senator CASE. I wish you would develop, if you would, your own thought, Mr. Findley, as to the difference between the administration view of what would happen in regard to NATO and your own, as to the necessity for a reservation. It is my understanding that it is not thought by the administration that this treaty would preclude the establishment of a NATO nuclear force.

Mr. FINDLEY. I think the administration's position is that this treaty would not alter present arrangements or make a continuation of present arrangements with NATO impossible, and I believe they are correct on that, as to their interpretation of transfer. But it is hard to see what the future holds, and I think it is very possible that in an assured time nuclear devices which are purely defensive, which can operate only over the territory of the country in which they are located only for specified time limits can be developed which would give the countries of Europe a greater assurance of protection in the event that the Soviet buildup continues.

NATO now owns a system called NADGE, it owns a lot of things and I would hope in time to come the institutional form and effectiveness and importance of NATO would grow, and a part of this growth might well be a purely defensive nuclear system which NATO would own as an organization, and which would not be subject to the veto of any individual state.

As we see the crises around the world I think the question would naturally rise in the mind of a citizen of West Berlin, for example, as to whether we would really push the nuclear button to defend their homes.

The same concern would arise in other parts of the world, and as time goes on and as other nations refine their nuclear weapons equipment, it seems to me less likely that the United States on its own initiative, would push the button and send its missiles against another country and thus risk destruction to its own cities, and in light of that likely trend, I think it is wise for us to keep the door open on the possibility that a purely defensive nuclear system can be developed for this most essential alliance for yourself.

Senator CASE. I thank you. I think the witness has called attention to a very important matter and I am sure the committee will take it fully into account.

EFFECT OF CZECHOSLOVAKIAN EVENTS ON RATIFICATION BY OTHER COUNTRIES

On another matter, just one question: Would you be willing to give or venture your opinion as to whether, if the Soviets should resort to the use of force in Czechoslovakia, this would affect the attitude of the West Germans and other nonnuclear states about this Nonproliferation Treaty, and perhaps then there wouldn't be any West German accession at a minimum, or there might be no ratification by other countries as well.

Mr. FINDLEY. Well, the presence of Soviet troops in the operations of Czechoslovakia certainly tend to support the concern and fears of West Germans, and, as they reflect upon what the future may hold, I would think they would see the need ultimately to have the advantage of nuclear defenses, not national nuclear defenses, I would hope, and I am sure that is their own feeling, but they would certainly see the need in future days of having nuclear defenses on which they could count, and which would not be subject to the veto of any single country.

Senator CASE. I think that is all, Mr. Chairman.

Senator SPARKMAN. Senator Pell?

Senator PELL. No questions.

Senator SPARKMAN. Senator Cooper?

EFFECT OF TREATY ON NATO ALLIANCE QUESTIONED

Senator COOPER. I can't quite follow your argument that this treaty would injure our NATO alliance. It seems to me history has shown that the NATO countries did not welcome the multilateral nuclear force, they have not desired, other than France, to build a nuclear offensive or defensive system. The NATO countries said they would rely on the deterrents of the United States. My own thinking is that maybe it would really disturb them if we precipitably withdrew all our forces or a great portion of them as is now being argued by some in the Congress.

Mr. FINDLEY. I think that precipitous withdrawal of troops from West Germany would be unfortunate, but I would hope that we could, through a number of steps, such as this, and this would be one such step, get a greater cohesion necessary in NATO, a greater feeling of common strength and purpose so that we can, in time, reduce the troop levels without weakening Western Europe's defense.

The presence of our troops doesn't automatically assure the intervention of our nuclear weapons to defend that area, because the presence of our troops in Vietnam has not induced American nuclear weapons.

Senator COOPER. That is all.

Senator SPARKMAN. Senator Curtis?

Senator CURTIS. No questions.

Senator SPARKMAN. Thank you very much, Congressman Findley; we appreciate your appearance and your statement.

Next is Dr. Edward Teller. Come around. We are glad to welcome you once more to the committee. We have your statement and it will be printed in full in the record and you may proceed as you see fit.

STATEMENT OF DR. EDWARD TELLER

Dr. TELLER. Thank you, Mr. Chairman, I have not given a statement, I have given a summary.

Senator SPARKMAN. Very well, that is what I had reference to.

Dr. TELLER. Actually I would like to expand on the summary in considerable detail but I will not do so because of your admonition to save time, to which I want to give full consideration.

Senator SPARKMAN. May I ask you this: Do you have a statement prepared?

Dr. TELLER. No. I would like to make some general remarks and then give maximum scope to questions.

Senator SPARKMAN. Well, you go ahead and you give us what we need to hear.

Senator HICKENLOOPER. Mr. Chairman, I agree with that. Dr. Teller is one of the greatest authorities in the world on this subject and I don't think we should try to curtail or circumscribe his testimony. I personally would like to hear what he has to say in whatever detail he cares to present it.

Dr. TELLER. Thank you very much, Senator Hickenlooper. I will try to be complete and clear. I will also try to be brief. In trying to reconcile these incompatible objectives I am in no worse position than you are in trying to oppose proliferation, and trying to do so in a rapidly changing world under very great stress. I am just participating in the general contradictory human conditions.

I would like to start with one general remark. A question of this overriding importance must not be treated too rapidly. I will try to confine myself primarily to my specialty, but I urge you not to hurry but to consider all sides of this issue. By reading carefully all the testimony that has been given here and listening to some more, I have a vivid impression, on the one hand, of great praise of accomplishments. On the other hand, serious doubts expressed in many and different quarters.

I hope that you will not brush aside either of these two considerations.

PROLIFERATION MUST BE LIMITED

Very particularly I hope that you will give full weight, and I am sure you will give full weight, to the need to do something effective about stopping further proliferation or at least limiting it. This is not a new question for me. Almost 30 years ago I and a few of my friends, heard and thought about the possibility of nuclear explosions. We thought about it very shortly after the discovery of fission itself. Half my life I have spent with this nightmare; and I don't want proliferation. At the same time I also do not want us to be in a position of offering a paper, an agreement, without any real safeguards. Nor am I happy about our taking even more responsibilities and getting entangled more deeply in the role of policeman of the world.

I hope that the complexity of the issues is vividly present in all your minds.

I have to add to the difficulties because my first remark will be this: Treaties are written in order to provide some safety, some permanance. A treaty which will lose its effectiveness within the 18 months now provided for the mere negotiation of verification conditions is not worth having. Yet the technical developments are proceeding so rapidly that it is exceedingly difficult to write a treaty which will continue to serve its initial objectives.

In spite of all these difficulties, I hope I can make constructive suggestions. But, first of all, let me remind you of the development of the present nuclear weapons situation which was not a straight escalation introduction all the time of bigger weapons but the introduction of great surprises, atomic weapons, the thermonuclear weapons, the means of delivery, technical developments concerning outer space, the great changes introduced by electronics, and now the nascent, the emerging, possibility of missile defense.

In this rapid and continuing technological revolution you won't put any genie back into the bottle. All you can do is to create new genies, and hope that they will be better and more benevolent ones.

DEPLOYMENT OF DEFENSIVE SYSTEM

Perhaps, just conceivably, missile defense may be a step in that direction. When it is said that missile defense will make matters worse because it will merely stimulate our opponents toward more offense, this is predicated on the assumption that defense will always remain more difficult than offense. It used to be said that the cost of offense is only 3 percent of the cost of defense. Now many estimate that the cost of offense is 50 percent of that for defense. The time may come when defense will be easier than offense. I do not know. But what I do know is that even today we can deploy, and because of wise decisions of the Senate we are in the way of deploying, a defense system, which has a good chance to be effective against the Chinese or any other newcomer to the nuclear club.

Whether it is presently possible to deploy a missile defense that would be effective against the Russians I don't know, and I claim nobody knows, and that is the reason why the present development, called Sentinel, is reasonable, because it is not only a defense in itself, it is also a pilot operation that can teach us whether further development will be reasonable.

I wanted to offer all this to you as a background on which to build, a background of rapidly changing technological situations.

OBJECTIONS TO PARTIAL TEST BAN TREATY

Now, let me go back to another fact that bears on present considerations, the partial Test Ban Treaty of 1963. At that time many people, many witnesses before you, I among them, raised some questions concerning the wisdom of provisions that would limit the peaceful applications of nuclear explosives in the Plowshare program. We have been assured that Plowshare will not be interfered with, but in fact the history since the signing of the partial Test Ban Treaty in 1963 is that Plowshare has been slowed down.

The new treaty now before you for ratification, by contrast, endorses Plowshare. There is no doubt in my mind that this is a great and important accomplishment, and I hope that whatever is needed will be done by spending the requisite scientific effort, in the political sphere in modifying earlier understandings in order, indeed, to make nuclear explosives serve peace. Plowshare explosions can make harbors, they can make waterways, they can help in the mining of raw materials, they can help the developing nations, and thereby strike at some of the causes of war. To strike at the causes of war, in my opinion, is probably the most important step one can make in the direction of lasting and stable peace.

At the time of the test ban my chief objections to the partial Test Ban Treaty, my chief worry, were of a different nature. I was worried lest this ban prevent us from acquiring needed knowledge for the development of missile defense. Many people, among them many excellent technical people, said that everything we need to know about nuclear explosives can be found out irrespective of the partial test ban.

Now, two of these advocates, Bethe and Garwin, have published an article in the March 1968 issue of the Scientific American, in which they argue that missile defense is ineffective and will remain so. I disagree that missile defense is ineffective.

One of their arguments, and I agree that the argument is worrisome, concerns "blackout", that is, interference with the seeing eye of the radar due to nuclear explosions. The 1963 partial Test Ban Treaty prohibits us from exploring this blackout problem experimentally. We are going into missile defense with one hand tied behind our backs. But we are at least moving.

I worry whether this Nonproliferation Treaty presently under consideration may go one step further in denying us certain important options, which could be more easily utilized if at present we exercise proper caution.

DISTINCTION BETWEEN DEFENSIVE AND OFFENSIVE WEAPONS

At this point I would like to come to the question that Senator Lausche brought up repeatedly this morning, the distinction between defensive and offensive weapons. Whatever your opinion is about the relative importance, the relative stabilizing or unstabilizing effect of these weapons in the hands of Russia and the United States, I think that an argument can be made in favor of the stabilizing effect of defense if defensive weapons and defensive weapons alone can be given to states which today do not possess either defensive or offensive capabilities.

Senator PASTORE. Dr. Teller, would you mind an interruption for a question?

Dr. TELLER. Of course not.

Senator PASTORE. Well, first of all let me say you know of the admiration and the affection that I have for you, and the great contribution that you have made not only to this country but to the world in your hydrogen bomb. You are the father of that. But the question I would like to ask you from the scientific point of view is this:

CAPABILITY OF A WEAPON BEING DEFENSIVE AND OFFENSIVE

Would it be possible for a nation to have exclusive control of an atomic defensive weapon without at the same time having revealed to it an offensive weapon?

Dr. TELLER. Sir, I am very happy you asked this question. Had you not asked it, I would have answered it in the next few sentences. [Laughter.]

The answer may not be what you expect. The answer is I don't know. The answer is I hope so. The answer is that with diligent work there is an excellent chance that this can be accomplished.

Now, let me say again what it is I want to accomplish. In our complex and interrelated world, questions concerning words like "sovereignty" have become ambiguous. But there is one sovereign right that every nation will be most unwilling to abandon, which will be the last to be abandoned, and that is the right to defend oneself from instant annihilation. It has been correctly said by Representative Holifield that we have weapons on allied territory which can be used, among other things, for defense. But these weapons are under the control of others than the natives of the country in which these weapons are placed.

185

There is an immense psychological drive, one that I think is unavoidable. Everybody wants to have the right to defend his own life. If the exercise of that right leads to defense alone, then this right, to my mind, is not easily questioned.

There is not only the problem, the psychological one which I have already stated; but there is a practical problem. When a missile is approaching, there is no chance for Tokyo to consult with Washington on appropriate actions. There is a reluctance to delegate responsibility for the nuclear release to an American official. He would necessarily be a minor official, because many such officials would be required. There are very practical reasons why it would be desirable to allow everyone to defend himself provided, Senator Pastore's question can be answered in the positive sense, provided the weapons transferred to this country's control can be used for defense and defense alone.

Unfortunately, I know of no presently viable ballistic missile defense system that does not utilize nuclear explosives. Possible alternative defense systems will evolve in the future. I would like to see alternative means of missile defense develop and I am not saying that they won't. I just cannot tell you that I really expect nonnuclear alternatives to be available in the foreseeable future.

Therefore, if we want to give that power to the person who wants to defend himself, we must give him control over nuclear weapons. In my opinion, the main objection to the multilateral force was that it did not give freedom of action to our allies, that it was always subject to American veto.

What I am looking for is defense in the hands of the person who defends himself, but given to him in such a way that it cannot be used for offense.

DIFFICULTY OF WEAPON REMAINING ONLY DEFENSIVE

Now, let me try to get to the technical point of this argument, which is really the answer that Senator Pastore wanted to have. The beginnings of his answer have been already mentioned by Representative Holifield in the "permissive action link." We can establish a defensive weapon. We can tie to it a nuclear warhead, and we can endow it with an electronic system which will permit this arrangement to explode only in a predetermined space which is clearly for the purpose of defense, because it is either directly above or in the immediate approaches to the country to be defended. Furthermore, it is easy to arrange so that the nuclear explosive will never explode in such a manner that it will do damage on the ground. All this, I am sure can be done.

The difficulty lies elsewhere. We give this device to a country X, and these people are very clever. They take an X-ray—excuse me, I said country X—I should say that if we give it to a country Y, they take an X-ray, they analyze all this devilish machinery and having understood it, they take a screwdriver, they take it apart, lift out the nuclear explosive and they are then ready to go on with their own nefarious purpose of aggression.

But we are more clever. We can make devices which will blow up if you X-ray it, and will certainly blow up if you take a screwdriver to it. I don't want to say that this problem is solved because I am claiming that we are clever, but in the end they may be more clever still.

Senator PASTORE. If you will permit me once again, they say that nothing is permanent excepting death and taxes. Now, this instrument here, if we should ever reach this day which you claim to be quite distant——

Dr. TELLER. I did not say that, sir.

POSSIBLE RELIEF CLAUSE

Senator PASTORE. There is a relief clause which we may consider if nonproliferation is bad as you have indicated and you would be against it for defense purposes. That is primarily what we are trying to avoid through this draft treaty. The day will come when possibly we can perfect this defensive instrument and it can be used exclusively for defense purposes—and you make a very strong and meritorious argument in that direction—what is there to preclude us from at that proper time of revising that treaty or excluding ourselves under the relief clause and bring ourselves in for peaceful objectives?

Dr. TELLER. I am very sorry you have taken away my testimony.

Senator PASTORE. I have?

Dr. TELLER. I want to steer in that direction, supporting this point of view with a few more arguments if you would permit me to proceed in my own way.

Senator PASTORE. Thank you, I am through.

Dr. TELLER. Let me try to recapture my line of thought.

I was just about to say, that in the end if you ask me the very serious question, Do I trust my electronic device, do I continue to trust our own inventiveness in preference to somebody else's inventiveness, even if we continue to develop safeguards, in the end I don't trust electronics just as I might say, if you don't mind, I don't trust treaties either. What I do trust because it is the best combination available is electronics plus treaties.

COOPERATION OF NATIONS TO DEFEND THEMSELVES

I would like to have an arrangement whereby we give to nations that want to defend themselves with nuclear warheads, the design of which need not be known to them. If necessary, their effectiveness can be demonstrated.

The recipients will have to cooperate: they will have to pay for and help to establish the necessary radar, and missile systems, but we would provide the warhead, which they would never see.

I say if we link the safeguards, the electronic safeguards, and the treaty with continuing inspection so that we see that none of these instruments has been tampered with, and that the treaties are being observed, if we furthermore put a time lock on each of these devices, so that after, let us say, 4 months they cease to function, they melt down, become unusable, unless somebody from this country goes there and renews the effectiveness of the defense. If we do all that, if we can

carefully create an environment that can be controlled and safeguarded and verified, then this verification has an excellent chance
to work, a better chance than we ever had to verify the partial test
ban or have to verify a nonproliferation treaty.

Therefore, if we do the best we possibly can, my answer is we do
not know, Senator Pastore, we do not know now, whether it can be
done. I hope it can be done, and I hope that if it is done that what you
have suggested, which is an excellent idea, will indeed be done, that
we will provide these means to stabilize the world, that we will help
to defend, the Japanese or Hindus or Pakistanese against the Chinese
or any other nuclear power.

DEPLOYMENT OF DEFENSIVE SYSTEMS URGED

I would explicitly like to read a very short statement. It is the final
segment of my summary.

It seems, therefore, necessary to declare that weapons which are
designed for defense and can be used for defense alone are in the
interest of peace; that when and if such defensive systems are properly
developed, the necessary steps will be taken to make them widely
available for self defense, and that this will be done even if it requires
modification of existing laws or treaties.

I therefore explicitly recommend that the Senate make it known
that it looks with favor on the development of effective defensive
systems and that by ratifying the treaty the Senate does not intend
to preclude the deployment of purely defensive arrangements, if and
when these become available.

This potential availability is not in the distant future, it is in the
unknown future which, by diligent work, could be soon.

If this condition, this reservation, is not stated explicitly then, I
cannot recommend ratification because in this case international stability and the prospect of peace may be jeopardized.

In fact, in this case, if such defensive means are not offered, some
of the important and powerful nations which presently object to the
treaty, will continue to object.

If, on the other hand, in order to finish on a positive note, we made
a declaration of intent of the general kind that I have suggested, this
will help to reassure our allies and to persuade nations which are now
reluctant, to join in the Nonproliferation Treaty. In a properly conceived form, and a willingly agreed form, the Nonproliferation Treaty
could be something very wonderful.

Thank you very much.

(The summary of testimony of Dr. Teller follows:)

SUMMARY OF TESTIMONY BY DR. EDWARD TELLER

Proliferation of nuclear weapons has increased the dangers of sudden and
violent conflict and it is most important to find proper means to prevent or
to limit future proliferation. Consideration of the Non-Proliferation Treaty,
whose ratification is under discussion, raises some general questions. Among
these are the question of verification, for which conditions may not be spelled
out for 18 months. Another is connected with the demands from non-nuclear
states for assurance against nuclear aggression. If these demands are to be

met in a truly effective manner the result may well be that the United States will have to assume, more than ever, the role of policing the world.

There are some technical considerations having a bearing on the treaty which may help to determine whether or not the intended beneficial results will be achieved. One is connected with Article V which permits and even encourages the use of nuclear explosives for peaceful and constructive purposes. This is to be welcomed as a great step forward. There is sound and cumulative evidence that nuclear explosives can indeed be used in an effective and safe manner for earth-moving and mining. This effort, known as Plowshare, may indeed help to eliminate shortages of essential raw materials, establish better harbors and other facilities, help the progress of developing nations, and thereby serve to reduce international tensions. To make this possible it is necessary for us to make a more determined effort to construct the devices best adapted to peaceful applications.

The second technical consideration concerns the question of offensive and defensive uses of nuclear weapons, and the more difficult problem of whether it is possible to establish that the weapons systems themselves are indeed of an offensive or defensive character. The immense offensive potential of nuclear weapons has been demonstrated and is firmly established in the public mind. The main motivation for the Non-Proliferation Treaty is the identification of nuclear weapons with aggression and destruction. It is therefore of particular importance to discuss the possibility of a purely defensive role for nuclear explosives.

Recent discussions have led to the important decision that the United States embark on the development of a defense against ballistic missiles. Even though there is not as yet full assurance that such defense will be effective, the determined effort to establish such a defense may turn out to be the greatest contribution to the security of the United States. The emphasis which has been placed on the program is apt to contribute to the clarification of the very question whether, and under what conditions, such a defense will turn out to be dependable and reasonably secure.

In considering non-nuclear states, it is of great interest to distinguish between the offensive or defensive use of nuclear weapons. Some states may indeed develop nuclear explosives for an offensive use and this will lead in additional countries to apprehensions, and further proliferation. If, on the other hand, an effective missile defense can be developed, and if furthermore, arrangements can be made to insure that these systems can be used for defense and only for defense, then a way may be found to decrease dangers, reduce apprehensions, persuade most or all non-nuclear states to forego the development of aggressive weapons and create peaceful and stable conditions.

Unfortunately, the only concrete way that has been proposed so far for missile defense, utilizes nuclear explosives. Because of this fact, the Non-Proliferation Treaty and in particular, Articles I and II of this treaty, may serve to limit the deployment of defensive systems. Without intending to do so, the treaty may therefore help to increase, rather than diminish the dangers to undefended countries and may thereby enhance rather than decrease the probability of war.

A purely defensive nuclear weapon may not be easily imagined but a long-term development has been underway which could provide equipment which guarantees that a missile defense system will certainly be used for defense and only for defense. The defensive missile could be given an electronic program which would permit its warhead to be detonated only in a predetermined space in which the defensive operation is to be carried out. One can elaborate this equipment in such a manner that any attempt to alter the general electronic program, or to remove the defensive warhead from the missile defense system, will render the weapon and its parts ineffective and unusable. While the user of the missile defense system need not even know the precise nature of the nuclear explosive, he will be able to employ it freely and instantly to remove a menacing object above his country. What I describe here is an advanced but incomplete program, rather than an accomplished fact, but I have strong hopes that this program can indeed be completed with full success.

We are faced with two important and interrelated problems. One is whether effective defense can be established in such a way that such defense cannot be misused for offensive purposes. If this can be done, and made available to nations in the pursuit of their justified aim of self-defense, greater stability may be achieved without further guarantees and obligations being undertaken by the great powers. It is my hope and my definite expectations that with diligent work such defense equipment can indeed be created.

The other question is whether the Non-Proliferation Treaty may act to discourage the development of such defensive weapons system and whether it may unnecessarily limit their use by non-nuclear powers.

It seems to me, therefore, necessary to declare that weapons which are designed for defense and can be used for defense alone are in the interest of peace. That when and if such defensive systems are properly developed, the necessary steps will be taken to make them widely available for self-defense, and that this will be done even if it requires modification of existing laws or treaties.

I therefore explicitly recommend that the Senate make it known that it looks with favor on the development of effective defensive systems and that by ratifying the treaty the Senate does not intend to preclude the deployment of purely defensive arrangements, if and when these become available.

If this condition is not met I cannot recommend ratification because in this case international stability and the prospect of peace may be jeopardized.

Senator SPARKMAN. Thank you, Dr. Teller. You have given us a very fine and forceful statement, and we all appreciate your appearing before us.

EFFECT OF TREATY ON UNITED STATES DEPLOYING ABM SYSTEM

I was interested in your concluding statement, and let me ask you this, in view of that: Is there anything in this proposed treaty that would prevent the United States from fully developing an ABM system?

Dr. TELLER. As I read the statement, there is nothing in the treaty that definitely prevents us from such a development. But the treaty puts on an equal footing the limitations on offensive and defensive weapons.

I think that this equal consideration, the implied equal condemnation of offensive and defensive weapons, is not sensible, is not just, and is not in the spirit of the United States.

At the same time, a declaration of this kind cannot help but lower the priority with which missile defense objectives are being pursued. There is no clear-cut legal obstacle to missile defense, but there is some implied discouragement.

Senator SPARKMAN. Yes.

Thank you very much.

Senator Pastore.

Senator PASTORE. No.

Senator SPARKMAN. Senator Hickenlooper.

Senator HICKENLOOPER. I think Dr. Teller has so clearly and in detail expressed his views that I do not know that any questioning of mine could amplify them.

I have the utmost respect for your views.

TEST BAN TREATY EFFECT ON PLOWSHARE PROGRAM

I recall your warnings at the time of the Test Ban Treaty, and while I eventually reluctantly voted for it, I felt it was extremely deficient in several of its provisions, especially the Plowshare prohibition which was written into it, and which has risen to plague us ever since. Why they put that in there, I do not know, but it is there.

I think you have explained the necessity for us to vigorously pursue the drive for a strictly and exclusively defensive weapons system as one of the great hopes for the possibility of assisting in the preservation of peace in the world.

I thank you very much for your contribution, Dr. Teller.

Dr. TELLER. Thank you, Senator Hickenlooper.

Senator SPARKMAN. I have a letter from the Disarmament Issues Committee of the United Nations Association, U.S.A. Without objection, it will be printed in the record.

(The letter referred to follows:)

UNITED NATIONS ASSOCIATION
OF THE UNITED STATES OF AMERICA,
New York, N.Y., July 16, 1968.

Senator JOHN SPARKMAN,
Acting Chairman, Senate Foreign Relations Committee,
Senate Office Building, Washington, D.C.

DEAR SENATOR SPARKMAN: The Disarmament Issues Committee of the United Nations Association USA, strongly supports the Nuclear Non-proliferation Treaty which was signed by the United States, the United Kingdom and the Soviet Union on July 1.

The program of our Committee is directed towards the dissemination of information on and the mobilization of support for disarmament agreements and a strengthened UN peacekeeping capacity. With the Committee on Arms Control and Disarmament for International Cooperation Year, with the Educational Committee to Halt Atomic Weapons Spread (a group we helped to initiate), with the UNA national policy panel on "Stopping the Spread of Nuclear Weapons", and with UNA Chapters and associated organizations throughout the country, we have worked intensively for this treaty for the past two years.

In our view, this historic pact which represents a landmark in the development of the United Nations, decisively reduces the threat of nuclear war by encouraging continued collaboration between the US and the USSR on measures of arms control, and by limiting the spread of nuclear weapons.

At the UN, where the basic terms of the treaty were suggested by the Irish delegation in 1958, the final draft was endorsed by an overwhelming vote of 95 nations on June 12. In the intervening years during which negotiations were underway, representatives of non-nuclear nations, speaking in UN bodies, took a leading part in the formation of the principles on which this agreement is based, acting also as catalytic agents in the negotiating process.

As Ambassador Arthur Goldberg pointed out in his statement in the recent UN debate, there are three chief advantages to the non-nuclear nations: the treaty will 1) establish effective controls through the International Atomic Energy Agency to halt the proliferation of nuclear weapons; 2) facilitate the sharing of the peaceful uses of nuclear energy among all nations; and 3) establish a solemn treaty obligation upon the nuclear powers to press forward in the search for nuclear disarmament.

It is this latter responsibility of the nuclear powers on which the non-nuclear states have placed the greatest emphasis. If the non-nuclear powers are to forego nuclear weapons, if the non-proliferation treaty is to remain in force and not be regarded as discriminatory or as a threat, the nuclear powers themselves will be expected to halt the strategic arms race and to reduce their nuclear weapons' arsenals.

It is worth noting in this connection that as many Congressmen have stated and many UN resolutions have indicated, the impact on the economy of successive arms control measures provides an opportunity for the defense industries to use their advanced technology on the solution of urgent domestic problems.

In the light of statements which have been made by American leaders in support of this treaty, and of the endorsement of a majority of nations, we feel assured the Senate will consent to ratification.

Sincerely yours,

JOSEPHINE W. POMERANCE, *Chairman.*

Senator SPARKMAN. Senator Lausche.

Senator LAUSCHE. I was impressed by your statement that the treaty deals equally with the transfer of offensive and strictly defensive nuclear devices or explosive devices.

Was I correct in my understanding of the interpretation which I have just made of your statement?

Dr. TELLER. Completely correct.

CONTROL OF EXPLOSIVE DEVICES

Senator LAUSCHE. I would like to read the language of article I:

Each nuclear weapon State Party to the Treaty undertakes not to transfer to any recipient whatsoever nuclear weapons or other nuclear explosive devices or—

I point out the disjunctive "or"—

control over such weapons or explosive devices directly or indirectly.

Is it your interpretation that this language means that even though an explosive device is so constructed to be used only for defensive purposes the treaty would prohibit the transfer?

Dr. TELLER. My understanding is that the treaty would clearly prohibit the transfer as soon as transfer of control is involved.

Now, I would like to expand on this point because it happens to be a very important one. The word "control" is a legal point rather than a factual point. If we have in some country nuclear weapons under our control, the control being exercised by a small number of GIs and an officer, then in the case of a deadly danger, are we really confident that these weapons will not be taken over by the other country? Yet, this form of transfer is permitted.

On the other hand, the offer of giving control but limiting the use to defense alone is not apt to do mischief, yet it is prohibited.

I am strongly tempted to suggest that this point be changed. But I am virtually certain that if we tried to change it then the Russians will object, and there will be no treaty, and I do not want to imperil the treaty itself, particularly because the devices that I am talking about are not in existence today, and, therefore, for a future benefit, and a benefit which I consider probable but not certain, we would be giving up an actual possibility which many of you, even now, regard as real progress.

I, therefore, would like to suggest a formulation which expresses your intent that when and if the technical situation develops to the point that defense, and pure defense, can be implemented, then you will use every means of reinterpretation, modification, or if needed, even abrogation, in order to serve the purposes we all share, a more perfect protection of peace.

MECHANISM TO LIMIT DESTRUCTION AREA OF EXPLOSION

Senator LAUSCHE. At one time you stated: "I have often been wrong when I have said that something could not be done. I have never been wrong when I have said that something could be done."

Now, you said today that, in your opinion, there could definitely be devised a mechanism that would limit the area in which the explosion would do destruction, and that could confine it within the area of the nation that is using the defensive weapon. Will you elaborate on that point?

Dr. TELLER. Yes, sir.

But let me, perhaps, make a little comment on your quote. It is not a quote from myself. That would be far too immodest. It is a quote from a very wonderful man who died 10 years ago, Ernest Lawrence. He said that about me, and I am proud of his statement.

I did say, and I do mean it, that we can devise the proper electronics. Proper functioning can be made very sure indeed, and it will allow detonation of a defensive device only in a prescribed space.

There is a point which I do not know. I am optimistic, but I cannot positively say that we will be successful. Will somebody find a way to interfere with this system? It is for this reason that I then went on to suggest the combination of strong technical development with continuing surveillance and a treaty that insures that if somebody tries to interfere he may have a small chance of success. But if he fails he will have a big chance of trouble stemming from his detected violation of agreements.

Senator LAUSCHE. I conclude, Dr. Teller, by saying to you that you are a tremendous inspiration, both from the standpoint of your unique knowledge in the scientific field and from the standpoint of your ability to present your case. I am fascinated to look at you and listen to you. You have been tremendously impressive to me, and very helpful in my approach to the problem that confronts us.

Dr. TELLER. Thank you.

Senator LAUSCHE. My conclusion with respect to this subject which you have raised will depend upon whether or not the right to withdraw will put us in the position to reform the treaty, abolish it, and thus make usable a purely defensive weapon or defensive instrumentality as distinguished from an offensive one for the achievement of peace among the different nations.

Senator SPARKMAN. I am going to ask before calling on Senator Case, if Senator Lausche would take charge of the hearings from here on out. I apologize but, I have a 12:30 appointment that I feel impelled to keep.

Dr. Teller and all of the other witnesses that we have had so far, and those who are to come yet, we are grateful to all of you for coming.

Dr. TELLER. Thank you.

Senator LAUSCHE (presiding). Senator Case.

Senator CASE. I have no questions at this time. Thank you very much.

Senator LAUSCHE. Senator Cooper.

Senator COOPER. I will be brief. I must say it is a great opportunity and privilege to hear you, Dr. Teller.

PROHIBITION OF TRANSFER OF OFFENSIVE WEAPONS FAVORED

As I understand it, you are not opposed to the treaty insofar as it prohibits the transfer of offensive weapons.

Dr. TELLER. I know that the problem is very complex indeed. The general idea of a nonproliferation treaty appeals to me. I know, and I have learned better by reading and listening to the testimony that has been offered here, that the questions are complex indeed, and they go far outside my field, and I do not feel that it is up to me to evaluate the effects on our alliances, on many other important questions.

I would very strongly urge the one recommendation I made. And I furthermore urge, as I have already urged, that whatever you do, whether you ratify or do not ratify, you do so after very thorough consideration of a problem which is far from being simply black or white.

UNITED STATES ASSISTS COUNTRIES TO DEPLOY DEFENSIVE SYSTEMS

Senator COOPER. You do argue that the United States should be permitted to assist a country, and you specifically referred to Europe, or to enable those countries to deploy defensive systems.

Dr. TELLER. Senator Cooper, I did not specifically refer to Europe, I specifically referred to Japan, India, and Pakistan, and I did so because these are the nations immediately threatened by the less developed, but possibly more aggressive, Chinese.

Because China is less developed, the chances of a valid missile defense are better. Because China is more aggressive, the danger could be greater.

I certainly do not want to exclude Europe, but I have not told you, because I cannot tell you, that we have a really dependable system or can develop one which will stop Russian missiles.

I would think that what can be done in this respect in Europe should depend on further development in the ABM field. And if we then find that missile defense can be made strong enough to have a real effect, even in the case of possible Russian aggression, in that case I would give the very highest priority to the defense of Europe, and I would give the highest priority to the defense of Europe in any case wherever I see a practical possibility of accomplishing such a defense.

EFFECTIVENESS OF A DEFENSIVE SYSTEM IN EUROPE

Senator COOPER. If a defensive system were installed in Europe could it be as effective as one deployed in the United States?

Dr. TELLER. Senator Cooper, I am very sorry I did not catch your question.

Senator COOPER. It has been said that under present conditions, at least, if an attack were launched on the United States by the Soviet Union that the United States would have about 15 minutes to prepare to meet that attack. Obviously, if there were an ABM system in Europe there would not be anything like that time, so it could not be as effective.

Dr. TELLER. In the case of Europe the time available might very well be 5 minutes. Therefore, if a button is to be pressed, it must be pressed right away. I believe that this can be done, but it can be done only if any unnecessary complication is avoided.

I should not say that it can be done. I should say, I hope it can be developed. The difficulty, the main difficulty, is not about the 5 minutes. The electronics, the radar, the missiles are fast enough to provide the defense.

The reason why I do not know today what can be done in Europe if it were to face a Russian attack simply flows from the mass of the Russian aggression capability and the sophistication of that capability and, therefore, in our early stage of ABM development, I am unable to say whether we can hope for a real defense against that. We should find out.

EFFECT OF DEPLOYMENT OF ABM SYSTEMS

Senator COOPER. One other question: the deployment of an ABM system against Russia would simply have the consequence of either country developing much more powerful offensive weapons. Already

MIRV is being developed to counter ABM systems. If one country, either the Soviet Union or the United States, puts in an ABM system, you would have the development of a higher level of offensive weapons designed to break through and penetrate any ABM system. That, of course, was Mr. McNamara's theory.

If that occured, the response to the development of ABM systems in the end both adopting those courses of action, then you would have gained nothing except to fill the world with thousands of more weapons. Is that view scientifically and technically of any value?

Dr. TELLER. Senator Cooper, I hoped you would not ask this question, but you did.

Senator COOPER. You are one of the greatest experts in the world on nuclear technology.

Dr. TELLER. Sir, the only scientific information I can give you is that the future is uncertain. If I were as clever as Secretary McNamara claimed to be, and if the technical development would stand still, and if the estimate, that defense is two or three times more expensive than offense, and will remain so, if I make all these assumptions, then I might come to a point where I might conceivably agree that more defense will simply generate more offense in the case of the United States and Russia.

The purely political aspects of escalation, the financial aspects, the relative wealth of the two countries make the equations so complex that no computing machine, no clever individual, can give you a good answer. If you add to this the possibility that defense might become cheaper than offense then Mr. McNamara's argument becomes most doubtful.

He is assuming that technology will not develop, as indeed it has not developed in the automobile industry. But in the defense field, technology is developing. To try to make general statements of the kind which you have quoted is a very hazardous business.

Senator COOPER. It certainly is. Mine would have to be a general statement because I am not an authority in this field, but we have to find, and study such information as we can get.

May I ask, have you been invited to testify before the preparedness subcommittee on this question of the establishment of the ABM system?

Dr. TELLER. No, sir; I have not.

Senator COOPER. I believe all these outstanding nuclear scientists should be invited. I think you should be, and I think others should be.

SOVIET DEVELOPMENT OF FOBS

I recall in the consideration by this committee of the Outer Space Treaty that no witness testified to the fact that the Soviets had developed what is now called FOBS. We approved the treaty, and then within a short time it was announced that they had developed this weapon.

It would seem inconceivable to me that the Department of Defense, the State Department, did not know of it, but they did not tell us about it. Was the development of FOBS in violation of the treaty?

Dr. TELLER. I do not know whether the FOBS was a violation of the treaty or not. They just present a small example of a small surprise that can put a treaty within a very short time of its ratification into a new context.

Senator LAUSCHE. Senator Curtis.

Senator CURTIS. Dr. Teller, I cannot add to the praise that has been heaped upon you, and what I am about to ask is probably something which has already been stated, but I will ask it in a particular manner.

TRANSFER OF DEFENSIVE WEAPONS UNDER PROPOSED TREATY

If this treaty is ratified without any reservation, then will the United States or any other signatory power be prevented from getting or transferring in any manner defensive nuclear weapons to any other nation?

Dr. TELLER. I believe that this would be the case. We would be prevented from doing so, and I am very worried about that, not in the case of land mines, whose operation would require some time in any case, because troops move with a smaller speed, but very particularly in the case of ballistic missiles and the defense against them where, as Senator Cooper has pointed out, speed is of the utmost importance.

NONNUCLEAR COUNTRY AUTHORITY TO DEVELOP NUCLEAR WEAPONS

Senator CURTIS. Now, I also want to ask you if this treaty were to be ratified without any reservation, could a nation that has no nuclear devices now, but which is a signatory to the treaty, could it develop its own nuclear defensive weapons?

Dr. TELLER. It could not without violating the treaty.

Senator CURTIS. And this is, perhaps, obvious, but a country that was not a signatory to this treaty could, if its technology permitted, both develop nuclear devices for defensive purposes and transfer them to other countries.

Dr. TELLER. It could do both and, Senator Curtis, you have pointed out some very strong reasons why countries may hesitate to sign this treaty.

On the other hand, we could make it clear that those nonnuclear countries which signed the treaty will be the first to get effective defenses, whether they are nuclear or nonnuclear. If these countries could be assured of self defense, I believe that the effectiveness of the treaty could be greatly improved.

ADVANCEMENT OF DEFENSE DEVICES

Senator CURTIS. In the case of the signatory states or in the case of any state, is there any scientific reason why we should assume that technology for nuclear defenses cannot advance and progress as fast or faster than offensive devices? We do not know what will happen, but is there any scientific reason to assume that they cannot?

Dr. TELLER. That defensive devices——

Senator CURTIS. Cannot——

Dr. TELLER. Advance faster?

Senator CURTIS. Advance as fast as offensive devices.

Dr. TELLER. I am not sure of my answer. History seems to show that aggressive devices, devices of attack, are more easily made than defensive devices. This stands to reason because for aggression you need an explosive and you need a delivery system, and that is all. In the case of defense you need detection, discrimination from decoys, penetration of chaff, timing, fast rockets, very fast rockets, excellent electronic control, and nuclear devices made for the purpose of having specific effects directed against an incoming missile and not directed, at objects on the ground.

I think it is a reasonable expectation that whoever embarks on his own on nuclear devices will get the capability of aggression first and defense later and this, as between two countries like India and Pakistan, is indeed an unstabilizing factor.

If we can break this situation by helping countries to obtain defensive devices, then this vicious situation of aggression coming before defense, could be broken.

SHOULD UNITED STATES DEVELOP DEFENSIVE SYSTEM?

Senator CURTIS. From a scientific standpoint, you regard the problems in developing a nuclear defensive system so overwhelming that the United States should not put forth every effort to develop it?

Dr. TELLER. I consider these problems—no, let me answer you differently, sir.

I would have said just 10 years ago that they are so overwhelming that we should not try. I now believe that I was wrong.

Starting from 1958, carefully looking at each proposal that came along, I did change my mind, and in four years have practically completed the process.

When I believed that offense will always predominate, the ratio of expenses appeared to be 30 to 1. Today estimates are between 2 and 3 to 1. You know how hard it is to predict costs even when you do something relatively conservative like designing an F-111. I would say that today my best judgment is that we should bend every effort toward the aim of developing defensive weapons for our own use, and that we should also keep in mind and prepare for the deployment of these weapons, for the self defense of others, if this can be done in a reasonable manner.

Senator CURTIS. And it is your opinion that there is a great likelihood that we could be successful in such an undertaking?

Dr. TELLER. I would say that there is a great likelihood that we will be successful if we try to defend ourselves or others against anybody except the Russians.

In the case of the Russians, I would say I do not know. Maybe yes, maybe no. Ask me in two years.

Senator CURTIS. If we were successful in building nuclear devices that were a effective defense against potential aggressors other than Russia, namely, Red China, that in itself would be the first step or a step toward accomplishing the same thing with respect to Russia, is that not right? Wouldn't we be better off than if we started from scratch?

Dr. TELLER. We would be much better off because we would have done on a small scale that which we would then have to repeat on a big scale. We would have a pilot operation. We would have made our mistakes on a smaller scale, and we would then be prepared to do the right thing when we have to spend the greater amounts of money, provided that during this first phase of operation we indeed gain enough confidence. Whether this will be so or not, I do not know.

I claim that the truth is that I do not know, and I furthermore claim that the whole truth is that nobody knows.

Senator CURTIS. If we could develop effective nuclear defenses, and if they were deployed to other countries for their use at their instigation, is it your opinion that it would have a twofold benefit, one, as a deterrent to an aggressor launching, and second, if the aggressor went ahead anyway it might save countless lives as well as the surrounding economy?

Dr. TELLER. I agree with both of these benefits. But I would also like to add a third. It would help to persuade the recipient country not to embark on a nuclear program of its own because its most urgent need would be satisfied. These needs might be satisfied precisely on the condition that the recipient does not embark on an independent development.

Senator CURTIS. In other words, if a small, economically weak or emerging nation is denied the right to acquire from other nations proven means of defense, then they are forced to try to develop them themselves.

Dr. TELLER. They very well may feel that they are forced to do so.

Senator CURTIS. Thank you very much.

Senator LAUSCHE. Any further questions?

Senator COOPER. Mr. Chairman, may I ask one further question?

Senator LAUSCHE. Yes. Senator Cooper.

Senator COOPER. I want to limit my question to make a distinction between research and development of the defensive system and the actual mass construction of its components and its deployment.

Can you state whether or not, in your judgment, the United States has reached that point in research—where it could proceed to actually construct the components of an effective ABM system and install them on the soil of another state?

Dr. TELLER. I believe that we have not reached that stage.

Senator COOPER. We are not at that stage?

Dr. TELLER. We have performed research at a slow rate over many years; the research has progressed far, and to the extent that I trust an ABM I tend to trust the safeguards, electronic safeguards, and the rest around it.

But while the research is in an advanced state, the development is not. The application of these ideas to ABM is in a very primitive stage indeed.

Development as contrasted with research, is a little more predictable. You can have more confidence in it, but it also is usually more expensive, and these expenditures, which will be millions of dollars, will not be committed, will not be made, if there is no hope to install these instruments.

Therefore, the treaty in its present form, without any statement of intent, may serve to prevent the development.

We, therefore, have to proceed cautiously, have to stimulate this essential research and development, and make sure that in some appropriate fashion the option is held open to install defensive equipment in another country when the technical and political conditions fully justify that.

Senator COOPER. This is the last question. I want to make my distinction as clear as I can.

I think I understood you to say that the heart of research has not reached the stage when an effective ABM can be built.

Dr. TELLER. I have said that and I mean it. The research is far advanced, the development needs much more work. I am optimistic about the outcome, but we have nothing that we can now offer as a ready product.

TIMING OF RESEARCH AND DEVELOPMENT

Senator COOPER. Now, if funds were made available for adequate research and construction of development prototypes, and for tests of prototypes that can be made without violating the nuclear Test Ban Treaty, would you consider that should be done before our country actually begins to construct the elements of this system and lays them on the soil of this country?

Dr. TELLER. I do not quite understand. Should we go ahead with research and development before we have the commitment to install it; is that the question?

Senator COOPER. Yes.

Dr. TELLER. I do not now, but I tend to believe that research and development should go on on an urgent basis because a commitment to install is a very serious political commitment, and should be done only if research and development are firm. I may be wrong in this judgment. It is a political statement rather than a technical one.

Senator CASE. Would the Senator permit a question here, because there may be some misunderstanding?

Dr. Teller, are you talking now about a so-called defensive system which you want us to be free to develop and even to offer to nonnuclear nations, or are you talking about the thin antiballistic missile system that has been announced as a program which has gone ahead?

Dr. TELLER. I am talking about the former, about the defense and defense only system which we might install on somebody else's territory.

As far as our thin system is concerned, I think research and development has progressed to the point where a first deployment is fully justified.

Senator CASE. Thank you very much, Mr. Chairman. I think that Senator Cooper had intended to ask the question which you just answered.

Dr. TELLER. Thank you very much for helping me out of this misunderstanding.

Senator LAUSCHE. Thank you very much for your help, Dr. Teller.

Dr. TELLER. Thank you.

Senator LAUSCHE. There are four more witnesses who are waiting to testify. We will meet at 2:30 in room S-116 at the Capitol.

The meeting will be recessed until that time.

(Thereupon, at 12:50 p.m. the hearing was recessed to reconvene at 2:30 p.m. this day.)

Senator LAUSCHE (presiding). The meeting will come to order. The hearings on the proposed Nonproliferation Treaty will be resumed. The first witness to testify will be Mr. William Huntington, director of the Quaker program at the United Nations, New York City.

Mr. Huntington, your statement will be printed in the record. You may read the entire statement or, if you would prefer, you may discuss what you want to present and highlight it for the record.

STATEMENT OF WILLIAM R. HUNTINGTON, DIRECTOR, QUAKER PROGRAM OF THE UNITED NATIONS

Mr. HUNTINGTON. Mr. Chairman, I thank you very much for the opportunity to appear, and I thank you for taking our statement and putting it into the record. I will not read it in its entirety, but I would like to comment on its essence.

Senator LAUSCHE. Take it up subject by subject, as you go along, if you will.

Mr. HUNTINGTON. As you noted, I represent Quaker interests and concerns at the United Nations, and these concerns seek to identify themselves with worldwide human interests and concerns.

It might be appropriate to comment at this point, Mr. Chairman, that the Society of Friends, puts its prime trust in neither electronics, treaties nor both, but, in the long run, in human commonsense and in the capacity for nobility of the human spirit.

TREATY RATIFICATION URGED

It is impossible for us to believe, Mr. Chairman, that after the initiative and leadership which the United States has taken in the preparation and promotion of this treaty, and the years its statesmen and experts have spent on it, that you will not recommend, and the Senate will not give, its advice and consent to its ratification.

We are here today to tell you of our support and our confidence that it will be ratified by this country, and to emphasize that its success depends on its being followed by next steps.

In his appearance before the General Assembly, President Johnson also stressed the promise of this treaty for future actions, and he stressed the U.S. commitment to this promise when he said that he was there:

To pledge, on behalf of the United States, our determination to make this but a first step toward ending the peril of nuclear war.

And when he said again:

We shall, as a major nuclear weapon power, promptly and vigorously pursue negotiations on effective measures to halt the nuclear arms race and to reduce existing nuclear arsenals.

In respect to the word "promptly" we would remind the Senate committee that it took the Disarmament Committee an unnecessarily long time to negotiate the Nonproliferation Treaty, to recall that agreement was delayed in part by the U.S. attachment to the theory of a multilateral nuclear force under NATO, and to express our concern that a similar attachment to the ABM defense system not be allowed to impede negotiations on measures to cut back nuclear arsenals.

DISARMAMENT DISCUSSIONS IN THE UNITED NATIONS

My experience at the U.N. has made me particularly conscious of the fact that many countries feel that the significance of the Nonproliferation Treaty lies in its potentials as a bridge which can open the way to further progress on disarmament, and I am particularly happy to be allowed to talk to you, Mr. Chairman, on this subject because I think it is appropriate for the Senate to be reminded of the very serious discussion that went on in the U.N. on the treaty.

Even the reservations to the treaty that were recorded by a number of nations underline its importance as a step.

We, Friends, have our reservations to the treaty, too, but we did not think it appropriate to go into them at this time because of the fact that we wanted to emphasize the next step.

But the countries who explained their abstentions in the U.N. were not opposed to preventing the proliferation of nuclear weapons. They felt only that the treaty did not go far enough, that it was unbalanced, discriminating against nonnuclear weapons, by preventing horizontal proliferation and not vertical proliferation; some felt that more time should have been spent considering some of the objections that were raised.

These countries were not, as some have suggested, interested in becoming nuclear powers themselves nor in practicing proliferation.

COMMENTS OF FRENCH AMBASSADOR

I think it is interesting to look at the comments of the French Ambassador in which he reiterated the seriousness of the question of disarmament and their long devotion to it, he said:

It is this question which haunts the minds of men who realize that the existence of the absolute weapon is not only a new step in military development but also, and above all, a permanent threat to individuals, not nations and to life itself.

France, for its part, which will not sign the nonproliferation treaty, will behave in the future in this field exactly as the States adhering to the treaty. There is certainly no doubt in that respect in the mind of anyone.

Again he said:

As has been said, as has been repeated so often by the highest French authorities, the only solution to the threat which results from the existence of these weapons is the complete stoppage of their manufacture and the complete destruction of the stockpiles.

France believes that the nations of the world will receive the guarantees of security to which they have the right to aspire only when the world has embarked on the road toward nuclear disarmament and on condition that such disarmament is carried out to the full.

HIGH QUALITY DEBATE IN THE U.N.

Now, as I said, Mr. Chairman, the debate in the U.N. was unprecedented in U.N. history for its high quality, its wide participation and constructive substantive analysis, and I have appended here in the footnote for the next couple of pages some statements that were made testifying to this.

I listened to most of it. I have been at the U.N. in this post for 5 years, and I have not ever seen such a long and protracted, widely participated in, debate on any subject.

The Arab nations, who wanted the Southwest Africa question in the Assembly at the same time, had to space their meetings separately because all the top men in all the delegations were in the meetings on the Nonproliferation Treaty. In the beginning, as you are well aware, the United States and U.S.S.R., the cosponsors of the draft treaty, made it very clear that there were not going to be any changes. They were adamant.

At the end of this long debate, in which there was none of the propaganda talk or the accusations going back and forth, that does, unfortunately, characterize some debates, the nonnuclear powers, and almost all of them spoke, gained the respect of the United States and the U.S.S.R., and some concessions were made. The nations in the end supported the revised draft because they had had a chance to register their most serious opinions, and because there had been wide participation and the promise of next steps had been reaffirmed and strengthened.

If there had been no concessions there would have been double as many abstentions; there would have been 40 abstentions instead of 20.

CONCESSIONS MADE TO NONNUCLEAR NATIONS

Senator LAUSCHE. Are you able to recall the concessions that were made?

Mr. HUNTINGTON. They included a strengthening of article VI by mentioning in the preamble that the nuclear powers intend to carry on with further steps toward nuclear disarmament. Then paragraph 4 in the resolution requests the nuclear states to pursue negotiations on effective measures.

Senator LAUSCHE. Was that provision not in the original proposal?

Mr. HUNTINGTON. In the original resolution, but it was strengthened by the adding of some words in the preamble of the draft, Mr. Chairman.

Senator LAUSCHE. Well, further emphasis was given to the need of carrying on for the purpose of reducing arms.

Mr. HUNTINGTON. Another addition was a clause recalling that in accordance with the Charter of the United Nations, states must refrain in their international relations from the threat or the use of force against the territorial integrity or political independence of any state, or in any other manner inconsistent with the purposes of the U.N., and that establishment and maintenance of international peace and security are to be presented with the least diversion for armaments of the world's human and economic resources.

This satisfied the small parties because it brought the major powers back into reaffirming the charter.

ACCESS TO SCIENTIFIC ADVANTAGES OF PEACEFUL USES

The third concession was in broader access to the scientific advantages of peaceful uses.

After all this, I do believe, Mr. Chairman, that if the United States does not ratify this treaty, the last bit of credibility and the last hope that exists among the nations for the United States taking serious initiatives for progress in disarmament will vanish. I think cynicism will take over again and people will say, as they have been saying, "Well, nuclear war, a third world war, is inevitable."

You will see in my printed testimony some samples from a whole host of quotations that could have been quoted to show the wide positive support for the treaty because of the hopeful future steps. I would just like to repeat a very few excerpts.

WIDE SUPPORT FOR TREATY

Mrs. Myrdal, who is the Minister for Disarmament of Sweden, made in her initial presentation a very careful and very pleading appeal for some minor revisions in the draft, which would push it further along the road. For instance, in regard to control of explosions, she said what we really ought to develop is an international body that is responsible for all nuclear explosions, that all nuclear explosions, so far as the human world is concerned, should be prohibited, unless this international body specifically permitted them. This is the kind of order we should look forward to, and she hoped that could come along at this stage.

But at the end of the debate, in early June, she said:

I wish to stress that it is only after a conscientious weighing of the pros and cons that we have arrived at this decision (to vote in favor of the draft resolution). The hesitation which my delegation, like so many others, has felt all through the complicated negotiations on this treaty is related to the fact that the treaty as such can only be characterized as a modest step toward nuclear disarmament. The hesitation does not, of course, stem from any lack of conviction about the desirability of contributing to nuclear disarmament. Gradually we have come to the conclusion that the treaty represents "a bridge we must cross before any further progress on disarmament can be made."

As you see, this same thought is repeated by the other Scandinavian nations in the next quotation.

Senator LAUSCHE. Are the expressions that you quote in here substantially similar to those made by the different nations such as Denmark, Ethiopia, Yugoslavia, Sudan, Malta, Mexico, Pakistan, on the basis that this is the first step and that it constitutes a bridge that must be crossed to reach a higher level?

Mr. HUNTINGTON. Precisely.

ATTITUDE OF PAKISTAN

I think it is interesting, if I might just read the last quotation which is the one of Pakistan, because Pakistan is an example of a nation who is, from everything that it said, not so much interested, even located as it is, in being provided with defensive weapons, whether nuclear or antiballistic or what, against the potential nuclear power of its neighbors, as it is in deescalating the nuclear race, so that this whole business will be unnecessary.

In paragraph 4 of the draft resolution, the 18-nation Committee on Disarmament and the nuclear-weapon states are requested urgently to pursue negotiations on effective measures relating to cessation of the nuclear arms race at an early date and to nuclear disarmament and on a treaty on general and complete disarmament. We note that the nuclear powers have made a declaration of intention in the preamble to the text of the treaty to undertake effective measures in the direction of nuclear disarmament, and in Article VI of the treaty, to pursue negotiations in good faith on such measures. Unless the nuclear arms race is halted by the three depository Governments and rapid and substantial steps are taken towards nuclear disarmament—in other words, towards vertical non-proliferation—the cooperation of the remaining two nuclear powers in the direction of nuclear disarmament as well as general and complete disarmament cannot be realistically expected. The vital interests of peace and security for all mankind, quite apart from the viability and stability of the Non-Proliferation treaty, will depend on the ability of the three nuclear power parties to the treaty to implement their solemn and binding pledges to end the nuclear arms race and carry out nuclear disarmament at an early date.

UNITED STATES-U.S.S.R. DISCUSSIONS ON DISARMAMENT MATTERS

Now, just a word about these next steps on the other side of this bridge. It is encouraging to read that our Government and the Governments of the United Kingdom and U.S.S.R. have already begun in the 18-Nation Disarmament Conference to look forward and to promise discussions on these issues.

The United States and the U.S.S.R. have said they are going to begin discussions on limiting nuclear delivery systems. This is what the world is looking for. There really will be despair if we turn away from this to perfect our own ABM system.

There are many areas that need to be explored: the comprehensive test ban; the ABM question I just mentioned; the cutoff of production of fiissionable materials; a freeze on manufacture of nuclear weapons; the adoption of a convention outlawing the use of nuclear weapons; the banning of nuclear weapons; and the banning of the use of chemical and biological weapons which the British gave special stress to yesterday. This new question, which is going to be discussed a great deal, I think, in the coming year, the prohibition of the use of the seabed for military purposes.

What we hope is that these things won't have to be taken up one by one as the Test Ban Treaty and the Nonproliferation Treaty have been. Why cannot the 18-Nation Disarmament Conference start studies on several simultaneously, so that we can make some progress.

PEACEFUL USES OF ATOMIC ENERGY

Finally, I should say a word about the peaceful uses, because our fellow members in the United Nations supported the treaty in the sincere hope and belief that it would lead us closer to disarmament and create conditions for sharing without discrimination the unlimited possibilities of atomic energy for peaceful purposes.

Our Latin American neighbors, who have already closed their continent to nuclear weaponry, are greatly interested in the opportunities this great universal source of energy opens for all nations. They speak for the developing world, and there follows the quotation from two of them, one being Costa Rica, who says:

We have no desire or possibility of ever acquiring atomic arms. We have renounced their use in our territory under the Treaty of Tlatelolco, but we do hope that we will be able to make peaceful use of nuclear energy if it is appropriate and possible, according to the new technology which is being prepared on the basis of new discoveries in this branch of human knowledge. This will greatly benefit the economic and social development of our country.

And Uruguay said:

We do not want war with atoms; we want peace with atoms. The inequality separating us from the nuclear powers in the use of the infernal machines that they possess is a matter of concern for us from the point of view of the general fate of mankind; but the inequality, greater and greater every day, in the benefits derived from atomic energy and from scientific and technical advances applied to economic and industrial development is of very acute interest to us because of the stagnation, the servitude, the backwardness and the poverty that beset our peoples. It would be tragic indeed if the era of colonialism, now in its last days in this world, were to experience a rebirth in consequence of the technological progress achieved by the great powers. Nuclear neo-colonialism on the economic level must also be banished; the doors to technological progress must be opened wide to the developing countries, thus avoiding new causes of upheaval, new seedbeds of conflict, new misfortunes and miseries, all resulting, paradoxically, from the very scientific progress of mankind.

Mr. Chairman, we look to the Foreign Relations Committee and to the Senate of the United States to go forward in the matter of this treaty, and in the directions it promises, because we believe that it is America's historical destiny not to be celebrated as the source of massive destruction in the world, but for its rising to the challenge of its role in the van of intelligent human social development.

Thank you.

(The prepared statement of Mr. Huntington follows:)

STATEMENT OF WILLIAM R. HUNTINGTON, DIRECTOR, QUAKER PROGRAM AT THE UNITED NATIONS, ON BEHALF OF THE AMERICAN FRIENDS SERVICE COMMITTEE AND THE FRIENDS COMMITTEE ON NATIONAL LEGISLATION

Mr. Chairman and Senators, my name is William Huntington and as Director of the Quaker United Nations Program I represent Quaker interests and concerns—which seek identification with world-wide human interests and concerns—at United Nations Headquarters in New York. Because the Society of Friends is highly decentralized and individualistic no individual or group can speak officially for all Friends, but no consensus among them is broader than a faith that mankind can and must rid itself of the scourge of war. The American Friends Service Committee, which supports our UN office, and the Friends Committee on National Legislation are grateful for this opportunity to be heard in connection with the Non-Proliferation Treaty because they believe its ratification is an essential though minor step on the path toward peace.

It is impossible for us to believe, Mr. Chairman, that after the initiative and leadership the United States has taken in the preparation and promotion of this treaty, and the years its statesmen and experts have spent on it, that you will not recommend and the Senate will not give its advice and consent to its ratification. Therefore we are here today to talk about next steps—to remind Senators that it took the Disarmament Committee an unnecessarily long time to negotiate the nonproliferation treaty—to recall that agreement was delayed in part by the U.S. attachment to the theory of a multilateral nuclear force under NATO and to express our concern that a similar commitment to the ABM not be allowed to impede negotiations on a treaty to cut back nuclear arsenals.

My experience at the UN has made me particularly conscious of the fact that many countries feel the significance of the nonproliferation treaty lies in its *potential as a bridge* which can open the way to further progress on disarmament.

In his appearance before the General Assembly, President Johnson also stressed the promise of this treaty for future actions, and the U.S. commitment to this promise, when he said that he was there "to pledge, on behalf of the United States, our determination to make this but a first step toward ending the peril of nuclear war," and when he said, again, "we shall, as a major nuclear-weapon Power, promptly and vigorously pursue negotiations on effective measures to halt the nuclear arms race and to reduce existing nuclear arsenals."

Even the reservations to the treaty that were recorded by a number of nations underline its importance as a step. Those who explained their abstentions were not opposed to preventing the proliferation of nuclear weapons. They felt only that the treaty does not go far enough, as in the case of France. In the opinion of India the treaty discriminates against non-nuclear powers. Zambia, which voted against the treaty, felt more time should have been spent considering the treaty and more of the objections that some of the non-nuclear nations had to specific provisions should have been taken into account.

It is interesting to note parts of the statement of the Ambassador of France, which had not participated in the Committee debate, in the General Assembly meeting on 12 June:

"The question of disarmament, which in the world of today is the question of nuclear disarmament, is the essential task that has faced mankind since in 1945 the first atomic bomb in history exploded at Hiroshima. It is this question which was before the United Nations at the very moment when it was born in San Francisco, a few months later. It is this question which haunts the minds of men who realize that the existence of the absolute weapon is not only a new step in military development but also, and above all, a permanent threat to individuals, to nations and to life itself.

"France, for its part, which will not sign the non-proliferation treaty, will behave in the future in this field exactly as the States adhering to the treaty. There is certainly no doubt in that respect in the mind of anyone.

"But the real question is not that. Nor can it be the mere confirmation by the international community of the monopoly of the Powers which at this time happen to possess this capability. The real question is—I said it at the beginning, and it is still our thought—the complete disappearance of nuclear weapons.

"As has been repeated so often by the highest French authorities, the only solution to the threat which results from the existence of these weapons is the complete stoppage of their manufacture and the complete destruction of the stockpiles.

"Our delegation wishes, first of all to recall that the great undertaking of disarmament, to which the French Government is ready to devote the best of its efforts, is always before us, and that it is essentially on this subject that each and every one should shoulder his own responsibilities.

"France believes that the nations of the world will receive the guarantees of security to which they have the right to aspire only when the world has embarked on the road towards nuclear disarmament and on condition that such disarmament is carried out to the full."

As I said earlier, Mr. Chairman, a host of quotations show that the wide positive support of the draft treaty was not just for the treaty per se, but because, in spite of imperfections, it was a step forward that had to be taken. Here are a few statements which were made during the more than 6 weeks of debate on the treaty. This debate in the General Assembly's First Committee was unprecedented in United Nations history for its high quality, wide participation and constructive substantive analysis.*

---

*The Chairman of the First Committee, Mr. Fahmy of the United Arab Republic, said at the close of the meeting after the vote (92 yes, 4 no, 22 abstentions) in the Committee commending the treaty for the General Assembly:

"As far as I can recall, there has been no debate on any other item in the field of disarmament in which so many representatives of medium and small Powers have participated with such full awareness of the complexity of the issues involved and their tremendous impact and the consequences of their contribution in debating, explaining, clarifying or seeking answers to questions of peace and security which will undoubtedly affect mankind for a long time to come.

"You have elevated the standard of the discussion by unprecedented statesmanship. You have proved that under the auspices of this world Organization it is not only possible but indeed feasible, through conciliation and confidence based on frank and honest discussion, to overcome difficulties which at the very beginning might have appeared insurmountable. You entered this room on 26 April, and for a long time there was a feeling of uneasiness and doubt; but with proper understanding and good spirit it became possible for you to disperse satisfied, having taken a historic decision which could be regarded, without any exaggeration, as having far-reaching effects on issues of peace and security, economic development and scientific and technological advance. Most important of all, you have reached an understanding on an international contractual instrument within the framework of which super, big, medium and small Powers must work together if this international treaty is to mean anything to humanity.

"I am sure that the positive decision you have taken will be hailed all over the world as a landmark and one of the crucial achievements of the United Nations."

The Representative of Mexico, on 6 June, said of the debate:

"The general Debate, as was recognized explicitly by the representatives of the two main cosponsors of the draft treaty, the Soviet Union and the United States, has been held at a singularly high level. It has been a most serious, careful and constructive debate in which almost all representatives of the non-nuclear States have participated. The delegations of the two co-Chairmen of the Eighteen-Nation Committee on Disarmament have, on their part, given obvious proof of flexibility and understanding and have endeavored to consider the legitimate concern expressed and to take into account the numerous suggestions expressed in the interest of improving the text. That has obviously led to a revision of the draft resolution as well as—and this is even more important—of the draft treaty itself. May I add that that has also safeguarded the dignity and prestige of the General Assembly. which is the most representative organ of the United Nations."

THE PROMISE

Mrs. Alva Myrdal, the distinguished Minister for Disarmament of Sweden, who had in the course of a very thoughtful statement on 9 May pleaded for a prohibition of all nuclear explosions—"The conduct of any explosions desirable for peaceful purposes would have to be dealt with as exceptions, which could be granted only by an international body"—said on 5 June:
"I wish to stress that it is only after a conscientious weighing of the pros and cons that we have arrived at this decision (to vote in favor of the draft resolution). The hesitation which my delegation, like so many others, has felt all through the complicated negotiations on this treaty is related to the fact that the treaty as such can only be characterized as a modest step towards nuclear disarmament. The hesitation does not, of course, stem from any lack of conviction about the desirability of contributing to nuclear disarmament. Gradually we have come to the conclusion that the treaty represents 'a bridge we must cross before any further progress on disarmament can be made.'"
Denmark, 7 May:
"We accept the draft. However, we do so on the clear understanding that it is a first link in a chain of developments. We must not confine ourselves to this treaty; it is not our ultimate goal. It is a treaty which shall create the conditions for further disarmament steps. I would like here to quote the following from the communique issued on 26 April of this year after the meeting of the Foreign Ministers of Finland, Iceland, Norway, Sweden and my own country: 'The Ministers also discussed the report from the Eighteen-Nation Disarmament Committee presenting an American-Soviet joint draft treaty on the non-proliferation of nuclear weapons. The Ministers stressed the great importance of a treaty being concluded without further delay and with the largest possible adherence. A non-proliferation treaty would be an important contribution to international security and relaxation of tension. Such a treaty should as soon as possible be followed up by an agreement on a complete nuclear test ban and by other disarmament measures.'"
Ethiopia, 6 May:
"Certainly this treaty is only the beginning. It is a choice between the perfect and the impossible and between the less than perfect and the attainable. The shortcomings in the treaty are but a reflection of the world situation in which we live. To say that the treaty is not all-embracing is to understate the obvious. After all it could hardly be otherwise when out of the five members of the nuclear club only three support the treaty while the fourth is an outsider and the fifth is much less than enthusiastic.
"In the view of my Government, the viability of a non-proliferation agree-ment lies in what will happen in the future, perhaps in the immediate future: it depends first on the speed with which the nuclear-weapon Powers will follow this agreement with real measures of nuclear disarmament. Secondly, it depends on how soon nuclear technology will become the technology of the day and to what extent a non-proliferation arrangement will meet the demands for non-discriminatory technological co-operation.
"Thirdly, the viability of this agreement will depend on the extent to which the nuclear Powers can co-operate to create a world atmosphere in which nuclear energy will become the means for human development and progress and not the device for mutual self-destruction."
Yugoslavia, 14 May:
"There is general agreement that it is most essential to have the non-prolifera-tion treaty serve as a step to facilitate the initiation of the process of nuclear disarmament and to pave the way to general and complete disarmament. For that reason we should highly appreciate any initial step which could be taken in this direction and which could create conditions conducive to further progress in this field. In this context we regard as a matter of utmost urgency the

requirement that the nuclear Powers undertake to pursue negotiations as soon as possible with the aim of achieving agreement on other measures."

Sudan, 29 May:

"If the treaty on the non-proliferation of nuclear weapons is not concluded now, if it does not become operative this year, then we can safely predict that the ranks of its supporters will have become visibly thinner by next year. If at the time this treaty becomes operative it is not followed by serious measures of nuclear disarmament, then we can be virtually certain that the nuclear-weapon States will have to admit some more members into their 'club.' The danger to peace will be more present and palpable, the urge for more States to join the 'club' will be more irresistible, and any further measures of disarmament will be more difficult. Should we not then interpret this treaty in the light of the urgency of our need, and should we not support it as a measure of defence against the menace of nuclear war, realizing that, defective though it may be, there is greater danger in its rejection?"

Malta, 6 June:

"The real test of its viability will be the seriousness and the rapidity with which the major nuclear-weapon Powers will now embark on other aspects of nuclear disarmament. It was mainly to ensure that consideration of the essential next steps, already long overdue, would be taken up without delay that we found ourselves anxious to finalize discussion on the non-proliferation treaty at this session."

Mexico, 6 June:

"I trust that the forthcoming meetings of the Eighteen-Nation Committee on Disarmament will show that even in that task the two co-Chairmen can come to agreements as effective as those that led them successfully, with the co-operation of other members of the Committee and of the members of the First Committee, to bring to a successful conclusion the drafting of a treaty on the non-proliferation of nuclear weapons."

Pakistan, 6 June:

"In paragraph 4 of the draft resolution the Eighteen-Nation Committee on Disarmament and the nuclear-weapon States are requested urgently to pursue negotiations on effective measures relating to cessation of the nuclear arms race at an early date and to nuclear disarmament and on a treaty on general and complete disarmament. We note that the nuclear Powers have made a declaration of intention in the preamble to the text of the treaty to undertake effective measures in the direction of nuclear disarmament and, in article VI of the treaty, to pursue negotiations in good faith on such measures. Unless the nuclear arms race is halted by the three depository Governments and rapid and substantial steps are taken towards nuclear disarmament—in other words, towards vertical non-proliferation—the co-operation of the remaining two nuclear Powers in the direction of nuclear disarmament as well as general and complete disarmament cannot be realistically expected. The vital interests of peace and security for all mankind, quite apart from the viability and stability of the non-proliferation treaty, will depend on the ability of the three nuclear powers parties to the treaty to implement their solemn and binding pledges to end the nuclear arms race and carry out nuclear disarmament at an early date."

Mr. Orn of Sweden, the Rapporteur of the First Committee, said on 12 June, in bringing to the Plenary Session of the Assembly the report of the Committee:

"I think I interpret the feelings of a vast majority of that Committee if I express the hope that in commending this treaty on non-proliferation of nuclear weapons the Committee has played a significant part in helping us to cross a bridge at the other end of which we expect substantial progress towards nuclear disarmament and arms control."

NEXT STEPS

What are the next steps to be taken on the other side of this bridge? All of them have been many times referred to in disarmament discussions here in Washington as well as in New York, Geneva, London, Moscow, and many other capitals. The United States and the U.S.S.R. have recently announced a willingness to begin discussions on limiting nuclear delivery systems. These are other areas that need to be explored as well: A Comprehensive Nuclear Test-Ban, the Anti-Ballistic Missile question, the Cut Off of the Production of Fissionable Materials, a Freeze on the Manufacture of Nuclear Weapons, the adoption of a Convention Outlawing the Use of Nuclear Weapons, the Banning of the use of Nuclear Weapons, the Banning of the Use of Chemical and Biological Weapons, the

Prohibition of the Use of the Sea-Beds for Military Purposes. But may we suggest that it may not be necessary to take them up only one at a time. Could not separate committees work on several of them simultaneously, whether in Geneva, New York, or elsewhere?

THE PEACEFUL ATOM

Finally, Mr. Chairman, we must stress the importance of this Treaty for the prospects of the peaceful uses of atomic energy. I have spoken chiefly of its purpose in overcoming the dangers of military uses, but, as Ambassador Vratusa of Yugoslavia put it, his country voted for it "in the sincere hope and belief that it leads us closer to disarmament and creates conditions for sharing, without discrimination, the unlimited possibilities of atomic energy for peaceful purposes."

Our Latin American neighbors, who have already closed their continent to nuclear weaponry, are deeply interested in the opportunities this great universal source of energy opens for all nations. They speak for the developing world, and I quote from two of them:

Costa Rica, 29 May:

"I hesitated to intervene in this debate, because Costa Rica is a country without an army, navy or air force, and we trust in the force of law to protect our interests. We have no desire or possibility of ever acquiring atomic arms. We have renounced their use on our territory under the Treaty of Tlatelolco, but we do hope that we will be able to make peaceful use of nuclear energy if it is appropriate and possible, according to the new technology which is being prepared on the basis of new discoveries in this branch of human knowledge. This will greatly benefit the economic and social development of our country."

Uruguay, 5 June: (quoting his country's statement on the Treaty of Tlatelolco)

"Latin America has said: We do not want war with atoms; we want peace with atoms. The inequality separating us from the nuclear Powers in the use of the infernal machines that they possess is a matter of concern for us from the point of view of the general fate of mankind; but the inequality, greater and greater every day, in the benefits derived from atomic energy and from scientific and technical advances applied to economic and industrial development is of very acute interest to us because of the stagnation, the servitude, the backwardness and the poverty that beset our peoples. It would be tragic indeed if the era of colonialism, now in its last days in this world, were to experience a rebirth in consequence of the technological progress achieved by the great Powers. Nuclear neo-colonialism on the economic level must also be banished; the doors to technological progress must be opened wide to the developing countries, thus avoiding new causes of upheaval, new seedbeds of conflict, new misfortunes and miseries, all resulting, paradoxically, from the very scientific progress of mankind."

Mr. Chairman, we look to the Foreign Relations Committee and to the Senate of the United States to go forward in the matter of this Treaty, and in the directions it promises, because we believe that it is America's historical destiny not to be celebrated as the source of massive destruction in the world, but for its rising to the challenge of its role in the van of intelligent human social development.

HOW TO IMPROVE THE TREATY

Senator LAUSCHE. In your study of this entire problem, and it is obviously quite broad, and especially in your study of the treaty, are there any aspects of the treaty which you feel are bad and dangerous to the United States?

I am looking at it from both sides. I have my own views of some weak aspects of it, and my question to you is, in your analysis of it, are there any phases of the treaty that stand out as possibly dangerous to our country?

Mr. HUNTINGTON. My views on that, sir, are that the greatest danger to our country is that we blindly pursue the chimera of military security. We are in danger of getting out of touch with the rest of the world, and failing in the opportunity to achieve security for ourselves and other peoples because of our obsession with military arrangements which could lead in the end to nuclear warfare and all other kinds of warfare, and I think that this is where the danger lies.

Senator LAUSCHE. All right. But you said that the treaty is not perfect. What more would you have done in order to make the treaty perfect under the present unstable conditions that exist?

Mr. HUNTINGTON. From our point of view, the treaty would have been better if it had been stronger, if it had included more concrete commitments on the part of the nuclear powers to deescalate their armaments.

The delegate of India, for instance, pointed out that up to 1965 this treaty had been referred to as the "nondissemination" treaty and the language was changed to the "nonproliferation" treaty because dissemination is only part of proliferation. Proliferation also includes the great increase in the number of nuclear weapons that are hanging over our head.

Sweden, again, said very forcefully:

We are here to talk about not the real essence. The real danger to us in the world having a nuclear war break out does not come from the nonnuclear powers. It comes from the fact that the nuclear powers are armed to the teeth and increasing their arms.

Senator LAUSCHE. Yes.

EFFECT OF TRANSFER PROHIBITION ON U.S.S.R.

Has any hint come into your mind that Russia is procuring an advantage under this treaty because of its supposed advancement in the development of antiballistic missiles, and that if the treaty prohibits the transfer of antiballistic missiles by the United States that that will inure to the benefit of Russia and to the hurt of the United States?

That is, let us assume that Turkey wanted defensive missiles, and under the treaty we cannot give them to her. Does that help Russia or hurt Russia?

Mr. HUNTINGTON. I believe that Russia is anxious, as anxious and, perhaps, more anxious, than we are to end the nuclear arms race. As long as the military escalation and arms race is going on, the Russians are going to weigh whether this or that is in their advantage or not. We are going to do the same thing. This is going to increase the arms race, and there is no end to it, because the military mind, whether it is in the Soviet Union or in our country, works the same way.

There is no solution to this problem of who has the advantage except to stop the arms race. I honestly believe from talking to many of the Eastern European delegations and the noncommitted delegates at the U.N., that their overwhelming desire is to end the arms race and deescalate this whole business.

Senator LAUSCHE. Yes; you will understand I am putting these questions for the sincere purpose of exploring the advantages and disadvantages, whatever they might be, Mr. Huntington.

Mr. HUNTINGTON. Yes.

Senator LAUSCHE. All right.

Thank you very much for your testimony.

Mr. HUNTINGTON. Thank you, sir.

Senator LAUSCHE. The next witness is Prof. Mason Willrich, professor of law and director of the Center for the Study of Science, Technology and Public Policy at the University of Virginia.

Your statement will be inserted in full in the record, Professor Willrich, and you may proceed to read it or you can discuss the different thoughts contained in it by highlighting them.

STATEMENT OF MASON WILLRICH, PROFESSOR OF LAW AND DIRECTOR, CENTER FOR THE STUDY OF SCIENCE, TECHNOLOGY AND PUBLIC POLICY, UNIVERSITY OF VIRGINIA

Mr. WILLRICH. Thank you, Mr. Chairman.

I will read sections of my paper.

Mr. Chairman, I welcome the opportunity to present for the consideration of this committee my views concerning the Treaty on Nonproliferation of Nuclear Weapons. At the outset, let me make clear that I believe the treaty is in the long term security interests of the United States in particular, and the world community of nations in general. I urge this committee to report favorably and the Senate to consent promptly and without reservation to its ratification.

With respect to the future course of nuclear weapons proliferation three major alternatives are open: (1) uncontrolled nuclear weapons proliferation; (2) selective or controlled nuclear weapons proliferation; and (3) a general effort to prevent any further nuclear weapons proliferation.

Both supporters and most critics of the Nonproliferation Treaty seem in agreement that it would and that uncontrolled proliferation of nuclear weapons is bad policy.

CONTROLLED PROLIFERATION

Disagreement between the treaty's critics and its supporters arises, however, over evaluation of the second major policy alternative—selective or controlled proliferation. Three kinds of selective proliferation should be distinguished: (1) acquisition of nuclear deterrent forces by selected additional states; (2) acquisition of nuclear deterrent forces by multilateral groups of states; and (3) acquisition of ballistic missile defense systems by additional states, or multilateral groups of states.

I would now like to focus on this third alternative. The third type of selective proliferation that has been suggested is the transfer of ballistic missile defense systems to certain nonnuclear weapon states. It has been asserted that it is technically possible to design a tamperproof system which would prevent an ABM warhead from being used as an offensive weapon.

In rebuttal on the technical level, it has been stated that the use of X-rays and other scientific techniques on the ABM warheads transferred could lead to the acquisition by the recipient of sensitive design information which could thereafter be used in the manufacture of other warheads, even though the ABM warheads themselves were not diverted from their intended use.

OBJECTIONS TO TRANSFER OF ABM SYSTEMS

In addition to these technical arguments, there are, I believe, more basic objections to the future transfer of ABM systems to either selected non nuclear weapon states or multilateral groups. The first is effectiveness. The problem of ABM defense of Japan, India or Nationalist China against Communist China's intermediate range missiles will materialize sooner and will be different in kind than the problem of U.S. defense against China's ICBMs. The problem of an ABM system for Europe seems overwhelming given the short warning time and the potential weight and sophistication of a Soviet nuclear attack.

My second objection is cost. Who would pay for the costs of a U.S. supplied ballistic missile defense system for Western Europe, Japan, or India? I would judge that any proposal for Western Europe to pay billions of dollars for an ABM system made in the United States would receive much rougher treatment in the parliaments of Europe than the Senate recently gave to the U.S. ABM deployment program.

My third objection is the chain reaction effect. We are already familiar with the fact that any ABM defense of particular cities in the United States would involve difficult problems of political choice. Similarly, once the United States transferred an ABM system to one nonnuclear weapon state, or regional group, it might be hard pressed to deny such a "technological fix" to others.

While the Nonproliferation Treaty would perpetuate the existing discrimination between nuclear weapon and nonnuclear weapon states, the discrimination inherent in selective proliferation would be worse. It would compound the security problems of all. Finally, a policy of selective proliferation under such pressures would seem to lead, seem to lead unavoidably, to the same result as uncontrolled proliferation.

FUTURE IMPLICATIONS OF PROPOSED TREATY

I would now like to turn to the future implications of the treaty.

The Nonproliferation Treaty provides that nuclear weapons must remain under the exclusive control of the present five nuclear weapon states for the indefinite future. While the treaty leaves the freedom of action on nuclear weapon states relatively untouched, along with this freedom comes serious responsibilities, for the United States and the Soviet Union in particular. The treaty inescapably implies that nonnuclear weapon states in general will have to rely for the indefinite future on one or more nuclear weapon states as guarantors of their security against nuclear attack.

This means that the U.S. guaranty of West German security must remain credible as long as the threat of a nuclear attack by the Soviet Union exists. In my judgment, such credibility can only be preserved by the continued deployment of substantial U.S. forces on West German territory.

Here the Soviet Union will bear a major responsibility for the creation of a political climate in Europe in which West Germany can continue to accept a nonnuclear weapon status.

In the case of Japan, as China's nuclear power continues to grow, the visibility of the U.S. commitment to the nuclear defense of Japan may well have to increase correspondingly to remain credible. With respect to India, which is not at present allied to either nuclear superpower, the Security Council resolution on security assurances may offer some solace, but only if India changes its mind and becomes a party to the Nonproliferation Treaty.

Since the veto limits the possible target of Council action, the proposed resolution is aimed squarely at Communist China and no other potential nuclear aggressor. In this respect, the Security Council may become a principal organ for future collaboration between the United States and the Soviet Union in the containment of Communist China.

At the same time that role of the two superpowers as guarantors of the security of nonnuclear weapon states is extended by the Nonproliferation Treaty and its accompanying Security Council resolution on security assurances, the responsibilities on the United States and the Soviet Union mutually to control their own future development, procurement, and deployment of nuclear armaments is increased—if they expect the nonnuclear weapon parties to continue to abide by their pledges of nuclear weapons abstinence.

I believe a freeze on further deployment of offensive and defensive nuclear delivery systems must be put into effect by the United States and the Soviet Union within the next few years if the Nonproliferation Treaty is to endure for its initial period of 25 years. Such a limitation must in my judgment be based on the principle of functional strategic nuclear parity which both sides must recognize and consciously seek to maintain. Thus, the containment of China's nuclear power, if it continues to grow, must become increasingly a shared responsibility of the United States and the Soviet Union.

While the Nonproliferation Treaty confirms for the time being the status quo regarding nuclear weapons, it looks forward to change concerning the peaceful uses of nuclear energy.

AVAILABILITY OF PLUTONIUM

As a result of the accelerating trend toward use of nuclear energy for a variety of peaceful purposes, a trend which the treaty will reinforce, we look forward to a world in which plutonium will be readily available in very large quantities in all industrially advanced states and in many developing states.

The amount of plutonium accumulated in the world as a result of production in civil nuclear power programs is estimated to reach 28,000 kilograms by 1970 and 300,000 to 450,000 kilograms by 1980. Thus, the stockpiles of plutonium used in civil nuclear programs will soon dwarf the amounts of fissionable materials in the nuclear weapons stockpiles of all nuclear weapon states. Yet less than 10 kilograms of plutonium is needed for a bomb which will destroy a medium sized city.

Control over plutonium and plutonium production capacity will in the 1970s and 1980s be an internal as well as international security problem of staggering dimensions. Moreover, a plutonium production capability, whether or not safeguarded, represents a latent threat to the security of a neighboring nonnuclear weapon state without any plutonium production capacity of its own.

Safeguards on peaceful nuclear activities will at most serve to flash a red warning light in case materials are diverted to weapons purposes in a nonnuclear weapon state. There is nothing that safeguards alone can do to prevent diversion from occurring once a nonnuclear weapon state decides to embark on a nuclear weapons program.

Therefore, safeguards are part of, but not a complete response to the challenge to the international system presented by continuing peaceful nuclear innovation. An adequate response to the exploitation of nuclear energy will require further structural innovation in the international political system.

The Nonproliferation Treaty could give us some sorely needed additional time to change our modes of thinking. It contains within it our best hope of survival in the nuclear era which has only just begun.

Thank you, Mr. Chairman.

(The prepared statement of Mr. Willrich follows:)

STATEMENT BY MASON WILLRICH

Mr. Chairman, I welcome the opportunity to present for the consideration of this Committee my views concerning the Treaty on Non-Proliferation of Nuclear Weapons. At the outset, let me make clear that I believe the Treaty is in the long-term security interests of the United States in particular, and the world community of nations in general. I urge this Committee to report favorably and the Senate to consent promptly and without reservation to its ratification.

The Non-Proliferation Treaty is the culmination of negotiations stretching over almost five years and involving many nations with diverse political and economic interests, and military and industrial capacities. Therefore, the Treaty is a complex legal document and necessarily contains compromises and ambiguities. In an article to appear in the July issue of the *Yale Law Journal* I have discussed at length the many difficult problems of interpretation which will be encountered by the Parties as the Treaty is implemented. Therefore, today I will focus on two fundamental concerns: first, an evaluation of the policy underlying the Treaty; and, second, an assessment of the implications of the Treaty for the future.

POLICY EVALUATION

One goal of overriding importance in the nuclear era is the avoidance of nuclear war. This goal must be achieved in a world of nation-states in which diverse value systems coexist and conflicts between value systems persist. It is primarily in relation to the goal of the avoidance of nuclear war that the Non-Proliferation Treaty should be evaluated.

With respect to the future course of nuclear weapons proliferation three major alternatives are open: (1) uncontrolled nuclear weapons proliferation; (2) selective or controlled nuclear weapons proliferation; and (3) a general effort to prevent any further nuclear weapons proliferation. The Non-Proliferation Treaty represents a basic policy decision, potentially by the entire world community, in favor of the third alternative.

What can be said about the probable effects of each of the other two alternative policies on the likelihood of nuclear war? How do these compare with an assessment of the effects in this regard of establishment of the rule of nuclear weapons containment embodied in the Non-Proliferation Treaty?

A policy favoring general uncontrolled nuclear weapons proliferation, the choice at the opposite extreme from the Non-Proliferation Treaty, is not likely to be adopted. Even Communist China, which has moved further than any other State toward espousing such a policy, has characteristically limited itself to verbal encouragement of Afro-Asian States, and has stated it would be "unrealistic" for non-nuclear-weapon States to expect material assistance from it for this purpose.

Occasionally the argument is made, however, that if all States possessed nuclear weapons no State would be able to use them without incurring an unacceptable risk of damage to its own territory and population. The argument goes on that if all States possessed nuclear weapons, the risk of escalation to use of nuclear weapons in any armed conflict would constitute a substantial deterrent to all use of force. The logic of the argument may have superficial appeal in the abstract, although even on this level it is in my judgment not persuasive. But the model of the world in which all States possessed nuclear weapons is absurd. Most States could not support a nuclear force even if it was given to them, much less develop a nuclear deterrent themselves. Many States would be incapable of providing the technical expertise to man such a force. Therefore, we will live in a world of nuclear-weapon and non-nuclear-weapon States for the foreseeable future. The consequence of a policy favoring general nuclear weapons proliferation would be a world of many—say fifteen to twenty-five—nuclear-weapon States, but not a world in which every State was a nuclear-weapon power.

Would the likelihood of nuclear war increase in such a world? Both supporters and most critics of the Non-Proliferation Treaty seem in agreement that it would and that uncontrolled proliferation of nuclear weapons is bad policy. The basic reasons for such a conclusion have been detailed by Secretary Rusk in his statement to this Committee on July 10, and I will not reiterate them here.

Disagreement between the Treaty's critics and its supporters arises, however, over evaluation of the second major policy alternative—selective or controlled proliferation. Three kinds of selective proliferation should be distinguished: (1) acquisition of nuclear deterrent forces by selected additional States; (2) acquisition of nuclear deterrent forces by multilateral groups of States; and (3) acquisition of ballistic missile defense systems by additional States, or multilateral groups of States. The consequences of each kind of selective proliferation will be analyzed in turn.

The United States has helped and is continuing to help the United Kingdom to develop and maintain an independent nuclear deterrent. In the past, the Soviet Union helped China in its nucelar weapons program. In the future, might it not be good policy to assist certain others to acquire nuclear weapons?—or at least to refrain from actively discouraging certain non-nuclear-weapon States from acquiring nuclear weapons on their own? Such a policy, it may be argued, could increase the balance and stability of certain key power relationships. Moreover, creation of certain additional national nuclear deterrent forces might reduce the need for existing nuclear-weapon States to extend guarantees against nuclear blackmail and thereby reduce the risk of their being drawn into local or regional conflicts.

The defects of a policy of controlled proliferation of nuclear deterrent forces to selected additional States, however, become apparent when concrete cases are considered. It has been recently estimated that seven non-nuclear-weapon States could produce nuclear weapons within less than two years. These are India, Japan, Canada, Switzerland, Sweden, Israel and West Germany. I believe four are of primary concern: Japan, India, Israel and West Germany. Each of these non-nuclear-weapon Nations faces a major security problem for which a nuclear deterrent might seem to offer a solution. Each possesses, although in varying degrees, the technological prerequisites for a nuclear weapons program. And each is also a claimant of United States assistance to resolve its future security dilemma.

Should not Japan acquire its own nuclear deterrent against Communist China, perhaps with United States assistance? Would this not help to stabilize Communist China's position in Asia and reduce the risk of a direct nuclear confrontation in the not-too-distant future between the United States and China? Japan is already allied to the United States, potentially against China, and it has the scientific, industrial and economic bases to support a secure second-strike nuclear deterrent. But there are a number of implications which need to be considered before a policy of selective proliferation is accepted with regard to Japan.

Since Japan has been the one target of nuclear attacks in the past, a strong psychological aversion to nuclear weapons exists among the Japanese people. It is my opinion that a decision by a Japanese Government to acquire nuclear weapons could not be taken without a substantial shift in public opinion toward a resurgence of nationalism, probably with militarist overtones. While, therefore, Japan's primary intention in acquiring nuclear weapons would be to offset Communist China, other nations in the Far East and Southeast Asia would probably perceive Japan's actions as aimed in more than one direction.

Furthermore, if the argument that Japan needs nuclear weapons to deter Communist China is persuasive, then there would seem to be all the more reason for India to have nuclear weapons. After all, China attacked India in 1962. India now faces a nuclear-armed China without benefit of a mutual defense treaty with the United States or any other nuclear-weapon State. India possesses the technological capability to acquire nuclear weapons, although in view of the geographical assymetry with respect to the delivery problem it would be more costly for India to acquire a credible nuclear deterrent against China than vice versa.

But if we concede that India should have a nuclear deterrent against China, and perhaps provide external support, what then do we do about Pakistan? Since their formation as States, India and Pakistan have had a continuing history of oscillation between armed conflict and armed truce, with armaments generously supplied on both sides, primarily by the United States and the United Kingdom, and to a lesser extent by France and the Soviet Union.

Japan and India together illustrate one major difficulty with a policy of selective or controlled proliferation, namely how to prevent the acquisition of nuclear weapons by one additional State from resulting in an uncontrollable "chain reaction." Another difficulty is that a consensus might not be reached among all States involved as to which ones, if any, should be encouraged or permitted to acquire nuclear weapons. If such a consensus were not reached, selective proliferation could quickly become competitive. Israel is a good illustration of this difficulty.

If Israel acquired nuclear weapons, whether alone or with outside help, the Soviet Union would probably respond with some form of offsetting assistance to the United Arab Republic. Since indigenous Arab capabilities are less than Israel's, the Soviet Union might offset the Israeli deterrent with a nuclear guarantee to the Arab States backed up by the transfer of some of its own nuclear forces to Egypt. Thereafter, the United States would have no choice but to grant a supporting commitment to Israel. The unhappy result of selective proliferation in the Middle East would then be the Soviet Union and the United States glaring at each other over nuclear barricades with Arab and Israeli fingers on the nuclear trigger.

A policy of selective proliferation with respect to either the Far East or Middle East would also have major repercussions in Europe. If Japan or India is justified in acquiring nuclear weapons to offset China's growing nuclear power, or Israel is justified in acquiring nuclear weapons to offset the Arab States' growing conventional power, how can the non-proliferation case be sustained against West Germany which is the major target for 700 nuclear warheads on missiles located in western Russia and which faces over 20 Soviet divisions deployed in East Germany? While the United States is presently obligated under the North Atlantic Treaty to assist West Germany if it is subject to an armed attack, after August 24, 1969 that Treaty obligation will be subject to termination on one year's notice. Secretary Rusk has made clear the United States has no intention of withdrawing from NATO. Nevertheless, we must recognize that from the West German perspective the possibility will exist, and that one year is insufficient lead time for any non-nuclear-weapon State to prepare for its own nuclear defense.

Despite these circumstances all responsible officials agree that West Germany must not acquire nuclear weapons in the future. A nuclear-armed West Germany would be destabilizing in the extreme. Whether the future of Europe is envisioned in an Atlantic Community or as a construction from the Atlantic to the Urals, whether Western Europe becomes united or remains composed of independent States, whether bridges between the Eastern and Western parts of Europe are built up or torn down, the future of Germany must be without nuclear weapons. On this point the United States, the Soviet Union, the United Kingdom and France share a common interest, together with the smaller and less powerful States of Europe, West and East. Fortunately, most West Germans recognize this as a fact of their political life. We can disagree with and resist Soviet foreign policy aimed at the break up of NATO and the isolation of West Germany from the United States. We can also discount the utility of the French nuclear weapons program, although the force de frappe seems to make sense as a hedge against the future growth of German military power, if not as a deterrent against the Soviet Union. Yet on this cardinal point of non-proliferation policy we should be clear that we are in agreement.

Therefore, I conclude that selective proliferation of nuclear deterrent forces would probably lead to a net decrease in the security of the non-nuclear-weapon State which acquired nuclear weapons, would generally destabilize the military relationships affected, and would produce in each case a chain reaction effect.

I turn now to consideration of the second type of selective proliferation, namely multilateral groups of States. In concept, the creation of multilaterally owned and controlled nuclear forces has considerable merit. This type of selective proliferation could lead to more fingers on the nuclear safety catch without increasing the number of decision-making centers which could fire nuclear weapons. Multilateral participation in the operational as well as planning phases of nuclear deterrence might reduce national aspirations for nuclear weapons and could become the cutting edge for political unification and structural change in the nation-state system.

The difficulty with the multilateral nuclear force, or "MLF," as a type of selective proliferation lies not so much with the concept as with its implementation. The concept depends for its viability on, first, a desire seriously shared among all participants to move toward meaningful forms of political unification, and, second, an external security threat that is perceived by the participants to be increasing. Of course, these two conditions are interrelated.

In my opinion, the shared interest never really existed in sufficient depth among the participants, including the United States, in the discussions between 1960 and 1966 of various proposals for a multilateral nuclear force within NATO. In West Germany itself a substantial element of political opinion saw an MLF primarily as something to be given up for reunification. In NATO, proposals for an MLF were divisive rather than unifying, and their implementation would have forced West Germany to make an irrevocable choice between France and the United States. In Europe as a whole, implementation of an MLF would have caused real, whether or not rational, concerns among the states of Eastern Europe and the Soviet Union about a West German finger on the nuclear trigger. Implementation of an MLF could well have forestalled the tendencies toward polycentrism and independence from the Soviet Union which are so apparent and welcome today throughout Eastern Europe. Moreover, the Soviet nuclear threat is not now perceived in Western Europe as increasingly dangerous, so as to require new steps to be taken.

Therefore, I conclude that, whether or not the MLF was good policy for the early 1960's in relation to NATO, the option need not be preserved for the 1970's or 1980's. Furthermore, the option of selective proliferation of nuclear deterrent forces to other multilateral groups outside NATO does not seem to be a serious possibility for the foreseeable future. In general, selective proliferation to multilateral groups is a policy option that may properly be closed.

The third type of selective proliferation that has been suggested is the transfer of ballistic missile defense systems to certain non-nuclear-weapon States. It has been asserted that it is technically possible to design a tamper-proof system which would prevent an ABM warhead from being used as an offensive weapon. In rebuttal on the technical level, it has been stated that the use of X-rays and other scientific techniques on the ABM warheads transferred could lead to the acquisition by the recipient of sensitive design information which could thereafter be used in the manufacture of other warheads, even though the ABM warheads themselves were not diverted from their intended use.

There are, I believe, more basic objections to the future transfer of ABM systems to either selected non-nuclear-weapon States or multilateral groups. The first is effectiveness. The problem of ABM defense of Japan, India or Nationalist China against Communist China's intermediate range missiles will materialize sooner and will be different in kind than the problem of United States defense against China's ICBM's. The problem of an ABM system for Europe seems overwhelming given the short warning time and the potential weight and sophistication of a Soviet nuclear attack. Therefore, it is doubtful whether the United States could, even if it wished, provide an ABM shield to non-nuclear-weapon States in which those States would have confidence.

My second objection is cost. Who would pay for the costs of a United States supplied ballistic missile defense system for Western Europe, Japan, or India? I would judge that any proposal for Western Europe to pay billions of dollars for an ABM system made in the U.S.A. would receive much rougher treatment in the Parliaments of Europe than the Senate recently gave to the United States ABM deployment program.

My third objection is the chain reaction effect. We are already familiar with the fact that any ABM defense of particular cities in the United States would involve difficult problems of political choice. Similarly, once the United States transferred an ABM system to one non-nuclear-weapon State, or regional group, it might be hard pressed to deny such a "technological fix" to others. It is my conclusion, therefore, that the transfer of ABM systems to selected non-nuclear-weapon States or groups of States is an option that it is wise to foreclose.

The basic difficulty in any policy of selective proliferation is how to be selective within a global system composed of interrelated units. While the Non-Proliferation Treaty would perpetuate the existing discrimination between nuclear-weapon and non-nuclear-weapon States, the discrimination inherent in selective proliferation would be worse. It would lead to more resentment on the part of the remaining non-nuclear-weapon States, and risk more competition among the nuclear-weapon States. It would compound the security problems of all. Finally, a policy of selective proliferation under such pressures would seem to lead unavoidably to the same result as general proliferation.

Would then a policy to prevent the acquisition of nuclear weapons by every non-nuclear-weapon State reduce the probability of nuclear war? There is no clear answer to this question. However, it is fair to conclude that any further nuclear weapons proliferation would, in the long-term, increase that probability. On balance, therefore, a flat prohibition on the further spread of nuclear weapons to additional States is the preferred policy alternative in relation to the goal of avoidance of nuclear war. A general nonproliferation policy is also justifiable as a way of buying time needed to take further steps which might effect an actual reduction in the risk of nuclear war in the future.

FUTURE IMPLICATIONS

The competitive forces inherent in the existing international system, reinforced by conflicts over basic values among competing States within the system have greatly accelerated the exploitation of nuclear energy. A series of upward and outward trends are established in both the military and the peaceful nuclear fields. The Non-Proliferation Treaty is an attempt to reverse the military trends, confirm the peaceful trends and establish a barrier between the two. In short, the Treaty is a major attempt to achieve political control on a global scale over the scientific and technological processes by which nuclear energy is exploited.

The Non-Proliferation Treaty provides that nuclear weapons must remain under the exclusive control of the present five nuclear-weapon States for the indefinite future. While the Treaty leaves the freedom of action of nuclear-weapon States relatively untouched, along with this freedom comes serious responsibilities, for the United States and the Soviet Union in particular. The Treaty inescapably implies that non-nuclear-weapon States in general will have to rely for the indefinite future on one or more nuclear-weapon States as guarantors of their security against nuclear attack from other nuclear-weapon States. This means that the United States guarantee of West German security must remain credible as long as the threat of a nuclear attack by the Soviet Union exists. In my judgment, such credibility can only be preserved by the continued deployment of substantial United States forces on West German territory. Hopefully but not necessarily, West German accession to the Non-Proliferation Treaty will lead to general improvement in relations between West Germany and the Soviet Union. Here the Soviet Union will bear a major responsibility for the creation of a political climate in Europe in which West Germany can continue to accept a non-nuclear-weapon status.

In the case of Japan, as China's nuclear power continues to grow, the visibility of the United States commitment to the nuclear defense of Japan may well have to increase correspondingly to remain credible. With respect to India, which is not at present allied to either nuclear superpower, the Security Council resolution on security assurances may offer some solace, but only if India changes its mind and becomes a Party to the Non-Proliferation Treaty.

This is the main purpose of the Security Council's resolution. The veto limits the possible target of Council action, and the proposed resolution is aimed squarely at Communist China and no other potential nuclear aggressor. In this respect, the Security Council may become a principal organ for future collaboration between the United States and the Soviet Union in the containment of Communist China—as long as Communist China is not a member of the United Nations. Such collaboration, increasingly in the open and institutionalized, would be an important ingredient of any meaningful security assurance to a non-nuclear-weapon State such as India. However, it is too early to tell whether the resolution should be properly characterized as an effort to move toward this kind of cooperation between the superpowers or as merely a short-term expedient to obtain subscriptions to the Non-Proliferation Treaty.

At the same time that role of the two superpowers as guarantors of the security of non-nuclear-weapon States is extended by the Non-Proliferation Treaty and its accompanying Security Council resolution on security assurances, the responsibilities on the United States and the Soviet Union mutually to control their own future development, procurement and deployment of nuclear armaments is increased—if they expect the non-nuclear-weapon Parties to continue to abide by their pledges of nuclear weapons abstinence. I believe a freeze on further deployment of offensive and defensive nuclear delivery systems must be put into effect by the United States and the Soviet Union within the next few years if the Non-Proliferation Treaty is to endure for its initial period of twenty-five years. Such a limitation must in my judgment be based on the principle of functional strategic nuclear parity which both sides must recognize and consciously seek to maintain. Thus, the containment of China's nuclear power, if it continues to grow, must become increasingly a shared responsibility of the United States and the Soviet Union.

At some point in the future, we will probably have to concede Communist China a second-strike capability against the United States.

I would argue that the United States should prepare to do this sooner rather than later. Thereafter, relations with Communist China will proceed, as they do now with the Soviet Union, on the basis of nuclear deterrence on both sides rather than a first-strike capability on one side. Such a posture of mutual deterrence among the United States, the Soviet Union and Communist China may not be comfortable. But it would lead to a more secure world than a resumption of the nuclear arms race between the United States and the Soviet Union which is the probable result if we thicken our ABM defenses in order to postpone as far as possible the day when we grant Communist China a nuclear strike capability against us.

Nuclear weapons will remain contained within the existing international structure only for a limited period of time. A question of fundamental importance is whether new solutions embracing necessary structural change can be found or will emerge during the period while the rule of nuclear weapons containment established by the Treaty lasts. Perhaps the greatest risk in the Treaty is that the search for new forms will be unsuccessful. Having maintained the status quo against increasing pressures, if the Treaty structure breaks down the ensuing instabilities could be more severe and dangerous than if the natural course of nuclear weapons proliferation had not been interrupted. This does not mean that the risks inherent in the Treaty outweigh the risks without the Treaty, but it highlights the need for receptivity to structural innovation in the international system in the critical interim period.

While the Non-Proliferation Treaty confirms for the time being the status quo regarding nuclear weapons, it looks forward to change concerning the peaceful uses of nuclear energy. Civil nuclear industries throughout the world, and in all of Eastern Europe except in the Soviet Union, will be open to international inspection. Non-nuclear-weapon States will come to rely mainly on an international system of accountability for assurance against nuclear weapons programs in other non-nuclear-weapon States. A new multilateral framework for peaceful applications of nuclear explosives is established.

As a result of the accelerating trend toward use of nuclear energy for a variety of peaceful purposes, a trend which the Treaty will reinforce, we look forward to a world in which plutonium will be readily available in very large quantities in all industrially advanced States and in many developing States. The magnitude of the security risk from the spread of plutonium and plutonium production technology throughout the world should not be underestimated. One recent and conservative estimate is that 8,000 kilograms of plutonium will be produced annually in civil nuclear power reactors by 1970 and 50,000–70,000 kilograms annually by 1980. The corresponding amounts of plutonium accumulated in the world as a result of past production is estimated to be 28,000 kilograms by 1970, and 300,000-450,000 kilograms by 1980. Thus, the stockpiles of plutonium used in civil nuclear programs will soon dwarf the amounts of fissionable materials in the nuclear weapons stockpiles of all nuclear-weapon States. Yet less than 10 kilograms of plutonium is needed for a bomb which will destroy a medium-sized city.

Control over plutonium and plutonium production capacity will in the 1970's and 1980's be an internal as wells as international security problem of staggering dimensions. Moreover, a plutonium production capability, whether or not safeguarded, represents a latent threat to the security of a neighboring non-nuclear-weapon State without any plutonium production capacity of its own. In fact, tendencies toward non-economic civil nuclear power races between various non-nuclear-weapon States are already developing.

Safeguards on peaceful nuclear activities will at most serve to flash a red warning light in case materials are diverted to weapons purposes in a non-nuclear-weapon State. There is nothing that safeguards alone can do to prevent diversion from occurring once a non-nuclear-weapon State decides to embark on a nuclear weapons program. There is no built-in enforcement mechanism in the safeguards concept. Therefore, safeguards are part of, but not a complete response to the challenge to the international system presented by continuing peaceful nuclear innovation. Here again, an adequate response to the exploitation of nuclear energy will require further structural innovation in the international political system.

Einstein once said: "The unleashed power of the atom has changed everything save our modes of thinking, and thus we drift to unparallelled catastrophe." The Non-Proliferation Treaty could give us some sorely needed additional time to change our modes of thinking. It contains within it our best hope of survival in the nuclear era which has only just begun.

Senator LAUSCHE. Senator Case.

Senator CASE. I do not think I have any questions, Mr. Chairman.

Senator LAUSCHE. I would like to ask a few questions.

CLARIFICATION OF TRANSFER PROHIBITION

Under the provisions of article I and article II, Mr. Willrich, what is your opinion about the right of the United States or any signatory nation possessed of the atomic explosive to allow the transfer of a genuine antiballistic missile defense system?

May I put it another way: Is the transfer of both offensive and defensive missiles prohibited by the treaty?

Mr. WILLRICH. Mr. Chairman, I think that I would not want to intrude upon the administration which, after all, is the one to interpret the treaty for you.

My understanding of the treaty, however, is that the treaty would prohibit the transfer to another country, it would not prohibit the deployment under U.S. control in that country of either offensive or defensive nuclear weapons.

Senator LAUSCHE. That is exactly the query or the doubt that I have. I cannot go along from a legal standpoint with the argument that you can transfer an explosive atomic device providing you keep control over the trigger. Have you the treaty with you?

Mr. WILLRICH. Yes, sir.

Senator LAUSCHE. I ask you these questions because you are a teacher of law, are you not?

Mr. WILLRICH. I am one of many teachers of law, sir.

Senator LAUSCHE. All right. Now, "Each nuclear weapon state party to the treaty undertakes not to transfer to any recipient whatsoever nuclear weapons or other nuclear explosive devices." I stop at this point.

Am I correct in my understanding that under the language which I have just read, no signatory nuclear power will be permitted to transfer nuclear weapons or other nuclear explosive devices?

Mr. WILLRICH. You are correct, sir.

Senator Lausche. From that point on it says "or"—and I emphasize this joining word "or" which is in the disjunctive—"or other nuclear explosive devices or control over such weapons or explosive devices directly or indirectly."

Doesn't that mean, first, that you cannot transfer the nuclear explosive device nor the control. You cannot transfer the control over them?

Mr. Willrich. That is correct, sir.

Senator Lausche. That would then mean, according to what I have read thus far, that a signatory nuclear state would be prohibited from transferring the explosive device or the control over an explosive device; is that correct?

Mr. Willrich. That is correct, sir.

Senator Lausche. You heard Dr. Teller's argument this morning?

Mr. Willrich. Yes, sir.

Senator Lausche. May I have your views on that, where he said that he does not oppose the treaty, and he said that he thinks it would be dangerous not to approve it because Russia would drop out. I think I am correct in my quotation of him. But he does have concern about the fact that under the treaty you cannot transfer defensive weapons.

Mr. Willrich. Well, as I indicated in my statement, Mr. Chairman, I do not feel that the option of transferring defensive weapons systems is a good option to preserve. Beyond that, I do not think that option exists at the moment, and I think it is a substantial number of years before we are at the point where we would be prepared to transfer those types of systems.

Third, I think that one of the issues which is squarely posed by this treaty, and which is going to be posed in many other phases of our national life and in our international existence in the future, is the issue of political control over the research and development process in the future. I would assert that control over this process is a political issue, and a political issue of fundamental importance to the security of our Nation.

U.S. WITHDRAWAL FROM TREATY

Senator Lausche. In the event an ABM should be developed in the future, one that is financially justifiable and effective—Senator Pastore this morning said that we had the power within 90 days of withdrawing from the treaty—and that that would enable us to restate and re-agree on what should be done.

What is your view of that?

Mr. Willrich. Well, I think there are a lot of uncertainties in that problem, and at this point I prefer to wait and see where the scientific development leads us, and not to think about withdrawal before we get into the treaty.

EXPANSION OF U.S. WORLD COMMITMENTS

Senator Lausche. What answer do you give to the argument that the signing of this treaty will expand our obligation to become the policeman of the world and burden us with subduing every disorder that occurs?

Mr. Willrich. Mr. Chairman, I am very sympathetic to the sense of the Senate concerning commitments, and commitments which may not appear to be when they are entered into what they seem to develop into very shortly.

On the other hand, I do feel that in this treaty there are substantial commitments, there are substantial commitments by the United States, and substantial commitments by the nonnuclear weapons states, and there are substantial commitments by the Soviet Union. But I do feel that in entering into these commitments that this is the way for a more reasonable future than without any treaty at all.

Now I understand the reluctance to enter into any form of commitment. But I would say one of the most dangerous things that can happen is for a reaction to occur whereby, because we have had problems with commitments in the past, that this is a ground for questioning, independently a ground for questioning, commitments of this kind which, I think, are fundamentally in the security interests of the United States.

Senator LAUSCHE. You do know that the Secretary of State and Mr. Foster testified that we are not assuming any new obligations of any character whatsoever in excess of the obligations that we have in the United Nations now?

Mr. WILLRICH. I am aware of that testimony, and I feel that there are always potential obligations that can be translated into reality.

What I am suggesting is that this treaty take some of those potential obligations which we ourselves and the Soviet Union have been under, for ever since the United Nations Charter was signed, and begins to move toward a translation of those obligations into more of a reality.

U.N. SECURITY COUNCIL ACTION

Senator LAUSCHE. Do you agree that when the moment for critical action arises, if it does, that the issue must go to the Security Council of the United Nations, and that there the United States, if it does not want to exercise its military force, will be able to do so by vetoing whatever resolution is sought to be passed by the Security Council?

Mr. WILLRICH. That is the effect of the resolution that the Security Council has passed.

Senator LAUSCHE. Is that your understanding?

Senator CASE. It is my understanding, and also the Secretary did state very clearly there were no commitments beyond what was stated in the treaty and in the declaration of intent, in the resolution of the United Nations Security Council.

I am not quite sure, either from your paper or from what you have just said, as to how much further you would go beyond this.

Mr. WILLRICH. I certainly would not disagree with what Secretary Rusk has said the treaty means.

I would prefer to use the word "responsibilities" rather than commitments and I do feel that this treaty, if it is going to work, is going to require the United States and the Soviet Union together to share some rather important responsibilities.

EXTENT OF U.S. COMMITMENT TO GO TO WAR

Senator CASE. The point, I think, that we are all jittery about is an advance commitment that takes out of the hands of the United

222

States a decision at some future time as to where its armed forces will or will not be employed beyond its own borders and, in effect, gives somebody else the right to do this.

I am not convinced that I would make any commitment for any purpose, or to be very specific, to go to war in defense of anybody else. How do you know how anybody else is going to act or what provocation a person is going to give to another person?

I think I would have to say my own present view is that the United States make up its own mind at the time it goes to war whether it is going to war and whether it is in its interests and in the interests of world peace to do it.

Mr. WILLRICH. I would respond at two levels. One is in terms of the treaty itself. This focuses, I believe, not so much in the commitment of force problem, which I share your concern about, but rather on the commitment to assume a posture whereby it will not become as likely that you will have to use that force.

But the commitment to assume that posture is, I think, in the treaty.

Now, sir, I think that there is a point here where if we expect non-nuclear weapon states to sign on in the treaty that we must make sure that those nonnuclear weapon states feel secure within the framework of the treaty.

In other words, just as we would not enter the treaty unless we felt more secure on the inside than on the outside, we must be sympathetic to the concerns of the nonnuclear weapon states who also want to feel more secure inside than outside.

RETAINING U.S. TROOPS IN WEST GERMANY

Senator CASE. One thing I did not mention. I did like very much your emphasis on the importance of our retaining our troops in West Germany.

I think far more than any promise that may be made or statement of intention is the fact that we are leaving the troops there in such substantial numbers as to contribute to a credible defense and a nonnuclear one.

Mr. WILLRICH. Yes, sir.

Senator CASE. And if you are to be credible, I think you have to mean really a nonnuclear defense because the incredibility of any defense based upon the use of nuclear weapons, whether strategic or tactical, it seems to me is almost self-evident, and especially for a country like ours in regard to involvement in something that is far away from our own territory.

Mr. WILLRICH. Senator Case, I would say that the commitment of troops is important at both levels, at the conventional level, as you say, and also at making sure that the other country understands that we are prepared to resort to the use of nuclear weapons if necessary because of the substantial numbers of troops that are there.

Senator CASE. I am not so sure I follow the last point, at least I do not exclude agreement with it. I think we should avoid, if we possibly can, any reliance upon that by keeping an adequate number there, and here is where I disagree, for example, with Senator Mansfield and others who have suggested just leaving a small handful—not a handful but a substantially smaller number than are there now.

I think the effect upon the NATO defense of a reduction of substantial numbers of our forces, and the effect upon other countries which would undoubtedly leap at a chance to follow our example, might well be the reduction of the NATO military to the point where it would not be credible as a defense against Russia except through the use of nuclear weapons and such a situation ought to be avoided by all in every way.

Mr. WILLRICH. I agree entirely.

Senator LAUSCHE. I want to put the same questions that I put to Mr. Huntington. Do you see in the treaty any pitfalls as far as the United States is concerned? Do you see in it advantages that Russia would have in joining the treaty that the United States would not have?

Mr. WILLRICH. No, on both counts.

Senator LAUSCHE. Now, Russia is supposed to possess the antiballistic missile. To what extent it is sophisticated and developed, I do not think we know. If Russia has a highly effective ABM, would that be an inducement for it to join in a treaty that would prohibit the nonatomic nations from getting either defensive or offensive weapons?

Mr. WILLRICH. First of all, from all the evidence that I have read in the public record, I do not believe that Russia is on the verge of acquiring the kind of ABM defense that you describe, Mr. Chairman.

Secondly, were they to acquire such a defensive system, I feel rather confident that the United States would follow or be developing its own system in parallel. I do not think that one side is going to get the jump on the other side in this development.

So that I think that you would wind up in a position of relative symmetry between the two as far as the ABM development and deployment is concerned.

Senator LAUSCHE. I think you have answered my question, that you do not see any pitfalls as far as we are concerned in the treaty.

Mr. WILLRICH. I think the treaty is greatly to the interests of the United States, sir.

Senator LAUSCHE. Finally, we do make some positive commitments in this treaty. But when it comes to the moment of making a decision as to whether we will become a policeman, we retain that judgment in our own hands and will express it in the United Nations Security Council; is that correct?

Mr. WILLRICH. I think that under the treaty and the Council resolution we retain that judgment, and we can express it in the Security Council or we might express it outside the Security Council.

Senator LAUSCHE. Yes.

But we do agree to go to the Security Council and there discuss it and act under the powers that we have.

Mr. WILLRICH. If we have time. Otherwise, we can proceed under article 51 of the charter, sir.

Senator LAUSCHE. All right. Thanks very much, Mr. Willrich.

Mr. WILLRICH. Thank you, Mr. Chairman.

Senator CASE. Mr. Chairman, I am sorry I have to leave, but I have some young people I have to see, and I will try to be back.

Senator LAUSCHE. The next witness is the Reverend Stanley M. Andrews, national executive secretary of Americans for National Security, an affiliate of Liberty Lobby.

Reverend Andrews, we are glad to have you here.

STATEMENT OF REV. STANLEY M. ANDREWS, NATIONAL EXECUTIVE SECRETARY, AMERICANS FOR NATIONAL SECURITY

Mr. ANDREWS. Thank you, Mr. Chairman.

I am going to submit the statement and then I will talk off the cuff from it, if I may.

Senator LAUSCHE. Yes.

Mr. ANDREWS. Our organization is opposed to the ratification of the treaty since we believe ratification of the treaty is historically meaningless at this time and that the United States will lose more than it can possibly gain by becoming a member of this pact.

I am going to try to make four points.

HISTORIC MEANING OF TREATY IS CHALLENGED

The first is that it is historically meaningless, because out of the five powers that now have nuclear know how, only three of the nations are considering ratification of the treaty. Someone has called this a "three-fifths treaty," and I rather think it is a good term, and it makes it meaningless because, unless Red China and France enter into this treaty, it leaves endless flexibility for those who are potential enemies to do what they want, to give their know how to countries to their advantage, and it places us at a disadvantage.

There has been a lot said about the treaty and the three powers promising not to give the bomb to nations that do not possess it. There is a lot of fuzzy thinking here because, first of all, many of the nations that do not possess the bomb, do not possess the bomb even if we gave them the know how, because they lack the financial resources; they lack the raw material resources and, therefore, they never would be interested in the bomb unless we gave it to them.

But certainly you cannot imagine a country like Iceland or Mongolia or Ghana or Kenya caring about this treaty except they are going to sign it and they are going to ratify it because the big nations want them to sign a piece of paper, and it is meaningless, absolutely meaningless to them.

It is noticeable that West Germany, India, Japan, Pakistan, Brazil, Argentina, who are possible threshold nations, who have the financial resources, some technical know how, and are able to cross into the A-bomb club, have not signed the treaty and, in fact, are giving strong indications that they will not sign the treaty, unless there are further commitments made which I will directly touch on.

I also want to point out that of the 34 nonnuclear nations that possess nuclear reactors from which the raw materials come for bombs, only 17 of these have so far signed the treaty.

Now we come to the second point which is the one that has caused Senator Case and others a lot of concern. This is the problem of commitments.

CLARIFICATION OF UNITED STATES COMMITMENTS

It is evident that West Germany is going to demand new American guarantees, and yet, at the same time, most Americans are increasingly reluctant to approve any new commitments or guarantees since our military authorities admit we are already overcommitted in many areas of potential conflict in the world.

Now, it is true that Mr. Rusk declared that the new treaty does not affect bilateral or other American defense pacts. But here, and here is one of the current credibility gaps, West German sources indicate a belief that the treaty ratification by the United States will destroy the present German faith in the NATO treaty.

I might say that is not——

Senator LAUSCHE. Where is the language in the treaty which removes the operation of this treaty from those bilateral and multilateral agreements?

Mr. ANDREWS. I think if you will let me in just a moment I will develop that, Senator.

Senator LAUSCHE. All right.

Mr. ANDREWS. Incidentally, the West German sources, which I see here, indicate a belief that the ratification will destroy the present German faith in the NATO treaty. This is by actual contact, Senator, in Bonn that I have had.

The West German Chancellor has indicated his dissatisfaction with President Johnson's pledge to uphold American commitments to Germany. He publicly stated that.

The Senate should not ratify the treaty until there are definite and binding statements from the President concerning possible new commitments and giving clear explanation of what would be involved by the ratifying nations in the way of providing possible force or quarantine of a violator of the treaty. The administration should also spell out what steps will be taken to contain the maverick Red China and French nuclear weapon systems.

After all, this treaty is meaningless unless we are able to contain the two big powers that will not sign the treaty. Otherwise the treaty is of no use at all.

We are just saying to each other that we love each other but Red China and France don't love us.

We ask the question, under this treaty will the Soviets come immediately to the aid—say, of the United States in case of nuclear attack by Red China.

It is our belief that these brief hearings have not provided an ample review of these possible ramifications.

We could quote Prime Minister Gandhi who said that the New Delhi government considers as unsatisfactory—and, incidentally, Mr. Rusk has said there have been no new pledges—but she says in an official statement she considers as unsatisfactory the "additional Soviet-American pledge to act at once through the United Nations Security Council in the case of nuclear aggression. This report certainly contradicts Mr. Rusk's assertion that 'no new promises or commitments will be made in order to secure signatories to the treaty.' Again, Mr. Rusk declares 'the effectiveness of the treaty depends in large measure upon the adherences of other nations.'" The realistic facts now demonstrate the unwillingness and failure of important nations in the world community to adhere or pledge their support to the treaty.

CREDIBILITY GAP IN ADMINISTRATION STATEMENTS CHARGED

Further—and I have given this quite a lot of space because I believe this thing of commitments is a vital weakness of the treaty from the American standpoint—there is a credibility gap between the statements of Mr. Rusk to this committee and the statement made by our American Ambassador to the United Nations, the Honorable Arthur J. Goldberg. The Ambassador appeared before the United Nations Security Council and formally pledged the United States to assist nonnuclear countries threatened by nuclear attack. The exact language was "the United States would act immediately through the U.N. Security Council to take the measures necessary to counter such aggression or to remove the threat of aggression."

The Washington Daily News, which I do not usually quote, but I found an editorial here with which I agree, ends their editorial saying:

This pledge to go to the aid of a nuclear victim is no small matter. For the Johnson administration to treat it as a matter of routine interest is to do the American public a disservice.

Again, Mr. Chairman it would seem like the administration's left hand, Mr. Rusk, is unaware of the administration's right hand, Mr. Goldberg's thinking and public statement. There are those who contend that the Gulf of Tonkin declaration was not meant to give the President authority to wage war. I regret that the Senators who have taken this position are not here this afternoon. It seems strange today that these same men do not see the trap for new commitments and U.N. directed nuclear wars which are contained in the statements and philosophy of the supporters of the treaty.

ADEQUACY OF INSPECTION SAFEGUARDS QUESTIONED

This is a treaty in which inspection safeguards are vital. It was President John F. Kennedy who declared that nuclear or general disarmament was only possible or wise if inspection safeguards were adequate. Unfortunately, there is no firm universal inspection system but rather the treaty provides that an international safeguards system be negotiated between IAEA and individual or groups of nonnuclear signatories. While in nuclear plan operations in signatory nations the inspectors would be forbidden access to "commercially sensitive" information. And certainly Congressman Craig Hosmer this morning pointed out all the weaknesses of this inspections system. At the present time he stated even the Inspector General has either quit or been fired, and they cannot find anyone to take the job. It is a difficult thing.

This committee needs to further study article III, before it consents to such a treaty. The Deputy Secretary of Defense admits that there is nothing in this treaty to prevent nonnuclear signatories from carrying military activities involving nuclear energy outside this inspection system. In other words, certainly any nation that does not sign this, say Red China, can do anything they want with nuclear energy. They can put it in their allies' lands, and so forth.

Further, the treaty does not prohibit the manufacture and possession of nuclear submarines on which much of our strategy is based.

A further vital weakness, and I interpolate this, is acknowledged by the Defense Department, that there is nothing in the treaty which prohibits the Soviet Union from exploding a nuclear device technically termed peaceful, say, in collusion with Egypt.

Another thing, and likewise, we could say that we are going to explode a peaceful test with one of our allies, and as long as we control the nuclear device, to get back to your problem of defensive-offensive weapons, as long as we keep the device and control it, even though we take it, say, and put it in one of our allied countries, as long as our men are there and control the buttons we can do this in spite of this treaty.

So can Soviet Russia. Soviet Russia can do the same thing, and we cannot accuse them of any violation. They can turn around and take their atomic weapon and move it over into Mongolia and have an explosion there. They can call it peaceful, and it is within the limits of this treaty, which makes this treaty more and more technically meaningless.

STATE OF U.S. NATIONAL DEFENSE

Then my fourth and last point, beyond these technical weaknesses in the treaty, there remains the important issue of the state of our national defense. Red China, a nonsignatory nation, presently is engaged in testing H-bombs and has developed an ICBM system.

Gen. Earle G. Wheeler in recent testimony before the Senate Military Preparedness Subcommittee stated he is apprehensive of the ability of the United States to maintain offensive or defensive capabilities in the event of a nuclear war. He stated that the Soviet nuclear capability is growing, that this country is lagging on development of new fighter planes and new submarines, and that we lacked a satisfactory defense system to destroy any Soviet manned bomber attack.

Actually, regarding the testimony dealing with the ratio of Soviet bombers that could successfully penetrate the U.S. defense line when it was revealed in secrecy to the members of the committee, the Congressmen said that it was just incredible and shocking how many could get through.

Again, in recent weeks the House Armed Services Committee just a week ago stated that "Russian submarines now pose one of the most critical military threats ever faced by the United States."

Certainly, it does not appear logical or practical to engage in a treaty which is not binding on potential enemies of the United States and when the facts of continued Russian expansion in Africa, the Mediterranean, and the Mideast all indicate the advisability of our Nation to shore up its defenses rather than weaken them by such unrealistic "peacemaking" playing as the proposed ratification of this treaty involves.

Proponents of nuclear disarmament have sold the idea that if we give up nuclear weapon warfare and "go back to conventional warfare" we will achieve a huge economy which then can be used for ghetto programs, conservation projects, urban renewal, all these other things.

Yet when you take a hard look, and military authorities will back this up, if we were to cut out our nuclear weapons and our plans for that and go back to conventional warfare and conventional weapons, we would find actually that the cost would be three to four times the cost of our present nuclear defenses.

Incidentally, this was an argument that McNamara used years ago when he first became Secretary. He said, "Let us go to nuclear weapons because they are cheaper and more efficient and we can kill more if the necessity comes, cheaper."

Now, they turned that argument over and they say, "Get rid of the nuclear weapons. Go back to conventional warfare and we can economize."

DELAY IN RATIFICATION URGED

In conclusion, Mr. Chairman, it is our sincere conviction that this is not the time for ratifying such a treaty. Until the technical problems which have been pointed out are worked out, until more definite understanding of "new commitments" are openly discussed with West Germany, our other NATO allies, with India, and other nations—this treaty as it stands carries all the explosive power of another Gulf of Tonkin declaration. Further, the international scene, with Red China emerging as a great and revolutionary world power, with Soviet Russia constantly scheming to expand its powers over the land, sea, and air spaces of the world—does not reveal in any hopeful manner a future without armed conflict and aggression. We, therefore, urge, Mr. Chairman, let this treaty lay on the table until the day comes when all of the big world powers together unite for peace.

Thank you, Mr. Chairman.

Senator LAUSCHE. Thank you very much, Reverend Andrews.

Your statement will be printed in the record. Thank you very much for your testimony.

(The prepared statement of Mr. Andrews follows:)

STATEMENT OF REV. STANLEY M. ANDREWS

Mr. Chairman, I am Rev. Stanley M. Andrews, National Executive Secretary of Americans for National Security. Our organization merged with Liberty Lobby in 1966 and we presently carry on our interest in national defense issues thru the media channels of Liberty Lobby. I am before you to present the views of our 200,000 subscribers and more than 14,000 Board of Policy members regarding the proposal of the Administration that the Senate advise and consent to the ratification of the Nuclear Nonproliferation Treaty.

Our organization is opposed to ratification of the Treaty since we believe ratificaton of the Treaty is historically meaningless at this time and that the United States will lose more than it can possibly gain by becoming a member of this Pact.

We believe it is historically meaningless since of the five nations that possess the ultimate power of the bomb only three of the nations, Russia, England and the United States have signed the Treaty and Red China and France will not, under any foreseeable future conditions ratify the Treaty. As someone recently said—this is a 3/5ths Treaty. There is no real protection to any nation, large or small, unless each possessor of the bomb joins in an all-inclusive agreement.

Those supporting the treaty point out the promise of the Russians, England and the United States to the nations not possessing nuclear weapons, that the means to make bombs will not be given to any of the other 59 nations which have signed the Treaty. This promise is full of loopholes. It is quite possible that El Salvador, Iceland, Mongolia, Ghana, Chad or Kenya enter into the agreement sincerely since they have neither the financial or technical resources to build nuclear weapons. It is noticeable that West Germany, India, Japan, Pakistan, Brazil and Argentina—all possible "threshold" nations—able to cross into the A bomb club—have not signed the Treaty. Further that of the 34 non-nuclear nations that possess nuclear reactors from which comes the raw material for bombs, only 17 so far have signed.

It is evident that West Germany will demand new American guarantees. Most Americans are increasingly reluctant to approve any new commitments or guarantees since we are already over-committed in many areas of potential conflict in the world. It is true that Mr. Rusk declared that the new Treaty does not affect bilateral or other American defense pacts but—and here one of the current credibility gaps appears—West German sources indicate a belief that the Treaty ratification by the United States will destroy the present German faith in the NATO Treaty. The West German Chancellor has indicated his dissatisfaction with President Johnson's pledge to uphold American commitments to Germany. The Senate should not ratify the Treaty until there are definite and binding statements from the President concerning possible new commitments and giving clear explanation of what would be involved by the ratifying nations in the way of providing possible force or quarantine of a violator of the Treaty. The Administration should also spell out what steps will be taken to contain the maverick Red China and French nuclear weapon systems. We ask the question—under this Treaty will the Soviets come immediately to the aid—say, of the United States in case of nuclear attack by Red China. It is our belief that these brief hearings have not provided an ample review of these possible ramifications. Prime Minister Indira Ghandi has stated that the New Delhi government considers as unsatisfactory the additional Soviet-American pledge to act at once through the United Nations Security Council in the case of nuclear aggression. This report certainly contradicts Mr. Rusk's assertion that "no new promises or commitments will be made in order to secure signatories to the Treaty." Again, Mr. Rusk declares the effectiveness of the treaty depends in large measure upon the adherences of other nations. The realistic facts now demonstrate the unwillingness and failure of important nations in the world community to adhere or pledge their support to the Treaty.

Further, it is evident that a credibility gap exists between the statement of Mr. Rusk to this Committee and the statement made by our American Ambassador to the United Nations, the Hon. Arthur J. Goldberg. The Ambassador appeared before the United Nations Security Council and formally pledged the United States to assist non-nuclear countries threatened by nuclear attack. The exact language was "the United States would act immediately thru the UN Security Council to take the measures necessary to counter such aggression or to remove the threat of aggression."

The Washington Daily News in commenting on Mr. Goldberg's statement stated editorially: "For Ambassador Goldberg to call this a matter of historical significance was putting it mildly. It is linked to the newly passed UN treaty to bar the further spread of nuclear weapons."

"It may be argued there are escape hatches. 'Aggression' has been interpreted as 'self-defense' in this age of double-talk. And acting 'thru the Security Council' provides ample chance for delay and evasion. Nonetheless, the U.S., Russia and Britain have made solemn pledges in clear language.

". . . This pledge to go to the aid of a nuclear victim is no small matter. For the Johnson Administration to treat it as a matter of routine interest is to do the American public a disservice."

Again, Mr. Chairman it would seem like the Administration's left hand, Mr. Rusk, is unaware of the Administration's right hand; Mr. Goldberg's thinking and public statement. There are those who contend that the Gulf of Tonkin declaration was not meant to give the President authority to wage war, it seems strange today, that these same men do not see the trap for new commitments and UN directed nuclear wars which are contained in the statements and philosophy of the supporters of the Treaty.

This is a treaty in which inspection safeguards are vital. It was President John F. Kennedy who declared that nuclear or general disarmament were only possible or wise if inspection safeguards were adequate. Unfortunately there is no firm universal inspection system but rather the Treaty provides that an international safeguards system "be negotiated between IAEA and individual or groups of non-nuclear signatories while in nuclear plan operations in signatory nations the inspectors would be forbidden access to "commercially sensitive" information. Article III needs further study by this Committee before it consents to such a treaty. The Deputy of Defense admits that there is nothing in this treaty to prevent non-nuclear signatories from carrying military activities involving nuclear energy outside this inspection system. Further, the treaty does not prohibit manufacture and possession of nuclear submarines.

Beyond these technical weaknesses in the treaty, there remains the important issue of the state of our national defense. Red China, a non-signatory nation, presently is engaged in testing H bombs and has developed an ICBM system. General Earle G. Wheeler in recent testimony before the Senate Military Preparedness Subcommittee stated he is apprehensive of the ability of the United States to maintain offensive or defensive capabilities in the event of a nuclear war. He stated that the Soviet nuclear capability is growing, that this country is lagging on development of new fighter planes and new submarines, and that we lacked a satisfactory defense system to destroy any Soviet manned bomber attack. It is understood that the ratio of Soviet bombers that would successfully penetrate the U.S. Defense lines, when revealed in secrecy to the Committee led members of the committee to describe the statistics as "incredible" and "shocking." Again, the House Armed Forces Committee just last week stated that "Russian submarines now pose one of the most critical military threats ever faced by the United States."

Certainly, it does not appear logical or practical to engage in a Treaty which is not binding on potential enemies of the United States and when the facts of continued Russian expansion in Africa, the Mediterranean, and the Mideast all indicate the advisability of our nation to shore up its defenses rather than weaken them by such unrealistic "peace-making" playing as the proposed ratification of this treaty involves.

Proponents of nuclear disarmament have sold the idea that if we give up nuclear weapon warfare and "go back to conventional warfare" we will achieve a huge economy which then can be used for ghetto programs, conservation projects, urban renewal and a host of other programs to raise the economic or educational standards of the nation. However, military authorities tell us that conventional type warfare would cost many times the cost of our nuclear defenses. This is just one of the fuzzy ideas the peaceniks have generated.

In conclusion, Mr. Chairman, it is our sincere conviction that this is not the time for ratifying such a treaty. Until the technical problems which have been pointed out are worked out, until more definite understanding of "new commitments" are openly discussed with West Germany, our other NATO allies, with India, and other nations—this treaty as it stands carries all the explosive power of another Gulf of Tonkin declaration. Further, the international scene, with Red China emerging as a great and revolutionary world power, with Soviet Russia constantly scheming to expand its powers over the land, sea and air spaces of the world—does not reveal in any hopeful manner a future without armed conflict and aggression. We therefore urge, Mr. Chairman, let this Treaty lay on the table until the day comes when all of the big world powers together unite for peace.

Thank you Mr. Chairman.

Senator LAUSCHE. The next witness is Dr. Arthur Larson, chairman of the Educational Committee To Halt Atomic Weapons Spread.

Dr. Larson, your statement will be printed in the record. You may proceed to give the highlights of your thoughts.

STATEMENT OF ARTHUR LARSON, CHAIRMAN, EDUCATIONAL COMMITTEE TO HALT ATOMIC WEAPONS SPREAD

Mr. LARSON. Mr. Chairman, thank you very much for this opportunity. I will try to select some points that have been prominent over the entire hearings, if I may, and particularly today, because even listening today, I have, I regret to say, heard quite a bit of confusion, misunderstanding, misreading of the treaty, obvious misstatements of fact and a number of very serious errors, large and small, that really ought to be corrected even though it is a little late in the hearing to do so. So I am going to try to pick the things out of this statement that might have some corrective effect.

Senator LAUSCHE. All right.

Mr. LARSON. This committee you referred to, the Educational Committee To Halt Atomic Weapons Spread, was formed a couple of years ago. I suppose it is the only national private group that was set up specifically to deal with this exact problem, the nonproliferation problem. And in our first effort, which was in September of 1966, we got a group of 290 distinguished Americans behind us and put out some educational materials, a letter to the President, and so on. We had 12 Nobel laureates, among others in our group, urging just some such treaty as this and trying to deal with some of what then appeared to be the major obstacles to the treaty.

We were all, of course, deeply moved the other day in the East Room to see the treaty actively signed by what now appears to be 60 countries, which I think is quite a remarkable number of countries to sign a treaty on such short notice. Rather than call attention to a few countries that have not got around to signing it yet, I think the emphasis should be on the astonishing fact that this many people somehow have gone through the machinery of their own government to get policy clearance for such a far reaching decision as this.

SPEEDY RATIFICATION URGED

The first note I would like to sound, Mr. Chairman, is this: That even though there seems to be overwhelming support for this treaty, I would like to urge that, in view of the pressures of bills necessary in the Senate that we are all aware of, we do not succumb to the sort of thing I have been hearing a little of lately which is this treaty is so strongly supported by everybody or almost everybody that we really do not have to worry about whether there is some delay in the ratification. This worries me much more than the question of whether the treaty will ultimately be ratified at all, and the reason it worries me is that this is such an accident prone world we live in that it would just take one such incident as the U-2 or a blowup in Czechoslovakia or goodness knows what, and we might first of all have the tragic episode itself on our hands, and we might just conceivably, if we wait until next year, even lose the treaty, and that, I think, would be a tragedy of unspeakable proportions.

I think the reason there is such wide support for this, in spite of some of the views that have been heard today, is very simple, and that is that whether you consider the specific interest of the United States or the interest of humanity at large, there is virtually everything to gain and nothing to lose in this treaty.

EFFECT ON U.S. SECURITY

There has been quite a bit of talk about security of the United States. I would make the unqualified statement that there is no conceivable way in which the Nonproliferation Treaty can injure the security of the United States, and there are a number of ways in which it could enhance it. It does not deprive us of any of the rights we now have, notably the right to deploy under our control nuclear weapons anywhere we are now deploying them, whatever suits our security needs most efficiently.

The American nuclear deterrent itself will not be diminished or damaged in any way.

There has been some considerable talk about the right—you raised the question yourself, Mr. Chairman—to deploy under the nuclear powers' own control weapons in other countries.

Senator LAUSCHE. Yes, I would like to hear about that.

Mr. LARSON. That situation is not changed at all one way or the other. It remains exactly as it is. But as matters now stand, of course the advantage is overwhelmingly with us. I have seen statements made in testimony that we should be concerned because in the exercise of this privilege there are 700 nuclear devices deployed by the Soviet Union in East Europe. We have 7,000 deployed under the same privilege, so to speak, 7,000; 10 times as many.

That is not counting the 1,750 ICBMs we have in the United States, and the Polaris missiles and so on.

The benefit to American security, I think, is threefold. First, we cut down considerably the risk of accidental outbreak of nuclear war by stopping this proliferation, and, second, we reduce the outbreak of small nuclear wars which could grow into big ones.

Let me just add a point here that I do not think has been sufficiently brought out in most of the discussions that I have seen.

Senator LAUSCHE. May I go upstairs to vote? That was a vote signal, and I will be back in about 5 minutes.

(Whereupon, a short recess was taken, after which the hearing was resumed.)

Senator LAUSCHE. All right, if you will proceed, Mr. Larson.

NUCLEAR DEADLOCK

Mr. LARSON. Mr. Chairman, I was going to try to make a point which seems to me has not been adequately made in most of the discussions I have heard about why there is a special danger in the kind of nuclear buildup that would occur if proliferation went beyond the countries that now have atomic weapons. Sometimes I think it is assumed that if a number of other countries, six or eight or 10 or 20 or 30 countries, got nuclear weapons, the situation would somehow be roughly comparable to what we have now, the so-called stable deterrent, two countries locked in a nuclear deadlock. This simply is not so, and the reason is a very simple technical one. What we now have between the Soviet Union and the United States is a situation in which, because of hardened missile silos, Polaris submarines, and the like, each side knows that it cannot knock out the other on a first strike. The other side can retaliate with a devastating blow which probably would completely or almost completely wipe out the civilization of the attacker. That is the famous stable deterrence so neither side attacks, and that is a situation we have been living with for quite a few years.

But if atomic weapons spread to new countries, this is not the kind of a system they would build. They could not afford it, they would not have the sophistication for it. It would be years before they could build anything like it. What they would acquire—the only thing they could possibly afford or build would be big, dirty, first strike weapons. That means that you would have a much more dangerous situation than we have now between the Soviet Union and the United States. It would be a little bit like some of the worrisome early periods of the atomic era. In other words, if you have nothing but a first strike capability, the only thing it is good for is to strike first and knock the other fellow out once and for all so that he cannot retaliate. This is why it must be appreciated that by proliferating nuclear weapons you do not merely proliferate the kind of problem we have now quantitatively. You introduce a whole new and radically more dangerous element which is the fact that the kind of nuclear weapons these countries would have would be the kind that would tempt them to wipe out their hated rival once and for all before there was any possibility of retaliation.

EFFECT OF TREATY ON NATO ALLIANCE

Now, the third advantage, it seems to me, for American security in the Nonproliferation Treaty is that proliferation of nuclear weapons would markedly alter the power balance in a way we cannot even predict and it might be very dangerous indeed.

At this point I think it would be appropriate if I said a word or two about NATO which has been brought up by a number of people.

It has been asserted that the treaty would somehow damage NATO. I have never seen this statement supported by anything except sheer opinion. Congressman Findley this morning said something that simply cannot be allowed to rest unchallenged in the record. He said several times that somehow this whole episode had damaged NATO because the NATO partners had been completely ignored in the discussions; we made this treaty over their heads. I cannot imagine anything further from the truth. As a matter of fact, the truth is that the occasion of this treaty led to some of the most intensive, protracted, and in the end productive consultations we have ever had within the NATO group. I happened to run into Ambassador Harland Cleveland some weeks ago, and he said he had not done anything for months—he is the Ambassador to NATO of course—except work on consultations on this treaty with the NATO powers, and I do not think anybody had better tell Ambassador Cleveland that no consultations were held with NATO powers, and this whole thing was done behind their backs or over their heads.

NATO has had its ups and downs, but you cannot blame this on the Nonproliferation Treaty. The reasons for it must be looked for somewhere else.

There is nothing that will be changed under this treaty that will affect any of the provisions of the alliance. None of the members of the alliance are seriously developing atomic weapons at this time. There is nothing to prevent the alliance from operating exactly the way it has done in the past.

Senator LAUSCHE. Mr. Larson, at this point I want to call attention to, although it is already contained in the record, the statement made by Secretary Rusk pertaining to the impact that this treaty would have on our obligations in NATO. (The material referred to appears on p. 5.)

Mr. Larson. Yes, very good. I might say in this connection, too, while we are talking about disruption of NATO, the most severe disruption of NATO, as we all know, has come not from nonproliferation of nuclear weapons, not from the countries that have been restrained from or that have refrained from producing nuclear weapons. It has come from the one country that has chosen to go out and develop its own independent atomic capabilities because it thinks that is the road to self sufficiency and away from collective security. That was the main damage to NATO in the past.

EFFECT OF U.S. ABM SYSTEM ON NATO

Now, as to damage to NATO in the future, I think people who are urging an anti ballistic missile system should be aware of the fact that the impact on NATO of that line of development would be potentially infinitely more damaging than the Nonproliferation Treaty for a very obvious reason.

If we proceed to rely for our security on a ring of intercontinental antiballistic missiles to protect our own soil, it would be only natural for the European partners to begin to think we are turning inward, that we are abandoning the whole concept of defenses that led to NATO in the first place, and we are beginning to adopt the fortress America concept with the ABM being the symbol of it. It is curious that the same people who have raised this argument about the Nonproliferation Treaty hurting NATO are frequently the same people who are for extensive development and deployment of an ABM system where the argument really has some substance.

I think, as we all know, the problem as to NATO is the same as it always was, which was that the real solution lies in more skillful and more intelligent use of it as a political organization and more skillful use of it as a source of consultation.

EFFECT ON INTERNAL POLITICAL PROBLEMS OF OTHER NATIONS

Now, since these advantages to the United States itself and to, of course, humanity at large are so obvious, it strikes me that very often when Americans raise objections to the treaty it is often not because of danger to Americans or damage to Americans but because of some supposed damage to some foreign country, and the most often mentioned is West Germany.

I am perfectly well aware of the fact that this treaty will raise and is raising internal political problems in a number of other important countries such as West Germany, India, Japan, Brazil, and others for reasons, by the way, that vary from one country to the other. It may be a problem concerned about security, the primary example being India. It may be development of peaceful uses of atomic energy which is the point so often raised by Brazil, or aversion to international inspection as in West Germany, among other things.

I would like to say simply this: If these countries have internal political difficulties with some of these issues, that is their problem. Our problem is to consider this treaty from the point of view of the interests of the United States of America and the world as a whole. I do not see why we should try to play both sides of the game and hesitate to approve a treaty because some other countries have got some faults to find with it from their own points of view.

Now, I have examined all of those arguments in this little booklet that many of you have called "Questions and Answers on the Spread of Nuclear Weapons," one by one taking up each of the principal countries that have raised objections and in great detail examining these problems that they have raised, and in my opinion there is a perfectly adequate answer to all of the objections raised either through the treaty itself or through the security assurances through the United Nations that have been given by the powers, the nuclear powers.

(A short recess was taken, after which the hearing was resumed.)

Senator LAUSCHE. The committee will come to order.

OBJECTIONS OF BRAZIL

Mr. LARSON. I was going to give one or two illustrations because the point has been raised that some of these countries are holding back from signing and that some of them have raised many objections throughout the negotiations. Take Brazil, for example. Brazil, for some reason, has been perhaps the outstanding exponent of the objection that it will not be allowed to develop peaceful nuclear explosions. Now just think of this a minute. Here we have the spectacle of a country that has not even matriculated in the atomic kindergarten and it is objecting because it cannot have the final rewards of something that atomic Ph. D.s are not even sure they can produce. As for expenditure of countless billions of dollars, because this sort of thing can only be developed as part of and as a consequence of and corollary of the most sophisticated advance imaginable to nuclear weapons development.

OBJECTIONS OF WEST GERMANY

Now, as for West Germany, I think a word should be said. First, of all, I think we should remember that the West Germans themselves, the responsible official West Germans, are not coming forward and objecting to this treaty because it will not let them become a nuclear power. As a matter of fact, West Germany has got a lot less to lose by this treaty than any country in the world because West Germany is already under a solemn obligation dating from 1954 not to manufacture nuclear weapons. Now there are some loopholes in that, but it is under a great deal more restraint than almost any other country in the world. What this would do would be to put West Germany on the same footing as everybody else and in that sense it is a relative net gain.

RUSSIAN FEAR OF GERMANY

Senator LAUSCHE. It has been argued that this treaty has been signed by Russia primarily because of the aim that it has on West Germany and the fear that West Germany will develop a nuclear weapon. May I hear your comment on that claim?

Mr. LARSON. I would say that the most profound force in Russian foreign policy since the war effort until recently at least with the emergence of the China question has been fear of West Germany. There is no question about that. And it still is very true today, but

I am not one to appraise the motivations of the Soviet Union. I think anyone who does so is more of a prophet than I am. But I am certain that the prospect of West Germany's remaining outside this nuclear group is certainly an important consideration to the Soviet Union in this total quid pro quo. But, you see, the Germans are sensitive to their position as the result of the last two wars, and a responsible German simply will not come forward and say, "I want my country to be a nuclear weapons power." They do not dare do that, for this reason: When this sort of idea, or some implication of it, some suggestion with the ultimate implications are raised, it usually comes from somebody presuming to speak for them and their interests.

The kind of objections the Germans were mostly raising, the specific ones, tend to be something like their fear that inspection by the IAEA will result in industrial espionage. It seems to me that is the one they seem to have made the most of, and the most emphatically.

INSPECTION SAFEGUARDS SYSTEM

In that connection, I think I might say a word about this whole question of inspection, because there has been a lot said about that today.

Senator LAUSCHE. I would like to ask you a question on that.

Mr. LARSON. And it needs a great deal of clarification. Some of the misconceptions are very much in need of being put right.

Senator LAUSCHE. Until now Russia has always fought any effort to allow outside individuals to come into their nation for the purpose of inspection.

Mr. LARSON. That is right.

Senator LAUSCHE. It has argued that they will come in as spies rather than with the purpose of legitimately learning what is happening in the development and distribution of the bomb. What will Russia do, in your opinion, if it is proposed that verification can only be effective by allowing outsiders to come within the country to see whether the treaty is being enforced and obeyed?

Mr. LARSON. I think we have to clear up an initial misconception. There is nothing in here about inspection inside the nuclear powers, no obligation on them at all, the United States, or the Soviet Union, or Britain.

Senator LAUSCHE .Why do you think that was put into the treaty, that all others shall be inspected but not Russia, France, China, and——

Mr. LARSON. It is simply realistic bargaining with the Soviet Union. You accurately summed up their attitude toward inspection, whether under this or any other kind of treaty.

U.S. ATTITUDE TOWARD INSPECTION

Senator LAUSCHE. Based upon the United States' insistence throughout the years that verification can only be effective through actual visits and inspections, what do you feel prompted our country to give up that accepted principle which it has always followed and now say, "Well, we will not ask for visitation of the lands of the nuclear powers"?

Mr. LARSON. The reason is that you do not really need it so badly in this case as you do in the case of, say, atomic testing or something like that, and that is because the transfer of nuclear weapons or nuclear materials is a two-ended thing. It has a beginning point, and it has a receiving point, and you can check it at the receiving point.

Now, I said that there was no internal inspection in Russia or the United States, but there is an obligation on Russia and the United States not to transfer nuclear materials or weapons or nuclear know-how or enriched uranium or plutonium or anything to a nonnuclear country unless the safeguards of this treaty are applied to it. So, in that sense, Russia is definitely subject to the entire inspection safeguards system. The only thing being that the point at which it takes hold is not on Russian soil.

I want to correct another misconception which has been expressed several times today that there simply are not any safeguards in this treaty. It amounts to zero. I think this is a misreading of the treaty itself. Some people seem to have the impression that because there will be specific agreements working out the details of an inspection system that there simply is not any inspection at all or there is not any safeguard at all until the agreements are made and therefore that the whole idea of the treaty could be frustrated by simply refusing to make agreements. But the obligation is cast not in conditional terms depending upon the making of agreements. It is cast in absolute terms. It says each nonnuclear weapons state party to the treaty— this is article III—undertakes to accept safeguards. That is an obligation as set forth in agreement to be negotiated and so forth.

Senator LAUSCHE. I want to be the devil's advocate for the moment.

Mr. LARSON. Yes.

AGREEMENT TO ACCEPT SAFEGUARDS

Senator LAUSCHE. Each party to the treaty agrees to accept safeguards reached through negotiation.

Mr. LARSON. As set forth in negotiations. But let me give you the other which when read with this gives you the full measure of the obligation. This is article II. Each state party to the treaty undertakes not to provide source or special fissionable material or equipment or material especially designed or prepared for the processing, and so forth, to any nonnuclear weapon state for peaceful purposes unless the source of special fissionable materials shall be subject to the safeguards required by this act.

Now, as I read this treaty, that means that there have to be some safeguards in force before these transfers can be made.

That is the operative language of the statute. I think we should also hasten to point out that this is not as much of a leap into the dark as many people seem to think. This is going on right now all the time. This is not a radical change. It is not as though we have to invent some whole new concept called inspection and find out how to do something we have never done before. The International Atomic Energy Agency is inspecting 50 or more reactors right now. The United States is constantly inspecting under bilateral arrangements the reactors that it has built in other countries, and Euratom is inspecting and so on. I think when people talk about whether the IAEA is competent to do this kind of work, there is one salient fact that ought to go into the record and be remembered, and that is that the United States has begun to turn over to the IAEA some of the inspections that it used to do under its bilateral agreements, both of power and research and reactors.

Now, I think this is the most eloquent possible factual evidence of the fact that we, the United States, believes that the IAEA can do this job. Not only that, but we have announced—although as I indicated a moment ago we do not have to—we have announced voluntarily we will accept inspection by the IAEA of all our peaceful nulcear facilities. It is a voluntary offer on our part, with no reciprocity required, just to show our good faith.

Now, it is true that the IAEA staff is small, and it is not as experienced as it is going to become. It has been inspecting mostly reactors. Last time I looked into it, it had not been inspecting any chemical plutonium separation plants. But remember that probably according to the explanatory statement furnished by Mr. Adrian Fisher at the time this treaty was negotiated that it is understood by the reference to arrangement made with groups by IAEA that what was in the minds of the negotiators was that Euratom would somehow be worked into the inspection process under the overall agencies of the IAEA.

POSSESSION OF FISSIONABLE MATERIALS

This fact that a country cannot receive fissionable materials and if it cannot receive fissionable materials it cannot go anywhere in the entire atomic program, peaceful or otherwise, the fact that it cannot receive atomic materials unless they are subject to the treaties, the kind of safeguards set forth in this treaty, means two things: First, there is, of course, a tremendous incentive to perfect the agreements as quickly as possible, and, secondly, there is a tremendous incentive to come within the treaty.

I have heard a lot of testimony today that seemed to assume that it is sort of a matter of indifference to countries whether they come within the treaty or not, or to put it another way, that it is sort of an option open to any country if it just happens to feel like it, it will move forward with atomic weapons development. Where is it going to get the materials? You have to have either enriched uranium or plutonium, and there are only a few places you can get those, and they are not something that you can just make yourself. You first of all have to have the natural uranium, and that occurs only in a few places in the world. Then you have to have the facilities to either enrich it or you have to develop plutonium, and there are only a few places where that can happen. There are only two chemical separation plants outside the nuclear powers: one in Euratom and one in India.

Senator LAUSCHE. May I ask you this, Mr. Larson: Is there anything in the treaty which would operate as a coercive force to compel the signatory nations to agree on strict proposals of certification by the IAEA?

Mr. LARSON. Yes, yes. It is the fact they cannot, as I read the treaty, they cannot get the necessary fissionable materials until there are safeguards under which the materials can be supplied.

239

Senator LAUSCHE. It has been suggested that the treaty ought to contain a provision cutting off nuclear aid for peaceful purposes to countries who do not come to an agreement with the IAEA within the 18 months specified.

Mr. LARSON. I have read the passages here, and I would think that was the effect of it now because it says that these materials shall only be furnished under safeguards, and, as I have indicated, this is also a strong incentive for countries to come within the treaty.

Now, it is conceivable, and this may happen, some people think, in the case of India——

Senator LAUSCHE. Mr. Larson, we will be having another vote pretty soon, and if you will take up your subjects that you still have in mind and enable Senator Cooper and myself to ask whatever questios we want, we would appreciate it.

Mr. LARSON. All right. I will do that. I am trying to work in your questions as I go along from one point to another.

Senator LAUSCHE. Yes.

EFFECT OF ABSENCE OF RED CHINA AND FRANCE

Mr. LARSON. Objection has been raised a number of times that the treaty is no good if it does not have Communist China and France in it. There is a quick answer to that, and that is: This is a very unusual and a special kind of treaty, and that contains a reason why this is not a very serious thing to worry about. If you worry about this, you have to start with the proposition that Communist China and France, the two most chauvinistic countries on earth, the two most nationalistic and inward-turning countries on earth, are just dying to break their own atomic monopoly and give their secrets and atomic know how and their atomic materials and atomic monopoly away to other countries. This is utterly unrealistic. They are the two last countries in the world that are going to want to give away what they have, and for this reason—although obviously it would be very fine to have them within the treaty—I just do not think we ought to lose too much sleep for the time being over the fact that they are not within the treaty because they are not going to do what the treaty forbids in any case, because it would be a violation of their own self interests.

COMMENTS ON DR. TELLER'S TESTIMONY

I would like to say, since I probably anticipate a question on this anyway, a word about Dr. Edward Teller's testimony this morning. I have known him for a long time, and I share everyone's admiration for him. I have spent 2- and 3-day sessions discussing this and other problems with him in the past. I can tell you a quick two-line story. During World War I the great menace was submarines, and somebody said to Will Rogers, "What do you think we ought to do with the submarine menace," just as the nuclear power is now. Will Rogers said, "I have got a perfect solution," and everybody perked up. Will Rogers said, "All you have to do is raise the temperature of the Atlantic Ocean to the boiling point, and then just let those submarines try to operate."

The questioner of course said, "Well, but how are you going to raise the temperature of the Atlantic Ocean to the boiling point?" And Will Rogers said, "Well, that is a technical question for the scientists."

Well, I had exactly the same reaction this morning. Here we are confronted with a situation and not a theory, and we have spent a very large part of the day in a never-never land of some kind of a world in which there is an airtight set of antiballistic missiles surrounding each of 140 countries that somehow can be pointed in the direction of every potential aggressor but cannot be steered enough so that they can be offensive, in which case they will self-destruct, as a famous television series says.

I have followed this ABM business ever since I used to attend Cabinet meetings some years ago and when the first possibility was raised during the Eisenhower administration. I am afraid everybody has been drawn along into a kind of an illusion because many have ignored the appalling technical difficulties. When I think, for example, that we are now talking about multiple warheads accompanied by hundreds, probably, of decoys.

I think Senator Pastore had the right idea. When that day comes, if it ever does, it will be time enough to introduce new kinds of treaties and security arrangements, but what we are talking about today is something terribly real. We are talking about a world in which there are at least seven countries that could have nuclear weapons systems within a couple of years, and perhaps 25 which within a few years more will have the industrial capacity.

Senator LAUSCHE. I am obliged to interrupt at this time. I do not think you are putting the proper construction on Dr. Teller's testimony. Dr. Teller suggested that we ought to be assured that there is some avenue on which we can travel to reap the benefit that would come at some future time through the achievement of a very effective antiballistic missile system, and I think you cannot discount his argument that many of the nations of the world will feel distressed to place their future life at the whims and mercy of Russia and the United States—aid what other nation is there, Britain—he did not say that he opposed the treaty.

OBJECTION TO PROPOSED RESERVATION TO TREATY

Mr. LARSON. That is right. I finally gathered that. But what worries me, Mr. Chairman, about Mr. Teller's suggestion is a very practical thing. I have seen this in connection with the Test Ban Treaty and other treaties. When it is pretty certain that a treaty is going to go through, the next line of defense of opponents is usually to fall back and try to introduce some sort of ragged reservation of some kind so that you do not quite wholeheartedly go all out and approve the treaty. This is what he was, I think, suggesting, that we somehow indicate a slight reservation through some sort of Senate action. This, I am suggesting, would be a most unfortunate addendum to an approval of the treaty. I think the most unfortunate thing about it, Mr. Chairman, would be that it would make the Senate of the United States look ridiculous because if the scientific community in this world and the other people who know this subject intimately, really believed the Senate of the United States thinks this kind of development that Dr. Teller was talking about this morning is so imminent, that it warrants some sort of special expression by the Senate, then I am afraid the Senate is going to be humiliated by having been talked into such a course. This is adequately taken care of by the fact that there are provisions for reopening the treaty if the situation is sufficiently urgent to the security of the United States, and I think it should be left at that. When the time comes that something like Dr. Teller suggests develops, an appropriate modification can be made.

That, Mr. Chairman, concludes as much as I would like to volunteer.

Senator LAUSCHE. I think you have covered the whole subject.

Mr. LARSON. Thank you.

Senator LAUSCHE. I think we have had the various views. Every time I examine a document with a view of ascertaining what it means, I try to find out what the advantages are, what the disadvantages are, and whether or not the document contains some hidden pitfalls. My questioning today dealt with what hidden pitfalls there might be in the bill, not implying that I believe they were in there, but anyone who rationally studies a document would try to make certain that he knew what it contained.

I thank you very much, Dr. Larson.

Mr. LARSON. Thank you.

Senator LAUSCHE. Your prepared statement along with the prepared statement of Leonard S. Rodberg, on behalf of the United World Federalists, will be entered in the record at this point.

(The statements referred to follow: material accompanying Mr. Larson's testimony is in the committee files.)

STATEMENT OF ARTHUR LARSON

Mr. Chairman and Members of the Committee, May I first express my sincere gratitude for being afforded this opportunity to testify on the ratification of the Treaty on Nonproliferation of Nuclear Weapons. I am appearing today in my capacity as Chairman of the Educational Committee to Halt Atomic Weapons Spread. This is a private group consisting of fifty-five American citizens, drawn from all walks of life, having in common a profound concern about the problem of spread of atomic weapons. It was formed about two years ago. One of its first acts was to prepare a public statement and a letter to the President of the United States, calling attention to the urgency of a treaty to curb proliferation of nuclear weapons, and making specific suggestions on how to overcome some of the most conspicuous obstacles. This statement and letter were subscribed to by 290 American leaders, distinguished in science, education, religion, business, labor, law, the arts and public affairs, including 12 Nobel Laureates. The Committee has continued from that day to this to carry on a program of public education, through informational publications, educational television programs, and the like.

Needless to say, for those who have been specially involved over the years in the effort to being about a nonproliferation treaty, it was a moving experience to observe the historic signing of the Treaty in the East Room of the White House on July 1, 1968, by the Soviet Union, Great Britain, the United States, and dozens of nonnuclear states. But even in this moment of gratification, there remains one cause for concern. This is the danger that the satisfaction of having achieved the initial signature of the Treaty, combined with the intense pressure of business in the Senate, might result in delay in ratification, unless the sense of urgency that led to the signing is maintained up to the moment of ratification.

My primary reason for worry about any delay is that this world has become so accident-prone—not least in recent times—that one simply cannot gamble on having the same international atmosphere next year that one has this year.

Some contemporary counterpart to the U-2 incident might intervene. Or, to take a specific example out of today's headlines, some people are even now expressing the fear that the situation in Czechoslovakia could blow up into another Hungary. If something like this should happen, and if the Treaty had not been ratified in the meantime, we would have not only the tragedy of the episode itself, but the added tragedy of the probable loss of the nonproliferation treaty. My first plea, then, is that we all beware of the kind of complacency that would assume the existence of such overwhelming support for the Treaty that there is no particular urgency about its early ratification.

I do believe it is true that the Treaty enjoys a degree of support not only from the general public but from informed specialists of all kinds that is rare for any public issue. The reason is clear. Whether you consult the interests of the United States itself, or of the world at large and the human race into the distant future, this is one of those unusual situations in which there is virtually everything to gain and nothing to lose.

So far as the security of the United States is concerned, there is no conceivable way in which the nonproliferation treaty can endanger United States security, and there are important ways in which that security will be enhanced. It does not deprive us of any of the rights we now are exercising to deploy our nuclear weapons in a way calculated to serve our national security needs most efficiently. Specifically, there is nothing in the Treaty to prevent the United States from placing nuclear weapons in other countries as long as they remain under American control. The American nuclear deterrent will be in no way diminished or damaged. It is true that the Soviet Union has 700 nuclear devices deployed in Warsaw Pact countries, but it is also true that the United States has 7,000 nuclear devices—ten times as many—deployed in Europe. This is in addition to the 1,750 ICBM's based in the United States.

The benefit to American security, as Secretary McNamara pointed out in his testimony before the Joint Committee on Atomic Energy on March 7, 1966, lies in the fact that the Treaty combats three risks inherent in proliferation. The first is the fact that the probability of the outbreak of nuclear war by accident increases with the increase in the prevalence of nuclear weapons, and in such a case there is severe danger that the major nuclear powers would be drawn in with disastrous consequences.

The second risk is the outbreak of "small nuclear wars which could catalyze a big one between the great powers."

To understand why the proliferation of nuclear weapons to present nonnuclear powers would markedly aggravate the danger of nuclear war, one must identify the difference between the kind of nuclear arsenal the great powers now use to maintain the nuclear deterrent, and the kind of nuclear arsenals future nuclear powers might develop.

Since the United States and the Soviet Union have shown that even their immense nuclear arsenals can be used to create a "stabilized deterrent," the skeptic may ask why the same kind of deadlock may not be expected if atomic weapons come into the hands of other natural rivals around the world.

The United States and the Soviet Union have a "stable deterrent" because each country now has sufficient nuclear missiles in hardened sites, submarines, and the like, to enable it to survive a first strike by its opponent and still retaliate with what the Pentagon calls "unacceptable" destruction on the attacker. This means that there is no advantage in a "first strike"; indeed, the result is national suicide. However, this will not be true of the countries that might set out to create nuclear weapons from now on—or at least it will not be true for a very long time. With the technology and materials at their disposal, the only kind of bombs they could build would be big, dirty bombs suitable only for use against cities. It follows that a new nuclear power would be under severe temptation to launch a first strike, if it thought it could without retaliation destroy its detested enemy once and for all by knocking out both its nuclear installations and its major centers of population.

The third risk of proliferation pointed out by Secretary McNamara is that it would "cause important and destabilizing shifts in the regional power balance."

It has sometimes been asserted that the nonproliferation treaty would have a damaging or even destructive effect on NATO. I have never seen this sort of statement supported by anything except sheer opinion. Such difficulties as NATO has experienced until now have certainly not been the fault of a nonproliferation treaty for the obvious reason that it has not existed. For the future, there will be no real change under the provisions of the Treaty in any of the conditions that have affected the health of this Alliance. No other member of the

Alliance is now seriously developing nuclear weapons. There is nothing to prevent the Alliance from operating in the future exactly as it has done in the past.

It is curious that people who make this charge are often the same people who are in favor of deployment of an anti-ballistic missile system—although when it comes to disrupting the Atlantic Alliance, the ABM is far more worrisome than the nonproliferation treaty could ever be. The obvious reason is that, once the United States starts down the road of consuming its security resources in a system of devices to try to protect its own continental territory, the European allies could understandably begin to wonder whether this signalled a turning-inward of the strategic concept of American defense, and a turning-away from the defensive concept which gave rise to NATO.

Nor should it be forgotten that the principal disruption of NATO has come, not from members that refrained from developing nuclear weapons, but from a member that has used independent nuclear weapons development as an avenue of asserting self-sufficiency.

It remains as true as it has been for years that the real clue to the future of NATO is the fuller and more intelligent use of NATO in the form of more effective consultation and more sophisticated and productive political arrangements.

Since the advantages to the United States are so obvious, it is not surprising that, when Americans raise objections to the Treaty, it is often not because of potential damage to American or broad human interests, but because of supposed damage to some foreign country such as West Germany.

I am quite aware of the fact that acceptance of this Treaty raises real internal political problems in some of the nonnuclear countries, such as West Germany, India, Japan, Brazil and others, for reasons that vary from one country to the other. Sometimes the problem is one of concern about security, as in the case of India. Sometimes it is one of development of peaceful uses of atomic energy, as in Brazil. Sometimes it is aversion to international inspection, as in West Germany, among other issues. My point today is simply that, if these other countries are worried about some of these implications of the Treaty, that is their problem. Our problem is to consider the interests of the United States and of humanity as a whole. I see no reason why we should try to play both sides of the chess game, and hesitate to approve a treaty because some other country might for its own reasons find some fault with it.

I have examined in detail the specific issues raised by the principal nonnuclear powers in my booklet *Questions and Answers on the Spread of Nuclear Weapons*, and it is my opinion that there is an adequate answer to the reservations of these various powers either in the Treaty itself or in the security assurances through the United Nations given by the nuclear powers.

Sometimes these objections are a bit difficult to take seriously. For example, partly for internal political reasons, Brazil has been repeatedly complaining that the Treaty would prevent it from developing peaceful nuclear explosives. Here we see the spectacle of a country that has not even matriculated in the atomic kindergarten complaining that it is being deprived of something that the atomic Ph. D.'s have not yet been able to achieve after billions of dollars worth of the most advanced and sophisticated development.

As for West Germany, it is important to remember that the Germans themselves are not objecting to the Treaty on the blunt ground that it will prevent their becoming a nuclear weapons power. Responsible Germans are too sensitive to their vulnerability to do anything of the sort. For this reason, if any such suggestion is raised, either expressly or by implication, it usually has to be done by someone else presuming to represent what is conceived to be the Germans' interest or concern. The most specific objection raised by West Germany itself has been the fear that inspection under the auspices of the International Atomic Energy Agency instead of EURATOM will amount to industrial espionage. Of course, the detailed inspection agreements are still to be worked out, but as a result of the negotiations and modifications that have taken place in the last few months, including a provision that nonnuclear signatories may seek agreements with IAEA in groups—obviously a concession to the EURATOM group—there is every reason to believe that inspection arrangements can be worked out that will satisfy the West Germans. This kind of fear should not be brushed aside, but is easy to exaggerate. The foreign editor of the West German newspaper *Die Zeit*, for example, has written:

"There is no need for us to indulge in shadowboxing with the spectres of hypothetical contingencies—Russian inspectors swarming through our factories, all our most advanced research and development withering away, Germany dropping to the level of an agricultural state. Some people may be obsessed by these nightmares, but there is nothing in the text of the Treaty draft to justify them." [*Die Zeit*, Feb. 24, 1967.]

It is obvious that the United States itself does not take this kind of apprehension seriously, since the United States has already voluntarily promised to submit its own nonmilitary nuclear activities to IAEA safeguards similar to those accepted by the nonnuclear signatories. Certainly the amount Germany has to lose by any imagined industrial espionage is small in comparison with what the United States might lose, if there were any substance to the fear. I can only add, as a result of my consultations on this point with a number of experts on West German affairs, that the great majority believe that West Germany, after some reluctance, will adhere to the Treaty.

Another objection sometimes heard is that the Treaty will not work without the adherence of France and Communist China. People who raise this objection have lost sight of the main purpose of the Treaty, which is to prevent the passage of nuclear weapons and nuclear information from the nuclear to the nonnuclear powers. Neither Communist China nor France has evidenced the slightest intention to assist any other country in acquiring nuclear weapons. They are now members of a nuclear weapons monopoly, and, in the light of the overall character of their foreign policy, it is reasonable to assume that they would be among the last to indulge in any voluntary abdication of this advantageous position. It is true, of course, that in the long run the success of the nonproliferation treaty will be strongly affected by the success of measures to curb the strategic arms race among nuclear powers, and that this in turn raises a question of involvement of France and Communist China in any such efforts. But the first step is to get the nonproliferation treaty into force, and as to that step, the nonadherence of France and Communist China is not a particularly serious problem. Indeed, on June 12 we had something approaching a confirmation of this fact when the representative of France at the United Nations, after a long period of remaining aloof from the discussions and negotiation of the Treaty, announced that "France will conduct herself in this field exactly like the states who decide to sign."

It happens all too often in discussions of this kind of issue that preoccupation with peripheral issues tends to obscure the tremendous central importance of the pending action. When everything has been said about problems of internal German politics, Brazilian industrial development, and Indian or Japanese special security needs, it must never be forgotten that the one momentous question at stake is: Do we in our lifetimes want to see a world in which nuclear weapons are in the hands, not only of every quarreling state, but perhaps even of revolutionary factions, dissident tribes, ruthless guerrillas, lawless gangsters, wealthy eccentrics, latter-day reincarnations of Adolf Hitler, and extremist groups of a kind which was found last August in New York to have an arsenal including automatic weapons, hand grenades, 250,000 rounds of ammunition, and an anti-tank gun?

Does this sound fanciful? An Ad Hoc Advisory Panel on Safeguarding Special Nuclear Material last year told the Atomic Energy Commission that the commission's standards must be strengthened to prevent theft of uranium by private parties interested in selling it on the black market. The panel commented that:

"Every effort should be made to insure timely notifications of the opening of black markets in the world for special nuclear materials. It is not clear that such markets exist today, although the Panel understands that a "fence" was involved in the recent theft of fuel elements (containing natural uranium) from the Bradwell Reactor in England."

Should weapons technology become as widespread as reactor technology, it seems reasonable to assume that there will be even greater incentives for a black market and that there can be no assurance that some of the thousands of persons who will have become skilled in weapons manufacture will not offer their services to the highest bidder. Actual operable weapons will also be much more vulnerable to theft and sale on a black market if they are in the arsenals of not five, but twenty or thirty governments.

The immediate problem, of course, is not so fantastic. It lies in the fact that six countries—India, Canada, West Germany, Japan, Sweden, and Israel—given the necessary political decision, could probably detonate a nuclear device in less than two years. In addition, on the basis of industrial capacity, wealth, experience with nuclear technology, and access to fissionable materials, the list of countries that could develop nuclear weapons in less than ten years would expand to a total of at least twenty-five, including Belgium, East Germany, Italy, Switzerland, Czechoslovakia, the Netherlands, Pakistan, Spain, Argentina, Australia, Brazil, Denmark, Indonesia, Poland, Portugal, Romania, South Africa, the United Arab Republic, and Yugoslavia.

Presently, in addition to the five nuclear weapons powers, forty-one countries possess operating nuclear reactors. Plutonium, one possible material for fission weapons, is produced as a by-product in nuclear reactors fueled with natural uranium. It is estimated that civilian nuclear reactors outside the United States will produce more than 5,000 kilograms of plutonium per year by 1970, and 25,000 to 50,000 kilograms per year by 1980. Since it takes about five kilograms of plutonium to make one bomb, there will soon be enough plutonium produced in civilian reactors outside the United States to manufacture more than 1,000 bombs per year—and 5,000 to 10,000 per year by 1980.

The urgency of this danger lies in the fact that several of the countries technologically best suited to develop nuclear weapons are now engaged in serious debate on whether to take this route. Pressure is building up in India as well as in Japan, where the proximity of Communist China makes the problem more pressing with every new advance in China's nuclear weapons development.

Seldom has the world been confronted with such a chilling deadline. If the problem of proliferation is not solved within the year, the chance to avoid the ultimate nightmare will probably have been lost forever. Suppose India decides it can wait no longer and sets out to create a nuclear arsenal—will Pakistan be far behind? Suppose Israel concludes that atomic weapons are necessary to its defense—will the Arab countries rest until they, too, have nuclear arms? And so on.

I should like to conclude with a point that contains both a note of hope and a warning. Not the least of the benefits of this Treaty is the fact that it has set the stage for moving on to the next phase of control of nuclear arms. Several days before the signing of the Treaty, the Russian Foreign Minister, Mr. Gromyko, suddenly announced Russia's readiness to join in negotiations with the United States about curbing offensive and defensive nuclear weapons. The President was therefore able to use the occasion of the Treaty signing to announce that such talks would definitely begin in the nearest future.

There was unquestionably a strong connection between the Treaty negotiations and this promising development. For several years, both in the General Assembly of the United Nations, and in the Eighteen Nation Disarmament Committee, there has been repeated insistence that agreement of the nonnuclear powers to forgo nuclear development must be accompanied by genuine efforts of the nuclear powers to curb "vertical proliferation" of nuclear weapons. As a result, the final version of the Treaty contains, not merely a preambular recitation on the topic, but an operative obligation in Article VI on the part of the nuclear powers "to pursue negotiations in good faith on effective measures relating to cessation of the nuclear arms race at an early date and to nuclear disarmament, and on a Treaty on general and complete disarmament under strict and effective international control." The hopeful note is that such negotiations will indeed now begin at an early date. The warning lies in the plain implication from the discussions that a failure to live up to this obligation on the part of the nuclear powers could eventually lead to a breakdown of the nonproliferation treaty itself. The implication for the current controversy about deployment of an antiballistic missile system is self-evident. The Treaty, then, is important not only for its own sake, but for the further opportunity it opens up for a more definitive solution of humanity's most pressing problem, that of eliminating not only the ultimate actuality but the pervasive dread of nuclear holocaust.

For all these reasons, therefore, I respectfully urge the early ratification of this Treaty, which many people including the heads of major nuclear powers have characterized as the most important international treaty since the dawn of the nuclear age.

STATEMENT BY LEONARD S. RODBERG ON BEHALF OF UNITED WORLD FEDERALISTS

Mr. Chairman and Members of the Committee, I am Leonard S. Rodberg, a long-time member of United World Federalists. I am also Associate Professor of Physics at the University of Maryland, am on the Executive Committee of the Federation of American Scientists, and was formerly a staff member of the United States Arms Control and Disarmament Agency.

On behalf of the United World Federalists and its president, Mr. James G. Patton, I express our appreciation to you for permitting us to appear before you and present our views on the Nuclear Non-Proliferation Treaty.

We believe it is of the utmost importance that this Treaty be approved at this time. The coming decade is likely to be the crucial one in determining whether or not nuclear weapons spread uncontrollably beyond the present five nuclear powers. The technical know-how required to construct nuclear weapons is now available worldwide, and nuclear reactors capable of producing the necessary fissionable materials are being constructed in many countries around the world. It has been estimated that 20 or more countries will have the capacity to produce nuclear weapons within the next decade, if they choose to do so. We believe that worldwide acceptance of this Treaty will have an important influence on this choice.

The spread of nuclear weapons to additional countries would seriously hinder the efforts of the United States, through the United Nations and in concert with many other countries, to establish a stable world order in which large-scale conflict can be prevented and disputes between nations can be resolved by peaceful means. Many of the countries which have the capacity to produce nuclear weapons in the near future are currently embroiled in local conflicts, and the dangers inherent in these disputes would be enormously magnified if nuclear weapons were to become a factor in them. We need only think of the disputes in the Middle East, or between India and Pakistan, and imagine what these would be like if the parties possessed nuclear weapons, to see the great danger to world security if nuclear weapons should spread beyond the present nuclear powers.

Besides making these local conflicts far more dangerous, the spread of nuclear weapons would reduce still further the ability of the United States to become a moderating influence in these areas. We would be reluctant to become involved because of the danger of escalation into a nuclear war. The ability of the United Nations to intervene through any of its various peacekeeping mechanisms would also be severely restricted, both because of the danger that peacekeeping forces would become involved in a nuclear conflict and because, in such a nuclear confrontation, the potential rate of destruction is likely to far exceed the speed with which the necessary political decisions can be made.

Not only would it be more difficult to maintain international order in a proliferated world, but the maintenance of internal order and of forward progress in the countries concerned would also become more difficult. With possession of nuclear weapons a factor, disputes between dissenting factions within a country would be sharper and far more dangerous. In addition, as we in the United States can testify, possession of nuclear weapons leads inevitably to an enhanced role for the military in a nation's government. We have seen how the demands of the military establishment have increased as it has developed a wide variety of nuclear weapons and nuclear delivery systems.

In addition, the need for centralized control of nuclear weapons and for immediate decision-making on their use has led to an expansion of the authority of the Executive Branch of the Government and a weakening of democratic control over the military. These problems are likely to be even more serious in countries which do not have as well-developed a democratic tradition as our own. Furthermore, these countries are just now attempting to develop their industrial base and reach economic self-sufficiency, and the enormous diversion of resources that would inevitably follow the acquisition of nuclear weapons would delay this process and increase the likelihood of revolutionary disorder within these countries.

We believe that the Non-Proliferation Treaty will make an important contribution in retarding the spread of nuclear weapons and preventing the kind of disastrous developments I have outlined. It will thus help to preserve an environment where steps toward strengthening the United Nations and improving its peacekeeping abilities can continue to move forward.

Its provisions for inspections and nuclear safeguards also will contribute to the development of mechanisms that will strengthen world order. The Treaty envisions the use of International Atomic Energy Agency safeguards for facilities capable of producing material for nuclear weapons. This agency is presently operating the beginnings of an effective international inspection system, and it is of the greatest importance for future steps towards arms control and disarmament that this mechanism be expanded and that the nations of the world gain experience in the inspection process. There have been some suggestions that the inspection provisions of this Treaty are not adequate to preserve our security. In fact, these provisions provide a significant strengthening of the measures presently available to ensure that the enormous quantities of plutonium that will be produced in the next decade are used only for peaceful purposes.

It has also been suggested that this Treaty is "only a scrap of paper" and will not solve the problem of nuclear proliferation. In the present anarchic world of independent nations, true enforcement of treaties is not possible. Yet, as suggested above, this Treaty is an important step in preserving an international climate where we can develop this legal machinery and create new means of international peacekeeping.

In today's world no treaty can alone prevent the spread of nuclear weapons, but it can create a situation in which non-nuclear countries can feel that they need not acquire them, and it can go a long way towards diminishing the importance of nuclear weapons to these countries. In the long run, the only way that the spread of nuclear weapons can be stopped is through a de-emphasis of these weapons and a shift toward a situation where countries would not need them in order to play a significant role in world affairs. This Treaty will, we believe, tend to reduce the pressures on additional countries to develop their own nuclear weapons.

In this regard, the United World Federalists is pleased at the announcement that there soon will be talks between our country and the Soviet Union on steps to halt the further buildup of strategic nuclear missiles and anti-missile systems. If the importance of nuclear weapons in world affairs is to be reduced, we and the Soviet Union must begin now to take significant steps to halt our own nuclear arms race. We believe that the upcoming talks are a most hopeful development, and we look forward to significant progress in them in the coming months.

After a five-year hiatus since the signing of the nuclear Test Ban Treaty it appears that we are again moving forward with steps which will reduce the danger of the nuclear arms race and lead toward the ultimate goal of general and complete disarmament. Only when a genuine world security system is established, and nations are prohibited from using force or the threat of force in international disputes, will we feel that the threat of nuclear holocaust is past. We believe that the Non-Proliferation Treaty is an extremely significant step in that direction, and we urge its early ratification. Thank you.

Senator LAUSCHE. The meeting will be adjourned.

(Whereupon, at 4:50 p.m., the committee was adjourned.)

APPENDIX

TEXT OF NONPROLIFERATION TREATY (EX. H, 90–2) AND RELATED DOCUMENTS

LETTER OF TRANSMITTAL

THE WHITE HOUSE, *July 9, 1968.*

To the Senate of the United States:

I am transmitting herewith, for the advice and consent of the Senate to ratification, the Treaty on the Non-Proliferation of Nuclear Weapons.

This treaty was opened for signature on July 1, 1968 in Washington, London and Moscow. Ninety-five members of the United Nations had voted to commend it, and to request that it be opened for signature and ratification at the earliest possible date.

On July 1 it was signed in Washington by the United States of America, the United Kingdom of Great Britain and Northern Ireland, the Union of Soviet Socialist Republics and 53 other states. Many others have indicated their intention to sign it promptly.

I consider this treaty to be the most important international agreement limiting nuclear arms since the nuclear age began. It is a triumph of sanity and of man's will to survive.

The treaty takes a major step toward a goal the United States has been seeking for the past twenty-two years. Beginning with the McMahon Act in 1946, our statutes have forbidden the transfer of our nuclear weapons to others.

In the Executive branch, efforts to prevent the spread of nuclear weapons have complemented those of the Congress. Ever since the Baruch Plan of 1946, we have sought to achieve an international consensus on this subject.

In making the first United States test ban proposal, President Eisenhower noted that his purpose was to curtail the uncontrolled spread of nuclear weapons.

When President Kennedy announced the successful negotiation of the Nuclear Test Ban Treaty in 1963, he expressed the hope that it would be the opening wedge in a campaign to prevent the spread of nuclear weapons. He pointed out that a number of other nations could soon have the capacity to produce such weapons, and urged that we use whatever time remained to persuade such countries not to follow that course.

In 1964, in the first message I submitted to the Geneva Disarmament Conference, I proposed an agreement that nuclear weapons not be transferred to non-nuclear countries, and that all transfers of nuclear materials for peaceful purposes take place under international safeguards.

In 1966, the United States Senate clearly showed its support for negotiations toward a non-proliferation treaty. Ninety-nine Senators declared themselves in favor of the Pastore resolution (Senate Resolution 179). It commended serious and urgent efforts to negotiate international agreements limiting the spread of nuclear weapons. It supported additional efforts by the President which were appropriate and necessary for the solution of nuclear proliferation problems.

The treaty I am submitting to you today is the product of these efforts by the legislative and executive branches. Its provisions are described in detail in the accompanying report of the Secretary of State.

Its central purpose is to prevent the spread of nuclear weapons. Its basic undertaking was deliberately patterned after United States atomic energy legislation, which forbids transfers of our nuclear weapons to others. The treaty not only makes such a prohibition binding on all nuclear powers; it reinforces the prohibition by barring nonnuclear countries from receiving them from any source, from manufacturing or otherwise acquiring them, and from seeking or receiving any assistance in their manufacture.

The treaty, however, does more than just prohibit the spread of nuclear weapons. It would also promote the further development of nuclear energy for peaceful purposes under safeguards.

This is the goal of the International Atomic Energy Agency (IAEA), which resulted from President Eisenhower's "Atoms for Peace" plan. The IAEA is charged with the primary responsibility for safeguards under the non-proliferation treaty. It already has considerable experience in applying safeguards under international agreements for cooperation in the civil uses of nuclear energy.

I believe that this treaty will greatly advance the goal of nuclear cooperation for peaceful purposes under international safeguards.

It will require that all parties which export nuclear materials and equipment to non-nuclear-weapon states for peaceful purposes make sure that such materials, and those used or produced in such equipment, are under international safeguards.

It will require all non-nuclear parties to accept international safeguards on *all* peaceful nuclear activities within their territories, under their jurisdiction, or carried out under their control anywhere.

It will help insure cooperation in the field of peaceful uses of nuclear energy, and the exchange of scientific and technological information on such peaceful applications.

It will enable all countries to assist non-nuclear parties to the treaty with their peaceful nuclear activities, confident that their assistance will not be diverted to the making of nuclear weapons.

It obligates the nuclear-weapon parties to make potential benefits from any peaceful applications of nuclear explosions available—on a non-discriminatory basis, and at the lowest possible cost—to parties to the treaty that are required to give up the right to have their own nuclear explosives.

By 1985 the world's peaceful nuclear power stations will probably be turning out enough by-product plutonium for the production of tens of nuclear bombs every day. This capability must not be allowed to result in the further spread of nuclear weapons. The consequences would be nuclear anarchy, and the energy designed to light the world could plunge it into darkness.

But the treaty has a significance that goes beyond its furtherance of these important aspects of United States nuclear policy. In the great tradition of the Nuclear Test Ban Treaty, it represents another step on the journey toward world peace. I believe that its very achievement, as well as its provisions, enhances the prospects of progress toward disarmament.

On Monday, July 1—as this treaty was signed on behalf of the United States—I announced that agreement had been reached with the Soviet Union to enter into discussions in the nearest future on the limitation and reduction of both offensive nuclear weapons systems, and systems of defense against ballistic missiles. Thus there is hope that this treaty will mark the beginning of a new phase in the quest for order and moderation in international affairs.

I urgently recommend that the Senate move swiftly to enhance our security and that of the entire world by giving its consent to the ratification of this treaty.

LYNDON B. JOHNSON.

LETTER OF SUBMITTAL

DEPARTMENT OF STATE,
Washington, July 2, 1968.

The PRESIDENT,
The White House:

I have the honor to submit to you, with the recommendation that it be transmitted to the Senate for its advice and consent to ratification, a certified copy of the Treaty on the Non-Proliferation of Nuclear Weapons, signed in Washington on July 1, 1968, on behalf of the United States of America, the United Kingdom of Great Britain and Northern Ireland, the Union of Soviet Socialist Republics, and 53 other states. It is open for signature by all other states, many of which have expressed their intention to sign it.

Since introducing the Baruch Plan in 1946, the United States has endeavored to prevent the spread of nuclear weapons. Beginning with the McMahon Act in that same year, United States legislation has consistently forbidden the transfer of such weapons to others.

In the spring of 1966, after extensive hearings by the Joint Committee on Atomic Energy, a broad consensus of the Senate was reached in support of negotiations toward a nuclear non-proliferation treaty under which other countries would be bound to follow this same policy. Senate Resolution 179, which was sponsored by Senator Pastore and co-sponsored by 58 other Senators, was adopted by a bipartisan vote of 84–0, with all absent Senators but one declaring themselves in favor. Since that time the negotiations of the treaty have been closely followed by the Congressional advisers to the Eighteen Nation Disarmament Committee, and have been the subject of annual reports to the Congress and numerous hearings. They were discussed at hearings held in May and June 1966 by the Subcommittee on National Security and International Operations of the Senate Committee on Government Operations; in June 1966 by the Committee on Foreign Relations; in February and March 1967 by that Committee's Subcommittee on Disarmament; and in February 1968 by the House Committee on Foreign Affairs.

International concern on the subject of proliferation was demonstrated on December 4, 1961 when the General Assembly of the United Nations unanimously approved a resolution calling on all states to conclude an international agreement to prevent the wider dissemination of nuclear weapons.

In a message to the Eighteen Nation Disarmament Committee (ENDC) on January 21, 1964, you proposed that there be agreement "to stop the spread of nuclear weapons to nations not now controlling them" and "that all transfers of nuclear materials for peaceful purposes take place under effective international safeguards".

On June 15, 1965, the United Nations Disarmament Commission passed a resolution by a vote of 83–1 (with 18 abstentions) urging that the ENDC give priority attention to a treaty to prevent the further spread of nuclear weapons. On August 15, 1965, after consultations within the Atlantic Alliance, the United States submitted to the ENDC a draft of such a treaty. The Soviet Union presented its version of a draft treaty at the Twentieth Session of the United Nations General Assembly in September 1965.

After almost two years of negotiations, including extensive consultations with our allies, the United States and the Soviet Union presented to the ENDC identical drafts of a treaty on August 24, 1967. The article on safeguards was left blank because of inability to reach agreement on a formulation that was acceptable to all. In the ensuing months, further efforts were made to reach agreement, and consideration was given to various proposals put forth by members of the Committee.

On December 19, 1967, the United Nations General Assembly adopted, by a vote of 112–1 (with 4 abstentions), a resolution calling upon the ENDC to resume negotiations of the treaty on an urgent basis, requesting submission of a full report to the General Assembly on or before March 15, 1968, and recommending resumption of the 22nd General Assembly to consider the treaty upon receipt of such report.

When the ENDC reconvened on January 18, 1968, the United States and the Soviet Union submitted a complete treaty draft, including an article on safeguards which had been formulated in light of the extensive consultations in the North Atlantic Council. The January 18 draft also contained new articles and revisions which addressed concerns raised by various non-nuclear-weapon states.

On March 11, 1968, the ENDC Co-Chairmen presented a revised treaty draft, responsive to additional suggestions made by non-nuclear-weapon states, which was reported to the United Nations General Assembly.

On April 24, 1968, the United Nations General Assembly reconvened to consider the new treaty draft. Following thorough debate in the First Committee, in which further suggestions were made by non-nuclear-weapon states for improving the draft text, the United States and the Soviet Union presented a final draft on May 31, 1968; the changes in the text were directed especially at strengthening provisions relating to the peaceful uses of nuclear energy.

On June 10, 1968, a resolution commending the treaty draft was approved in the First Committee of the United Nations General Assembly by a vote of 92–4 (with 22 abstentions). On June 12, 1968, the General Assembly in plenary session approved the same resolution by a vote of 95–4 (with 21 abstentions).

On July 1, 1968, the treaty was signed in Washington by 56 states.

The treaty consists of a preamble and eleven articles, the first seven of which contain its principal substantive provisions.

In broadest outline, the treaty is designed to (a) prevent the spread of nuclear weapons (Articles I and II); (b) provide assurance, through international safeguards, that the peaceful nuclear activities of states which have not already developed nuclear weapons will not be diverted to making such weapons (Article III); (c) promote the peaceful uses of nuclear energy to the maximum extent consistent with the treaty's other purposes and provisions (Articles IV and V); and (d) give recognition to the determination of the parties that the treaty should lead to further progress toward arms control and disarmament (Articles VI and VII).

The preamble has twelve paragraphs expressing the consensus of the parties. The first three reflect the importance and urgency of preventing nuclear proliferation; the next two express support for international safeguards on peaceful nuclear activities and for improvements in safeguards techniques; the next two deal with the principle of sharing the benefits of peaceful applications of nuclear energy, and of making technological by-products of work on nuclear explosives available for peaceful purposes; the next four express the urgent need for further progress toward disarmament and limitations on the nuclear arms race; and the last reaffirms the principles of the United Nations Charter regarding the use of force and threats of force in international relations. It should be noted that Article VIII of the treaty provides for review conferences, the first of which is to be held five years after the treaty enters into force, to review the operation of the treaty "with a view to assuring that the purposes of the Preamble and the provisions of the Treaty are being realized."

Articles I and II contain the basic undertakings to prevent the proliferation of nuclear weapons.

Article I deals with the obligations of parties that are nuclear-weapon states, which are limited to those that had manufactured and exploded a nuclear weapon or other nuclear explosive device prior to January 1, 1967 (Article IX, paragraph 3). First, such states undertake not to transfer nuclear weapons, or control over them, to any recipient whatsoever. This provision deliberately parallels United States atomic energy legislation, which has always prohibited such transfers. Second, nuclear-weapon states must not assist non-nuclear-weapon states to manufacture or otherwise acquire nuclear weapons. Third, these prohibitions apply not only to nuclear weapons but also to other nuclear explosive devices. Inclusion of the latter was necessary because a nuclear explosive device intended for peaceful purposes can be used as a weapon or can be easily adapted for such use, and because the technology for making such devices is essentially indistinguishable from that of making nuclear weapons. But while Article I covers all such devices, it will not deprive non-nuclear-weapon parties of the potential benefits from any peaceful applications of nuclear explosions, which are dealt with in Article V.

Article II deals with the obligations of all parties that are not nuclear-weapon states as defined above. Such non-nuclear-weapon states undertake first, not to receive the transfer of nuclear weapons or other nuclear explosive devices, or control over them, from any transferor whatsoever. Second, they must not manufacture or otherwise acquire such weapons or devices or seek or receive assistance in such manufacture.

Articles I and II were the first substantive articles to be included in their present form in the treaty text. Before any of the other substantive articles had been added, these two articles prompted several questions from our NATO allies. The questions, and the answers given by the United States, are enclosed.

Article III provides for verification of compliance with the treaty by means of international safeguards designed to insure that nuclear energy is not diverted from peaceful uses to nuclear weapons or other nuclear explosive devices.

The first paragraph of Article III provides that such safeguards shall be applied on all source or special fissionable material in all peaceful nuclear activities within the territory, jurisdiction or control of non-nuclear-weapon parties. Such parties undertake to accept safeguards on such material for the exclusive purpose of verification of the fulfillment of their obligations under the treaty. The safeguards are to be as set forth in agreements to be negotiated and concluded with the International Atomic Energy Agency (IAEA) in accordance with the Statute of the IAEA and the IAEA safeguards system.

The second paragraph of Article III prohibits the provision by any of the parties of (a) source or special fissionable material or (b) equipment or material especially designed or prepared for the processing, use or production of special fissionable material, to any non-nuclear-weapon state for peaceful purposes, unless the source or special fissionable material shall be subject to the safeguards required by Article III.

The third paragraph of Article III prescribes that the safeguards be implemented so as to comply with Article IV of the treaty—which deals with furthering the peaceful uses of nuclear energy—and to avoid hampering the economic and technological development of the parties or international cooperation in the field of peaceful nuclear activities.

The fourth paragraph of Article III permits the agreements with the IAEA to be concluded by non-nuclear-weapon parties either individually or together with other states in accordance with the Statute of the IAEA. The remainder of the paragraph provides schedules for commencing negotiations of safeguards agreements, as well as for their entry into force. In effect, they provide a transition period after the treaty's entry into force within which the detailed arrangements for the safeguards required by the treaty can be worked out and put into operation.

An integral part of the negotiating history of Article III is the statement of principles enumerated by the United States Co-Chairman of the Eighteen Nation Disarmament Committee when the Article was first publicly presented on January 18, 1968, and reiterated by Ambassador Goldberg when the treaty was presented to the First Committee of the United Nations General Assembly on May 31, 1968. These principles regarding the safeguards, and the safeguards agreements, called for by Article III, are as follows:

"1. There should be safeguards for all non-nuclear-weapon parties of such a nature that all parties can have confidence in their effectiveness. Therefore safeguards established by an agreement negotiated and concluded with the IAEA in accordance with the Statute of the IAEA and the Agency's safeguards system must enable the IAEA to carry out its responsibility of providing assurance that no diversion is taking place.

"2. In discharging their obligations under Article III, non-nuclear-weapon parties may negotiate safeguards agreements with the IAEA individually or together with other parties; and, specifically, an agreement covering such obligations may be entered into between the IAEA and another international organization the work of which is related to the IAEA and the membership of which includes the parties concerned.

"3. In order to avoid unnecessary duplication, the IAEA should make appropriate use of existing records and safeguards, provided that under such mutually agreed arrangements the IAEA can satisfy itself that nuclear material is not diverted to nuclear weapons or other nuclear explosive devices."

Adherence to these principles should facilitate the timely conclusion of safeguards agreements meeting the requirements of the treaty by all non-nuclear-weapon parties, including those which are subject to Euratom safeguards.

Article III does not require nuclear-weapon states to subject their peaceful nuclear activities to international safeguards. This fact led to criticism of the treaty as being discriminatory, and charges that it gave the nuclear-weapon states an unfair commercial advantage unrelated to the basic purpose of the treaty. It was in this context that you stated on December 2, 1967 that the United States was not asking any country to accept safeguards that we were unwilling to accept ourselves. Thus you announced that "when such safeguards are applied under the treaty, the United States will permit the International Atomic Energy Agency to apply its safeguards to all nuclear activities in the United States—excluding only those with direct national security significance." A parallel announcement was made by the United Kingdom.

Article IV insures that nothing in the treaty will be interpreted as affecting the right of all parties, without discrimination, to use nuclear energy for peaceful purposes in conformity with Articles I and II. It also contains an undertaking by all parties to facilitate, and affirms their right to participate in, the fullest possible exchange of equipment, materials and scientific and technological information for the peaceful uses of nuclear energy. Finally it requires those parties in a position to do so to cooperate in contributing to the further development of peaceful applications of nuclear energy, especially in the territories of non-nuclear-weapon states and with due consideration for the needs of the developing areas of the world.

Article V is designed to compensate for the undertaking by non-nuclear-weapon parties in Article II not to acquire nuclear explosive devices even for peaceful purposes. It provides assurance to such parties that they will not lose, by such renunciation, the potential benefits from peaceful applications of nuclear explosions. It is also designed to assure them there would be no economic incentive for them to try to develop their own nuclear explosive devices for such purposes. Specifically, the parties to the treaty undertake to take appropriate measures to insure that the potential benefits of such peaceful applications will be made available to non-nuclear-weapon parties on a nondiscriminatory basis and that the charge to such parties for the explosive devices used will be as low as possible and exclude any charge for research and development. The article requires that such benefits shall be made available in accordance with the treaty—which would preclude non-nuclear-weapon states from acquiring the nuclear explosive devices themselves or control over them. Thus the devices would remain under the custody and control of a nuclear-weapon state, which would in effect provide a nuclear explosion service. The Article requires that such explosions be carried out under appropriate international observation and through appropriate international procedures. It contemplates that non-nuclear-weapon states will be able to obtain such services pursuant to a special international agreement or agreements, through an appropriate international body with adequate representation of non-nuclear-weapon states. It provides that negotiations on this subject shall commence as soon as possible after the treaty enters into force. But it preserves the option of obtaining nuclear explosion services pursuant to bilateral agreements.

Article VI is an undertaking by all parties to pursue negotiations in good faith on effective measures relating to cessation of the nuclear arms race at an early date and to nuclear disarmament, and on a treaty on general and complete disarmament under strict and effective international control.

Article VII makes clear that nothing in the treaty affects the right to conclude regional treaties establishing nuclear-free zones.

Article VIII establishes the procedures for amending the treaty. Paragraph 1 is derived from the Nuclear Test Ban Treaty. It requires the Depositary Governments to convene a conference to consider a proposed amendment if requested to do so by one-third or more of the parties to the treaty. Paragraph 2 provides that for an amendment to enter into force it must be ratified by a majority of all parties to the treaty, including all nuclear-weapon parties and all other parties which, on the date the amendment is circulated, are members of the Board of Governors of the IAEA. No amendment will enter into force for any party that does not ratify it.

Article VIII also provides for a conference, five years after the treaty enters into force, to review the operation of the treaty. Further review conferences, at five year intervals thereafter, will be held if requested by a majority of the parties.

Article IX designates the United States, the United Kingdom and the Soviet Union as Depositary Governments and provides that the treaty shall enter into force upon the deposit of instruments of ratification by those states and forty other signatory states. It specifies how other states may become parties and contains provisions of a formal nature relating to ratification, accession, and registration with the United Nations, all derived from the corresponding provisions of the Nuclear Test Ban Treaty.

The provisions for signature and accession have been designed to permit the widest possible application of the treaty. At the same time adherence to the treaty will in no way imply recognition or change in status of regimes the United States does not now recognize. Nor will it in any way result in according recognition or change in status to any regime not now recognized by any other party.

Article X provides a right of withdrawal upon three months notice if a party finds that extraordinary events related to the subject matter of the treaty have jeopardized its supreme interests. This provision is the same as the withdrawal provision in the Nuclear Test Ban Treaty except that it requires notice of such withdrawal to be given to the United Nations Security Council as well as to the other treaty parties and requires the notice to include a statement of the extraordinary events involved.

In addition, Article X provides for a conference, to be held twenty-five years after the treaty enters into force, at which a majority of the parties will decide whether the treaty shall continue in force indefinitely, or be extended for an additional fixed period or periods.

Article XI provides that the English, Russian, French, Spanish and Chinese texts of the treaty are equally authentic, and deals with the deposit of the original treaty instruments and transmittal of certified copies to signatory and acceding states.

In the course of the negotiation of the treaty, a number of non-nuclear-weapon states, including especially non-aligned states, expressed the need for some form of assurance with respect to their security that would be appropriate in light of their renunciation of the right to acquire nuclear weapons. While there is no provision on this subject in the treaty, a resolution on this subject was adopted by the United Nations Security Council on June 19, 1968 by a vote of 10–0 (with 5 abstentions). The United States, the United Kingdom, and the Soviet Union each issued substantially identical declarations in explanation of their votes for such resolution. Copies of the resolution, and of the declaration by the United States are enclosed.

The signing of this treaty is, I believe, an event of unique significance. Wide adherence to it will greatly reduce the threat of an increasing number of states with nuclear weapons at their disposal, and will thus enhance the security of the United States, its allies, and the rest of the world. At the same time, it will give new impetus to international cooperation in the peaceful uses of nuclear energy and to further efforts toward disarmament.

Because of the great interest shown by so many nations in this historic effort as well as its significance to world peace, I sincerely hope that the United States will be in a position to ratify this treaty as soon as possible.

Respectfully submitted.

DEAN RUSK.

(Enclosures: (1) Certified copy of treaty; (2) questions asked by U.S. allies and answers given by the United States; (3) United Nations Security Council Resolution 255 (1968); and (4) declaration of the Government of the United States of America.)

Treaty on the Non-Proliferation of Nuclear Weapons

The States concluding this Treaty, hereinafter referred to as the "Parties to the Treaty",

Considering the devastation that would be visited upon all mankind by a nuclear war and the consequent need to make every effort to avert the danger of such a war and to take measures to safeguard the security of peoples,

Believing that the proliferation of nuclear weapons would seriously enhance the danger of nuclear war,

In conformity with resolutions of the United Nations General Assembly calling for the conclusion of an agreement on the prevention of wider dissemination of nuclear weapons,

Undertaking to cooperate in facilitating the application of International Atomic Energy Agency safeguards on peaceful nuclear activities,

Expressing their support for research, development and other efforts to further the application, within the framework of the International Atomic Energy Agency safeguards system, of the principle of safeguarding effectively the flow of source and special fissionable materials by use of instruments and other techniques at certain strategic points,

Affirming the principle that the benefits of peaceful applications of nuclear technology, including any technological by-products which may be derived by nuclear-weapon States from the development of nuclear explosive devices, should be available for peaceful purposes to all Parties to the Treaty, whether nuclear-weapon or non-nuclear-weapon States,

Convinced that, in furtherance of this principle, all Parties to the Treaty are entitled to participate in the fullest possible exchange of scientific information for, and to contribute alone or in cooperation with other States to, the further development of the applications of atomic energy for peaceful purposes,

Declaring their intention to achieve at the earliest possible date the cessation of the nuclear arms race and to undertake effective measures in the direction of nuclear disarmament,

Urging the cooperation of all States in the attainment of this objective,

Recalling the determination expressed by the Parties to the 1963 Treaty banning nuclear weapon tests in the atmosphere in outer space and under water in its Preamble to seek to achieve the discontinuance of all test explosions of nuclear weapons for all time and to continue negotiations to this end,

Desiring to further the easing of international tension and the strengthening of trust between States in order to facilitate the cessation of the manufacture of nuclear weapons, the liquidation of all their existing stockpiles, and the elimination from national arsenals of nuclear weapons and the means of their delivery pursuant to a treaty on general and complete disarmament under strict and effective international control.

Recalling that, in accordance with the Charter of the United Nations, States must refrain in their international relations from the threat or use of force against the territorial integrity or political independence of any State, or in any other manner inconsistent with the Purposes of the United Nations, and that the establishment and maintenance of international peace and security are to be promoted with the least diversion for armaments of the world's human and economic resources,

Have agreed as follows:

ARTICLE I

Each nuclear-weapon State Party to the Treaty undertakes not to transfer to any recipient whatsoever nuclear weapons or other nuclear explosive devices or control over such weapons or explosive devices directly, or indirectly; and not in any way to assist, encourage, or induce any non-nuclear-weapon State to manufacture or otherwise acquire nuclear weapons or other nuclear explosive devices, or control over such weapons or explosive devices.

ARTICLE II

Each non-nuclear-weapon State Party to the Treaty undertakes not to receive the transfer from any transferor whatsoever of nuclear weapons or other nuclear explosive devices or of control over such weapons or explosive devices directly, or indirectly; not to manufacture or otherwise acquire nuclear weapons or other nuclear explosive devices; and not to seek or receive any assistance in the manufacture of nuclear weapons or other nuclear explosive devices.

ARTICLE III

1. Each non-nuclear-weapon State Party to the Treaty undertakes to accept safeguards, as set forth in an agreement to be negotiated and concluded with the International Atomic Energy Agency in accordance with the Statute of the International Atomic Energy Agency and the Agency's safeguards system, for the exclusive purpose of verification of the fulfillment of its obligations assumed under this Treaty with a view to preventing diversion of nuclear energy from peaceful uses to nuclear weapons or other nuclear explosive devices. Procedures for the safeguards required by this article shall be followed with respect to source or special fissionable material whether it is being produced, processed or used in any principal nuclear facility or is outside any such facility. The safeguards required by this article shall be applied on all source or special fissionable material in all peaceful nuclear activities within the territory of such State, under its jurisdiction, or carried out under its control anywhere.

2. Each State Party to the Treaty undertakes not to provide: (a) source or special fissionable material, or (b) equipment or material especially designed or prepared for the processing, use or production of special fissionable material, to any non-nuclear-weapon State for peaceful purposes, unless the source or special fissionable material shall be subject to the safeguards required by this article.

3. The safeguards required by this article shall be implemented in a manner designed to comply with article IV of this Treaty, and to avoid hampering the economic or technological development of the Parties or international cooperation in the field of peaceful nuclear

activities, including the international exchange of nuclear material and equipment for the processing, use or production of nuclear material for peaceful purposes in accordance with the provisions of this article and the principle of safeguarding set forth in the Preamble of the Treaty.

4. Non-nuclear-weapon States Party to the Treaty shall conclude agreements with the International Atomic Energy Agency to meet the requirements of this article either individually or together with other States in accordance with the Statute of the International Atomic Energy Agency. Negotiation of such agreements shall commence within 180 days from the original entry into force of this Treaty. For States depositing their instruments of ratification or accession after the 180-day period, negotiation of such agreements shall commence not later than the date of such deposit. Such agreements shall enter into force not later than eighteen months after the date of initiation of negotiations.

ARTICLE IV

1. Nothing in this Treaty shall be interpreted as affecting the inalienable right of all the Parties to the Treaty to develop research, production and use of nuclear energy for peaceful purposes without discrimination and in conformity with articles I and II of this Treaty.

2. All the Parties to the Treaty undertake to facilitate, and have the right to participate in, the fullest possible exchange of equipment, materials and scientific and technological information for the peaceful uses of nuclear energy. Parties to the Treaty in a position to do so shall also cooperate in contributing alone or together with other States or international organizations to the further development of the applications of nuclear energy for peaceful purposes, especially in the territories of non-nuclear-weapon States Party to the Treaty, with due consideration for the needs of the developing areas of the world.

ARTICLE V

Each Party to the Treaty undertakes to take appropriate measures to ensure that, in accordance with this Treaty, under appropriate international observation and through appropriate international procedures, potential benefits from any peaceful applications of nuclear explosions will be made available to non-nuclear-weapon States Party to the Treaty on a non-discriminatory basis and that the charge to such Parties for the explosive devices used will be as low as possible and exclude any charge for research and development. Non-nuclear-weapon States Party to the Treaty shall be able to obtain such benefits, pursuant to a special international agreement or agreements, through an appropriate international body with adequate representation of non-nuclear-weapon States. Negotiations on this subject shall commence as soon as possible after the Treaty enters into force. Non-nuclear-weapon States Party to the Treaty so desiring may also obtain such benefits pursuant to bilateral agreements.

ARTICLE VI

Each of the Parties to the Treaty undertakes to pursue negotiations in good faith on effective measures relating to cessation of the nuclear arms race at an early date and to nuclear disarmament, and on a treaty on general and complete disarmament under strict and effective international control.

ARTICLE VII

Nothing in this Treaty affects the right of any group of States to conclude regional treaties in order to assure the total absence of nuclear weapons in their respective territories.

ARTICLE VIII

1. Any Party to the Treaty may propose amendments to this Treaty. The text of any proposed amendment shall be submitted to the Depositary Governments which shall circulate it to all Parties to the Treaty. Thereupon, if requested to do so by one-third or more of the Parties to the Treaty, the Depositary Governments shall convene a conference, to which they shall invite all the Parties to the Treaty, to consider such an amendment.

2. Any amendment to this Treaty must be approved by a majority of the votes of all the Parties to the Treaty, including the votes of all nuclear-weapon States Party to the Treaty and all other Parties which, on the date the amendment is circulated, are members of the Board of Governors of the International Atomic Energy Agency. The amendment shall enter into force for each Party that deposits its instrument of ratification of the amendment upon the deposit of such instruments of ratification by a majority of all the Parties, including the instruments of ratification of all nuclear-weapon States Party to the Treaty and all other Parties which, on the date the amendment is circulated, are members of the Board of Governors of the International Atomic Energy Agency. Thereafter, it shall enter into force for any other Party upon the deposit of its instrument of ratification of the amendment.

3. Five years after the entry into force of this Treaty, a conference of Parties to the Treaty shall be held in Geneva, Switzerland, in order to review the operation of this Treaty with a view to assuring that the purposes of the Preamble and the provisions of the Treaty are being realized. At intervals of five years thereafter, a majority of the Parties to the Treaty may obtain, by submitting a proposal to this effect to the Depositary Governments, the convening of further conferences with the same objective of reviewing the operation of the Treaty.

ARTICLE IX

1. This Treaty shall be open to all States for signature. Any State which does not sign the Treaty before its entry into force in accordance with paragraph 3 of this article may accede to it at any time.

2. This Treaty shall be subject to ratification by signatory States. Instruments of ratification and instruments of accession shall be deposited with the Governments of the United States of America, the United Kingdom of Great Britain and Northern Ireland and the Union of Soviet Socialist Republics, which are hereby designated the Depositary Governments.

3. This Treaty shall enter into force after its ratification by the States, the Governments of which are designated Depositaries of the

Treaty, and forty other States signatory to this Treaty and the deposit of their instruments of ratification. For the purposes of this Treaty, a nuclear-weapon State is one which has manufactured and exploded a nuclear weapon or other nuclear explosive device prior to January 1, 1967.

4. For States whose instruments of ratification or accession are deposited subsequent to the entry into force of this Treaty, it shall enter into force on the date of the deposit of their instruments of ratification or accession.

5. The Depositary Governments shall promptly inform all signatory and acceding States of the date of each signature, the date of deposit of each instrument of ratification or of accession, the date of the entry into force of this Treaty, and the date of receipt of any requests for convening a conference or other notices.

6. This Treaty shall be registered by the Depositary Governments pursuant to article 102 of the Charter of the United Nations.

ARTICLE X

1. Each Party shall in exercising its national sovereignty have the right to withdraw from the Treaty if it decides that extraordinary events, related to the subject matter of this Treaty, have jeopardized the supreme interests of its country. It shall give notice of such withdrawal to all other Parties to the Treaty and to the United Nations Security Council three months in advance. Such notice shall include a statement of the extraordinary events it regards as having jeopardized its supreme interests.

2. Twenty-five years after the entry into force of the Treaty, a conference shall be convened to decide whether the Treaty shall continue in force indefinitely, or shall be extended for an additional fixed period or periods. This decision shall be taken by a majority of the Parties to the Treaty.

ARTICLE XI

This Treaty, the English, Russian, French, Spanish and Chinese texts of which are equally authentic, shall be deposited in the archives of the Depositary Governments. Duly certified copies of this Treaty shall be transmitted by the Depositary Governments to the Governments of the signatory and acceding States.

IN WITNESS WHEREOF the undersigned, duly authorized, have signed this Treaty.

DONE in triplicate, at the cities of Washington, London and Moscow, this first day of July one thousand nine hundred sixty-eight.

QUESTIONS ON THE DRAFT NON-PROLIFERATION TREATY ASKED BY U.S. ALLIES TOGETHER WITH ANSWERS GIVEN BY THE UNITED STATES

1. Q. What may and what may not be transferred under the draft treaty?

A. The treaty deals only with what is prohibited, not with what is permitted.

It prohibits transfer to any recipient whatsoever of "nuclear weapons" or control over them, meaning bombs and warheads. It also prohibits the transfer of other nuclear explosive devices because a nuclear explosive device intended for peaceful purposes can be used as a weapon or can be easily adapted for such use.

It does not deal with, and therefore does not prohibit, transfer of nuclear delivery vehicles or delivery systems, or control over them to any recipient, so long as such transfer does not involve bombs or warheads.

2. Q. Does the draft treaty prohibit consultations and planning on nuclear defense among NATO members?

A. It does not deal with allied consultations and planning on nuclear defense so long as no transfer of nuclear weapons or control over them results.

3. Q. Does the draft treaty prohibit arrangements for the deployment of nuclear weapons owned and controlled by the United States within the territory of non-nuclear NATO members?

A. It does not deal with arrangements for deployment of nuclear weapons within allied territory as these do not involve any transfer of nuclear weapons or control over them unless and until a decision were made to go to war, at which time the treaty would no longer be controlling.

4. Q. Would the draft prohibit the unification of Europe if a nuclear-weapon state was one of the constituent states?

A. It does not deal with the problem of European unity, and would not bar succession by a new federated European state to the nuclear status of one of its former components. A new federated European state would have to control all of its external security functions including defense and all foreign policy matters relating to external security, but would not have to be so centralized as to assume all governmental functions. While not dealing with succession by such a federated state, the treaty would bar transfer of nuclear weapons (including ownership) or control over them to any recipient, including a multilateral entity.

UNITED NATIONS SECURITY COUNCIL RESOLUTION 255 (1968)

ADOPTED BY THE SECURITY COUNCIL AT ITS 1433RD MEETING
ON 19 JUNE 1968

The Security Council,
Noting with appreciation the desire of a large number of States to subscribe to the Treaty on the Non-Proliferation of Nuclear Weapons, and thereby to undertake not to receive the transfer from any transferor whatsoever of nuclear weapons or other nuclear explosive devices or of control over such weapons or explosive devices directly, or indirectly; not to manufacture or otherwise acquire nuclear weapons or other nuclear explosive devices; and not to seek or receive any assistance in the manufacture of nuclear weapons or other nuclear explosive devices,
Taking into consideration the concern of certain of these States that, in conjunction with their adherence to the Treaty on the Non-Proliferation of Nuclear Weapons, appropriate measures be undertaken to safeguard their security,

Bearing in mind that any aggression accompanied by the use of nuclear weapons would endanger the peace and security of all States,

1. *Recognizes* that aggression with nuclear weapons or the threat of such aggression against a non-nuclear-weapon State would create a situation in which the Security Council, and above all its nuclear-weapon State permanent members, would have to act immediately in accordance with their obligations under the United Nations Charter;

2. *Welcomes* the intention expressed by certain States that they will provide or support immediate assistance, in accordance with the Charter, to any non-nuclear-weapon State Party to the Treaty on the Non-Proliferation of Nuclear Weapons that is a victim of an act or an object of a threat of aggression in which nuclear weapons are used;

3. *Reaffirms* in particular the inherent right, recognized under Article 51 of the Charter, of individual and collective self-defense if an armed attack occurs against a Member of the United Nations, until the Security Council has taken measures necessary to maintain international peace and security.

***

DECLARATION OF THE GOVERNMENT OF THE UNITED STATES OF AMERICA

(Made in the United Nations Security Council in explanation of its vote for Security Council Resolution 255 (1968))

The Government of the United States notes with appreciation the desire expressed by a large number of States to subscribe to the treaty on the non-proliferation of nuclear weapons.

We welcome the willingness of these States to undertake not to receive the transfer from any transferor whatsoever of nuclear weapons or other nuclear explosive devices or of control over such weapons or explosive devices directly, or indirectly; not to manufacture or otherwise acquire nuclear weapons or other nuclear explosive devices; and not to seek or receive any assistance in the manufacture of nuclear weapons or other nuclear explosive devices.

The United States also notes the concern of certain of these States that, in conjunction with their adherence to the treaty on the non-proliferation of nuclear weapons, appropriate measures be undertaken to safeguard their security. Any aggression accompanied by the use of nuclear weapons would endanger the peace and security of all States.

Bearing these considerations in mind, the United States declares the following:

Aggression with nuclear weapons, or the threat of such aggression, against a non-nuclear-weapon State would create a qualitatively new situation in which the nuclear-weapon States which are permanent members of the United Nations Security Council would have to act immediately through the Security Council to take the measures necessary to counter such aggression or to remove the threat of aggression in accordance with the United Nations Charter, which calls for taking "* * * effective collective measures for the prevention and removal of threats to the peace, and for the suppression of acts of aggression or other breaches of the peace * * *". Therefore, any State which commits aggression accompanied by the use of nuclear weapons or which threatens such aggression must be aware that its actions are to be countered effectively by measures to be taken in accordance with the United Nations Charter to suppress the aggression or remove the threat of aggression.

The United States affirms its intention, as a permanent member of the United Nations Security Council, to seek immediate Security Council action to provide assistance, in accordance with the Charter, to any non-nuclear-weapon State party to the treaty on the non-proliferation of nuclear weapons that is a victim of an act of aggression or an object of a threat of aggression in which nuclear weapons are used.

The United States reaffirms in particular the inherent right, recognized under Article 51 of the Charter, of individual and collective self-defense if an armed attack, including a nuclear attack, occurs against a Member of the United Nations, until the Security Council has taken measures necessary to maintain international peace and security.

The United States vote for the resolution before us and this statement of the way in which the United States intends to act in accordance with the Charter of the United Nations are based upon the fact that the resolution is supported by other permanent members of the Security Council which are nuclear-weapon States and are also proposing to sign the treaty on the non-proliferation of nuclear weapons, and that these States have made similar statements as to the way in which they intend to act in accordance with the Charter.

COMPARISON OF THE EURATOM SAFEGUARDS SYSTEM AND THE IAEA SAFEGUARDS SYSTEM

U.S. Atomic Energy Commission, January 13, 1967

1. OBJECTIVE OF ORGANIZATION

IAEA safeguards	Euratom safeguards — Euratom Treaty	Euratom safeguards — Euratom-U.S. bilateral	Comment
"The Agency shall seek to accelerate and enlarge the contribution of atomic energy to peace, health and prosperity throughout the world." (Statute, Article II)	"It shall be the aim of the Community to contribute to the raising of the standard of living in Member States and to the development of commercial exchanges with other countries by the creation of conditions necessary for the speedy establishment and growth of nuclear industries." (Article 1)	"The Parties (U.S. and Euratom) will cooperate in programs for the advancement of the peaceful applications of atomic energy." (Article 1, original Agreement which Entered into Force August 27, 1958)	IAEA and Euratom-U.S. Bilateral restrict to peaceful use only. Euratom Treaty does not restrict to peaceful use only.

2. AIMS OF SAFEGUARDS SYSTEM

IAEA safeguards	Euratom safeguards — Euratom Treaty	Euratom safeguards — Euratom-U.S. bilateral	Comment
"It shall ensure, so far as it is able, that assistance provided by it or at its request or under its supervision or control is not used in such a way as to further any military purpose." (Statute, Article II)	"The Community shall guarantee, by appropriate measures of control, that nuclear materials are not diverted for purpose other than those for which they are intended. (Article 2.e)	"The Community undertakes the responsibility for establishing and implementing a safeguards and control system designed to give maximum assurance that any material, equipment or devices made available pursuant to this Agreement and any source or special nuclear material, equipment and devices, will be utilized solely for peaceful purposes." (Article XII)	The Euratom Treaty establishes as the aim of safeguards assurance that materials are not diverted to uses other than those to which they are intended without placing any limitation on permissible intended purposes. As far as U.S. supplied material is concerned, however, the U.S.—Euratom Bilateral limits the use to peaceful purposes.

3. GENERAL PRINCIPLES

IAEA safeguards	Euratom safeguards — Euratom Treaty	Euratom safeguards — Euratom-U.S. bilateral	Comment
"To establish and administer safeguards designed to ensure that special fissionable and other materials, services, equipment, facilities, and information made available by the Agency or at its request or under its supervision or control are not used in such a way as to further any military purpose; and to apply safeguards, at the request of the parties, to any bilateral or multilateral arrangement, or at the request of a State, to any of that State's activities in the field of atomic energy." (Statute, Article III.A.5)	"The Commission shall satisfy itself that in the territories of Member States: a. ores, source materials and special fissionable materials are not diverted from their intended uses as stated by the users; and b. the provisions concerning supplies and any special undertaking concerning measures of control entered into by the Community in an agreement concluded with a third country or an international organization are observed." (Article 77)	"The Community guarantees that: No material, including equipment and devices, transferred pursuant to this Agreement to the Community or to persons within the Community, will be used for atomic weapons, or for research on or development of atomic weapons, or for any other military purpose." (Article XI)	IAEA safeguards are applied only to facilities and material covered by an agreement between the IAEA and a Member State. IAEA safeguards are made applicable to U.S. supplied materials and equipment by a "safeguards transfer agreement". Euratom Treaty covers all facilities (except weapons establishments) and materials in the Community except those "intended for the purpose of defense." Euratom safeguards apply to material and

COMPARISON OF THE EURATOM SAFEGUARDS SYSTEM AND THE IAEA SAFEGUARDS SYSTEM

U.S. Atomic Energy Commission, January 13, 1967

IAEA safeguards	Euratom safeguards		Comment
	Euratom Treaty	Euratom-U.S. bilateral	

1. OBJECTIVE OF ORGANIZATION

IAEA safeguards	Euratom Treaty	Euratom-U.S. bilateral	Comment
"The Agency shall seek to accelerate and enlarge the contribution of atomic energy to peace, health and prosperity throughout the world." (Statute, Article II)	"It shall be the aim of the Community to contribute to the raising of the standard of living in Member States and to the development of commercial exchanges with other countries by the creation of conditions necessary for the speedy establishment and growth of nuclear industries." (Article 1)	"The Parties (U.S. and Euratom) will cooperate in programs for the advancement of the peaceful applications for the atomic energy." (Article 1, original Agreement which Entered into Force August 27, 1958)	IAEA and Euratom-U.S. Bilateral restrict to peaceful use only. Euratom Treaty does not restrict to peaceful use only.

2. AIMS OF SAFEGUARDS SYSTEM

IAEA safeguards	Euratom Treaty	Euratom-U.S. bilateral	Comment
"It shall ensure, so far as it is able, that assistance provided by it or at its request or under its supervision or control is not used in such a way as to further any military purpose." (Statute, Article II)	"The Community shall guarantee, by appropriate measures of control, that nuclear materials are not diverted for purpose other than those for which they are intended. (Article 2.e)	"The Community undertakes the responsibility for establishing and implementing a safeguards and control system designed to give maximum assurance that any material, equipment or devices made available pursuant to this Agreement and any source or special nuclear material, equipment and devices, shall be utilized solely for peaceful purposes." (Article XII)	The Euratom Treaty establishes as the aim of safeguards assurance that materials are not diverted to uses other than those to which they are intended without placing any limitation on permissible intended purposes. As far as U.S. supplied material is concerned, however, the U.S.—Euratom Bilateral limits the use to peaceful purposes.

3. GENERAL PRINCIPLES

IAEA safeguards	Euratom Treaty	Euratom-U.S. bilateral	Comment
"To establish and administer safeguards designed to ensure that special fissionable and other materials, services, equipment, facilities, and information made available by the Agency or at its request or under its supervision or control are not used in such a way as to further any military purpose; and to apply safeguards, at the request of the parties, to any bilateral or multilateral arrangement, or at the request of a State, to any of that State's activities in the field of atomic energy." (Statute, Article III.A.5)	"The Commission shall satisfy itself that in the territories of Member States: a. ores, source materials and special fissionable materials are not diverted from their intended uses as stated by the users; and b. the provisions concerning supplies and any special undertaking concerning measures of control entered into by the Community in an agreement concluded with a third country or an international organization are observed." (Article 77)	"The Community guarantees that: No material, including equipment and devices, transferred pursuant to this Agreement to the Community or to persons within the Community, will be used for atomic weapons, or for research on or development of atomic weapons, or for any other military purpose." (Article XI)	IAEA safeguards are applied only to facilities and material covered by an agreement between the IAEA and a Member State. IAEA safeguards are made applicable to U.S. supplied materials and equipment by a "safeguards transfer agreement". Euratom Treaty covers all facilities (except weapons establishments) and materials in the Community except those "intended for the purpose of defense." Euratom safeguards apply to material and

268

COMPARISON OF THE EURATOM SAFEGUARDS SYSTEM AND THE IAEA SAFEGUARDS SYSTEM—Continued

6. RECORDS

IAEA safeguards	Euratom safeguards		Comment
	Euratom Treaty	Euratom-U.S. bilateral	
"The State shall arrange for the keeping of records with respect to principal nuclear facilities and also with respect to all safeguarded nuclear material outside such facilities. For this purpose the State and the Agency shall agree on a system of records with respect to each facility and also with respect to such material, on the basis of proposals to be submitted by the State in sufficient time to allow the Agency to review them before the records need to be kept." (INFCIRC/66, paragraph 33)	"The Commission shall require the maintenance and production of operating records in order to permit accountability for ores, source materials and special fissionable materials used or produced. The same shall apply to the transport of source materials and special fissionable materials". (Article 79). The above requirements are implemented by a regulation (#8) which states that records must be maintained which will enable the producers or users to submit suitable reports to the Euratom Commission.	The Euratom Commission will require "the maintenance and production of operating records to assure accountability for source or special nuclear material made available, or source or special nuclear material used, recovered, or produced as a result of the use of source or special nuclear material, moderator material or any other material relevant to the effective application of safeguards, or as a result of equipment, devices and facilities made available pursuant to this Agreement."	In practice the records kept under Euratom safeguards are very similar to those kept under IAEA safeguards.

7. REPORTS

IAEA safeguards	Euratom safeguards		Comment
	Euratom Treaty	Euratom-U.S. bilateral	
The Agency shall have the right and responsibility "to call for and receive progress reports;". (Statute, Article XII.A.4) "The State shall submit to the Agency reports with respect to the production, processing and use of safeguarded nuclear material in or outside principal nuclear facilities". (INFCIRC/66, paragraph 37) Special procedures apply to the reports pertaining to reactors. "The frequency of submission of routine reports shall be agreed between the Agency and the State, taking into account the frequency established for routine inspections. However, at least two such reports shall be submitted each year and in no case shall more than 12 such reports be required in any year. (INFCIRC/66, paragraph 55)	Producers of ores and producers and users of source materials or special fissile materials shall report to the Commission detailed information regarding material production, inventories, transfers, locations and losses. (Regulation #8)	The Euratom Commission will require "that progress reports be prepared and delivered to the Euratom Commission with respect to projects utilizing material, equipment, devices and facilities referred to in paragraph 2 of this Annex." (Item 6 above) (Annex B, paragraph 3)	The Euratom Treaty specifies when certain reports shall be submitted; this requirement applies to all Member States. IAEA and the States reach agreement individually on the reporting frequency; for CPP the routine reports shall be submitted monthly to the IAEA. The IAEA and the Euratom-U.S. Bilateral require use reports; the Euratom Treaty does not.

8. APPROVAL OF CPP PROCESSES

The IAEA Statute states that the Agency shall have the right and responsibility "to approve the means to be used for the chemical processing of irradiated material." (Statute, Article XII.A.5)	"The processes to be used for the chemical processing of irradiated material shall be subject to the approval of the Commission." (Article 78)	These provisions are comparable.

9. STOCKPILE STORAGE

The IAEA Statute states that the Agency shall have the right "To require deposit with the Agency of any excess of special fissionable materials recovered or produced as a byproduct over what is needed … in order to prevent stockpiling of these materials." (Statute, Article XII.A.5)	The Euratom Treaty states that "The Commission may require that any excess of any special fissionable materials recovered or produced as a byproduct, not being actually in use or ready for use, be deposited with the (Euratom Supply) Agency or in storage premises which are or can be controlled by the Commission." (Article 80)	The Euratom Commission will "require the deposit and storage, under continuing safeguards, in Euratom facilities of any special nuclear material referred to in paragraph 2 of this Annex which is not currently being utilized for peaceful purposes in the Community or otherwise transferred as provided in the Agreement for Cooperation between the Government of the United States of America and the Community." (Annex B, paragraph 4) These provisions are comparable.

10. INSPECTORATE AND DUTIES

The IAEA Statute states that "The Agency shall as necessary, establish a staff of inspectors." (Article XII.B) The staff of inspectors shall have the responsibility of accounting for the material supplied and verifying that facilities and materials subject to safeguards are not used in furtherance of any military purpose. (Statute, Article XII.A.6)	The Euratom Treaty states that "Inspectors shall be recruited by the Commission." The inspectors shall have the responsibility of obtaining and verifying the accountability for ores, source materials and special fissionable materials used or produced. (See Article 82)	The Euratom Commission will establish an inspection organization as "necessary to assure accounting for source or special nuclear material … to determine whether there is compliance with the guarantees of the Community. The inspection organization will also be in a position to make and will make such independent measurements as are necessary to assure compliance with the provisions of this Annex and the Agreement for Cooperation." (Annex B, paragraph 5) Under the IAEA and the Euratom-U.S. Bilateral the inspectors must verify material and facility use. Under Euratom Treaty the inspectors have material accountability responsibilities.

COMPARISON OF THE EURATOM SAFEGUARDS SYSTEM AND THE IAEA SAFEGUARDS SYSTEM—Continued

11. APPOINTMENT OF INSPECTORS

IAEA safeguards	Euratom safeguards		Comment
	Euratom Treaty	Euratom-U.S. bilateral	
"The Director General of the IAEA shall inform the State in writing of the name, nationality and grade of the Agency inspector proposed, shall transmit a written certification of his relevant qualifications and shall enter into such other consultations as the State may request." (GC(V)/ INF/39, paragraph 1). "If a State, either upon proposal of a designation or at any time after a designation has been made, objects to the designation of an Agency inspector for that State, it shall inform the Director General of its objection." (GC(V)/INF/39, paragraph 2)	The Commission shall, "prior to the first visit of an inspector to the territories of any State, enter into consultations, which shall cover all future visits of this inspector, with the Member State concerned." (Article 81)		

12. ACCESS BY INSPECTORS

The IAEA shall have the right and responsibility "To send into the territory of the recipient State or States, designated by the Agency after consultation with the State or States concerned, who shall have access at all times to all places and data and to any person who by reason of his occupation deals with materials, equipment, or facilities which are required by this Statute to be safeguarded, as necessary to account for source and special fissionable materials supplied and fissionable products and to determine whether there is compliance with the undertaking against use in furtherance of any military purpose." (Statute XII.A.6) (See also GC(V)/INF/39, paragraph 9)	"On presentation of their credentials, inspectors shall at all times have access to all places and data and to any person who by reason of his occupation deals with materials, equipment or facilities subject to the control provided for in this Chapter, to the extent necessary to control ores, source materials and special fissionable materials, and to satisfy themselves" that the items are not diverted from their intended uses as stated by the users. (Article 81)	The Euratom Commission will establish "an inspection organization which will have access at all times: a. to all places and data, and b. to any person who by reason of his occupation deals with materials, equipment, devices or facilities safeguarded under this Agreement, necessary to assure accounting for source or special nuclear material subject to paragraph 2 of this Annex and to determine whether there is compliance with the guarantees of the Community." (Annex B, paragraph 5)	The IAEA may make unannounced inspections when the Agency has the right of access at all times.

13. ACCOMPANIMENT OF INSPECTORS

"Inspectors designated by the Agency shall be accompanied by representatives of the State concerned, if that State so requests, provided that the	"Inspectors appointed by the Commission shall be accompanied by representatives of the authorities of the State concerned, if that State so re-		

COMPARISON OF THE EURATOM SAFEGUARDS SYSTEM AND THE IAEA SAFEGUARDS SYSTEM—Continued

11. APPOINTMENT OF INSPECTORS

IAEA safeguards	Euratom safeguards			Comment
	Euratom Treaty	Euratom-U.S. bilateral		
"The Director General of the IAEA shall inform the State in writing of the name, nationality and grade of the Agency inspector proposed, shall transmit a written certification of his relevant qualifications and shall enter into such other consultations as the State may request." (GC(V)/INF/39, paragraph 1). "If a State, either upon proposal of a designation or at any time after a designation has been made, objects to the designation of an Agency inspector for that State, it shall inform the Director General of its objection." (GC(V)/INF/39, paragraph 2)	The Commission shall, "prior to the first visit of an inspector to the territories of any State, enter into consultations, which shall cover all future visits of this inspector, with the Member State concerned." (Article 81)			

12. ACCESS BY INSPECTORS

IAEA safeguards	Euratom safeguards			Comment
	Euratom Treaty	Euratom-U.S. bilateral		
The IAEA shall have the right and responsibility "To send into the territory of the recipient State or States inspectors, designated by the Agency after consultation with the State or States concerned, who shall have access at all times to all places and data and to any person who by reason of his occupation deals with materials, equipment, or facilities which are required by this Statute to be safeguarded, as necessary to account for source and special fissionable materials supplied and special fissionable products and to determine whether there is compliance with the undertaking against use in furtherance of any military purpose." (Statute XII.A.6) (See also GC(V)/INF/39, paragraph 9)	"On presentation of their credentials, inspectors shall at all times have access to all places and data and to any person who by reason of his occupation deals with materials, equipment or f cilities subject to the control provided for in this Chapter, to the extent necessary to control ores, source materials and special fissionable materials, and to satisfy themselves" that the items are not diverted "from their intended uses as stated by the users. (Article 81)	The Euratom Commission will establish "an inspection organization which will have access at all times: a. to all places and data and, and b. to any person who by reason of his occupation deals with materials, equipment, devices or facilities safeguarded under this Agreement, necessary to assure accounting for source or special nuclear material subject to paragraph 2 of this Annex and to determine whether there is compliance with the guarantees of the Community." (Annex B, paragraph 5)		

13. ACCOMPANIMENT OF INSPECTORS

IAEA safeguards	Euratom safeguards			Comment
	Euratom Treaty	Euratom-U.S. bilateral		
"Inspectors designated by the Agency shall be accompanied by representatives of the State concerned, if that State so requests, provided that the	"Inspectors appointed by the Commission shall be accompanied by representatives of the authorities of the State concerned, if that State so re-			The IAEA may make unannounced inspections when the Agency has the right of access at all times.

inspectors shall not thereby be delayed or otherwise impeded in the exercise of their functions." (Statute, Article XII, paragraph 6)

quests, provided that the inspectors shall not thereby be delayed or otherwise impeded in the exercise of their functions." (Article 81)

14. NOTICE OF INSPECTIONS

"The State shall be given at least one week's notice of each inspection, including the names of the Agency's inspectors, the place and approximate time of their arrival and departure, and the facilities and materials to be inspected. Such notice need not exceed 24 hours for any inspection to investigate any incident requiring a 'special inspection'." (GC(V)/INF/39, paragraph 4)

Euratom Treaty does not specifically state that any notice need be given prior to an inspection. However, since "inspectors appointed by the Commission shall be accompanied by representatives of the authorities of the State concerned, if that State so requests", some notice is, obviously, necessary. Under certain conditions the IAEA may make unannounced inspections.

15. PRIVILEGES AND IMMUNITIES OF INSPECTORS

"Agency inspectors shall be granted the privileges and immunities necessary for the performance of their functions. Suitable provision shall be included in each project or safeguards agreement for the application, in so far as relevant to the execution of that agreement, of the provisions of the Agreement on the Privileges and Immunities of the International Atomic Energy Agency excepting Articles V and XII thereof, provided that all parties to the project or safeguards agreement so agree." (GC(V)/INF/39, paragraph 13)

"In the territory of each Member State and whatsoever their nationality, the officials and other employees of the Community . . . shall be immune from legal process for acts performed by them in their official capacity, including their words spoken or written; they shall continue to benefit from such immunity after their functions have ceased." (Article 11, Protocols)

Euratom inspectors are covered by immunities as specified in the Euratom Treaty.

The IAEA obtains agreement individually from each State on the privileges and immunities of inspectors.

16. INSPECTION REPORT

"After an inspection has been carried out, the State concerned shall be duly informed by the Agency of its results. In case the State disagrees with the report of the Agency's inspectors, it shall be entitled to submit a report on the matter to the Board of Governors." (GC(V)/INF/39, paragraph 12)

Euratom has advised that the practice is to allow the inspected facility to review the report in draft prior to its issuance.

19. NONCOMPLIANCE

"In the event of noncompliance and failure by the recipient State or States to take corrective steps within a reasonable time", the Board of Governors may "direct curtailment or suspension of assistance being provided by the Agency or by a member and call for the return of materials and equipment made available to the recipient member or group of members. The Agency may also suspend any noncomplying member from the exercise of the privileges and rights of membership."

"The Board shall report the noncompliance to all members and to the Security Council and General Assembly of the United Nations". (Statute, Article XII)

In the event of noncompliance, the Commission may withdraw from the offending persons or enterprises "financial or technical assistance", may place the enterprise "under the administration of a person or board appointed by the Commission and the State" and may order "the complete or partial withdrawal of source materials or special fissionable materials." (Article 83)

"Forced execution shall be governed by the rules of civil procedure in force in the State in whose territory it takes place." (Article 164)

"It is understood by the Parties that a continuation of the cooperative program between the Government of the United States of America and the Community will be contingent upon the Community's establishing and maintaining a mutually satisfactory and effective safeguards and control system which is in accord with the principles set forth in Annex "B" to this agreement". (Article XII, paragraph E)

20. CIRCUMSTANCES REQUIRING SAFEGUARDS

Nuclear material shall be subject to Agency safeguards if it is being or has been:

a. supplied under a project agreement
b. submitted to safeguards under a safeguards agreement by the parties to a bilateral or multilateral agreement
c. unilaterally submitted to a safeguards agreement
d. produced, processed or used in a principal nuclear facility to which any of the above three items apply
e. produced in or by the use of safeguarded nuclear material
f. substituted for safeguarded nuclear material

(See INFCIRC/66, paragraph 19)

"The Commission shall satisfy itself that in the territories of Member States: ores, source materials and special fissionable materials are not diverted from their intended uses as stated by the users". (Article 77)

"The Community undertakes the responsibility for establishing and implementing a safeguards and control system designed to give maximum assurance that any material, equipment or devices made available pursuant to this Agreement and any source or special nuclear material derived from the use of such material, equipment and devices, shall be utilized solely for peaceful purposes". (Article XII)

COMPARISON OF THE EURATOM SAFEGUARDS SYSTEM AND THE IAEA SAFEGUARDS SYSTEM—Continued

21. EXEMPTIONS FROM SAFEGUARDS APPLICATION

IAEA safeguards	Euratom safeguards		Comment
	Euratom Treaty	Euratom-U.S. bilateral	
The Agency permits the exemption from safeguards at the request of the State concerned of nuclear material provided it does not at any time exceed:			Euratom has not specified any deminimus quantities to be exempted from the active implementation of safeguards. The IAEA exemption is concerned only with exempting the application of safeguards and not the peaceful use guarantee relating to the material in question.
a. 1 kilogram total of special fissionable material consisting of one or more of the following: Plutonium or U-235 (calculated from the uranium enrichment).			
b. 10 metric tons of natural and depleted uranium (above 0.5%).			
c. 20 metric tons of depleted uranium (0.5% or below).			
d. 20 metric tons of thorium.			
With regard to reactors, produced or used nuclear material shall be exempted from safeguards if:			
a. it is plutonium produced in the fuel of a reactor whose rate of production does not exceed 100 grams of Pu annually;			
b. it is produced in a reactor having a maximum power of 3 MWt.			
(See INFCIRC/66, paragraph 21)			

22. SUSPENSION OF SAFEGUARDS

Safeguards may be suspended while nuclear material is transferred within the State, to another Member State or to an international organization provided the total at any times does not exceed:	The Euratom safeguards system does not employ the concept of suspension.	Similar to Euratom Treaty obligations.---------	
a. 1 effective kilogram of special fissionable material.			
b. 10 tons of natural and depleted uranium enriched above 0.5%.			
c. 20 metric tons of depleted uranium below 0.5%.			

d. 20 metric tons of thorium.

Safeguards may be suspended on special nuclear material in irradiated fuel transferred for reprocessing if other nuclear material is substituted for it. (See INFCIRC/66, paragraph 24)

23. TERMINATION OF SAFEGUARDS

Safeguards will be terminated on nuclear material returned to the State that originally supplied it provided:

a. it was not improved while under safeguards;

b. special fissionable material produced in it has been removed;

c. it was subject to safeguards only by reason of its use in a principal nuclear facility;

d. it has been diluted or consumed so it no longer has safeguards significance;

e. it has been replaced by substitute material;

f. it has been transferred out of the States to the State that originally supplied it, safeguards have been suspended, it will be subject to safeguards other than those of the Agency but accepted by the Agency;

g. the applicable safeguards agreement has expired.

(See INFCIRC/66, paragraph 26)

In addition, safeguards may be terminated by State-Agency agreement on material to be used for nonnuclear purposes. (See INFCIRC/66, paragraph 27)

Euratom Treaty safeguards terminate when the material is transferred out of the Community.

Similar to Euratom Treaty obligations.

276

Comparison of the Euratom Safeguards System and the IAEA Safeguards System—Continued

24. TRANSFER OF MATERIAL OUT OF STATE

IAEA safeguards	Euratom safeguards		Comment
	Euratom Treaty	Euratom-U.S. bilateral	

No safeguarded nuclear material shall be transferred outside the jurisdiction of the State in which it is being safeguarded unless:
  a. the material is being returned to the State that originally supplied it; or
  b. the material is being transferred subject to substitution provisions; or
  c. the material will be subject to Agency safeguards in the State to which it is being transferred; or
  d. the material was not subject to safeguards pursuant to a project agreement and will be subject to other safeguards acceptable to the Agency in the State to which it is being transferred.
(See INFCIRC/66 paragraph 28)
	Euratom safeguards follow all material transferred between any establishments in the Community if not for a military use. If any material is transferred out of the Community, Euratom safeguards cease to apply. (See Articles 77 and 79)	"No such material will be transferred to unauthorized persons or beyond the control of the Community, except as the Government of the United States of America may agree to such transfer and then only if the transfer of the material is within the scope of an Agreement for Cooperation between the Government of the United States of America and another nation or group of nations". (Article XI)	

ANALYSES OF IAEA SAFEGUARDS SYSTEMS

A. INTERNATIONAL RESEARCH AND TECHNOLOGY CORPORATION

Notes About Minimum Manpower and Money Requirements for Nuclear Safeguards

(By T. B. Taylor, Krassnigg Gasse 22, 1140 Vienna, Austria, September 20, 1967)

I have made some preliminary estimates of the numbers of inspectors and amounts of money required as a function of time for safeguarding the world's non-military nuclear technology, based on assumptions that I believe correspond to minimum requirements. I have also estimated the requirements, on the same basis, for safeguarding only the nuclear technology of those nations that do not now have nuclear weapons. These estimates are summarized in Tables I and II.

The assumptions made in this survey are the following:

1. One full time inspector requires $40,000 per year for his salary, all technical and administrative support, and equipment. I believe this may be too low by as much as a factor of two.

2. The equivalent of one full time inspector is required for every six research, test, and training reactors or critical or subcritical facilities. This is roughly the number allocated by the IAEA now. If this, as it should eventually, includes provision for inspection of fuel fabrication, fuel reprocessing, fuel transportation, storage and isotope enrichment facilities required for support of the reactors, then I believe the number of inspectors per reactor should be increased. Further increases will also be required as more large critical facilities for fast power breeder experiments are built.

3. Three hundred research, test, or training reactors and critical and subcritical facilities were in operation in 1966. About 315 are listed in Volume VI of the IAEA Directory of Research and Test Reactors. Some of these are no longer in operation, but perhaps several dozen reactors and critical facilities in operation then are not listed because they were not reported by the IAEA Member States.

4. Twenty-five research, test, or training reactors and critical and subcritical facilities that require safeguards will be added each year in the future. Additions listed per year in the IAEA Reactor Directory from 1957 to 1963 are 30, 29, 47, 22, 33, 29, and 20. The assumed 25 per year is therefore probably too low.

5. The equivalent of four full time inspectors per 1000 MWe of installed power plant capacity, plus one full time additional inspector for every two power plants is assumed for all activities associated with power production—isotope enrichment, fuel element fabrication and chemical reprocessing, fuel transport and storage, and power production itself. I believe this is in line with some of the current thinking in the Safeguards and Inspection Department of the IAEA. I also believe it is likely to be an underestimate of the manpower required for adequate inspection, but probably not by a very large factor. The allocation of a small fraction of the inspectors on the basis of numbers of reactors, rather than power level, was to assure adequate inspection of new reactor prototypes and power reactor experiments that operate at low power levels, but may contain large amounts of highly enriched uranium or plutonium.

6. Until 1971, the numbers of power reactors and their cumulative electrical generating capacity are derived from the IAEA power reactor summaries in the IAEA Bulletins and from the July 1967 issue of the Atomic Industrial Forum's *Nuclear Industry*. After 1971, additions to these summaries have been made by referring to an unpublished IR&T summary obtained by a review of periodicals and trade journals for announcements of new contracts and plans for construction of new power plants, particularly outside the United States. From 1975 on, I have assumed the following: world energy production will increase steadily at a rate of 6% per year, 50% of all new energy sources built between 1975–1980 will be nuclear, and 75% of all new sources will be nuclear after 1980. Much of

the power produced by nuclear sources after 1975 will not be for production of electricity, but reactor power plant outputs have been listed in equivalent electrical units, assuming 30% efficiency for production of electricity. The basis for all these assumptions is that nuclear energy sources will be definitely cheaper than other energy sources for most purposes by about 1970, so that very strong economic forces will tend to push the world into "going nuclear" very fast. That has already happened in the United States, at least in the plans for production of electric power. Large scale desalting of sea water, use of electricity for automobiles, increased use of electricity for space heating as it becomes cheaper, can all help lead to forecasts of considerably larger rates of nuclear power production than are shown in Table I.

In the extrapolations after about 1972, it is assumed that the average electrical output of nuclear power plants will be 700 MWe. This may be reduced considerably if new developments in reactor technology lead to competitive power costs at lower power levels, because, at the same power cost, smaller plants are often more desirable. Such developments will increase the need for safeguards inspectors.

7. Nuclear electric power costs are arbitrarily assumed to decrease from 8 mils per kwh in 1966 to 4 mils per kwh in 1970, and remain constant thereafter.

8. In Table II, it is assumed that 15 research, test, and training reactors and critical and subcritical facilities will be added each year in the non-nuclear-weapon-nations. This is about equal to the average number added per year during the last ten years, and is believed to be a low estimate because the number of nations in this category is very much larger than the number that have nuclear weapons.

9. Estimates of the money and inspectors required for safeguards do not include any allowances for supporting safeguards research and development. Especially during the next few years, the financial and manpower requirements for R&D will be very significant, and could even be larger than the requirements for operation of a safeguards system.

COMMENTS

1. Note that the costs of safeguards operations based on these assumptions never amount to more than 1% of the cost of the total electric power produced, and approach 0.7% of power costs when research and test reactors become a relatively trivial part of the cost. This is approximately correct even if a large fraction of the nuclear power produced by, say, 1985 is used for process heat, because 4 mils per kwh of electricity corresponds to about 1.3 mils per kwh of heat from a controlled heat source. That is a reasonable cost, equivalent to about $13 per ton of coal consumed in a controlled heat source.

2. An increase of as much as a factor of ten in the money and manpower requirements assumed in Tables I and II would not be a catastrophic blow to the nuclear power industry. I am confident that even a 7% increase in the cost of nuclear power, as the result of the development and operation of a highly effective international safeguards system, would be considered a small and very worthwhile price to pay for preventing the development of large illegal markets in special nuclear materials, frequent national and criminal threats of nuclear blackmail, further proliferation of large national military stockpiles of nuclear weapons, and eventually, a chaos of nuclear violence.

TABLE 1.—FORECASTS OF MINIMUM SAFEGUARDS REQUIREMENTS FOR WORLDWIDE NUCLEAR TECHNOLOGY

Year	Number of research and test reactors	Number of power reactors	Total power-MWE (×1000)	Number of inspectors for research and test reactors	Number of inspectors for power
1966	300	73	8. 4	50	70
1967	325	81	11. 6	54	87
1968	350	99	16. 5	58	115
1969	375	113	25. 0	62	155
1970	400	137	40. 0	67	228
1971	425	162	57. 0	71	309
1972	450	193	77. 0	75	405
1973	475	237	100. 0	79	518
1974	500	287	135. 0	83	684
1975	525	350	180. 0	87	896
1980	650	950	600. 0	108	2, 875
1985	775	2, 250	1, 500. 0	129	7, 125
1990	900	4, 000	2, 700. 0	150	12, 800

Year	Total inspectors	Cost at 40K/ inspector ($×10−6)	Cost per year of power at 4m/kw.-hr. and 80 per-cent load factor ($×10−6)	
1966	120	4. 8	470	8m/kw.-hr
1967	141	5. 6	570	7
1968	173	6. 9	690	6
1969	217	8. 7	865	5
1970	295	11. 8	1, 120	4
1971	380	15. 2	1, 600	
1972	480	19. 2	2, 160	
1973	597	23. 8	2, 800	
1974	767	30. 7	3, 800	
1975	993	39. 7	5, 000	
1980	2, 983	119. 0	16, 200	
1985	7, 254	290. 0	42, 000	
1990	12, 290	518. 0	75, 000	

TABLE II.—FORECASTS OF MINIMUM SAFEGUARDS INSPECTION REQUIREMENTS FOR NON-NUCLEAR-WEAPONS-NATIONS.

Year	Number of research and test reactors	Number of power reactors	MWE (×1000)	Number of inspectors for research and test reactors	Number of inspectors for power	Total Number of inspectors	Cost $×10−6
1966	111	14	1. 36	19	12	31	1. 25
1967	126	15	1. 82	21	15	36	1. 4
1968	141	25	3. 36	24	26	50	2. 0
1969	156	29	4. 85	26	34	60	2. 4
1970	171	33	6. 98	29	45	74	3. 0
1971	186	40	9. 8	31	59	90	3. 6
1972	201	53	16. 0	34	91	125	5. 0

B. Analysis by Representative Hosmer

Article III of the proposed treaty deals with the matter of safeguards to prevent cheating. No safeguards whatever are provided to police promises by non-nuclear states not to receive nuclear weapons or promises by nuclear states not to spread them around. To police the non-nuclear states' promises not to make weapons Article III calls for signatories to sign ancillary agreements with the International Atomic Energy Agency calling for inspection of their nuclear supplies and facilities by the IAEA. As an inducement to non-nuclear powers the United States has offered to place all its peaceful nuclear facilities under IAEA inspection and is encouraging other nuclear powers to do the same.

Doubts have been expressed as to the IAEA's technical and organizational capability to carry out inspection duties. These doubts are not my subject today. Rather, I want to discuss the probable cost of IAEA's proposed worldwide inspection duties. The subject has been almost universally ignored. The only authoritative study of costs which has come to my attention was made in September, 1967, by Dr. T. R. Taylor, founder and President of International Research and Technology Corporation, Vienna, Austria. Taylor's study has had private circulation only.

In making the calculations presented in the accompanying Table I have used Dr. Taylor's estimates to 1990 of the numbers of research, training and test reactors and the numbers of power reactors and total nuclear power megawatts. Footnotes to the table indicate the method by which these extrapolations were made.

I have assumed a need for one full-time inspector for each four research, test and training reactors or critical or subcritical assemblies. This is in excess of the number allocated by the IAEA, about one per six, but my number also provides for inspection of fuel fabrication, fuel reprocess, fuel transportation and storage, and isotope enrichment facilities required for support of these reactors and assemblies. Increased demand for inspectors over my figure should be anticipated as more large critical facilities for fast power breeder experiments are built.

In determining numbers of inspectors required for power reactors I have allowed five full-time inspectors for each 1000 megawatts of installed nuclear power plant capacity, plus one and one-half full-time inspectors for every two power plants. This is intended to cover not only plants themselves, but also associated activities such as isotope separation, fuel element fabrication and reprocessing, fuel transportation and fuel storage.

Determination of numbers of inspectors required, of course, is somewhat "iffy" and somewhat arbitrary. However, I have tried to specify reasonable numbers which take into consideration not only the wide variety of duties involved, but also such things as vacations, transfers, training, indoctrination and retraining and other practical factors. Any increase in confidence in the inspection system would be a factor of both improvement in inspection technology and expansion of the inspection force.

In calculating the total costs of IAEA inspection efforts I have assumed that one full-time inspector will need some $70,000 annually for his support. This figure includes salary, benefits, technical and administrative support and equipment. It also includes a relatively large sum in the early years of the program for supporting safeguards research and development. I have assumed that as R&D requirements diminish over the years that cost escalation will consume the savings and have therefore kept the cost per inspector steady throughout the years represented in the Table.

From the Table it is apparent that to do the job the United States wants IAEA to do in the inspection area during this year 1968 it should be employing 245 inspectors and spending $17,150,000 on the job. By way of contrast it actually is spending $498,815 and employs 22 professional inspectors, plus the Inspector General and one director. It is spending 2.8 percent and employing less than 10 percent of the people needed. Its expenditure on R&D is negligible. As a matter of fact, IAEA will spend only around $13 million this year for all its activities, about ¾th what might be required for inspection functions alone. Again referring to the Table, the staggering estimate of possible safeguards expenditures at a rate of over $1 billion annually by 1990, just slightly more than two decades hence, should elicit some study and discussion of finances in relation to the NPT.

Of course, the U.S. might recede from its position that inspection ought to be worldwide, covering nuclear as well as non-nuclear states. The U.S.S.R. probably never would agree to it anyway. France, Red China and others will be treaty holdouts. But even absent inspection of the nuclear powers non-weapons atomic efforts, the bill for inspection still will be high. Cut the 1990 figure by 90% and still over $100 million will be required and it raises the question : Where is the money coming from?

I respectfully suggest that those who are so carefully weighing the merits of this Treaty at the United Nations and elsewhere should expand their horizons and their oratory and come to grips with this question. If there is to be reliance on safeguards, they should be adequate safeguards adequately financed. Inadequate safeguards, the concomitant of inadequate financing, are essentially useless. They may, in fact, be dangerous, since they allay universal suspicion which might otherwise arise and afford some protection to the otherwise unwary.

TABLE SHOWING NONPROLIFERATION TREATY SAFEGUARD COSTS

Year	Number of research and test reactors [1]	Number of power reactors [2]	Total power in mega-watts [2]	Inspectors required for R. & T. reactors	Inspectors required for power reactors	Total inspectors	Safeguards cost total
1966	300	73	8,400	75	97	172	$12,040,000
1967	325	81	11,600	81	119	200	14,000,000
1968	350	99	16,500	88	157	245	17,150,000
1969	375	113	25,000	94	210	304	21,280,000
1970	400	137	40,000	100	303	403	28,210,000
1971	425	162	57,000	107	407	514	35,980,000
1972	450	193	77,000	113	580	643	45,010,000
1973	475	237	100,000	119	678	797	55,790,000
1974	500	287	135,000	125	890	1,015	71,050,000
1975	525	350	180,000	132	1,163	1,295	90,650,000
1980	650	950	600,000	163	3,713	3,876	271,320,000
1985	775	2,250	1,500,000	194	9,188	9,382	656,740,000
1990	900	4,000	2,700,000	225	16,500	16,725	1,170,750,000

[1] Facts and assumptions: 300 research, test, or training reactors and critical and subcritical assemblies were in operation in 1966. About 315 are listed in vol. VI of the IAEA Directory of R. & T. Reactors. Some of these are no longer in operation, but perhaps several dozen in operation then are not listed because they were not reported by IAEA member states. 25 R.,T. or T. reactors and assemblies that require safeguards will be added each year in the future. Additions per year listed in the IAEA Directory from 1957 to 1963 are 30, 29, 47, 22, 33, 29, and 20. Therefore the assumed 25 per year addition rate is conservative and probably low.

[2] Facts and assumptions: Until 1971 the numbers of power reactors and their cumulative electrical generating capacity are derived from IAEA power reactor summaries found in IAEA bulletins and from the July 1967 issue of Atomic Industrial Forum's Nuclear Industry. After 1971, additions to these have been made by reference to an unpublished summary by International Research & Technology Corp. (Vienna, Austria), obtained by a review of periodicals and trade journals for announcements of new contracts and plans for construction of new powerplants, particularly outside the United States. From 1975 on it is assumed that world energy production will increase steadily at a rate of 6 percent per year, 50 percent of all new energy sources built between 1975–80 will be nuclear, and 75 percent will be nuclear after 1980. Much of the power production after 1975 from nuclear sources will not be for production of electricity, but reactor powerplant outputs have been listed in equivalent electrical units, assuming 30 percent efficiency for production of electricity, a low assumption. The basis for all these assumptions is that nuclear energy sources will be cheaper than other energy sources for most purposes by about 1970—so that very strong economic forces will tend to push the world into "going nuclear" at a fast rate. Large-scale desalting of seawater, use of electricity for automobiles, space heating, etc., all help lead to forecasts considerably larger for nuclear power production than those shown. In the estimates after about 1972 it is assumed that the average electrical output of nuclear powerplants will be 700 MWE. This may be reduced considerably if new developments in reactor tecnology lead to competitive power costs at lower size plants, because, at the same power cost, smaller plants are often more desirable. Such development will increase the need for safeguards inspectors by ¾ per plant.

C. Brookhaven Analysis

IAEA COST AND MANPOWER REQUIREMENTS UNDER THE NON-PROLIFERATION TREATY

I. Introduction

This report provides estimates of the manpower and funding that will be needed by the International Atomic Energy Agency, to discharge its obligations under the Non-Proliferation Treaty.

Since details of the means by which the IAEA is to perform these duties have not yet been decided, it has been necessary to base the estimates on a number of assumptions. These assumptions fall in two general classes. The first concerns the level of inspection that will be undertaken by the IAEA. The second class includes assumptions on the magnitude of the industry to which IAEA inspection must be directed, and the method of performing the inspection.

The Office of Safeguards and Materials Management of the AEC has requested that the estimates be based on three of several possible levels of inspection. The assumptions include facilities in different countries as follows:

(a) All U.S., U.K., and U.S.S.R. peaceful activities and all non-nuclear-weapons country peaceful activities.

(b) All peaceful activities in non-nuclear-weapons countries, and selected peaceful activities in nuclear countries that are of a type competitive with those in non-nuclear countries.

(c) Representative samples of peaceful activities in both nuclear and non-nuclear-weapon countries of competitive types, with dependence on appraisals of the national systems of safeguards of the remaining peaceful activities in non-nuclear-weapons countries.

It is also assumed that the present IAEA safeguards criteria are in effect. The principal effect of this assumption is that continuous inspection is to be applied to plants whose inventory, annual throughput, or maximum potential annual production of special fissionable material exceeds 60 effective kilograms.

The estimates provided in this report are preliminary, and subject to considerable uncertainty. The major sources of uncertainty are discussed at appropriate points. In addition, the brief space of time available for arriving at the estimates presented here did not allow the use of a number of subtleties that could have improved the accuracy of the prediction. Most of the approximations used are discussed in the following section, which presents the assumptions upon which the study has been made.

II. Assumptions

The results of the study are based upon detailed consideration of the requirements for safeguards for central station power reactors, research and test reactors, research facilities, fuel fabrication plants, chemical processing plants and isotope separation facilities, and they include provision for a central headquarters organization which assimilates information gained by field representatives.

The assumptions on the growth of the industry are taken from the following publications. The document entitled "Power and Research Reactors in Member States," issued by the IAEA in January, 1968, lists the power reactors now existing, under construction, or planned in member states. This document was issued to project the number of power reactor sites through 1973. WASH–1084, "Forecast of Growth of Nuclear Power" (December, 1967), was used to extrapolate the installed nuclear capacity through the year 1980. A quadratic fit to the data in WASH–1084 was used to obtain further prediction of installed nuclear generating capacity in 1985 and 1990. The prediction of installed nuclear electric capacity in non-weapon states to 1980 is taken from a memorandum from Nakicenovic to the Director General of the IAEA, dated January 30, 1968, and entitled *Staff Requirements for the Control Function Under NPT*. This document was also used to obtain predicted nuclear electric capacity in the U.K. over the same interval. The data on U.K. capacity in the Nakicenovic memorandum are in turn based on extrapolation of information given in the October, 1967 issue of *The Journal of the British Nuclear Energy Society*. The predicted growth of nuclear power in the U.S.S.R. is based on present plans for installation of reactors, and information obtained informally from the IAEA liaison office to the United Nations. The latter information is soon to be improved. Extrapolation of installed capacity in the U.K. and non-weapons states was made from a least-squares quadratic fit to the data in the Nakicenovic memorandum. The growth in installed capacity in the U.S.S.R. after 1980 is assumed to be the same as that in the U.K.

The number of high-powered research and test reactors in the various areas is taken from the 1968 IAEA document "Power and Research Reactors in Member States." The number of such reactors has remained constant for some time, and it is not expected that this number will increase in the future. As new and more advanced facilities are brought on line, older ones will be decommissioned. Likewise, there is little tendency for appreciable increase in the number of low-powered research reactors or research facilities using large amounts of fissionable material. The predicted future number of these installations is taken to be the number now existing. Because most research facilities are of the low-powered research reactor variety, for which resident inspectors are not needed, and for which IAEA inspection will be infrequent, the effect of this assumption on overall IAEA staffing and costs will be small.

A review of future requirements in fuel fabrication plants, chemical processing plants, and isotope separation plants reveals many points in common. Cost analyses on all three kinds of facility indicate that benefits can be reached by increasing size to about 10 tonnes/day of throughput. Existing plants are much smaller, with the exception of the U.S. isotope separation facilities. It is assumed that fuel fabrication for future power reactors takes place in existing fuel fabrication facilities, and that in all cases the sizes of plants are increased as needs arise, until plants reach a throughput of 10 tonnes/day. Not until this time are new plants added. It is assumed that chemical reprocessing plants and isotope separation plants are added in modules of 5 and 10 tonnes/day throughput, whichever appears to be most economical at the time the requirement appears. The requirement for slightly enriched uranium for the power cycle is assumed to be met by existing U.S. facilities until the middle of the next decade. At that time, installation of a separate isotope separation facility is assumed, in the grouping of non-weapons-countries. Additional facilities as required are added in areas where the power generation demands the fuel.

It is assumed that production of hexafluoride, chemical reduction to fuel form, and reprocessing of scrap take place as adjunct activities at the same large facilities provided for other purposes (fuel fabrication, etc.).

There is a strong trend in the U.S. and the U.K. to install several nuclear generating plants on the same site. This practice reflects decreased costs from a variety of sources, as well as a growing difficulty in finding suitable sites for large nuclear reactors. It is assumed that after 1973, reactors in the U.S. and the U.K. are installed in pairs at reactor sites. It is assumed that in the remainder of the world, reactors are located one at each site.

The reactors built in the U.S., the U.S.S.R., and the non-weapons-countries after 1973 are assumed to be of the water-moderated and water-cooled variety. Those in the U.S. are assumed to generate 1,000 electrical megawattts each. Those in the U.S.S.R. and non-weapons-countries are assumed to generate 600 electric magawatts each until 1980. At this time, a change to the larger size is assumed to take place in this remainder of the world.

Where the assumption of the study and the criteria in use by the IAEA call for continuous inspection of a facility, the following assumptions are made on staffing required for this inspection: It is assumed that one inspector can adequately discharge the responsibility of the IAEA at a single power reactor site. The same assumption is made as regards high-powered reasearch and test reactors. It is assumed that research facilities requiring continuous inspection because of large inventories of fissionable material require one inspector per shift. In addition to this staff of resident inspectors for reactor activities, it is assumed that a traveling staff of inspectors satisfies the needs for additional personnel at peak levels of activity, and at times of illness and vacation. This traveling staff consists of 10% as many personnel as the IAEA staff resident inspectors.

The number of resident inspectors required for a fuel fabrication facility, fuel processing facility, or isotope separation facility is obtained from Table I. This table is consistent with current thinking in the AEC on suitable sizes of staff for continuous resident inspection. However, since plants of the large capacity envisioned in this study have not yet been designed or built, the requirement for resident inspection staff for these must be viewed as still very much in question.

It is assumed that a central IAEA staff provides several functions in addition to those of resident inspectors. This staff administers IAEA's safeguard functions, provides a pool for forming teams of inspectors and auditors of activities in the field, and performs a central function of data gathering and data analysis on safeguards, using information obtained from the field.

The budget for support for this activity is estimated as follows. It is assumed that the annual cost of maintaining one resident inspector is $25,000. This amount includes salary, overhead, and minor incidental expenses such as travel. It is assumed that the cost to the IAEA of one member of its general staff is $35,000 per year. This higher number reflects the need for additional secretarial overhead, higher amounts of travel cost, and a staff of personnel associated with gathering and analyzing information on the whereabouts and characteristics of the fissionable material being controlled. In addition to these administrative costs, it is assumed that the various plants at which resident inspectors are located are also furnished with certain kinds of equipment supplied by the IAEA. This equipment includes various kinds of devices used for non-destructive assay of fissonable material, and a data compiling and analyzing system. In accordance that this data gathering system is computer-based, and that inventory of the plant is therefore maintained on a true-time basis. The possibility of automatic continuous or periodic transmission of information to a central data handling unit at the headquarters of the IAEA is included in the estimates.

The above assumptions are adequate to lead to the conclusions generated in connection with assumption a of the three that have been analyzed. The conclusions of assumption b are based upon regarding chemical processing plants, fuel fabrication facilities, and isotope separation plants as competitive for world markets. It is thus assumed that no competition will exist for electrical power being supplied from the electrical generating plants of weapons countries and non-weapons countries. Thus the analysis under assumption b involves the assumption that one chemical processing plant, one fuel fabrication plant, and one isotope separation plant is inspected on a continuous basis in each of the three weapon states. No other facilities in these states are directly subjected to IAEA safeguards.

The analysis under assumption c is at best very difficult to perform in the absence of suitable guidelines. It appears that it would be necessary to inspect representative plants in each of the non-weapons states as these are built. Furthermore, the number of national systems to be verified could range anywhere from one per signatory of the treaty to only a few, the latter case assuming that safeguards are everywhere managed by regional groupings, such as Euratom in Western Europe and Comecon in eastern Europe.

In fact, it appears that no single non-weapons state would construct and operate more than one of the large plants visualized in this report for fuel fabrication, chemical processing, and isotope separation. With all of the added capacity that is visualized being constructed in different states or groups of states, all of the large plants would be inspected on a continuous basis under the guidelines given in connection with alternative c of the asumptions. Thus the only major change under alternative c as contrasted with alternative b is a large reduction in the number of power reactors inspected in the different countries. Inspection of Table III, giving costs associated with the alternatives, shows that until the year 1985, agency activities associated with reactors per se account for a minor fraction of the total budget.

The best conclusions that can be drawn at this time on the staffing and cost of discharge by the IAEA of its duties under the NPT, according to alternative c, are that these will fall between the limits of the numbers appropriate to alternative b, and the same numbers reduced by the amount of money and staff required for reactors. We therefore list the results of analysis under alternative c as the upper and lower limits obtained in this way.

Two additional simplifying assumptions that have been made throughout should be mentioned. The first is that for the most part the difference in fuel requirements for water reactors and for gas cooled reactors of the kind used in the UK have been neglected for the purposes of this first round study. The principal effect of this assumption is on the requirements for chemical processing, fuel fabrication, and isotope separation in the UK. The second assumption is related to the time at which various facilities will be needed. In the analysis, it has been assumed that these facilities are needed at the time that the appropriate nuclear capacity has been installed. In fact, fuel fabrication plants are required earlier than the related power reactors, and isotope separation plants are needed earlier still. On the other hand, the requirements for chemical processing plants lag behind those for the nuclear capacity they are to serve. The effect of time advance of some needs for some plants and time delay for needs of others tends to cancel. Though the assumptions will be revised in later studies of this kind, it is not expected that the changes will appreciably affect the conclusions drawn here.

TABLE I.—REQUIREMENTS FOR RESIDENT INSPECTION STAFF

Capacity	Fuel fabrication	Chemical processing	Isotope separation
Less than:			
1 tonne/day	7	10	7
5 tonnes/day	13	13	12
10 tonnes/day	19	16	17

TABLE II.—ESTIMATED IAEA STAFF FOR IMPLEMENTATION OF THE NPT

Year	Alternative a	Alternative b	Alternative c	
			Upper limit	Lower limit
1970	734	461	461	392
1971	775	476	476	394
1972	813	494	494	395
1973	855	521	521	411
1974	908	534	534	415
1975	956	549	549	419
1976	1,040	619	619	472
1977	1,073	634	634	473
1978	1,152	675	675	490
1979	1,203	706	706	493
1980	1,302	758	758	514
1985	1,766	1,033	1.033	668
1990	2,374	1,387	1,378	829

TABLE III.—ESTIMATED IAEA ANNUAL COSTS FOR IMPLEMENTATION OF THE NPT

[In millions of dollars assuming 3 percent per year escalation]

Year	Alternative a	Alternative b	Alternative c	
			Upper limit	Lower limit
1970	[1] 58.6	31.4	31.4	27.1
1971	29.8	16.0	16.0	13.0
1972	31.9	17.2	17.2	14.6
1973	34.1	19.0	19.0	15.0
1974	37.7	19.2	19.2	14.9
1975	40.1	20.4	20.4	15.4
1976	45.7	26.3	26.3	20.4
1977	46.0	25.2	25.2	18.6
1978	52.3	28.4	28.4	20.5
1979	54.3	30.1	30.1	20.7
1980	60.6	34.1	34.1	23.1
1985	93.5	52.7	52.7	35.5
1990	143.4	69.5	69.5	40.3

[1] Purchase of equipment for existing facilities is reflected in this year's figure.

D. COMPARISON OF ASSUMPTIONS ON IAEA COSTS OF ADMINISTERING SAFEGUARDS

IAEA COST AND MANPOWER REQUIREMENTS UNDER THE NON-PROLIFERATION TREATY:
A COMPARISON OF THE ESTIMATES OF T. B. TAYLOR AND TSO

I. Introduction

Three recent reports estimating prospective manpower requirements and costs of IAEA nuclear materials safeguards activities have led to divergent results. The first of these, dated September 20, 1967, was prepared by T. B. Taylor of the International Research and Technology Corporation; the second, which was also prepared by T. B. Taylor, is contained in a speech by the Honorable Craig Hosmer, in the House of Representatives on May 1, 1968; and the third, under date of June 13, 1968, was a draft report to the Office of Safeguards and Materials Management, USAEC, by its Technical Support Organization (TSO) at Brookhaven National Laboratory.

This analysis will compare the basic assumptions of the reports, to the extent that we know them, and describe the effects of differences in those assumptions on the resulting manpower and cost projections to 1990. At the outset, it must be noted that the TSO estimates assume that the safeguards of the IAEA are superposed on adequate national, regional, or plant safeguards supplying physical security and nuclear materials management to guard against theft and other diversion attempts. TSO estimates are based on continuation of current IAEA criteria, which include provisions for continuous inspection of major plants.

Since all assumptions in the first two estimates are the same except for the number of inspectors and the cost per inspector, the comparison will be made essentially only between the study by the TSO and the one prepared by Taylor in 1967. The relation to the estimate given in Congressman Hosmer's speech will be made at the end.

II. Assumptions

The assumptions of the Taylor and TSO studies are in some cases quite similar, in others highly divergent. A comparison follows:

A. Factors Affecting Staff Size and Equipment Costs
1. Size of the Nuclear Power Industry

The Taylor assumption is based on unpublished data generated by his own organization, plus a set of assumptions about the growth of world power requirements and the nuclear fraction of the total power generated for other purposes than producing electricity, beyond 1975.

The TSO assumption is based on the following sources, all post-dating the Taylor study:

(a) U.S.: WASH–1084, "Forecast and Growth of Nuclear Power," December, 1967; a quadratic fit to the data in this document was used to predict values for 1985 to 1990.

(b) U.K.: Extrapolation of 1980 of data given in the October, 1967 issue of The Journal of the British Nuclear Energy Society, taken from a memorandom from Nakicenovic to the Director General of IAEA, dated January 30, 1968. Extrapolation to 1985 and 1990 was made by a least-squares quadratic fit to these data.

(c) USSR: Present announced plans for installation of reactors, and information obtained informally from the IAEA liaison office to the United Nations. Growth beyond 1980 is assumed to be the same as that in the U.K.

(d) Non-Nuclear-Weapons States: The Nakicenovic memorandum predicts to 1980; a least-squares-fit quadratic extrapolation was made for 1985 and 1990.

Comparative typical results from the two studies are:

Year	World installed capacity in electrical megawatts ($\times 10^{-3}$)	
	Taylor	TSO
1975	180	115
1980	600	300
1985	1,500	620
1990	2,700	1.050

2. Non-Power Users of Large Reactors

Taylor states that reactor use for desalting of sea water, process heat, space heating, etc., might significantly increase the values in his forecast. It appears that he may have already included some of these uses in his totals.

TSO believes these uses will not begin to have a significant impact on the industry before the late 1980's. TSO estimates do not allow for these uses.

3. Power Level of Reactors

The Taylor study assumes a world average of 700 MWe.

TSO assumes the following:
U.S.: 1,000 MWe.
Other: 600MWe until 1980, then new installations at 1,000 MWe.

4. Multiple Reactors Siting

The trend toward installation of more than one nuclear power plant at a single site is not recognized by Taylor.

TSO assumes that, after 1973, reactors in the U.S. and U.K. are installed in pairs, elsewhere singly.

5. Number and Size of Fuel Fabrication and Processing Plants, and Isotope Separation Facilities

The Taylor study assumes inspectorate staff and equipment costs will increase linearly with installed electric generating capacity. Thus, it does not allow for the effect of increase in size of related nuclear industrial facilities.

TSO has assumed that the industry will grow in an economical fashion, that plant sizes will increase toward more economical levels, and that new installations will be made when and where needed. These assumptions on sizes and dates of installation of new plants were based on throughput of fuel consistent with the assumed power levels for the individual nations (U.S., U.K., U.S.S.R.) and for the non-weapons nations as a group.

6. *Research and Test Reactors*

Taylor assumes that 25 research, test, and training reactors and other small facilities requiring safeguards will be added each year, extrapolating IAEA data for the period 1957–1963.

TSO assumes no net increase in such facilities.

Despite these highly disparate assumptions, these reports agree that inspection of such facilities will have little impact on inspection costs.

B. *Staff and Equipment Requirements as a Function of Size and Number of Facilities*

1. *Staff*

The Taylor assumption for the *entire* nuclear industry is four full-time inspectors per 1000 MWe of installed capacity, plus one additional for every two power plants.

Details of the TSO assumption are as follows:

Reactors require one inspector at each power reactor site, or each high-power research or test reactor site, plus a traveling staff of inspectors (the size of this staff is 20% of the number of resident inspectors).

Research facilities having large inventories of fissionable material require one inspector per shift.

Fuel fabrication, fuel processing, and isotope separation facilities have requirements for numbers of continuous resident inspectors that are based on plant size.

Capacity	Fuel fabrication	Chemical processing	Isotope separation
1 tonne per day	7	10	7
5 tonnes per day	13	13	12
10 tonnes per day	19	16	17

In addition, a headquarters staff of 50 persons, plus 10% of the total inspectors in the field is assumed.

2. *Equipment*

Requirements for equipment are not detailed in the Taylor paper.

The TSO study allows for costs of a computer, software, assay equipment, radiation detectors, and installation, at each plant, in amounts appropriate to plant size and function.

C. *Cost Factors*

The Taylor cost estimates are derived from an assumed annual cost of $40,000 per inspector, to cover salary, all technical and administrative support, and equipment.

TSO assumes $25,000 annually for each inspector, and $35,000 for each headquarters staff member, to cover salary, travel, and overhead. Equipment costs are detailed as appropriate to the assumptions described above. Cost impact from initial purchase of equipment may be noted in the total cost estimate for 1970 in the table of Part III below.

III. *Comparison of Estimates*

Cost and manpower estimates arising from the two sets of assumptions are compared in the following table. For convenience, Congressman Hosmer's values are also given.

Year	Manpower			Costs (in millions)			Mills killowatt-hour TSO
	Hosmer	Taylor	TSO	Hosmer	Taylor		
1970	403	295	734	28.2	11.8	[2]58.6	
1971	514	380	775	36.0	15.2	29.8	0.16
1972	643	480	813	45.0	19.2	31.9	.09
1973	797	597	855	55.8	23.8	34.1	.07
1974	1,015	767	908	71.1	30.7	37.7	.06
1975	1,295	993	956	90.7	39.7	40.1	.05
1980	3,876	2,983	1,302	271.3	119.0	60.6	.03
1985	9,382	7,254	1,766	656.7	290.0	93.5	'.02
1990	16,725	12,290	2,374	1,170.8	518.0	143.4	.02

[1] A 3-percent annual cost escalation is included in the TSO estimates.
[2] Purchase of equipment for existing facilities is reflected in this estimate.

288

IV. Comparison With Congressman Hosmer's Estimates

Congressman Hosmer uses Taylor's predictions of number of power plants and installed nuclear capacity. He uses a different formula to calculate number of inspectors, this leads to more inspectors needed than Taylor estimates. Congressman Hosmer also assumes that each inspector needs $70,000 for salary, benefits, technical and administrative support, and equipment. This compares with Taylor's estimate of $40,000. Congressman Hosmer includes R&D in his $70,000 for early years. He keeps the $70,000 constant to allow for inflation. Taylor does not allow for R&D or inflation. The TSO estimate includes inflation but not R&D.

V. Summary

The greatest differences are as follows:

1. Taylor and Hosmer assume many more reactors than does the TSO. There is a factor of nearly 3 in assumed installed electric megawatts in 1990, and a factor of 2 in 1980.

2. Taylor and Hosmer do not take into account reductions in numbers of inspectors as fuel fabrication and spent fuel reprocessing plants become larger.

3. TSO assumptions on cost per inspector are close to Taylor's when put on the same basis (equipment included). Hosmer's assumed cost per inspector is larger, but includes R&D. TSO believes the increase to allow for R&D is too big.

U.S. ATOMIC ENERGY COMMISSION,
Washington, D.C., August 1, 1968.

Hon. JOHN J. SPARKMAN,
Committee on Foreign Relations,
U.S. Senate.

DEAR SENATOR SPARKMAN: As you know I accompanied Chairman Seaborg and Commissioner Tape at the presentation of the Commission's testimony on the Non-Proliferation Treaty during the recent hearings that were held before the Senate Committee on Foreign Relations. I would appreciate it if I could have the privilege of having this letter incorporated as part of the Committee's record of the hearings since I would like to add my voice to the many other expressions of support that have been given to the Treaty.

In his testimony Dr. Seaborg stressed that the Non-Proliferation Treaty should serve to foster peaceful atomic cooperation to a great extent as a result of the obligations found in the Treaty itself and more importantly as a result of the greater assurances that the Treaty will provide that peaceful atomic efforts will not be diverted to the production of nuclear weapons. President Johnson in his dramatic message at the UN on June 12, 1968, and in his statement at the signing of the Treaty emphasized that, pursuant to the Treaty, the United States shall engage in the fullest possible exchange of equipment, material and scientific and technological information, with particular attention given to the needs of the developing nations. I should like to briefly summarize where the peaceful atom now stands and to describe some of the more dramatic technical returns that are readily within our grasp.

On a previous occasion, specifically on October 19, 1967, I had the pleasure of appearing before the Senate Committee on Foreign Relations to testify in support of Senate Resolution 155 which advocated the construction of combined nuclear power desalting plants in the Middle East as an important means of hopefully bringing peace and prosperity in the area. In response to the Senate Resolution the Atomic Energy Commission has initiated a major study on the potential of using nuclear energy centers in the Middle East, and I am enclosing the AEC press release of June 11, 1968 which describes this effort in some detail.

At that time I described the great progress that has been made in the development of nuclear power as well as the great contribution that nuclear energy promises to make in the production of fresh water, as well as agricultural development. I believe it would be useful to now recall a few of these factors since they bear significantly on the kinds of peaceful atomic developments that should be facilitated by the Non-Proliferation Treaty. I will concentrate my remarks on nuclear power and on the use of large-scale nuclear plants for desalting and other purposes since they are the areas in which I have had the closest association over many years, first as Executive Director of the Joint Committee on Atomic Energy and then as a member of the Atomic Energy Commission since 1962.

As Chairman Seaborg indicated, nuclear power plants are now being constructed or planned in many countries throughout the world and in the U.S. alone we have seen a tremendous upsurge in the number of such stations which are being planned or ordered. As of June 30, 1968, 102 nuclear power plants having a total installed electrical capacity of almost 73,000,000 kilowatts were planned, under construction or in operation in the United States, and by the year 1980 we estimate that about 150,000,000 kilowatts of nuclear power will be installed in this country. Comparable developments are taking place elsewhere and there should be a vast growth in the nuclear industry as well as international cooperation and commerce in this field. The Non-Proliferation Treaty should serve to facilitate this growth and cooperation by removing doubts that the plutonium produced in atomic plants will be diverted to the production of nuclear weapons. The Treaty also should make it even easier for the United States to cooperate and do business with other countries even though we have already done a great deal.

When I appeared before the Senate Foreign Relations Committee on October 19, 1967, I underscored that even further advances in nuclear power technology are achievable and needed. I stated that the economy of today's reactor types can be further improved. Even more importantly, new reactor types producing more fissionable material than they consume, known as breeder reactors, are being developed. I also stressed that today's technology provides a solid foundation for an effective program of nuclear desalting and development and that we are now contemplating uses for cheap nuclear power that simply stagger the imagination of their importance. Our near term technology should allow us to produce desalted water in large quantities at costs which are attractive for municipal and industrial use in many water-short metropolitan areas. Moreover, water at the lower range of presently attainable costs can be attractive for specialized agriculture purposes as well. The longer range goal of desalted water at costs sufficiently low for general agricultural purposes is still ahead of us but the engineering judgment and our experience in nuclear power gives us every reason to expect that it can be achieved.

This, however, is still only part of the story. It now appears that the cheap nuclear energy produced in large amounts may help us not only in the important field of desalting but also in the production of the nitrogen and phosphorus based fertilizers as well as other chemicals important to agricultural and industrial development. These considerations have led to the development of an exciting new concept, the "nuclear energy center" which is now being studied intensively at our Oak Ridge National Laboratory. In such centers the amount of low cost energy derived from nuclear reactors will be applied in an integrated agro-industrial complex in the production of fresh water, fertilizer, and other products. The prospects are tremendous and they have a global significance. By breaking the vicious cycle of high cost energy due to low energy consumption and by fostering intensive agricultural development through the production of water and fertilizer, these centers may make a major contribution to a better life in many developing nations.

What has this all to do with the Non-Proliferation Treaty? I have already stated that the Treaty should facilitate our ability to assist others by sharing our latest advances with them. However, our ability to assist others is only as good as the strength of the technological progress we make and continue to make in this field. The prospect of using nuclear energy for desalting and to run vast new energy centers shows that we are not at the end of the road in our atomic progress but have some enormous new returns yet to come. The studies that we have been conducting in these fields alone also demonstrate the earnestness with which the United States plans to pursue such further progress and share its advances with other countries. The U.S. "Atoms-for-Peace-Program" has been an unbroken and effective element of our foreign policy since President Eisenhower made his landmark speech before the U.S. General Assembly on December 8, 1953. The program has received the staunch support of President Kennedy and President Johnson as well as the true bipartisan support of both Houses of Congress and I am sure this support will continue. President Johnson and a number of members of Congress also have shown a special vision in foreseeing the great role that large-scale nuclear desalting plants can play in agricultural and industrial development in critical areas of the globe.

I frankly am excited about the even greater technological advances that I see coming within our grasp. I also am delighted to give support to the Non-

Proliferation Treaty since it should contribute to the progress I foresee assuring that the nuclear plants and centers being constructed only will serve their intended peaceful purposes.

Sincerely,

JAMES T. RAMEY, *Commissioner.*

Enclosure.

AEC STUDYING POTENTIAL OF NUCLEAR ENERGY CENTERS IN THE MIDDLE EAST

The potential of nuclear-powered "energy centers" in the Middle East is being studied by the Atomic Energy Commission through its Oak Ridge National Laboratory.

The study will explore the technical and economic feasibility of using nuclear power-desalting plants to provide large amounts of fresh water and electricity in agro-industrial production complexes (energy centers) for development in arid regions of the Middle East.

The study is to serve, in part, as a response to Senate Resolution 155, adopted last year, calling on the Administration to consider the application of large scale nuclear desalting plants as a means of supporting a stable and durable peace in the Middle East.

An initial study of the basic nuclear powered agro-industrial concept was also conducted by the AEC at its Oak Ridge National Laboratory last summer. The purpose of the study was to appraise the possibilities of using the most advanced nuclear power, agricultural and industrial techniques on a large scale to provide badly needed energy, water and industrial products, especially fertilizer, in developing countries. Power from a nuclear plant would be used to desalt water to irigate arid land in which the complex would be located. The electricity would be used in industrial plants such as chemical factories and metal refineries, and in fertilizer production. (A report on this study will be available this summer.)

Based on the preliminary results and in collaboration with Oak Ridge National Laboratory, the Government of India has recenly initiated a similar study of the agro-industrial complex as it might apply to conditions in India. Such a complex might be expected to be heavily related to those products, such as fertilizer, which could assist in increasing food production in that country.

The new study is applying the information developed in the initial investigations to the specific conditions of the Middle East and is expected to be completed in about one year. The AEC will collaborate with the Interior Department on the nuclear desalting aspects of the study in accordance with established relationships.

Other agencies of the U.S. Government will carry out related studies which will be coordinated with the study of the Atomic Energy Commission. Policy guidance will be provided by an interagency panel chaired by the Director of the Office of Water for Peace of the Department of State.

The study group, including experts from Government, industry, foundations and universities, will estimate the power and water requirements of the Middle East; survey the sources and availability of raw materials for industrial products; survey the domestic and export markets including price and demand relationships for the products from such a complex; identify specific locations where the soil, climate and other conditions are suitable for agricultural development using desalted water for irrigation; design and estimate costs for agri-industrial complexes at specific locations; and define the need for experimental or pilot projects to assure the success of larger projects. Specific attention will be devoted to planning for new jobs in industrial plants and on farms in the region.

The concept of nuclear-powered agro-industrial complexes has grown out of studies by the AEC and the Office of Saline Water, Department of the Interior, of the use of nuclear energy to supply heat for desalting sea water and the generation of electricity. These studies have shown that the increase in size of nuclear power-desalting facilities results in the reduction of power and water costs.

STATEMENT BY MAURICE B. VISSCHER, ON BEHALF OF THE COUNCIL FOR HUMANIST AND ETHICAL CONCERNS, JULY 19, 1968

Mr. Chairman and Members of the Committee, I am Maurice B. Visscher, member of the American Humanist Association, which, together with the American Ethical Union, sponsors the Council for Humanist and Ethical Concerns, with offices at 312 Pennsylvania Avenue S.E., Washington, D.C. I am Professor and Head of the Department of Physiology at the University of Minnesota and President of the National Society for Medical Research.

The Council for Humanist and Ethical Concerns urges the prompt ratification of this proposed Treaty. It represents a useful first step toward reduction of the threat of thermonuclear war. Obviously this step will not eliminate the danger of such war, but in the present state of international anarchy it is unrealistic to suppose that the major powers would agree to a more drastic limitation in their freedom of action, regardless of how desirable such additional limitations might be.

A major advantage that would accrue to the people of the United States in the ratification and full implementation of this proposed Treaty is the possible reduction in the future cost of self-defense measures. The armaments race and the Vietnam war costs are now wasting the substance of the American economy. In the absence of a non-proliferation pact American largesse will be demanded by its allies and there will be further demands by the United States Department of Defense for additional funds to meet new real or imagined threats to American security. A move toward limitation of nuclear armaments would be not only a hopeful sign that the Senate and the President of the United States intended to decrease the danger of thermonuclear war, but would also be an indication that the United States government would be prepared to de-escalate the armaments race and proceed toward setting up a system of enforceable world law.

It is unfortunate that the proposed Treaty does not include a pledge by the nuclear-power nations never to use atomic weapons against a non-nuclear nation. It is also unfortunate that it does not include a pledge on the part of the nuclear powers never to engage in a "first strike" use of thermonuclear weapons. However, the Treaty would provide mechanisms, as in Article VIII, for amendments and extensions, subject to great power veto so as to avoid criticism from those nations. It also provides a mechanism for withdrawal upon three-months' notice. Consequently militaristic elements in the United States or other countries cannot claim that they would be having their hands tied forever by such a Treaty.

A major reason for the United States Senate to ratify this Treaty is to give assurance to the rest of the world that this country is prepared to participate as a partner with other countries, rather than as an independent dictator of world order in the solution of international problems.

This Council believes that ethical considerations and concern for human values demand that the United States take the lead in bringing an end as soon as possible to the threat of nuclear annihilation that hangs over the heads of all mankind. Ratification of the Non-Proliferation Treaty would be a small step in that direction.

NATIONAL SOCIETY DAUGHTERS OF THE AMERICAN REVOLUTION,
NATIONAL DEFENSE COMMITTEE.
Washington, D.C., July 18, 1968.

Senator FRANK J. LAUSCHE,
Senate Office Building,
Washington, D.C.

DEAR SENATOR LAUSCHE: This letter is prompted by reports of testimony which has been given before the Senate Foreign Relations Committee in the Hearings on the Nuclear Nonproliferation Treaty. These present an alarming disparity of so-called facts.

A careful study of the Text of this Treaty leads me to the conclusion that by again following the communist Pied Piper of Peace the United States is being further drawn into a trap from which there may be no escape. The United States is agreeing to cooperate with a country whose word cannot be trusted, a country that has never lived up to its commitments except in rare instances when it has been to its own interest to do so.

Restrictions already placed upon United States nuclear development by previous Treaty agreements have left untested many nuclear devices upon which the security, and even the survival, of our Nation may someday depend.

Added to this awesome prospect is the omission of realistic provisions for inspection under the Treaty. The proffered inspection of the Warsaw Pact nations made by the Soviet Union can only be recognized as an idle gesture. Should the Soviet Union permit these satellite countries to develop or manufacture nuclear arms—which is doubtful—we may be certain that such facilities will be well hidden.

The recommendation that the International Atomic Energy Commission be entrusted with the policing of this Treaty constitutes another example of gullibility on the part of our representatives. Both communist and noncommunist countries belong to the IAEC whose headquarters in Vienna are alarmingly and strategically situated for quick access to communist-held territory.

Furthermore, can an informed American actually believe that any opportunity will be granted for inspection within Soviet territory? On the other hand, United States eagerness to cooperate exposes our defense facilities to "inspection" by an avowedly unfriendly nation.

The commitment by the United States, to assist nonnuclear countries in the development of nuclear energy for peaceful use and to come to the aid of those threatened by nuclear attack, constitutes an extension of United States involvement in the international arena even beyond existing obligations which were previously assumed through the United Nations and other Treaties.

Why, instead of cooperating so earnestly with our sworn enemies, are we not suspicious of this attempt to restrict our further development of modern weapons? The only safeguard against an implacable enemy is the very strength which such treaties are intended to limit and destroy. This Nuclear Nonproliferation Treaty is another step in the planned program for the disarmament of the United States in the name of "peace"—a peace which can never come to fruition so long as our Nation's leaders continue to compromise and even cooperate with world communism.

Sincerely,

ENID H. GRISWOLD
Mrs. Frederick Griswold, Jr.,
National Chairman.

FEDERAL BAR ASSOCIATION,
Washington, D.C., July 23, 1968.

Hon. J. W. FULBRIGHT,
Chairman, Foreign Relations Committee,
U.S. Senate, Washington, D.C.

MY DEAR MR. CHAIRMAN: The Federal Bar Association wishes to go on record in support of ratification of the Treaty on the Non-Proliferation of Nuclear Weapons, signed in Washington on July 1, 1968 (Executive H, 90th Congress, 2d Session).

Our Association hereby submits the following resolution, as proposed by its International Law Committee, adopted upon ballot, and approved this date by its National Executive Committee:

"RESOLUTION

"Whereas nuclear weapons, with their vast destructive capabilities, pose a constant threat to international peace and security; and

Whereas the spread of nuclear weapons tends to further increase this threat, thereby perverting the rule of Law as the foremost principle of government and international intercourse; and

Whereas the fear of abuse of atomic power has long impeded the peaceful development and sharing of nuclear science among all the nations; and

Whereas the governments of more than fifty nations have recognized and accepted their responsibility to halt the proliferation of nuclear weapons and to provide for the peaceful use of the atom as a source of power for the benefit of all men, by signing the Treaty on the Non-Proliferation of Nuclear Weapons on July 1, 1968; and

Whereas the said Treaty has been transmitted by the President of the United States to the United States Senate for its advice and consent, where it is currently pending before the Senate Committee on Foreign Relations for the purpose of public hearing; and

Whereas the principles of this Treaty can serve to commit the nuclear nations to move forward towards effective measures of arms control and disarmament, thereby reducing the threat of aggression and restoring law and international agreement to their proper place in the management of the foreign affairs of nations; be it

Resolved, That the President of the Federal Bar Association be, and he hereby is, requested to direct a communication to the Chairman of the Committee on Foreign Relations, United States Senate, expressing support for the ratification of the Non-Proliferation Treaty, and to incorporate in such communication a true copy of this Resolution for the public record."

As lawyers, we recognize, of course, the trying task ahead in implementing this treaty through future negotiations. Particularly, we are aware that Article VI, a key principle, remains to be implemented. We are also aware of the arguments advanced against the treaty, notably those relating to nuclear weapons control among nuclear nations, and those dealing with the sharing of nuclear science with non-nuclear nations. We note that considerations giving rise to these arguments have prevented some major countries, both nuclear and non-nuclear, from subscribing to the treaty at this time. We believe, however, that this treaty, and the principles it embodies, can serve as a major first step in ending the threat of nuclear holocaust and in restoring international law and agreement as a force for peace in our strife-torn world.

We therefore endorse the purposes of the Non-Proliferation Treaty and urge the Senate to advise and consent thereto.

Respectfully submitted.

JAMES McI. HENDERSON,
President.

WOMEN'S INTERNATIONAL LEAGUE FOR PEACE AND FREEDOM,
LEGISLATIVE OFFICE,
Washington, D.C., July 29, 1968.

Hon. J. WILLIAM FULBRIGHT,
Chairman, Senate Foreign Relations Committee,
U.S. Senate, Washington, D.C.

DEAR SENATOR FULBRIGHT: The United States Section of the Women's International League for Peace and Freedom has asked me to send you the enclosed resolution which was adopted at the Annual Meeting in Painesville, Ohio, June 28–July 2, 1968.

In view of the initiative and leadership of the U.S. in negotiating this treaty, we assume that the Foreign Relations Committee will recommend ratification and that the Senate will ratify. However, it is our very great concern that consideration be given to the next steps to be undertaken by the U.S. in order to carry out the pledge made by President Johnson at the United Nations General Assembly "on behalf of the United States . . . to make this but a first step toward ending the peril of nuclear war."

We are gratified that between the time of the adoption of this resolution and its transmittal, the President announced on the occasion of the signing of the treaty that "agreement has been reached between the governments of the U.S.S.R. and the U.S. to enter in the nearest future into discussions on the limitation and the reduction of both offensive strategic nuclear weapons delivery systems and systems of defense against ballistic missiles."

It is our hope that even while these discussions are going on, the U.S. will pursue as vigorously as possible the additional measures recommended in the enclosed resolution.

Sincerely,

JUDITH McFADDEN,
Legislative Director.

Enclosure.

To : The President of the U.S.

Secretary of State,
The Secretary of Defense,
The Secretary of the Army,
The Secretary of the Navy,
The Secretary of the Air Force,
Chairman, Senate Committee on Foreign Relations,
Chairman, Senate Committee on Armed Services,
Chairman, House Foreign Affairs Committee,
Chairman, House Armed Services Committee,
Chairman, Joint Atomic Energy Committee,
Arms Control and Disarmament Agency,
William C. Foster, Rep. to 18-Nation Committee on Disarmament,
U.S. Ambassador to the U.N., George Ball,

RESOLUTION ON TREATY ON NON-PROLIFERATION OF NUCLEAR WEAPONS

The Women's International League for Peace and Freedom, U.S. Section, in Annual Meeting at Painesville, Ohio, June 28 to July 2, 1968, recognizing the desire of the members of the United Nations, as expressed in resolutions of the General Assembly, to end the nuclear arms race as a step toward general and complete disarmament, deplores the fact that the Treaty on the Non-Proliferation of Nuclear Weapons does not include fixed commitments binding on the nuclear weapons States to cease the manufacture of nuclear weapons, to ban *all* nuclear weapons tests, to ban the use of nuclear weapons and to provide for the destruction of existing stockpiles.

We note the provisions of Article VI of the treaty which states :

"Each of the parties to the treaty undertakes to pursue negotiations in good faith on effective measures relating to cessation of the nuclear arms race at an early date and to nuclear disarmament, and on a treaty on general and complete disarmament, under strict and effective international control."

We now call upon the U.S. Government to take immediate steps to implement the provisions of this article. Such steps should include :

1. Entering into discussions with the USSR towards a mutual limitation of the deployment of delivery systems of nuclear weapons—both offensive and defensive.

2. Initiating and pursuing vigorously negotiations :

    a. to complete a comprehensive test ban treaty prohibiting underground tests.

    b. to secure treaties to outlaw the production and use of nuclear weapons and to provide for the destruction of existing stockpiles.

These negotiations must begin immediately, be pursued vigorously and completed as soon as possible in order that the nuclear weapons treaty serve its announced purpose of ending the nuclear arms race and bringing about nuclear disarmament, leading to general and complete disarmament.

SUMMARY INDEX

(LIST OF WITNESSES APPEARS ALPHABETICALLY IN CONTENTS)

○

www.ingramcontent.com/pod-product-compliance
Lightning Source LLC
Chambersburg PA
CBHW022349280326
41935CB00007B/130